31/0089

Critical Essays from The Spectator

Critical Essays from The Spectator

by Joseph Addison

with four Essays by Richard Steele

edited by **Donald F. Bond**

1970 Clarendon Press, Oxford

Oxford University Press *Ely House, London W.1.*

Glasgow   Bombay
New York   Calcutta
Toronto   Madras
Melbourne Karachi
Wellington Lahore
           Dacca
Cape Town
Salisbury Kuala Lumpur
Ibadan   Singapore
Nairobi   Hong Kong
Dar es Salaam Tokyo
Lusaka
Addis Ababa

Made and printed in Great Britain by
William Clowes and Sons Ltd
London and Beccles

Preface

The present volume contains the most important critical essays from the *Spectator*—the three series on true and false wit, on the pleasures of the imagination, and on *Paradise Lost*, as well as a number of single papers, on taste, language, humour, original genius, and so on, fifty-six in all. In addition to these, which are all by Addison, four papers by Steele are included, his critiques on *The Man of Mode*, *The Scornful Lady*, *The Distressed Mother*, and *The Self-Tormentor* of Terence.

It is perhaps unnecessary to remind the reader that there is much criticism to be found elsewhere in the *Spectator*. A glance at the index in the Clarendon Press edition, under such topics as 'allegory', 'ancients and moderns', 'imitation', 'nature', 'Sappho', 'Spenser', or 'Tasso', will show how frequently these and other literary matters are commented on, sometimes at length, in essays not entirely devoted to criticism.

D. F. B.

University of Chicago.

Contents

Introduction

The series of daily essays published by Addison and Steele in 1711–12, from the pen of 'Mr. Spectator', ranged in subject-matter from the follies of contemporary fashion to the more serious problems of ethics and religion. From the beginning an imaginary club was devised, with members of broadly varying interests, whose topics of conversation might presumably be drawn upon as material for the essays. Besides Mr. Spectator, who acted as secretary, the club included an old-fashioned country squire, a prosperous City merchant, a young lawyer of the Inner Temple (and frequenter of the play-houses) a soldier, an elderly beau, and a grave clergyman.

The omission of a professional critic from the group seems at first sight a little strange, unless Mr. Spectator himself was designed for the role. (At the University, he tells us in the opening essay, 'I applied myself with so much diligence to my studies, that there are few celebrated books, either in the learned or the modern tongues, which I am not acquainted with.') But the label of literary critic is not applied to him. To the ordinary reader of Queen Anne's day 'critic' would no doubt call to mind the unlovable Richard Bentley, formidable classicist of Cambridge and victor over the Christ Church wits in the recent Phalaris controversy, or it might suggest the 'sour, undistinguishing' John Dennis, who cast a severe eye over contemporary literature and found most of it bad.

'Criticism', Dryden had remarked, shortly before his death in 1700, 'is now become mere hangman's work, and meddles only with the faults of authors.' Dryden himself was responsible for some of the best criticism of the age, mainly in the form of prefaces to his own work, but his verdict doubtless met with general endorsement. A generation earlier, in 'The Author's Apology for Heroic Poetry and Poetic Licence', he had characterized the 1670s as 'an age of illiterate, censorious, and detracting people who, thus qualified, set up for critics', but in the same important essay he formulated an admirable statement of critical procedure.

I must take leave to tell them that they wholly mistake the nature of criticism who think its business is principally to find fault. Criticism, as it was first instituted by Aristotle, was meant a standard of judging well; the chiefest part of which is to observe those excellencies which should delight a reasonable reader. If the design, the conduct, the thoughts, and the expressions of a poem be generally such as proceed from a true genius of poetry, the critic ought to pass his judgment in favour of the author.[1]

Dryden, throughout his life, had insisted that the best judges of literary merit were the creative artist and the gentleman of liberal education. Before his death, however, he had seen a change in the world of letters—the rise of a professional class of critics. On the one hand there were the scholarly reviewers for such serious journals as the *History of the Works of the Learned*, and on the other the contributors to periodicals like the *Gentleman's Journal* of Motteux, each issue of which generally carried a 'critique' of a new play, romance, or book of poems. The Rymers, Gildons, and Bentleys of the seventeenth century were of course not all given to fault-finding, but there was enough to cause uneasiness on the part of creative writers like Dryden. The 'image' of the professional critic had become—even before Addison and Steele had begun to write for the polite world of the age of Anne—decidedly unamiable, a creature of pedantry and dullness, inhabiting the musty cell of a university library or a garret in Grub Street.

It was less than a decade before the commencement of the *Spectator* that Swift, in a notable passage in the *Battle of the Books*, had drawn an allegorical portrait of the goddess Criticism—a frightful creature with 'claws like a cat', and with head, ears, and voice resembling those of an ass.

At her right hand sat Ignorance, her father and husband, blind with age; at her left, Pride her mother, dressing her up in the scraps of paper herself had torn. There, was Opinion her sister, light of foot, hoodwinkt, and headstrong, yet giddy and perpetually turning. About her play'd her children, Noise and Impudence, Dullness and Vanity, Positiveness, Pedantry, and Ill-Manners.

Similar views continued to be expressed throughout the reigns of Anne and the first Georges—by Swift himself in Part III of *Gulliver's Travels*; by Dr. Arbuthnot and other 'Scriblerians' in the *Memoirs of Martinus Scriblerus*; and most notably, of course, by Pope in the *Dunciad*, with its elaborate panoply of footnotes and other learned apparatus. Addison too, in No. 470 of the *Spectator*, parodied the scholar-critic's approach to literature by presenting a short poem 'in a new edition, with the several various readings which I find of it in former editions, and in ancient manuscripts'.

There were good reasons, therefore, for not making a professional critic a member of the Spectator Club. But the lively and constructive

---

[1] *Of Dramatic Poesy and Other Critical Essays*, ed. George Watson (Everyman's Library, 1962), i. 196–7. The sentence quoted earlier is from the *Life of Lucian* published in 1711 (ii. 213).

comment on books which forms the subject-matter of some of the best essays in the new journal doubtless helped to a considerable degree in creating a better 'public image' of the literary critic. More important, it brought the reasonable discussion of literature within the range of the ordinary middle-class reader. 'I shall be ambitious to have it said of me', Addison had announced in a well-known passage in No. 10, 'that I have brought philosophy out of closets and libraries, schools and colleges, to dwell in clubs and assemblies, at tea-tables, and in coffee-houses.' An important part of such 'philosophy' would be literature itself, and there is a great deal of evidence, as the *Spectator* went on, of an encouraging 'reader response'— at tea-tables as well as in coffee-houses—to papers dealing with literary subjects, both ancient and modern.

A year or so earlier, in *Tatler* 165, Addison had devoted an entire paper to a description of 'that importunate, empty, and conceited animal' known as a critic.

> This, in the common acceptation of the word, is one that, without entering into the sense and soul of an author, has a few general rules, which, like mechanical instruments, he applies to the works of every writer, and as they quadrate with them, pronounces the author perfect or defective. He is master of a certain set of words, as unity, style, fire, flegm, easy, natural, turn, sentiment, and the like; which he varies, compounds, divides, and throws together, in every part of his discourse, without any thought or meaning.

From this point he goes on to what looks like a reminiscence of an actual critic pontificating in the coffee-house.

> The marks you may know him by are, an elevated eye, and dogmatical brow, a positive voice and a contempt for every thing that comes out, whether he has read it or not. He dwells altogether in generals. He praises or dispraises in the lump. He shakes his head very frequently at the pedantry of universities, and bursts into laughter when you mention an author that is not known at Will's. He hath formed his judgment upon Homer, Horace, and Virgil, not from their own works, but from those of Rapin and Bossu. He knows his own strength so well, that he never dares praise any thing in which he has not a French author for his voucher.[1]

The satiric portrait is interesting as a sketch of all that Addison abhorred. The physical description—the elevated eye, dogmatical brow, and positive voice—would be the very opposite of his own cautious and reserved manner. It applies, on the other hand, to all we know of John Dennis, who, in Pope's words,

---

[1] One may compare the general remarks on criticism and critics in *Spectator* 291 (pages 80–3 of the present volume). Molière, whom Addison must have read, had expressed similar views in the *Critique de l'École des femmes*. See K. E. Wheatley in *RES*, N.S. 1 (1950), 245–7.

> . . . Stares tremendous, with a threatening eye,
> Like some fierce tyrant in old tapestry.

More important, however, than the physical description is the point made in the opening lines—the bad critic's habit of judging by mechanical rules, 'without entering into the sense and soul of an author'. To perceive the qualities in a writer which affect and please us, to discover *why* we are moved by great works of art, and left cold and indifferent by others—this Addison seems always to have had in mind as the job of the critic. He uses almost identical words in *Spectator* 409, the essay which introduces the series on the pleasures of the imagination. 'I could wish there were authors', he writes, 'who would enter into the very spirit and soul of fine writing, and show us the several sources of that pleasure which rises in the mind upon the perusal of a noble work.'

Thus although in poetry it be absolutely necessary that the unities of time, place and action, with other points of the same nature should be thoroughly explained and understood; there is still something more essential to the art, something that elevates and astonishes the fancy, and gives a greatness of mind to the reader, which few of the critics besides Longinus have considered.

The two longest sustained pieces of criticism in the *Spectator*—the eighteen Saturday papers on *Paradise Lost* and the eleven essays on the pleasures of the imagination—are addressed to this problem, the first an exercise in 'practical criticism', the other an attempt to explore the theoretical foundations.

The earliest critical essays in the *Spectator*, however, are prompted by current excesses—in opera, in modern tragedy, and in poetry. It is on the absurdities of Italian opera, then at the height of its popularity, that Addison levels his first attacks. A half-dozen lively papers point out the mixture of representational and realistic stage effects in the opera, with live birds and animals introduced on the stage, 'painted dragons spitting wild-fire . . . and real cascades in artificial landscapes'. A few days later he turns to a more important subject, with four papers on contemporary tragedy, as it succeeds or falls short of the great aim of this 'noblest production of human nature. . . . Diversions of this kind wear out of our thoughts every thing that is mean and little. They cherish and cultivate that humanity which is the ornament of our nature. They soften insolence, soothe affliction, and subdue the mind to the dispensations of Providence.' While the works of the Ancients—and those of Corneille and Racine—reach this ideal, modern English tragedies, by contrast, frequently prove to be empty and devoid of substance. 'Their language is very often noble and sonorous, but the sense either very trifling or very common.'

Addison then specifies some of the methods used by modern writers to compensate for this emptiness—high-sounding language (including rants), extravagant costume, drums and trumpets, ghosts and spectres, daggers, poniards, and other instruments of death. These are all futile if the play itself is hollow. 'Can all the trappings or equipage of a king or hero', he asks, 'give Brutus half that pomp and majesty which he receives from a few lines in Shakespeare?' These stage-effects are not in themselves bad, but only as they are offered in place of 'proportionable sentiments and expressions in the writing'. In *Hamlet* the appearance of the Ghost is made effective 'by the discourses that precede it: his dumb behaviour at his first entrance, strikes the imagination very strongly; but every time he enters, he is still more terrifying. Who can read the speech with which young Hamlet accosts him, without trembling?' Addison draws his illustrations for the most part from the current repertory at Drury Lane Theatre, and he effectively contrasts contemporary plays which depend on extraneous spectacle with the tragedies of the Ancients and those of Corneille, Racine, and Shakespeare.

It was his attack on 'the ridiculous doctrine of poetic justice', however, which remains the most interesting feature of these early papers on drama. The dogma itself had the authority of most of the influential seventeenth-century French critics, and to a certain degree the support of Dryden. According to its advocates, the writer of tragedy, since drama is ideally an agent of moral instruction, must see that virtue is recompensed and vice punished. It receives its most pronounced expression in *The Tragedies of the Last Age* (1678) of Rymer, and it is not always put in such extreme terms; but in most moralistic critics—Dennis, for example—there is the same assumption, implicit if not expressed, of an equal distribution of rewards and punishments.

Steele, in *Tatler* 82, had deplored the playwrights' method of 'disposing the fortune of the persons represented . . . and letting none be unhappy, but those who deserve it'. The remark, however, is made only incidentally, in a general discussion of the calamities incident to human life. Addison's objection to poetic justice is that it is contrary to the very purpose of tragedy. 'We find that good and evil happen alike to all men on this side the grave; and as the principal design of tragedy is to raise commiseration and terror in the minds of the audience, we shall defeat this great end, if we always make virtue and innocence happy and successful.' Restoration adaptations of Shakespeare—providing happy endings to *Romeo and Juliet* and *King Lear*—Addison sees as conspicuous examples of poetic justice which defeat the end of tragedy. *Lear*, he observes, is an admirable tragedy as Shakespeare wrote it, 'but as it is reformed according to the chimerical notion of poetical justice, in my humble opinion it has lost half its beauty'.

It was this paper that aroused the wrath of one of the principal advocates of the doctrine. According to a satirical account written by Pope two years later, John Dennis had walked into the bookshop of Bernard Lintott on the morning of 17 May 1712, 'and opening one of the volumes of the Spectator, in the large paper, did suddenly, without the least provocation, tear out that of No. 40 where the author treats of poetical justice, and cast it into the street'.[1] Dennis in fact composed a reply, 'To the Spectator, upon his Paper on the 16th of April', which he published in 1712 with his *Essay on the Genius and Writings of Shakespeare*. His indignation seems to have been prompted in great part by personal resentment against Steele (who he thought had written the offending paper), since he believed that Steele was at this time systematically attempting to undermine his reputation.[2] Although his objections do not seem to have attracted much attention, a later *Spectator* (No. 548) alludes to the attack and gives a more detailed defence of Addison's views.[3]

The most perfect man has vices enough to draw down punishments upon his head, and to justify Providence in regard to any miseries that may befall him. For this reason I cannot think, but that the instruction and moral are much finer, where a man who is virtuous in the main of his character falls into distress, and sinks under the blows of fortune at the end of a tragedy, than when he is represented as happy and triumphant. Such an example corrects the insolence of human nature, softens the mind of the beholder with sentiments of pity and compassion, comforts him under his own private affliction, and teaches him not to judge of men's virtues by their successes.

Besides these papers on Italian opera and modern tragedy Addison printed a single short essay (No. 35) on humour, without naming names but calling attention to the popularity of 'several writers, who set up for men of humour'. Here the general theme of cruelty inherent in satire and lampoons is stressed, but there is also condemnation of the 'irregular fancies' and 'unnatural distortions of thought' to be found in these would-be humorists. The paper concludes with contrasting genealogical tables of True and False

[1] *The Narrative of Dr. Robert Norris* (*Pope's Prose Works*, ed. Norman Ault, i. 166).

[2] E. N. Hooker, *Critical Works of Dennis*, ii. 435–6.

[3] Although this number is unsigned, it is almost certainly the work of Addison himself. Curiously enough, it has more than once been ascribed to Dennis. On the general subject see Arthur N. Wilkins, 'John Dennis and Poetic Justice', *N & Q*, 102 (1957), 421–4; and Amrih Singh, 'The Argument on Poetic Justice (Addison versus Dennis)', *Indian Journal of English Studies*, 3 (1962), 61–77.

Humour. The essay itself is rather slight, and seems to have been written partly to find out whether readers of the *Spectator* would welcome these ventures into criticism.

The reaction was favourable. 'I find by my bookseller', Addison writes just a month later (in No. 58), 'that these papers of criticism [those upon Italian opera and modern tragedy], with that upon humour, have met with a more kind reception than indeed I could have hoped for from such subjects'. Accordingly, he then gave his readers a consecutive series of six papers, lasting the entire week (7 to 12 May), on the larger topic of true and false wit in poetry (Nos. 58–63).

As in the papers on opera and tragedy, current trends provide the point of departure. 'I observed there were attempts on foot last winter to revive some of those antiquated modes of wit that have been long exploded out of the commonwealth of letters.' Addison is thinking of poems in acrostics, and this leads naturally into a discussion of all forms of 'false wit'—poems in typographical shapes, rebuses, 'echo poems', anagrams, chronograms, *bouts rimés*, and similar tricks with words and sounds. The greater part of the series is taken up with these matters, all supported by examples from literature ancient and modern. After engaging his readers' interest, Addison then (in No. 62) enlarges the scope of the inquiry into a serious discussion of true *versus* false wit, or, if we take the terms in the broadest sense, the difference between poetry enlivened by creative genius and that which depends for its effects on manipulation of verbal counters.

The function of wit, Locke had said, lay in the assemblage of ideas—'putting those together with quickness and variety, wherein can be found any resemblance or congruity thereby to make up pleasant pictures and agreeable visions in the fancy'. This definition Addison quotes with approval, but he adds an important element: the resemblance of ideas must give not only delight but surprise to the reader. Comparing a white object with milk or snow does not constitute true wit, unless there is some further, surprising resemblance. 'Thus when a poet tells us, the bosom of his mistress is as white as snow, there is no wit in the comparison; but when he adds, with a sigh, that it is as cold too, it then grows into wit.'

The resemblance, moreover, must be between ideas and not between mere words, syllables, or letters. It is in this respect that the typographical poems, anagrams, and acrostics described in the earlier essays fail—and by implication much of the eccentric and 'private' poetry of the seventeenth century. As for poets who have a share of true wit but who also indulge in some of these vagaries—

whose wit consists partly in the congruity of ideas and partly in that of words—these may be called poets of 'mixed wit'.

This kind of wit is that which abounds in Cowley, more than in any author that ever wrote. Mr. Waller has likewise a great deal of it. Mr. Dryden is very sparing in it. Milton had a genius much above it. Spenser is in the same class with Milton. . . . If we look into the Latin writers, we find none of this mixed wit in Virgil, Lucretius, or Catullus; very little in Horace, but a great deal of it in Ovid, and scarce any thing else in Martial.

Of the poets named, none, of course, is a poet of false wit, but Ovid and Martial among the ancients, and Waller and Cowley among the moderns, are guilty of a great deal of mixed wit.[1] Milton and Spenser 'had a genius much above it'. Addison clearly has in mind the difference between the metaphysical poets of the previous century (Herbert is singled out particularly in No. 58) and those whom he would place in the first rank—Virgil among the Ancients and Milton among the Moderns. The entire neo-classical movement was essentially one of reformation, toward a poetry which is without idiosyncrasy, simple in structure, and universal in appeal. Addison consistently judges a work of art by these standards, and it is for these reasons that he can praise the popular ballads as well as *Paradise Lost*. In each case it is

that natural way of writing, . . . which we so much admire in the compositions of the ancients; and which no body deviates from, but those who want strength of genius to make a thought shine in its own natural beauties. Poets who want this strength of genius to give that majestic simplicity of nature . . . are forced to hunt after foreign ornaments, and not to let any piece of wit of what kind soever escape them. I look upon these writers as Goths in poetry, who, like those in architecture, not being able to come up to the beautiful simplicity of the old Greeks and Romans, have endeavoured to supply its place with all the extravagancies of an irregular fancy [No. 62].

The three papers (Nos. 70, 74, and 85) devoted to the two popular ballads, 'Chevy Chase' and 'The Children in the Wood', attracted perhaps more attention than any of the others on literary topics. 'Chevy Chase' Addison probably knew in the form of a broadside ballad, printed frequently in song collections of the time. The many allusions to it in contemporary literature show that it was by no means unknown, but that it was associated with an old-fashioned and somewhat rustic taste. For his praise of these ballads Addison has been hailed as a pre-romanticist, since ballads were admired and imitated at the height of the Romantic movement. One does not have to read far, however, to see that the qualities that Addison

[1] Cf. R. L. Morris, 'Addison's *mixt wit*', *MLN*, 57 (1942), 666–8.

praises in the ballads are those he admires in Virgil and Milton—
simplicity, truth to nature, and universality of appeal.

The same standards, with added emphasis on sublimity, appear
in the series of papers on *Paradise Lost*. Addison had been anticipated
in praise of Milton by Dennis, who a few years earlier (chiefly in
The Grounds of Criticism in Poetry, 1704) had taken many of his
examples from *Paradise Lost* to illustrate the importance of sublimity
and enthusiasm in poetry.[1] Neither Addison nor Steele, of course,
held Dennis in high esteem, and although Dennis does anticipate the
Spectator in a few points, Addison's series of papers, covering
systematically the whole poem and written with more literary grace,
was undoubtedly of greater importance in advancing Milton's
reputation throughout the century and making *Paradise Lost*
better understood and appreciated by the ordinary cultivated reader.[2]
By the middle of the century the *Lives of the Poets* published under
Theophilus Cibber's name could affirm that owing to Addison's
papers 'it had become even unfashionable not to have read' Milton.
The prestige which they long maintained is suggested by Thomas
Newton's statement in the Preface to his edition of *Paradise Lost* in
1749.

It was recommended to me indeed to print entire Mr. Addison's Spectators
upon the Paradise Lost, as ingenious essays which had contributed greatly
to the reputation of the poem, and having been added to several editions
they could not well be omitted in this edition: and accordingly those
papers, which treat of the poem in general, are prefixed in the nature of a
preliminary discourse; and those, which are written upon each book
separately, are inserted under each book, and interwoven in their proper
places.

The eighteen essays were collected and further revised in 1719, as
*Notes upon the Twelve Books of Paradise Lost, written by Mr.
Addison*. A French translation was frequently reprinted with French
editions of Milton's poem, notably by Louis Racine in 1755.

So far as we know, these essays—published on Saturdays from

---

[1] For a general discussion of the subject see the long note (i. 511–14) in Hooker's
Critical Works of John Dennis, which lists the passages in *Paradise Lost* selected
for praise by both Dennis and Addison (less than a dozen in all), and points out
aspects of the poem in which both critics concur.

[2] 'Almost every turn of thought in Addison's mind seems to have found some
illustration in *Paradise Lost*; and he had the ability to make others feel this vital
connection between Milton and all that was most worth thinking about in life'
(John Walter Good, *Studies in the Milton Tradition* (University of Illinois
Studies in Language and Literature, Vol. I, nos. 3–4, 1915), p. 153). See further
Raymond D. Havens, *The Influence of Milton in English Poetry* (Cambridge,
Mass., 1922), Ch. i.

January to May 1712—were written directly for publication in the
Spectator. For his other extended series of critical essays, those on
'the pleasures of the imagination', Addison drew on an earlier work,
composed probably during his college days.[1] As the work of a
young man, written presumably for the eye of a college tutor, it is a
remarkable document, going as it does directly to the problem of
the imaginative response to art. In the essay on taste (No. 409),
which Addison composed as an introduction to the series, he relates
the inquiry to the general movement of reform he had undertaken in
earlier *Spectator* essays, particularly those on false wit.

I have endeavoured in several of my Speculations to banish this Gothic
taste which has taken possession among us. I entertained the town for a
week together with an essay upon wit, in which I endeavoured to detect
several of those false kinds which have been admired in the different ages
of the world; and at the same time to show wherein the nature of true wit
consists. I afterwards gave an instance of the great force which lies in a
natural simplicity of thought to affect the mind of the reader, from such
vulgar pieces as have little else besides this single qualification to recommend them. I have likewise examined the works of the greatest poet which
our nation or perhaps any other has produced, and particularized most of
those rational and manly beauties which give a value to that divine work.
I shall next Saturday enter upon an essay on the pleasures of the imagination. . . .

These 'pleasures', it is clear from the context, are those which the
mind receives in response to outside stimuli—from scenes of
external nature or from the productions of art—the kind of thing
that moves it strongly, which 'lifts it out of itself', which 'elevates
and astonishes the fancy' (No. 409). Imagination, as used here, is
not the creative faculty of the poet, but the mind's apprehension of
sense-impressions or 'phantasms'.[2] We find ourselves moved in a
pleasurable way by certain kinds of natural scenery, by certain kinds
of poetry, painting, architecture, and so on. What are these kinds,
and why is the response to them pleasing?

The sensation is immediate and spontaneous. 'It is but the opening
of the eye and the scene enters. . . . We are struck we know not how,
with the symmetry of any thing we see, and immediately assent to the
beauty of an object.' Those which are striking because of their

---

[1] The manuscript, now in the library of Harvard University, was first published
by J. Dykes Campbell in 1864. It contains a number of revisions, made probably
at the time Addison divided the material for publication as daily essays in the
Spectator.

[2] A writer a few years later than the *Spectator* defines it as 'that faculty which
presents to the mind's view the images or ideas of external sensible objects, or by
which the mind perceives them' (Zachary Mayne, *Two Dissertations concerning
Sense and the Imagination*, 1728, pp. 69–70).

novelty, or their grandeur and size, or their symmetry and colour (the uncommon, the great, and the beautiful) arouse emotions which are pleasurable, even though the pleasure may be mixed with melancholy and sorrow, or with apprehension and terror.

Not only here but throughout the *Spectator* one notes how frequently Addison calls attention to the effects of outward phenomena upon the mind. In one essay he remembers the 'pleasing astonishment' and 'agreeable horror' inspired by the ocean,[1] in others the vastness of the heavens and the universe, 'adorned with stars and meteors'.[2] The beauty of the country 'disposes us to be serious',[3] particularly the 'rude kind of magnificence' in mountains and precipices, and other 'stupendous works of nature'.[4] At Sir Roger de Coverley's country place the ivy-covered ruined abbey and other rural scenes 'naturally raise seriousness and attention', especially when 'night heightens the awfulness of the place'.[5] The world of minute nature revealed by the microscope also fills the mind with a pleasurable awe.[6] Devotion 'opens the mind to great conceptions',[7] and the reading of poetry awakens the mind to a pleasurable exercise and the realization of its capacities. 'The reader comes in for half of the performance' and is 'both a reader and a composer'.[8]

Addison's purpose, he had said in No. 409, was to determine 'the several sources of that pleasure which rises in the mind upon the perusal of a noble work', and in the series on the pleasures of the imagination he applies these categories of the Great, the Uncommon, and the Beautiful to the works respectively of Homer, Ovid, and Virgil—and, as he says, to a writer who combines the three in his own work, namely Milton. Here, as throughout the *Spectator*, what is noteworthy is not so much the originality of the ideas as the ease and sureness with which they are expressed, in terminology and with illustrations readily understood by the common reader.

Homer strikes the imagination with scenes of violence and heroic

---

[1] '[Of all objects] there is none which affects my imagination so much as the sea or ocean' (No. 489).

[2] Nos. 565, 412.

[3] 'In our retirements every thing disposes us to be serious; in courts and cities we are entertained with the works of man, in the country with those of God' (No. 465).

[4] No. 412.

[5] No. 110.

[6] 'Every part of matter is peopled; every green leaf swarms with inhabitants' (No. 519).

[7] No. 201.

[8] 'The mind is never so much pleased as when she exerts her self in any action that gives her an idea of her own perfections and abilities' (No. 512).

greatness, so that he often inspires terror; Virgil, with his peculiar note of beauty tinged with melancholy, often leaves the reader with a sensation of sadness and pity (what the French critics call the *tendre*); while Ovid, particularly in the enchanted ground of the *Metamorphoses*, affects the imagination with a pleasing sense of the uncommon and strange. These sensations are directly felt, and their province is that of the imagination, not the reason or judgement. They are not to be discovered by the formal critic, who is likely to judge by rules and hence to find imperfections while overlooking 'concealed beauties' (No. 291). Throughout the critical papers in the *Spectator* one finds the assumption that two kinds of writers exist— the 'little genius' who obeys all the rules, and the great 'natural genius' whose work, though it may violate the critic's standards, universally pleases. (No. 160, on the two kinds of genius, gives the most complete statement of this point, in a comparison between the learned and the natural genius.) 'Our inimitable Shakespeare is a stumbling-block to the whole tribe of these rigid critics. Who would not rather read one of his plays, where there is not a single rule of the stage observed, than any production of a modern critic, where there is not one of them violated?' (No. 592.)

The series on the pleasures of the imagination, then, may be considered the foundation for the whole programme of reform undertaken by the *Spectator*, so far as criticism is concerned. The first precept in poetry is to please (No. 592), and the greatest artists are not those who conform to rule but those whose beauties are to be apprehended by the universal consent of mankind. The principles of the arts, Addison had written in an early number of the *Spectator*, are to be deduced 'from the general sense and taste of mankind, and not from the principles of those arts themselves; or in other words, the taste is not to conform to the art, but the art to the taste' (No. 29).

In stressing simplicity and universality of appeal the *Spectator* was, of course, expressing the central doctrine of neo-classicism, but in his emphasis on taste and what has recently been called 'the perspective of receptivity',[1] Addison, more than any other critic of his time, opened up a line of speculation which was to gain increasing adherence in the time of Wordsworth. His critical essays, in short,

---

[1] 'Addison has well formulated what we may call the perspective of receptivity' (Herbert Dieckmann, 'Esthetic Theory and Criticism in the Enlightenment: Some Examples of Modern Trends', in *Introduction to Modernity: A Symposium on Eighteenth Century Thought*, ed. Robert Mollenauer (Austin, 1965), p. 73. Professor Dieckmann points out the shift of emphasis at this time, 'away from the consideration of the work of art itself and the norms to which it has to conform, towards the study of the process of its creation, the faculties that create it, and towards the response to art, that is, towards the nature of esthetic pleasure'.

not only stated perfectly the dominant opinion in his own day but charted paths which others were to follow.

Wherever we go in eighteenth-century criticism, whatever the specific subject of speculation, we almost invariably find that Addison has been there. If it is Hutcheson on beauty and aesthetic response, we find parallels to or echoes of Addison's 'Pleasures of the Imagination'; if it is Burke on taste and sublimity and beauty, Young and Tucker on original genius, Hume and Gerard, and Kames, Blair and Alison on taste, imagination, sublimity and novelty, the association of ideas and original genius, we are again in the presence of theory partially developed or at least adumbrated in the *Spectator* papers.[1]

It is worth noting, finally, that these critical essays (with the exception of the series on the pleasures of the imagination) were written as articles for a daily paper rather than as chapters in a formal treatise. They are addressed not to the world of the learned but to the ordinary man and woman, to be read in the coffee-house or at the tea-table. Addison was well aware of the difficulties in such writing. 'We must immediately fall into our subject and treat every part of it in a lively manner, or our papers are thrown by as dull and insipid. Our matter must lie close together, and either be wholly new in itself, or in the turn it receives from our expressions' (No. 124). It was, in fact, this very informality that made them so popular on their first appearance, and helped to create a taste for reading among many who had hitherto taken little heed of 'literature'. What Johnson said of Addison's papers on Milton is true of the entire range of critical essays.

Had he presented *Paradise Lost* to the public with all the pomp of system and severity of science, the criticism would perhaps have been admired, and the poem still have been neglected; but by the blandishments of gentleness and facility he has made Milton an universal favourite, with which readers of every class think it necessary to be pleased.

[1] C. D. Thorpe, 'Addison's Contribution to Criticism', in *The Seventeenth Century: Studies in the History of English Thought and Literature from Bacon to Pope, by Richard Foster Jones and Others Writing in his Honor* (Stanford, 1951), p. 324.

Chronological Table

1672   Richard Steele born Dublin (baptized 12 Mar.).
       Joseph Addison born Milston (near Amesbury), Wilts (1 May).

1684   Steele enters Charterhouse School, London (17 Nov.).

1686   Addison enters Charterhouse.

1687   Addison enters Queen's College, Oxford (18 May).

1689   Addison elected Demy at Magdalen College, Oxford (30 July).
       Steele enters Christ Church, Oxford (21 Dec.).

1691   Steele elected Postmaster at Merton College, Oxford (Aug.).

1692   Steele enters Life Guards as cadet (June).

1695   Steele enters Coldstream Guards.

1698   Addison elected Fellow of Magdalen College.

1699   Addison travels on the Continent (to early 1704).

1701   Steele's *The Christian Hero* (Apr.). His comedy *The Funeral* produced (Dec.).

1703   Steele's *The Lying Lover* produced (2 Dec.).

1704   Addison's poem, *The Campaign* (14 Dec.).

1705   Steele's *The Tender Husband* produced (23 Apr.); his marriage to Mrs. Margaret Stretch (d. 1706).
       Addison appointed Under-Secretary of State (July). His *Remarks on Italy* (Nov.).

1706   Steele appointed gentleman-waiter to Prince George of Denmark (Aug.).

1707   Addison's opera *Rosamond* produced (4 Mar.).
       Steele appointed Gazetteer (Apr. or May); his marriage to Mary Scurlock (9 Sept.).

1708   Addison elected M.P. for Lostwithiel.

1709   Addison in Dublin as chief Secretary to Lord Lieutenant Wharton (to autumn 1710).
       The Tatler begun by Steele, with contributions by Addison and others (12 Apr. 1709 to 2 Jan. 1711).

1710   Addison elected M.P. for Malmesbury (11 Mar.).

1711   *The Spectator* begun by Addison and Steele (1 Mar. 1711 to 6 Dec. 1712).

1713   Steele's *The Guardian* (12 Mar. –1 Oct.).
       Addison's *Cato* produced (14 Apr.).
       Steele elected M.P. for Stockbridge.
       Steele's *The Englishman* (6 Oct. 1713 to 11 Feb. 1714).

1714   Steele's *The Crisis* (19 Jan.), followed by his expulsion from the House (18 Mar.). His *Apology* (22 Oct.).
       The Spectator, 2nd ser., by Addison (18 June–20 Dec.).
       Addison chosen Secretary to the Regents (3 Aug.).
       Steele made supervisor of Drury Lane Theatre (18 Oct.).

1715   Steele elected M.P. for Boroughbridge (2 Feb.) and knighted (Apr.).
       The Englishman, 2nd ser., by Steele (11 July–21 Nov.).
       The Freeholder by Addison (23 Dec. 1715 to 25 June 1716).

1716   Addison's comedy *The Drummer* produced (10 Mar.); his marriage to the Dowager Countess of Warwick (9 Aug.).

1717   Addison appointed Secretary of State (15 Apr. 1717 to Mar. 1718).

1718 Estrangement between Addison and Steele over the Peerage Bill.
1719 Addison dies (17 June) and is buried in Westminster Abbey.
1720 *The Theatre* by Steele (2 Jan.–5 Apr.).
1722 Steele's *The Conscious Lovers* produced (7 Nov.).
1729 Steele dies at Carmarthen (1 Sept.).

Note on the Text

The first printing of the *Spectator* was that of the daily numbers (folio half-sheets) from 1 March 1711 to 6 December 1712 (555 issues), followed by a second series (Nos. 556–635), which appeared three times a week from 18 June to 20 December 1714. The 635 numbers were then reprinted in eight volumes, both 8vo and 12mo, in 1712–15, and subsequently many times throughout the eighteenth century.

The text used in this selection is based on that of the present writer's edition, published in five volumes (Oxford: Clarendon Press, 1965). In that edition the copy-text used is that of the original folio sheets, with the authorial revisions of the first 8vo and 12mo reprints incorporated into the text. (For details see the Introduction to the Clarendon Press edition, vol. i, pp. cvi–cix.)

In the present volume the text has been modernized in conformity with the principles adopted for the series.

Reading list

1. *Editions:*

By J. Nichols. London, 1788, 8 vols. This edition was originally undertaken by Thomas Percy in 1762, after 1768 continued by John Calder, and finally brought out by John Nichols. Percy's notes are marked 'P' and Calder's 'A' (for Annotator).

By Robert Bisset. London and Edinburgh, 1793-4, 8 vols. 'A new edition . . . with illustrative notes. To which are prefixed the lives of the authors.'

By Alexander Chalmers. London, 1806, 8 vols.

By Henry Morley, London, 1868. 'A new edition, reproducing the original texts, both as first issued, and as corrected by its authors.'

By G. Gregory Smith. London, 1897-8, 8 vols. With an introductory essay by Austin Dobson. Reprinted, without Dobson's essay, in Everyman's Library, 1907 (8 vols. in 4); revised, 1945.

By George A. Aitken. London, 1898-9, 8 vols. Reprinted, 1905.

By Donald F. Bond. Oxford, 1965, 5 vols.

2. *Important Books:*

BELJAME, ALEXANDRE, *Men of Letters and the English Public in the Eighteenth Century, 1660-1744: Dryden, Addison, Pope.* Trans. E. O. Lorimer. London: Kegan Paul, 1948. (Originally published Paris, 1881.)

LANNERING, J., *Studies in the Prose Style of Joseph Addison.* Uppsala: Lundequistska, 1951.

SMITHERS, PETER, *The Life of Joseph Addison.* Oxford: Clarendon Press, 1954; 2nd edn., 1968.

TUVESON, ERNEST LEE, *The Imagination as a Means of Grace: Locke and the Aesthetics of Romanticism.* Berkeley: University of California Press, 1960.

3. *Important Articles:*

THORPE, CLARENCE DEWITT, 'Addison and Hutcheson on the Imagination', *ELH*, 2 (1935), 215-34.

—— 'Two Augustans Cross the Alps: Dennis and Addison on Mountain Scenery', *SP*, 32 (1935), 463-82.

—— 'Addison's Theory of the Imagination as Perceptive Response', *Papers, Michigan Academy*, 21 (1936), 509-30.

—— 'Addison and Some of his Predecessors on "Novelty"', *PMLA*, 52 (1937), 1114-29.

—— 'Addison's Contribution to Criticism', in *The Seventeenth Century: Studies in the History of English Thought and Literature from Bacon to Pope, by Richard Foster Jones and Others Writing in his Honor.* Stanford: Stanford University Press, 1951, pp. 316-29.

CARRITT, E. F., 'Addison, Kant, and Wordsworth', *E & S*, 22 (1937), 26-36.

LEWIS, C. S., 'Addison', in *Essays on the Eighteenth Century Presented to David Nichol Smith in Honour of his Seventieth Birthday.* Oxford: Clarendon Press, 1945, pp. 1-14.

EVANS, G. BLAKEMORE, 'Addison's Early Knowledge of Milton', *JEGP*, 49 (1950), 204-7.

FRIEDMAN, ALBERT B., 'Addison's Ballad Papers and the Reaction to Metaphysical Wit', *CL*, 12 (1960), 1–13.

WILKINSON, JEAN, 'Some Aspects of Addison's Philosophy of Art', *HLQ*, 28 (1964), 31–44.

MAHONEY, JOHN L., 'Addison and Akenside: The Impact of Psychological Criticism on Early English Romantic Poetry', *British Journal of Aesthetics*, 6 (1966), 365–74.

HANSEN, DAVID A., 'Addison on Ornament and Poetic Style', in *Studies in Criticism and Aesthetics, 1660–1800: Essays in Honor of Samuel Holt Monk*. Minneapolis: University of Minnesota Press, 1967, pp. 94–127.

Wit and Humour

TRUE AND FALSE WIT

58   *Monday May 7 1711*

Ut pictura poesis erit .... Hor.

Nothing is so much admired and so little understood as wit. No
author that I know of has written professedly upon it; and as for
those who make any mention of it, they only treat on the subject as
it has accidentally fallen in their way, and that too in little short
reflections, or in general declamatory flourishes, without entering
into the bottom of the matter. I hope therefore I shall perform an
acceptable work to my countrymen if I treat at large upon this subject;
which I shall endeavour to do in a manner suitable to it, that I may
not incur the censure which a famous critic[n] bestows upon one who
had written a treatise *Upon the Sublime* in a low grovelling style. I
intend to lay aside a whole week for this undertaking, that the scheme
of my thoughts may not be broken and interrupted; and I dare
promise myself, if my readers will give me a week's attention, that
this great city will be very much changed for the better by next
Saturday night. I shall endeavour to make what I say intelligible to
ordinary capacities; but if my readers meet with any paper that in
some parts of it may be a little out of their reach, I would not have
them discouraged, for they may assure themselves the next shall be
much clearer.

As the great and only end of these my speculations is to banish
vice and ignorance out of the territories of Great Britain, I shall
endeavour as much as possible to establish among us a taste of
polite writing. It is with this view that I have endeavoured to set my
readers right in several points relating to operas and tragedies;
and shall from time to time impart my notions of comedy, as I think
they may tend to its refinement and perfection. I find by my bookseller that these papers of criticism, with that upon humour, have
met with a more kind reception than indeed I could have hoped for
from such subjects; for which reason I shall enter upon my present
undertaking with greater cheerfulness.

Motto: Horace, *Ars poetica*, 361: A poem will be like a picture.
critic : the superior character 'n' is used throughout to direct the reader to the
    Notes, pp. 257–89.

In this and one or two following papers I shall trace out the history of False Wit, and distinguish the several kinds of it as they have prevailed in different ages of the world. This I think the more necessary at present, because I observed there were attempts on foot last winter to revive some of those antiquated modes of wit that have been long exploded out of the Commonwealth of Letters. There were several satires and panegyrics handed about in acrostic, by which means some of the most arrant undisputed blockheads about the town began to entertain ambitious thoughts, and to set up for polite authors. I shall therefore describe at length those many arts of false wit, in which a writer does not show himself a man of a beautiful genius, but of great industry.

The first species of false wit which I have met with is very venerable for its antiquity, and has produced several pieces which have lived very near as long as the *Iliad* itself: I mean those short poems printed among the minor Greek poets, which resemble the figure of an egg,[n] a pair of wings, an axe, a shepherd's pipe, and an altar.

As for the first, it is a little oval poem, and may not improperly be called a scholar's egg. I would endeavour to hatch it, or, in more intelligible language, to translate it into English, did not I find the interpretation of it very difficult; for the author seems to have been more intent upon the figure of his poem, than upon the sense of it.

The pair of wings consist of twelve verses, or rather feathers, every verse decreasing gradually in its measure according to its situation in the wing. The subject of it (as in the rest of the poems which follow) bears some remote affinity with the figure, for it describes a god of love, who is always painted with wings.

The axe methinks would have been a good figure for a lampoon, had the edge of it consisted of the most satirical parts of the work; but as it is in the original, I take it to have been nothing else but the posy of an axe which was consecrated to Minerva, and was thought to have been the same that Epeus made use of in the building of the Trojan horse; which is a hint I shall leave to the consideration of the critics. I am apt to think that the posy was written originally upon the axe, like those which our modern cutlers inscribe upon their knives; and that therefore the posy still remains in its ancient shape, though the axe itself is lost.

The shepherd's pipe may be said to be full of music, for it is composed of nine different kinds of verses, which by their several lengths resemble the nine stops of the old musical instrument, that is likewise the subject of the poem.

Epeus: *Aeneid*, 2. 264.

The altar is inscribed with the epitaph of Troilus the son of Hecuba; which, by the way, makes me believe, that these false pieces of wit are much more ancient than the authors to whom they are generally ascribed; at least I will never be persuaded, that so fine a writer as Theocritus[n] could have been the author of any such simple works.

It was impossible for a man to succeed in these performances who was not a kind of painter, or at least a designer: he was first of all to draw the outline of the subject which he intended to write upon, and afterwards conform the description to the figure of his subject. The poetry was to contract or dilate itself according to the mould in which it was cast. In a word, the verses were to be cramped or extended to the dimensions of the frame that was prepared for them; and to undergo the fate of those persons whom the tyrant Procrustes used to lodge in his iron bed; if they were too short he stretched them on a rack, and if they were too long chopped off a part of their legs, till they fitted the couch which he had prepared for them.

Mr. Dryden hints at this obsolete kind of wit in one of the following verses, in his *Mac Flecknoe*; which an English reader cannot understand, who does not know that there are those little poems above-mentioned in the shape of wings and altars.

> . . . Choose for thy command
> Some peaceful province in Acrostic Land;
> There may'st thou wings display and altars raise,
> And torture one poor word a thousand ways.

This fashion of false wit was revived by several poets of the last age, and in particular may be met with among Mr. Herbert's poems;[n] and if I am not mistaken, in the translation of Du Bartas.[n] I do not remember any other kind of work among the Moderns which more resembles the performances I have mentioned, than that famous picture of King Charles the First, which has the whole book of Psalms written in the lines of the face and the hair of the head.[n] When I was last at Oxford I perused one of the whiskers; and was reading the other, but could not go so far in it as I would have done, by reason of the impatience of my friends and fellow-travellers, who all of them pressed to see such a piece of curiosity. I have since heard, that there is now an eminent writing-master in town, who has transcribed all the Old Testament in a full-bottomed periwig; and if the fashion should introduce the thick kind of wigs which were in vogue some few years ago, he promises to add two or three super-

---

Troilus: killed by Achilles at the siege of Troy.   *Mac Flecknoe*: 205–8.

numerary locks that shall contain all the Apocrypha. He designed
this wig originally for King William, having disposed of the two
Books of Kings in the two forks of the foretop; but that glorious
monarch dying before the wig was finished, there is a space left in
it for the face of any one that has a mind to purchase it.

But to return to our ancient poems in picture, I would humbly
propose, for the benefit of our modern smatterers in poetry, that
they would imitate their brethren among the Ancients in those
ingenious devices. I have communicated this thought to a young
poetical lover of my acquaintance, who intends to present his mistress with a copy of verses made in the shape of her fan; and if he
tells me true, has already finished the three first sticks of it. He has
likewise promised me to get the measure of his mistress's marriage-
finger, with a design to make a posy in the fashion of a ring which
shall exactly fit it. It is so very easy to enlarge upon a good hint, that
I do not question but my ingenious readers will apply what I have
said to many other particulars; and that we shall see the town filled
in a very little time with poetical tippets, handkerchiefs, snuff-boxes,
and the like female ornaments. I shall therefore conclude with a
word of advice to those admirable English authors who call themselves Pindaric writers,[n] that they would apply themselves to this
kind of wit without loss of time, as being provided better than any
other poets with verses of all sizes and dimensions.

59   *Tuesday May 8 1711*

Operose nihil agunt,   Sen.

There is nothing more certain than that every man would be a wit
if he could, and notwithstanding pedants of pretended depth and
solidity are apt to decry the writings of a polite author, as 'flash' and
'froth', they all of them show upon occasion that they would spare
no pains to arrive at the character of those whom they seem to
despise. For this reason we often find them endeavouring at works of
fancy, which cost them infinite pangs in the production. The truth of
it is, a man had better be a galley-slave than a wit, were one to gain

foretop: the lock of hair growing on the forepart of the crown; the similar part of
    the wig.
Motto: Seneca, *De brevitate vitae*, 13. 1: They laboriously do nothing.

that title by those elaborate trifles which have been the inventions of such authors as were often masters of great learning but no genius.

In my last paper I mentioned some of these false wits among the Ancients, and in this shall give the reader two or three other species of 'em that flourished in the same early ages of the world. The first I shall produce are the lipogrammatists or letter-droppers of antiquity, that would take an exception, without any reason, against some particular letter in the alphabet, so as not to admit it once into a whole poem. One Tryphiodorus was a great master in this kind of writing. He composed an Odyssey or epic poem on the adventures of Ulysses, consisting of four and twenty books, having entirely banished the letter *A* from his first book, which was called *Alpha* (as *Lucus a non lucendo*)[n] because there was not an alpha in it. His second book was inscribed *Beta*, for the same reason. In short, the poet excluded the whole four and twenty letters in their turns, and showed them, one after another, that he could do his business without them.

It must have been very pleasant to have seen this poet avoiding the reprobate letter, as much as another would a false quantity, and making his escape from it through the several Greek dialects, when he was pressed with it in any particular syllable. For the most apt and elegant word in the whole language was rejected, like a diamond with a flaw in it, if it appeared blemished with a wrong letter. I shall only observe upon this head, that if the work I have here mentioned had been now extant, the *Odyssey* of Tryphiodorus, in all probability, would have been oftener quoted by our learned pedants, than the *Odyssey* of Homer. What a perpetual fund would it have been of obsolete words and phrases, unusual barbarisms and rusticities, absurd spellings and complicated dialects? I make no question but it would have been looked upon as one of the most valuable treasuries of the Greek tongue.

I find likewise among the Ancients that ingenious kind of conceit, which the Moderns distinguish by the name of a rebus, that does not sink a letter but a whole word, by substituting a picture in its place. When Caesar was one of the masters of the Roman Mint, he placed the figure of an elephant upon the reverse of the public

lipogrammatists: writers of poems in which one particular letter of the alphabet was omitted.

Tryphiodorus: Greek grammarian and poet, *fl.* A.D. 450.

rusticities: rustic expressions (the earliest example of the word in this sense in *OED*).

money; the word *Caesar* signifying an elephant in the Punic language. This was artificially contrived by Caesar, because it was
not lawful for a private man to stamp his own figure upon the coin
of the Commonwealth. Cicero, who was so called from the founder
of his family, that was marked on the nose with a little wen like
a vetch (which is *cicer* in Latin) instead of Marcus Tullius Cicero,
ordered the words Marcus Tullius with the figure of a vetch at the
end of 'em to be inscribed on a public monument. This was done
probably to show that he was neither ashamed of his name or
family, notwithstanding the envy of his competitors had often
reproached him with both. In the same manner we read of a famous
building that was marked in several parts of it with the figures of a
frog and a lizard: those words in Greek having been the names of the
architects, who by the laws of their country were never permitted to
inscribe their own names upon their works. For the same reason it is
thought, that the forelock of the horse in the antique equestrian
statue of Marcus Aurelius, represents at a distance the shape of an
owl, to intimate the country of the statuary, who, in all probability,
was an Athenian.[n] This kind of wit was very much in vogue among
our own countrymen about an age or two ago, who did not practise
it for any oblique reason, as the Ancients above-mentioned, but
purely for the sake of being witty. Among innumerable instances
that may be given of this nature, I shall produce the device of one
Mr. Newberry, as I find it mentioned by our learned Camden in his
Remains. Mr. Newberry, to represent his name by a picture, hung
up at his door the sign of a yew-tree, that had several berries upon it,
and in the midst of them a great golden *N* hung upon a bough of the
tree, which by the help of a little false spelling made up the word
N-ew-berry.

I shall conclude this topic with a rebus, which has been lately
hewn out in free stone, and erected over two of the portals of
Blenheim House,[n] being the figure of a monstrous lion tearing to
pieces a little cock. For the better understanding of which device,
I must acquaint my English reader that a cock has the misfortune
to be called in Latin by the same word that signifies a Frenchman,
as a lion is the emblem of the English nation. Such a device in so
noble a pile of building looks like a pun in an heroic poem; and I am
very sorry the truly ingenious architect would suffer the statuary
to blemish his excellent plan with so poor a conceit: but I hope what
I have said will gain quarter for the cock, and deliver him out of the
lion's paw.

I find likewise in ancient times the conceit of making an echo talk sensibly, and give rational answers. If this could be excusable in any writer it would be in Ovid, where he introduces the echo as a nymph, before she was worn away into nothing but a voice. The learned Erasmus, though a man of wit and genius, has composed a dialogue[n] upon this silly kind of device, and made use of an echo who seems to have been a very extraordinary linguist, for she answers the person she talks with in Latin, Greek, and Hebrew, according as she found the syllables which she was to repeat in any of those learned languages. Hudibras, in ridicule of this false kind of wit, has described Bruin bewailing the loss of his bear to a solitary echo, who is of great use to the poet in several distichs, as she does not only repeat after him, but helps out his verse, and furnishes him with rhymes.

> He raged, and kept as heavy a coil as
> Stout Hercules for loss of Hylas;
> Forcing the valleys to repeat
> The accents of his sad regret:
> He beat his breast, and tore his hair,
> For loss of his dear crony bear,
> That echo from the hollow ground
> His doleful wailings did resound
> More wistfully, by many times,
> Than in small poets' splay-foot rhymes,
> That make her, in their rueful stories,
> To answer to interrogatories,
> And most unconscionably depose
> Things of which she nothing knows:
> And when she has said all she can say,
> 'Tis wrested to the lover's fancy.
> Quoth he, O whither, wicked Bruin,
> Art thou fled to my—Echo, *Ruin*?
> I thought thou hadst scorned to budge a step
> For fear. (Quoth Echo) *Marry guep*.
> Am not I here to take thy part!
> Then what has quelled thy stubborn heart?
> Have these bones rattled, and this head
> So often in thy quarrel bled?
> Nor did I ever winch or grudge it,
> For thy dear sake. (Quoth she) *Mum budget*.
> Thinkest thou 'twill not be laid i'th' dish
> Thou turnedst thy back? Quoth Echo, *Pish*.

Ovid: Metamorphoses, 3. 356 ff.
Rhymes: *Hudibras*, I. iii. 183–220. (It is Orsin who is bewailing the loss of the bear.)
Marry guep: originally the oath 'by Mary gypsy' or 'by St. Mary of Egypt'.
Mum budget: Keep quiet!

To run from those thou hadst overcome
Thus cowardly? Quoth Echo, *Mum.*
But what a-vengeance makes thee fly
From me too, as thine enemy?
Or if thou hadst no thought of me,
Nor what I have endured for thee,
Yet shame and honour might prevail
To keep thee thus from turning tail:
For who would grudge to spend his blood in
His honour's cause? Quoth she, *A pudding.*

60   *Wednesday May 9 1711*

Hoc est quod palles? Cur quis non prandeat, hoc est?   Per. *Sat.* 3.

Several kinds of false wit that vanished in the refined ages of the world, discovered themselves again in the times of monkish ignorance.

As the monks were the masters of all that little learning which was then extant, and had their whole lives entirely disengaged from business, it is no wonder that several of them who wanted genius for higher performances, employed many hours in the composition of such tricks in writing as required much time and little capacity. I have seen half the *Aeneid* turned into Latin rhymes by one of the *beaux esprits* of that dark age; who says in his preface to it, that the *Aeneid* wanted nothing but the sweets of rhyme to make it the most perfect work in its kind. I have likewise seen an hymn in hexameters to the Virgin Mary, which filled a whole book, though it consisted but of the eight following words;

> Tot, tibi, sunt, Virgo, dotes, quot, sidera, coelo.
> Thou hast as many virtues, O Virgin, as there are stars in heaven.[n]

The poet rung the changes upon these eight several words, and by that means made his verses almost as numerous as the virtues and the stars which they celebrated. It is no wonder that men who had so much time upon their hands, did not only restore all the antiquated pieces of false wit, but enriched the world with inventions of their own. It was to this age that we owe the production of anagrams,[n]

Motto: Persius, *Satires*, 3. 85: Is it for this that you are pale? Is it for this that you go without your dinner?

which is nothing else but a transmutation of one word into another, or the turning of the same set of letters into different words; which may change night into day, or black into white, if Chance, who is the goddess that presides over these sorts of composition, shall so direct. I remember a witty author, in allusion to this kind of writing, calls his rival, who (it seems) was distorted, and had his limbs set in places that did not properly belong to them, 'The Anagram of a Man'.

When the anagrammatist takes a name to work upon, he considers it at first as a mine not broken up, which will not show the treasure it contains till he shall have spent many hours in the search of it: for it is his business to find out one word that conceals itself in another, and to examine the letters in all the variety of stations in which they can possibly be ranged. I have heard of a gentleman who, when this kind of wit was in fashion, endeavoured to gain his mistress's heart by it. She was one of the finest women of her age, and known by the name of the Lady Mary Boon. The lover not being able to make any thing of Mary, by certain liberties indulged to this kind of writing converted it into Moll; and after having shut himself up for half a year, with indefatigable industry produced an anagram. Upon the presenting it to his mistress, who was a littled vexed in her heart to see herself degraded into Moll Boon, she told him, to his infinite surprise, that he had mistaken her surname, for that it was not Boon but Bohun.

> . . . Ibi omnis
> Effusus labor . . . .

The lover was thunderstruck with his misfortune, insomuch that in a little time after he lost his senses, which indeed had been very much impaired by that continual application he had given to his anagram.

The acrostic[n] was probably invented about the same time with the anagram, though it is impossible to decide whether the inventor of the one or the other were the greater blockhead. The simple acrostic is nothing but the name or title of a person or thing made out of the initial letters of several verses, and by that means written, after the manner of the Chinese, in a perpendicular line. But besides these there are compound acrostics, where the principal letters stand two or three deep. I have seen some of them where the verses have

---

Effusus labor: Virgil, *Georgics*, 4. 491–2:

> Straight all his hopes exhaled in empty smoke;
> And his long toils were forfeit for a look. DRYDEN.

not only been edged by a name at each extremity, but have had the same name running down like a seam through the middle of the poem.

There is another near relation of the anagrams and acrostics, which is commonly called a chronogram.[n] This kind of wit appears very often on many modern medals, especially those of Germany, when they represent in the inscription the year in which they were coined. Thus we see on a medal of Gustavus Adolphus the following words: CHRIStVs DuX ERGO TRIVMPHVS. If you take the pains to pick the figures out of the several words, and range them in their proper order, you will find they amount to MDCXVVVII, or 1627, the year in which the medal was stamped: for as some of the letters distinguish themselves from the rest, and overtop their fellows, they are to be considered in a double capacity, both as letters and as figures. Your laborious German wits will turn over a whole dictionary for one of these ingenious devices. A man would think they were searching after an apt classical term, but instead of that they are looking out a word that has an L, an M, or a D in it. When therefore we meet with any of these inscriptions, we are not so much to look in 'em for the thought, as for the year of the Lord.

The *bouts-rimés* were the favourites of the French nation for a whole age together, and that at a time when it abounded in wit and learning. They were a list of words that rhyme to one another, drawn up by another hand, and given to a poet, who was to make a poem to the rhymes in the same order that they were placed upon the list: the more uncommon the rhymes were, the more extraordinary was the genius of the poet that could accommodate his verses to them. I don't know any greater instance of the decay of wit and learning among the French (which generally follows the declension of empire), than the endeavouring to restore this foolish kind of wit. If the reader will be at the trouble to see examples of it, let him look into the new *Mercure Galant*;[n] where the author every month gives a list of rhymes to be filled up by the ingenious, in order to be communicated to the public in the *Mercure* for the succeeding month. That for the month of November last, which now lies before me, is as follows.

- - - - - - - - - - - - - - - - - Lauriers
- - - - - - - - - - - - - - - - - Guerriers
- - - - - - - - - - - - - - - - - Musette
- - - - - - - - - - - - - - - - - Lisette

Gustavus II (1594–1632), King of Sweden, was killed at Lützen 16 November 1632.

```
– – – – – – – – – – – – – – – – Cesars
    – – – – – – – – – – – – – – – Etendars
  – – – – – – – – – – – – – – – – Houlette
 – – – – – – – – – – – – – – – – Folette
```

One would be amazed to see so learned a man as Ménage talking seriously on this kind of trifle in the following passage.

Monsieur de la Chambre has told me, that he never knew what he was going to write when he took his pen into his hand; but that one sentence always produced another. For my own part, I never knew what I should write next when I was making verses. In the first place I got all my rhymes together, and was afterwards perhaps three or four months in filling them up. I one day showed Monsieur Gombaud a composition of this nature, in which among others I had made use of the four following rhymes, Amaryllis, Phillis, Marne, Arne, desiring him to give me his opinion of it. He told me immediately, that my verses were good for nothing. And upon my asking his reason, he said, because the rhymes are too common; and for that reason easy to be put into verse. Marry, says I, if it be so, I am very well rewarded for all the pains I have been at. But by Monsieur Gombauld's leave, notwithstanding the severity of the criticism, the verses were good. Vid. Menagiana.

Thus far the learned Ménage, whom I have translated word for word.

The first occasion of these *bouts-rimés* made them in some manner excusable, as they were tasks which the French ladies used to impose on their lovers. But when a grave author, like him above-mentioned, tasked himself, could there be any thing more ridiculous? Or would not one be apt to believe that the author played booty, and did not make his list of rhymes till he had finished his poem?

I shall only add, that this piece of false wit has been finely ridiculed by Monsieur Sarasin in a poem entitled, *La Défaite des bouts-rimés, The Rout of the Bouts-Rimés*.

I must subjoin to this last kind of wit the double rhymes,[n] which

---

Ménage: Giles Ménage (1613–92).

de la Chambre: Marin Cureau de la Chambre (1594–1669), physician to the king, was author of the *Art de connaître les hommes*.

Gombauld: Jean-Ogier de Gombauld (d. 1666) was admitted to the Académie Française in 1635, the year of its founding, with a discourse on the *je ne sais quoi*.

played booty: here used in the sense of 'not playing fairly'. Originally the phrase meant 'to join with confederates in order to "spoil" or victimize another player; to play into the hands of confederates in order to share the booty with them'.

Jean-François Sarasin: 1603–54.

are used in doggerel poetry, and generally applauded by ignorant readers. If the thought of the couplet in such compositions is good, the rhyme adds little to it; and if bad, it will not be in the power of the rhyme to recommend it. I am afraid that great numbers of those who admire the incomparable *Hudibras*, do it more on account of these doggerel rhymes than of the parts that really deserve admiration. I am sure I have heard the

> Pulpit, drum ecclesiastic,
> Was beat with fist instead of a stick

and

> There was an ancient sage philosopher
> Who had read *Alexander Ross* over

more frequently quoted, than the finest pieces of wit in the whole poem.

61   *Thursday May 10 1711*

Non equidem hoc studeo, bullatis ut mihi nugis
pagina turgescat, dare pondus idonea fumo.   Pers.

There is no kind of false wit which has been so recommended by the practice of all ages, as that which consists in a jingle of words, and is comprehended under the general name of punning.[n] It is indeed impossible to kill a weed, which the soil has a natural disposition to produce. The seeds of punning are in the minds of all men, and though they may be subdued by reason, reflection and good sense, they will be very apt to shoot up in the greatest genius, that is not broken and cultivated by the rules of art. Imitation is natural to us,

---

stick: *Hudibras*, I. i. 11–12; I. ii. 1–2.
Alexander Ross: (1590–1654), a Scottish clergyman and chaplain to Charles I, was author of *Pansebia, or a View of all Religions* (1653).
Motto: Persius, *Satires*, 5. 19–20:

> 'Tis not, indeed, my talent to engage
> In lofty trifles, or to swell my page
> With wind and noise. DRYDEN

and when it does not raise the mind to poetry, painting, music, or other more noble arts, it often breaks out in puns and quibbles.

Aristotle, in the eleventh chapter of his *Book of Rhetoric*, describes two or three kinds of puns, which he calls paragrams, among the beauties of good writing, and produces instances of them out of some of the greatest authors in the Greek tongue. Cicero has sprinkled several of his works with puns, and in his book where he lays down the rules of oratory, quotes abundance of sayings as pieces of wit, which also upon examination prove arrant puns. But the age in which the pun chiefly flourished, was the reign of King James the First. That learned monarch was himself a tolerable punster, and made very few Bishops or Privy Counsellors that had not some time or other signalized themselves by a clinch, or a conundrum. It was therefore in this age that the pun appeared with pomp and dignity. It had before been admitted into merry speeches and ludicrous compositions, but was now delivered with great gravity from the pulpit, or pronounced in the most solemn manner at the council-table. The great authors, in their most serious works, made frequent use of puns. The sermons of Bishop Andrewes, and the tragedies of Shakespeare,[n] are full of them. The sinner was punned into repentance by the former, as in the latter nothing is more usual than to see a hero weeping and quibbling for a dozen lines together.

I must add to these great authorities, which seem to have given a kind of sanction to this piece of false wit, that all the writers of rhetoric have treated of punning with very great respect, and divided the several kinds of it into hard names, that are reckoned among the figures of speech, and recommended as ornaments in discourse. I remember a country schoolmaster of my acquaintance told me once, that he had been in company with a gentleman whom he looked upon to be the greatest paragrammatist among the Moderns. Upon enquiry, I found my learned friend had dined that day with Mr. Swan[n], the famous punster; and desiring him to give me some account of Mr. Swann's conversation, he told me that he generally talked in the

---

Aristotle: Rhetoric, 3. 11.7.

paragram: defined in *OED* as 'a kind of play upon words, consisting in the alteration of one letter or group of letters of a word'.

puns: De Oratore, 2. 61–3.

conundrum: here used in the obsolete sense of 'pun' or 'word-play'.

Andrewes: Lancelot Andrewes (1555–1626), Bishop of Winchester. His sermons had long been criticized for their metaphysical and 'witty' adornments.

paragrammatist: the earliest example of the word in English (*OED*). For paragram see note on preceding paragraph.

2*

paranomasia, that he sometimes gave into the ploce, but that in his
humble opinion he shined most in the antanaclasis.

I must not here omit, that a famous university of this land was
formerly very much infested with puns; but whether or no this
might not arise from the fens and marshes in which it was situated,
and which are now drained, I must leave to the determination of
more skilful naturalists.[n]

After this short history of punning, one would wonder how it
should be so entirely banished out of the learned world, as it is at
present, especially since it had found a place in the writings of the
most ancient polite authors. To account for this, we must consider,
that the first race of authors, who were the great heroes in writing,
were destitute of all rules and arts of criticism; and for that reason,
though they excel later writers in greatness of genius, they fall short
of them in accuracy and correctness. The Moderns cannot reach their
beauties, but can avoid their imperfections. When the world was
furnished with these authors of the first eminence, there grew up
another set of writers, who gained themselves a reputation by the
remarks which they made on the works of those who preceded them.
It was one of the employments of these secondary authors, to
distinguish the several kinds of wit by terms of art, and to consider
them as more or less perfect, according as they were founded in
truth. It is no wonder therefore, that even such authors as Isocrates,
Plato and Cicero, should have such little blemishes as are not to be
met with in authors of a much inferior character, who have written
since those several blemishes were discovered. I do not find that
there was a proper separation made between puns and true wit by
any of the ancient authors, except Quintilian and Longinus. But
when this distinction was once settled, it was very natural for all men
of sense to agree in it. As for the revival of this false wit, it happened
about the time of the revival of letters,[n] but as soon as it was once
detected, it immediately vanished and disappeared. At the same time
there is no question, but as it has sunk in one age and rose in another,
it will again recover itself in some distant period of time, as pedantry
and ignorance shall prevail upon wit and sense. And, to speak the
truth, I do very much apprehend, by some of the last winter's
productions,[n] which had their sets of admirers, that our posterity
will in a few years degenerate into a race of punsters: at least, a man
may be very excusable for any apprehensions of this kind, that has

---

ploce: lit. 'plaiting'. 'The repetition of a word in an altered or more expressive
 sense, or for the sake of emphasis' (*OED*).
antanaclasis: the repetition of a word in a different or even contrary sense.

seen acrostics handed about the town with great secrecy and applause; to which I must also add a little epigram called the 'Witch's Prayer,' that fell into verse when it was read either backward or forward, excepting only, that it cursed one way and blessed the other.[n] When one sees there are actually such painstakers among our British wits, who can tell what it may end in? If we must lash one another, let it be with the manly strokes of wit and satire; for I am of the old philosopher's opinion, that if I must suffer from one or the other, I would rather it should be from the paw of a lion,[n] than the hoof of an ass. I do not speak this out of any spirit of party. There is a most crying dullness on both sides. I have seen Tory acrostics and Whig anagrams, and do not quarrel with either of them, because they are Whigs or Tories, but because they are anagrams and acrostics.

But to return to punning. Having pursued the history of a pun, from its original to its downfall, I shall here define it to be a conceit arising from the use of two words that agree in the sound, but differ in the sense. The only way therefore to try a piece of wit is to translate it into a different language, if it bears the test you may pronounce it true; but if it vanishes in the experiment, you may conclude it to have been a pun. In short, one may say of a pun as the countryman described his nightingale, that it is *vox et praeterea nihil*, a sound, and nothing but a sound. On the contrary, one may represent true wit by the description which Aristaenetus makes of a fine woman, When she is dressed she is beautiful, when she is undressed she is beautiful: or, as Mercerus has translated it more emphatically, *Induitur, formosa est: exuitur, ipsa forma est.*

62 *Friday May 11 1711*

Scribendi recte sapere est et principium et fons. Hor.

Mr. Locke has an admirable reflection upon the difference of wit and

---

vox et praeterea nihil: Plutarch, 'Sayings of Spartans', *Moralia* 233A.

Aristaenetus: (*fl.* mid-fifth century A.D.), a Greek writer of 'love epistles'. The quotation is from Book I, Letter 1.

Mercerus: Josias Mercier (d. 1626), French humanist. His edition of the *Epistolae Graecae* of Aristaenetus, with notes in Latin, was published at Paris in 1595.

Motto: Horace, *Ars poetica*, 309: Of writing well the source and fount is wisdom.

Locke: *Essay concerning Human Understanding*, II. xi. 2.

judgment, whereby he endeavours to show the reason why they are not always the talents of the same person. His words are as follow:

And hence, perhaps, may be given some reason of that common observation, that men who have a great deal of wit and prompt memories, have not always the clearest judgment, or deepest reason. For wit lying most in the assemblage of ideas, and putting those together with quickness and variety, wherein can be found any resemblance or congruity thereby to make up pleasant pictures and agreeable visions in the fancy; judgment, on the contrary, lies quite on the other side, in separating carefully one from another, ideas wherein can be found the least difference, thereby to avoid being misled by similitude and by affinity to take one thing for another. This is a way of proceeding quite contrary to metaphor and allusion; wherein, for the most part, lies that entertainment and pleasantry of wit which strikes so lively on the fancy, and is therefore so acceptable to all people.

This is, I think, the best and most philosophical account that I have ever met with of wit, which generally, though not always, consists in such a resemblance and congruity of ideas as this author mentions. I shall only add to it, by way of explanation, that every resemblance of ideas is not that which we call wit, unless it be such an one that gives delight and surprise to the reader: these two properties seem essential to wit, more particularly the last of them. In order therefore that the resemblance in the ideas be wit, it is necessary that the ideas should not lie too near one another in the nature of things; for where the likeness is obvious, it gives no surprise. To compare one man's singing to that of another, or to represent the whiteness of any object by that of milk and snow, or the variety of its colours by those of the rainbow, cannot be called wit, unless, besides this obvious resemblance, there be some further congruity discovered in the two ideas that is capable of giving the reader some surprise. Thus when a poet tells us, the bosom of his mistress is as white as snow, there is no wit in the comparison; but when he adds, with a sigh, that it is as cold too, it then grows into wit. Every reader's memory may supply him with innumerable instances of the same nature. For this reason, the similitudes in heroic poets, who endeavour rather to fill the mind with great conceptions, than to divert it with such as are new and surprising, have seldom anything in them that can be called wit. Mr. Locke's account of wit, with this short explanation, comprehends most of the species of wit, as metaphors, similitudes, allegories, enigmas, mottos, parables, fables, dreams, visions, dramatic writings, burlesque, and all the methods of allusion: as there are

---

heroic poets: writers of epic poetry.

many other pieces of wit (how remote soever they may appear at
first sight from the foregoing description) which upon examination
will be found to agree with it.

As true wit generally consists in this resemblance and congruity
of ideas, false wit chiefly consists in the resemblance and congruity
sometimes of single letters, as in anagrams,[n] chronograms, lipograms, and acrostics: sometimes of syllables, as in echoes and
doggerel rhymes; sometimes of words, as in puns and quibbles;
and sometimes of whole sentences or poems, cast into the figures
of eggs, axes, or altars: nay some carry the notion of wit so far, as to
ascribe it even to external mimicry; and to look upon a man as an
ingenious person, that can resemble the tone, posture, or face of
another.

As true wit consists in the resemblance of ideas, and false wit in
the resemblance of words, according to the foregoing instances;
there is another kind of wit which consists partly in the resemblance
of ideas, and partly in the resemblance of words; which for distinction sake I shall call mixed wit. This kind of wit is that which
abounds in Cowley,[n] more than in any author that ever wrote. Mr.
Waller has likewise a great deal of it. Mr. Dryden is very sparing in
it. Milton had a genius much above it. Spenser is in the same class
with Milton. The Italians, even in their epic poetry, are full of it.
Monsieur Boileau, who formed himself upon the ancient poets, has
everywhere rejected it with scorn. If we look after mixed wit among
the Greek writers, we shall find it nowhere but in the epigram-
matists. There are indeed some strokes of it in the little poem
ascribed to Musaeus,[n] which by that, as well as many other marks,
betrays itself to be a modern composition. If we look into the Latin
writers, we find none of this mixed wit in Virgil, Lucretius, or Catullus;
very little in Horace, but a great deal of it in Ovid, and scarce any
thing else in Martial.

Out of the innumerable branches of mixed wit, I shall choose one
instance which may be met with in all the writers of this class.
The passion of love in its nature has been thought to resemble fire;
for which reason the words fire and flame are made use of to signify
love. The witty poets therefore have taken an advantage from the
doubtful meaning of the word fire, to make an infinite number of
witticisms. Cowley[n] observing the cold regard of his mistress's
eyes, and at the same time their power of producing love in him,
considers them as burning-glasses made of ice; and finding himself
able to live in the greatest extremities of love, concludes the torrid
zone to be habitable. When his mistress has read his letter written in
juice of lemon by holding it to the fire, he desires her to read it over a

second time by love's flames. When she weeps, he wishes it were inward heat that distilled those drops from the limbeck. When she is absent he is beyond eighty, that is, thirty degrees nearer the pole than when she is with him. His ambitious love is a fire that naturally mounts upwards, his happy love is the beams of Heaven, and his unhappy love flames of Hell. When it does not let him sleep, it is a flame that sends up no smoke; when it is opposed by counsel and advice, it is a fire that rages the more by the wind's blowing upon it. Upon the dying of a tree in which he had cut his loves, he observes that his written flames had burnt up and withered the tree. When he resolves to give over his passion, he tells us that one burnt like him for ever dreads the fire. His heart is an Etna, that instead of Vulcan's shop encloses Cupid's forge in it. His endeavouring to drown his love in wine, is throwing oil upon the fire. He would insinuate to his mistress, that the fire of love, like that of the sun (which produces so many living creatures) should not only warm but beget. Love in another place cooks pleasure at his fire. Sometimes the poet's heart is frozen in every breast, and sometimes scorched in every eye. Sometimes he is drowned in tears, and burnt in love, like a ship set on fire in the middle of the sea.

The reader may observe in every one of these instances, that the poet mixes the qualities of fire with those of love; and in the same sentence speaking of it both as a passion and as real fire, surprises the reader with those seeming resemblances or contradictions that make up all the wit in this kind of writing. Mixed wit therefore is a composition of pun and true wit, and is more or less perfect as the resemblance lies in the ideas or in the words: its foundations are laid partly in falsehood and partly in truth: reason puts in her claim for one half of it, and extravagance for the other. The only province therefore for this kind of wit, is epigram, or those little occasional poems that in their own nature are nothing else but a tissue of epigrams. I cannot conclude this head of mixed wit, without owning that the admirable poet out of whom I have taken the examples of it, had as much true wit as any author that ever writ; and indeed all other talents of an extraordinary genius.

It may be expected, since I am upon this subject, that I should take notice of Mr. Dryden's definition of wit; which, with all the deference that is due to the judgement of so great a man, is not so properly a definition of wit, as of good writing in general. Wit, as he defines it, is 'a propriety of words and thoughts adapted to the subject.'[n] If this be a true definition of wit, I am apt to think that

---

epigram: here used in the sense of 'a pointed or antithetical saying'.

Euclid was the greatest wit that ever set pen to paper: it is certain there never was a greater propriety of words and thoughts adapted to the subject, than what that author has made use of in his *Elements*. I shall only appeal to my reader, if this definition agrees with any notion he has of wit: if it be a true one, I am sure Mr. Dryden was not only a better poet, but a greater wit than Mr. Cowley, and Virgil a much more facetious man than either Ovid or Martial.

Bouhours,[n] whom I look upon to be the most penetrating of all the French critics, has taken pains to show that it is impossible for any thought to be beautiful which is not just, and has not its foundation in the nature of things: that the basis of all wit is truth; and that no thought can be valuable, of which good sense is not the ground-work. Boileau[n] has endeavoured to inculcate the same notion in several parts of his writings, both in prose and verse. This is that natural way of writing, that beautiful simplicity, which we so much admire in the compositions of the Ancients; and which nobody deviates from, but those who want strength of genius to make a thought shine in its own natural beauties. Poets who want this strength of genius to give that majestic simplicity to nature, which we so much admire in the works of the Ancients, are forced to hunt after foreign ornaments, and not to let any piece of wit of what kind soever escape them. I look upon these writers as Goths in poetry, who, like those in architecture, not being able to come up to the beautiful simplicity of the old Greeks and Romans, have endeavoured to supply its place with all the extravagancies of an irregular fancy. Mr. Dryden makes a very handsome observation on Ovid's writing a letter from Dido to Aeneas in the following words: 'Ovid (says he, speaking of Virgil's fiction of Dido and Aeneas) takes it up after him, even in the same age, and makes an ancient heroine of Virgil's new-created Dido; dictates a letter for her just before her death to the ungrateful fugitive; and, very unluckily for himself, is for measuring a sword with a man so much superior in force to him, on the same subject. I think I may be judge of this, because I have translated both. The famous author of the *Art of Love* has nothing of his own; he borrows all from a greater master in his own profession, and, which is worse, improves nothing which he finds: nature fails him, and being forced to his old shift, he has recourse to witticism. This passes indeed with his soft admirers, and gives him the preference to Virgil in their esteem.'

Were not I supported by so great an authority as that of Mr. Dryden, I should not venture to observe, that the taste of most of

Virgil: 'Dedication of the Aeneis', 1697 (*Essays*, ed. Ker, ii. 193–4).

our English poets, as well as readers, is extremely Gothic. He quotes
Monsieur Segrais for a threefold distinction of the readers of poetry:
in the first of which he comprehends the rabble of readers, whom
he does not treat as such with regard to their quality, but to their
numbers and the coarseness of their taste. His words are as follow:

Segrais has distinguished the readers of poetry, according to their capacity
of judging, into three classes. [He might have said the same of writers
too if he had pleased.] In the lowest form he places those whom he calls
les petits esprits, such things as are our upper-gallery audience in a play-
house; who like nothing but the husk and rind of wit, prefer a quibble,
a conceit, an epigram, before solid sense and elegant expression: these are
mob-readers. If Virgil and Martial stood for Parliament-men, we know
already who would carry it. But though they make the greatest appearance
in the field, and cry the loudest, the best on't is they are but a sort of
French Huguenots, or Dutch Boors, brought over in herds, but not
naturalized; who have not lands of two pounds per annum in Parnassus,
and therefore are not privileged to poll. Their authors are of the same level,
fit to represent them on a mountebank's stage, or to be masters of the
ceremonies in a bear-garden: yet these are they who have the most
admirers. But it often happens, to their mortification, that as their readers
improve their stock of sense, (as they may by reading better books, and by
conversation with men of judgment) they soon forsake them.

I must not dismiss this subject without observing, that as Mr.
Locke in the passage above-mentioned has discovered the most fruitful source of wit, so there is another of a quite contrary nature to
it, which does likewise branch itself out into several kinds. For not
only the *resemblance* but the *opposition* of ideas does very often
produce wit; as I could show in several little points, turns, and anti-
theses, that I may possibly enlarge upon in some future speculation.

Segrais: Jean Regnauld de Segrais (d. 1701) was a member of the circle of the
   Hôtel de Rambouillet. His dissertation on Virgil, prefixed to his translation of
   the *Aeneid* and the *Georgics*, is quoted by Dryden (Watson, ii. 243).

63   *Saturday May 12 1711*

Humano capiti cervicem pictor equinam
jungere si velit et varias inducere plumas
undique collatis membris, ut turpiter atrum
desinat in piscem mulier formosa superne;
spectatum admissi risum teneatis, amici?
Credite, Pisones, isti tabulae fore librum
Persimilem, cujus, velut aegri somnia, vanae
finguntur species . . . .   Hor.

It is very hard for the mind to disengage itself from a subject in
which it has been long employed. The thoughts will be rising of
themselves from time to time, though we give them no encouragement; as the tossings and fluctuations of the sea continue several
hours after the winds are laid.

It is to this that I impute my last night's dream or vision, which
formed into one continued allegory the several schemes of wit,
whether false, mixed, or true, that have been the subject of my late
papers.

Methoughts I was transported into a country that was filled with
prodigies and enchantments, governed by the goddess of Falsehood, and entitled the Region of False Wit. There was nothing in the
fields, the woods, and the rivers, that appeared natural. Several
of the trees blossomed in leaf-gold, some of them produced bone-
lace, and some of them precious stones. The fountains bubbled in
an opera tune, and were filled with stags, wild boars, and mer-
maids, that lived among the waters, at the same time that dolphins
and several kinds of fish played upon the banks, or took their
pastime in the meadows. The birds had many of them golden

Motto: Horace, *Ars poetica*, 1–8.

> If in a picture (*Piso*) you should see
> A handsome woman with a fish's tail,
> Or a man's head upon a horse's neck,
> Or limbs of beasts of the most different kinds,
> Covered with feathers of all sorts of birds,
> Would you not laugh, and think the painter mad?
> Trust me, that book is as ridiculous,
> Whose incoherent style (like sick men's dreams)
> Varies all shapes, and mixes all extremes.   ROSCOMMON

Methoughts: an obsolete form of 'methought', the past tense of 'methinks'.
leaf-gold: gold beaten into a thin sheet, used in gildings. Now 'gold-leaf'.
bone-lace: lace made by knitting with bobbins originally of bone; formerly called
  'bone-work-lace'.

beaks, and human voices. The flowers perfumed the air with smells of incense, amber-grease and pulvillios, and were so interwoven with one another, that they grew up in pieces of embroidery. The winds were filled with sighs and messages of distant lovers. As I was walking to and fro in this enchanted wilderness, I could not forbear breaking out into soliloquies upon the several wonders which lay before me, when to my great surprise I found there were artificial echoes in every walk, that by repetitions of certain words which I spoke, agreed with me, or contradicted me, in everything I said. In the midst of my conversation with these invisible companions, I discovered in the centre of a very dark grove a monstrous fabric built after the Gothic manner, and covered with innumerable devices in that barbarous kind of sculpture. I immediately went up to it, and found it to be a kind of heathen temple consecrated to the god of Dullness. Upon my entrance I saw the deity of the place dressed in the habit of a monk, with a book in one hand and a rattle in the other. Upon his right hand was Industry, with a lamp burning before her; and on his left Caprice, with a monkey sitting on her shoulder. Before his feet there stood an altar of a very odd make, which, as I afterwards found, was shaped in that manner, to comply with the inscription that surrounded it. Upon the altar there lay several offerings of axes, wings, and eggs, cut in paper, and inscribed with verses. The temple was filled with votaries, who applied themselves to different diversions, as their fancies directed them. In one part of it I saw a regiment of anagrams, who were continually in motion, turning to the right or to the left, facing about, doubling their ranks, shifting their stations, and throwing themselves into all the figures and counter-marches of the most changeable and perplexed exercise.

Not far from these was a body of acrostics, made up of very disproportioned persons. It was disposed into three columns, the officers planting themselves in a line on the left hand of each column. The officers were all of them at least six foot high, and made three rows of very proper men; but the common soldiers, who filled up the spaces between the officers, were such dwarfs, cripples, and scarecrows, that one could hardly look upon them without laughing. There were behind the acrostics two or three files of chronograms, which differed only from the former, as their officers were equipped

---

pulvillios: (Ital. *polviglio*), cosmetic or perfumed powder for powdering the wig or perfuming the person.

Dullness: a general term for slowness, obtuseness, and bad writing generally—the eighteenth-century equivalent of bad art.

(like the figure of Time) with an hourglass in one hand, and a scythe in the other, and took their posts promiscuously among the private men whom they commanded.

In the body of the temple, and before the very face of the deity, methoughts I saw the phantom of Tryphiodorus the lipogrammatist, engaged in a ball with four and twenty persons, who pursued him by turns through all the intricacies and labyrinths of a country dance, without being able to overtake him.

Observing several to be very busy at the western end of the temple, I enquired into what they were doing, and found there was in that quarter the great magazine of Rebuses. These were several things of the most different natures tied up in bundles, and thrown upon one another in heaps like faggots. You might behold an anchor, a night-rail, and an hobby-horse bound up together. One of the workmen seeing me very much surprised, told me, there was an infinite deal of wit in several of those bundles, and that he would explain them to me if I pleased. I thanked him for his civility, but told him I was in very great haste at that time. As I was going out of the temple, I observed in one corner of it a cluster of men and women laughing very heartily, and diverting themselves at a game of crambo. I heard several double rhymes as I passed by them, which raised a great deal of mirth.

Not far from these was another set of merry people engaged at a diversion, in which the whole jest was to mistake one person for another. To give occasion for these ludicrous mistakes, they were divided into pairs, every pair being covered from head to foot with the same kind of dress, though, perhaps, there was not the least resemblance in their faces. By this means an old man was sometimes mistaken for a boy, a woman for a man, and a blackamoor for an European, which very often produced great peals of laughter. These I guessed to be a party of puns. But being very desirous to get out of this world of magic, which had almost turned my brain, I left the temple, and crossed over the fields that lay about it with all the speed I could make. I was not gone far before I heard the sound of trumpets and alarms, which seemed to proclaim the march of an enemy; and, as I afterwards found, was in reality what I apprehended it. There appeared at a great distance a very shining light, and in the midst of it a person of a most beautiful aspect; her name was Truth. On her right hand there marched a male deity, who bore several quivers on his shoulders, and grasped several

---

Tryphiodorus: see No. 59, p. 5.

night-rail: a dressing-gown or negligee.

arrows in his hand. His name was Wit. The approach of these two
enemies filled all the territories of False Wit with an unspeakable
consternation, insomuch that the goddess of those regions appeared
in person upon her frontiers with the several inferior deities, and the
different bodies of forces which I had before seen in the temple, who
were now drawn up in array, and prepared to give their foes a warm
reception. As the march of the enemy was very slow, it gave time to
the several inhabitants who bordered upon the regions of Falsehood
to draw their forces into a body, with a design to stand upon their
guard as neuters, and attend the issue of the combat.

I must here inform my reader, that the frontiers of the enchanted
region, which I have before described, were inhabited by the species
of Mixed Wit, who made a very odd appearance when they were
mustered together in an army. There were men whose bodies were
stuck full of darts, and women whose eyes were burning-glasses:
men that had hearts of fire, and women that had breasts of snow.
It would be endless to describe several monsters of the like nature,
that composed this great army; which immediately fell asunder, and
divided itself into two parts; the one half throwing themselves behind
the banners of Truth, and the others behind those of Falsehood.

The goddess of Falsehood was of a gigantic stature, and advanced
some paces before the front of her army; but as the dazzling light,
which flowed from Truth, began to shine upon her, she faded insensibly; insomuch that in a little space she looked rather like an
huge phantom, than a real substance. At length, as the goddess of
Truth approached still nearer to her, she fell away entirely, and
vanished amidst the brightness of her presence; so that there did not
remain the least trace or impression of her figure in the place where
she had been seen.

As at the rising of the sun the constellations grow thin, and the
stars go out one after another, till the whole hemisphere is ex-
tinguished; such was the vanishing of the goddess; and not only of
the goddess herself, but of the whole army that attended her, which
sympathized with their leader, and shrunk into nothing, in proportion as the goddess disappeared. At the same time the whole
temple sunk, the fish betook themselves to the streams, and the wild
beasts to the woods: the fountains recovered their murmurs, the
birds their voices, the trees their leaves, the flowers their scents, and
the whole face of nature its true and genuine appearance. Though I
still continued asleep, I fancied myself as it were awakened out of a
dream, when I saw this region of prodigies restored to woods and
rivers, fields and meadows.

Upon the removal of that wild scene of wonders, which had very much disturbed my imagination, I took a full survey of the persons of Wit and Truth, for indeed it was impossible to look upon the first, without seeing the other at the same time. There was behind them a strong and compact body of figures. The Genius of Heroic Poetry appeared with a sword in her hand, and a laurel on her head. Tragedy was crowned with cypress, and covered with robes dipped in blood. Satire had smiles in her look, and a dagger under her garment. Rhetoric was known by her thunderbolt; and Comedy by her mask. After several other figures, Epigram marched up in the rear, who had been posted there at the beginning of the expedition, that he might not revolt to the enemy, whom he was suspected to favour in his heart. I was very much awed and delighted with the appearance of the god of Wit; there was something so amiable and yet so piercing in his looks, as inspired me at once with love and terror. As I was gazing on him to my unspeakable joy, he took a quiver of arrows from his shoulder, in order to make me a present of it, but as I was reaching out my hand to receive it of him, I knocked it against a chair, and by that means awaked.

HUMOUR

Risu inepto res ineptior nulla est.   Mart.

Among all kinds of writing, there is none in which authors are more apt to miscarry than in works of humour, as there is none in which they are more ambitious to excel.[n] It is not an imagination that teems with monsters, an head that is filled with extravagant conceptions, which is capable of furnishing the world with diversions of this nature; and yet if we look into the productions of several writers, who set up for men of humour, what wild irregular fancies, what unnatural distortions of thought, do we meet with? If they speak nonsense, they believe they are talking humour; and when they have drawn together a scheme of absurd, inconsistent ideas, they are not able to read it over to themselves without laughing. These poor gentlemen endeavour to gain themselves the reputation of wits and humorists, by such monstrous conceits as almost qualify them for Bedlam;[n] not considering that humour should always lie under the check of reason, and that it requires the direction of the nicest judgment, by so much the more as it indulges itself in the most boundless freedoms. There is a kind of nature that is to be observed in this sort of compositions, as well as in all other, and a certain regularity of thought which must discover the writer to be a man of sense, at the same time that he appears altogether given up to caprice: for my part, when I read the delirious mirth of an unskilful author, I cannot be so barbarous as to divert myself with it, but am rather apt to pity the man, than to laugh at anything he writes.

The deceased Mr. Shadwell,[n] who had himself a great deal of the talent, which I am treating of, represents an empty rake, in one of his plays, as very much surprised to hear one say that breaking of windows was not humour; and I question not but several English readers will be as much startled to hear me affirm, that many of those raving incoherent pieces, which are often spread among us, under odd chimerical titles, are rather the offsprings of a distempered brain, than works of humour.

Motto: Catullus, *Carmina*, 39. 16: Nothing is sillier than a silly laugh. Wrongly attributed to Martial.

It is indeed much easier to describe what is not humour, than what is; and very difficult to define it otherwise than as Cowley has done wit, by negatives. Were I to give my own notions of it, I would deliver them after Plato's manner, in a kind of allegory, and by supposing humour to be a person, deduce to him all his qualifications, according to the following genealogy. Truth was the founder of the family, and the father of Good Sense. Good Sense was the father of Wit, who married a lady of a collateral line called Mirth, by whom he had issue Humour. Humour therefore being the youngest of this illustrious family, and descended from parents of such different dispositions, is very various and unequal in his temper; sometimes you see him putting on grave looks and a solemn habit, sometimes airy in his behaviour and fantastic in his dress: insomuch that at different times he appears as serious as a judge, and as jocular as a Merry-Andrew. But as he has a great deal of the mother in his constitution, whatever mood he is in, he never fails to make his company laugh.

But since there is an impostor abroad, who takes upon him the name of this young gentleman, and would willingly pass for him in the world; to the end that well-meaning persons may not be imposed upon by cheats, I would desire my readers, when they meet with this pretender, to look into his parentage, and to examine him strictly, whether or no he be remotely allied to Truth, and lineally descended from Good Sense? if not, they may conclude him a counterfeit. They may likewise distinguish him by a loud and excessive laughter, in which he seldom gets his company to join with him. For as True Humour generally looks serious, whilst everybody laughs about him; False Humour is always laughing, whilst everybody about him looks serious. I shall only add, if he has not in him a mixture of both parents, that is, if he would pass for the offspring of Wit without Mirth, or Mirth without Wit, you may conclude him to be altogether spurious, and a cheat.

The impostor of whom I am speaking, descends originally from Falsehood, who was the mother of Nonsense, who was brought to bed of a son called Frenzy, who married one of the daughters of Folly, commonly known by the name of Laughter, on whom he begot that monstrous infant of which I have been here speaking. I shall set down at length the genealogical table of False Humour, and, at the same time, place under it the genealogy of True Humour, that the reader may at one view behold their different pedigrees and relations.

Cowley: 'Of Wit', especially stanzas 3–7 (*Poems*, ed. Waller, pp. 16–18).

FALSEHOOD
NONSENSE
FRENZY—LAUGHTER
FALSE HUMOUR

TRUTH
GOOD SENSE
WIT—MIRTH
HUMOUR

I might extend the allegory, by mentioning several of the children of False Humour, who are more in number than the sands of the sea, and might in particular enumerate the many sons and daughters which he has begot in this island. But as this would be a very invidious task, I shall only observe in general, that False Humour differs from the True, as a monkey does from a man.

First of all, he is exceedingly given to little apish tricks and buffooneries.

Secondly, he so much delights in mimicry, that it is all one to him whether he exposes by it vice and folly, luxury and avarice; or, on the contrary, virtue and wisdom, pain and poverty.

Thirdly, he is wonderfully unlucky, insomuch that he will bite the hand that feeds him, and endeavour to ridicule both friends and foes indifferently. For having but small talents, he must be merry where he *can*, not where he *should*.

Fourthly, being entirely void of reason, he pursues no point either of morality or instruction, but is ludicrous only for the sake of being so.

Fifthly, being incapable of anything but mock-representations, his ridicule is always personal, and aimed at the vicious man, or the writer; not at the vice, or at the writing.

I have here only pointed at the whole species of false humorists, but as one of my principal designs in this paper is to beat down that malignant spirit, which discovers itself in the writings of the present age, I shall not scruple, for the future, to single out any of the small wits, that infest the world with such compositions as are ill-natured, immoral and absurd. This is the only exception which I shall make to the general rule I have prescribed myself, of *attacking multitudes*. Since every honest man ought to look upon himself as in a natural state of war with the libeller and lampooner, and to annoy them wherever they fall in his way, this is but retaliating upon them and treating them as they treat others.

47 *Tuesday April 24 1711*

Ride si sapis. . . . Mart.

Mr. Hobbes, in his discourse of *Human Nature*, which, in my humble opinion, is much the best of all his works, after some very curious observations upon laughter, concludes thus: 'The passion of laughter is nothing else but sudden glory arising from some sudden conception of some eminency in ourselves, by comparison with the infirmity of others, or with our own formerly: for men laugh at the follies of themselves past, when they come suddenly to remembrance, except they bring with them any present dishonour.'

According to this author therefore, when we hear a man laugh excessively, instead of saying he is very merry, we ought to tell him he is very proud. And indeed, if we look into the bottom of this matter, we shall meet with many observations to confirm us in his opinion. Everyone laughs at somebody that is in an inferior state of folly to himself. It was formerly the custom for every great house in England to keep a tame fool[n] dressed in petticoats, that the heir of the family might have an opportunity of joking upon him, and divert himself with his absurdities. For the same reason idiots are still in request in most of the courts of Germany, where there is not a prince of any great magnificence who has not two or three dressed, distinguished, undisputed fools in his retinue, whom the rest of the courtiers are always breaking their jests upon.

The Dutch, who are more famous for their industry and application, than for wit and humour, hang up in several of their streets what they call the sign of the Gaper, that is, the head of an idiot dressed in a cap and bells, and gaping in a most immoderate manner: this is a standing jest at Amsterdam.

Thus everyone diverts himself with some person or other that is below him in point of understanding, and triumphs in the superiority of his genius, whilst he has such objects of derision before his eyes. Mr. Dennis has very well expressed this in a couple of humorous lines, which are part of a translation of a satire in Monsieur Boileau.[n]

> Thus one fool lolls his tongue out at another,
> And shakes his empty noddle at his brother.

Motto: Martial, *Epigrams*, 2. 41. 1: Laugh if you are wise.
Hobbes: Thomas Hobbes, *Human Nature* (1650), ix. 13 (*Elements of Law*, I. ix. 13).

Mr. Hobbes' reflection gives us the reason why the insignificant people above-mentioned are stirrers up of laughter among men of a gross taste: but as the more understanding part of mankind do not find their risibility affected by such ordinary objects, it may be worth the while to examine into the several provocatives of laughter in men of superior sense and knowledge.

In the first place I must observe, that there is a set of merry drolls, whom the common people of all countries admire, and seem to love so well, 'that they could eat them', according to the old proverb: I mean those circumforaneous wits whom every nation calls by the name of that dish of meat which it loves best. In Holland they are termed Pickled Herrings; in France, Jean Pottages; in Italy, Macaronies; and in Great Britain, Jack Puddings. These merry wags, from whatsoever food they receive their titles, that they may make their audiences laugh, always appear in a fool's coat, and commit such blunders and mistakes in every step they take, and every word they utter, as those who listen to them would be ashamed of.

But this little triumph of the understanding, under the disguise of laughter, is nowhere more visible than in that custom which prevails everywhere among us on the first day of the present month, when everybody takes it in his head to make as many fools as he can. In proportion as there are more follies discovered, so there is more laughter raised on this day than on any other in the whole year. A neighbour of mine, who is a haberdasher by trade, and a very shallow conceited fellow, makes his boasts that for these ten years successively he has not made less than an hundred April fools.[n] My landlady had a falling out with him about a fortnight ago, for sending every one of her children upon some sleeveless errand, as she terms it. Her eldest son went to buy an halfpenny worth of inkle at a shoe-maker's; the eldest daughter was dispatched half a mile to see a monster; and, in short, the whole family of innocent children made April Fools. Nay, my landlady herself did not escape him. This empty fellow has laughed upon these conceits ever since.

This art of wit is well enough, when confined to one day in a twelvemonth; but there is an ingenious tribe of men sprung up of late years, who are for making April Fools every day in the year. These gentlemen are commonly distinguished by the name of

---

circumforaneous: strolling from market to market; vagrant.

Pickled Herring: a clown, buffoon, Merry-Andrew.

sleeveless errand: a common April Fool's joke, in which a person is sent on a pretended errand to find some non-existent object.

inkle: linen tape, or the thread or yarn from which it is made.

'Biters';[n] a race of men that are perpetually employed in laughing at those mistakes which are of their own production.

Thus we see, in proportion as one man is more refined than another, he chooses his fool out of a lower or higher class of mankind; or, to speak in a more philosophical language, that secret elation and pride of heart which is generally called laughter, arises in him from his comparing himself with an object below him, whether it so happens that it be a natural or an artificial fool. It is indeed very possible that the persons we laugh at may in the main of their characters be much wiser men than ourselves, but if they would have us laugh at them, they must fall short of us in those respects which stir up this passion.

I am afraid I shall appear too abstracted in my speculations, if I show that when a man of wit makes us laugh, it is by betraying some oddness or infirmity in his own character, or in the representation which he makes of others; and that when we laugh at a brute or even at an inanimate thing, it is at some action or incident that bears a remote analogy to any blunder or absurdity in reasonable creatures.

But to come into common life, I shall pass by the consideration of those stage coxcombs that are able to shake a whole audience, and take notice of a particular sort of men who are such provokers of mirth in conversation, that it is impossible for a club or merry-meeting to subsist without them; I mean, those honest gentlemen that are always exposed to the wit and raillery of their well-wishers and companions; that are pelted by men, women and children, friends and foes, and, in a word, stand as butts in conversation, for everyone to shoot at that pleases. I know several of these butts, who are men of wit and sense, though by some odd turn of humour, some unlucky cast in their person or behaviour, they have always the misfortune to make the company merry. The truth of it is, a man is not qualified for a butt, who has not a good deal of wit and vivacity, even in the ridiculous side of his character. A stupid butt is only fit for the conversation of ordinary people: men of wit require one that will give them play, and bestir himself in the absurd part of his behaviour. A butt with these accomplishments, frequently gets the laugh of his side, and turns the ridicule upon him that attacks him. Sir John Falstaff was an hero of this species, and gives a good description of himself in his capacity of a butt, after the

---

abstracted: used in the now obsolete sense of 'abstruse, difficult'.
merry-meeting: any festive or convivial gathering.
Falstaff: 2 *Henry IV*, I. ii. 7–12.

following manner; 'Men of all sorts' (says that merry knight)
'take a pride to gird at me. The brain of man is not able to invent
anything that tends to laughter more than I invent, or is invented on
me. I am not only witty in myself, but the cause that wit is in other
men.'

249   *Saturday December 15 1711*

Γέλως ἄκαιρος ἐν βροτοῖς δεινὸν κακόν.   Frag. Vet. Po.

When I make choice of a subject that has not been treated of by
others, I throw together my reflections on it without any order or
method, so that they may appear rather in the looseness and freedom
of an essay, than in the regularity of a set discourse. It is after this
manner that I shall consider laughter and ridicule in my present
paper.

Man is the merriest species of the creation, all above and below
him are serious.[n] He sees things in a different light from other
beings, and finds his mirth rising from objects which perhaps cause
something like pity or displeasure in higher natures. Laughter is
indeed a very good counterpoise to the spleen; and it seems but
reasonable that we should be capable of receiving joy from what is
no real good to us, since we can receive grief from what is no real
evil.

I have in my forty-seventh paper raised a speculation on the
notion of a modern philosopher, who describes the first motive of
laughter to be a secret comparison which we make between ourselves and the persons we laugh at; or in other words, that satisfaction which we receive from the opinion of some pre-eminence in
ourselves, when we see the absurdities of another, or when we reflect
on any past absurdities of our own. This seems to hold in most cases,
and we may observe that the vainest part of mankind are the most
addicted to this passion.

I have read a sermon of a conventual in the Church of Rome, on
those words of the wise man, 'I said of laughter it is mad, and of
mirth what does it?' Upon which he laid it down as a point of

Motto: Menander, *Monostichoi*, 88: Unseasonable laughter is a grievous ill.
(One of the 'Sententiae singulis versibus contentae e diversis Poetis' in
Winterton, *Poetae Minores Graeci*, Cambridge, 1677, p. 507.)
The wise man: Eccl. 2. 2.

doctrine, that laughter was the effect of original sin, and that Adam could not laugh before the Fall.[n]

Laughter, while it lasts, slackens and unbraces the mind, weakens the faculties, and causes a kind of remissness and dissolution in all the powers of the soul: and thus far it may be looked upon as a weakness in the composition of human nature. But if we consider the frequent reliefs we receive from it, and how often it breaks the gloom which is apt to depress the mind, and damp our spirits with transient unexpected gleams of joy, one would take care not to grow too wise for so great a pleasure of life.

The talent of turning men into ridicule, and exposing to laughter those one converses with, is the qualification of little ungenerous tempers. A young man with this cast of mind cuts himself off from all manner of improvement. Every one has his flaws and weaknesses; nay, the greatest blemishes are often found in the most shining characters; but what an absurd thing is it to pass over all the valuable parts of a man, and fix our attention on his infirmities; to observe his imperfections more than his virtues; and to make use of him for the sport of others, rather than for our own improvement.

We therefore very often find that persons the most accomplished in ridicule are those who are very shrewd at hitting a blot, without exerting anything masterly in themselves. As there are many eminent critics who never writ a good line, there are many admirable buffoons that animadvert upon every single defect in another, without ever discovering the least beauty of their own. By this means these unlucky little wits often gain reputation in the esteem of vulgar minds, and raise themselves above persons of much more laudable characters.

If the talent of ridicule were employed to laugh men out of vice and folly, it might be of some use to the world; but instead of this, we find that it is generally made use of to laugh men out of virtue and good sense, by attacking everything that is solemn and serious, decent and praiseworthy in human life.

We may observe, that in the first ages of the world, when the great souls and masterpieces of human nature were produced, men shined by a noble simplicity of behaviour, and were strangers to those little embellishments which are so fashionable in our present conversation. And it is very remarkable, that notwithstanding we fall short at present of the Ancients in poetry, painting, oratory, history, architecture, and all the noble arts and sciences which depend more upon genius than experience, we exceed them as much in doggerel, humour, burlesque, and all the trivial arts of ridicule. We meet with more raillery among the Moderns, but more good sense among the Ancients.

The two great branches of ridicule in writing are comedy and
burlesque.[n] The first ridicules persons by drawing them in their
proper characters, the other by drawing them quite unlike themselves. Burlesque is therefore of two kinds, the first represents mean
persons in the accoutrements of heroes, the other describes great
persons acting and speaking, like the basest among the people.
Don Quixote is an instance of the first, and Lucian's *Gods*[n] of the
second. It is a dispute among the critics, whether burlesque poetry
runs best in heroic verse, like that of *The Dispensary*,[n] or in doggerel,
like that of *Hudibras*. I think where the low character is to be raised
the heroic is the proper measure, but when an hero is to be pulled
down and degraded, it is done best in doggerel.

If Hudibras had been set out with as much wit and humour in
heroic verse as he is in doggerel, he would have made a much more
agreeable figure than he does; though the generality of his readers
are so wonderfully pleased with the double rhymes, that I do not
expect many will be of my opinion in this particular.

I shall conclude this essay upon laughter with observing, that the
metaphor of laughing, applied to fields and meadows when they are
in flower, or to trees when they are in blossom, runs through all
languages; which I have not observed of any other metaphor,
excepting that of fire, and burning, when they are applied to love.
This shows that we naturally regard laughter, as what is in itself both
amiable and beautiful. For this reason likewise Venus has gained the
title of φιλομμειδής the laughter-loving dame, as Waller has translated it, and is represented by Horace as the goddess who delights in
laughter. Milton, in a joyous assembly of imaginary persons, has
given us a very poetical figure of laughter. His whole band of mirth is
so finely described that I shall set the passage down at length.

> But come thou Goddess fair and free,
> In heaven yclept Euphrosyne,
> And by men, heart-easing Mirth,
> Whom lovely Venus at a birth
> With two sister Graces more
> To ivy-crowned Bacchus bore:
> Haste thee Nymph, and bring with thee
> Jest and youthful Jollity,
> Quips and cranks, and wanton wiles,
> Nods, and becks, and wreathed smiles,

φιλομμειδής: the epithet used by Homer (*Iliad*, 4. 10; 5. 375; 14. 211).
Waller: *The Countess of Carlisle in Mourning*, 13.
Horace: *Odes*, 2. 8. 12, etc.
Milton: *L'Allegro*, 11–16, 25–40.

Such as hang on Hebe's cheek,
And love to live in dimple sleek;
Sport that wrinkled Care derides,
And Laughter holding both his sides.
Come, and trip it as you go
On the light fantastic toe,
And in thy right hand lead with thee,
The mountain nymph, sweet Liberty;
And if I give thee honour due,
Mirth, admit me of thy crew
To live with her, and live with thee,
In unreproved pleasures free.

Poetry

THE BALLAD

Interdum vulgus rectum videt. Hor.

When I travelled, I took a particular delight in hearing the songs and
fables that are come from father to son, and are most in vogue among
the common people of the countries through which I passed; for it is
impossible that any thing should be universally tasted and approved
by a multitude, though they are only the rabble of a nation, which
hath not in it some peculiar aptness to please and gratify the mind of
man. Human nature is the same in all reasonable creatures; and
whatever falls in with it, will meet with admirers amongst readers
of all qualities and conditions. Molière, as we are told by Monsieur
Boileau,[n] used to read all his comedies to an old woman who
was his housekeeper, as she sat with him at her work by the chimney-
corner; and could foretell the success of his play in the theatre, from
the reception it met at his fireside: for he tells us the audience always
followed the old woman, and never failed to laugh in the same place.

I know nothing which more shows the essential and inherent
perfection of simplicity of thought, above that which I call the
Gothic manner in writing, than this, that the first pleases all kinds
of palates, and the latter only such as have formed to themselves a
wrong artificial taste, upon little fanciful authors and writers of
epigram. Homer, Virgil, or Milton, so far as the language of their
poems is understood, will please a reader of plain common sense,
who would neither relish nor comprehend an epigram of Martial or a
poem of Cowley: so, on the contrary, an ordinary song or ballad
that is the delight of the common people, cannot fail to please all
such readers as are not unqualified for the entertainment by their
affectation or ignorance; and the reason is plain, because the same
paintings of nature which recommend it to the most ordinary reader,
will appear beautiful to the most refined.

The old song of *Chevy Chase* is the favourite ballad of the common

---

Motto: Horace, *Epistles*, 2. 1. 63: At times the public see and judge aright.
Chevy Chase: (Child, No. 162) deals with the rivalry between the houses of Percy
  and Douglas, but also introduces the combat between the English and Scots at
  the battle of Otterburn (1388), in which Sir Henry Percy (Hotspur) and his
  brother were captured and James (2nd Earl of Douglas and Mar) was killed.

people of England; and Ben Jonson[n] used to say he had rather have
been the author of it than of all his works. Sir Philip Sidney in his
discourse of poetry[n] speaks of it in the following words; 'I never
heard the old song of Percy and Douglas, that I found not my heart
more moved than with a trumpet; and yet is it sung by some blind
crowder with no rougher voice than rude style; which being so evil
apparelled in the dust and cobweb of that uncivil age, what would it
work trimmed in the gorgeous eloquence of Pindar?' For my own
part, I am so professed an admirer of this antiquated song, that I shall
give my reader a critique upon it, without any further apology for so
doing.

The greatest modern critics have laid it down as a rule, that
an heroic poem should be founded upon some important precept
of morality,[n] adapted to the constitution of the country in which
the poet writes. Homer and Virgil have formed their plans in this
view.[n] As Greece was a collection of many governments, who
suffered very much among themselves, and gave the Persian emperor,
who was their common enemy, many advantages over them by their
mutual jealousies and animosities, Homer, in order to establish
among them an union, which was so necessary for their safety,
grounds his poem upon the discords of the several Grecian princes[n]
who were engaged in a confederacy against an Asiatic prince, and
the several advantages which the enemy gained by such their discords. At the time the poem we are now treating of was written,
the dissensions of the barons, who were then so many petty princes,
ran very high, whether they quarrelled among themselves or with
their neighbours, and produced unspeakable calamities to the
country: the poet, to deter men from such unnatural contentions,
describes a bloody battle and dreadful scene of death, occasioned
by the mutual feuds which reigned in the families of an English and
Scotch nobleman. That he designed this for the instruction of his
poem, we may learn from his four last lines, in which, after the
example of the modern tragedians, he draws from it a precept for the
benefit of his readers.

> God save the King and bless the land
>   In plenty, joy, and peace;
> And grant henceforth that foul debate
>   'Twixt noblemen may cease.

The next point observed by the greatest heroic poets, hath been to
celebrate persons and actions which do honour to their country:

---

crowder: fiddler. The ancient Welsh 'crowd' was an early form of the fiddle.

thus Virgil's hero was the founder of Rome, Homer's a prince of Greece; and for this reason Valerius Flaccus[n] and Statius, who were both Romans, might be justly derided for having chosen the Expedition of the Golden Fleece and the Wars of Thebes, for the subjects of their epic writings.

The poet before us, has not only found out an hero in his own country, but raises the reputation of it by several beautiful incidents. The English are the first who take the field, and the last who quit it. The English bring only fifteen hundred to the battle, the Scotch two thousand. The English keep the field with fifty-three: the Scotch retire with fifty-five: all the rest on each side being slain in battle. But the most remarkable circumstance of this kind, is the different manner in which the Scotch and English kings receive the news of this fight, and of the great men's deaths who commanded in it.

> This news was brought to Edinburgh,
>   Where Scotland's King did reign,
> That brave Earl Douglas suddenly
>   Was with an arrow slain.
>
> O heavy news, King James did say,
>   Scotland can witness be,
> I have not any captain more
>   Of such account as he.
>
> Like tidings to King Henry came
>   Within as short a space,
> That Percy of Northumberland
>   Was slain in Chevy-Chase.
>
> Now God be with him, said our King,
>   Sith 'twill no better be,
> I trust I have within my realm
>   Five hundred as good as he.
>
> Yet shall not Scot nor Scotland say
>   But I will vengeance take,
> And be revenged on them all
>   For brave Lord Percy's sake.
>
> This vow full well the King performed
>   After on Humble-down,
> In one day fifty knights were slain
>   With lords of great renown.
>
> And of the rest of small account
>   Did many thousands die, etc.

At the same time that our poet shows a laudable partiality to his countrymen, he represents the Scots after a manner not unbecoming so bold and brave a people.

> Earl Douglas on a milk-white steed,
>   Most like a baron bold,
> Rode foremost of the company
>   Whose armour shone like gold.

His sentiments and actions are every way suitable to an hero. One of us two, says he, must die: I am an earl as well as yourself, so that you can have no pretence for refusing the combat: however, says he, 'tis pity, and indeed would be a sin, that so many innocent men should perish for our sakes; rather let you and I end our quarrel in single fight.

> Ere thus I will out-braved be,
>   One of us two shall die;
> I know thee well, an earl thou art,
>   Lord Percy, so am I.

> But trust me, Percy, pity it were,
>   And great offence, to kill
> Any of these our harmless men,
>   For they have done no ill.

> Let thou and I the battle try,
>   And set our men aside;
> Accurst be he, Lord Percy said,
>   By whom this is denied.

When these brave men had distinguished themselves in the battle and in single combat with each other, in the midst of a generous parley, full of heroic sentiments, the Scotch earl falls; and with his dying words encourages his men to revenge his death, representing to them, as the most bitter circumstance of it, that his rival saw him fall.

> With that there came an arrow keen
>   Out of an English bow,
> Which struck Earl Douglas to the heart
>   A deep and deadly blow.

> Who never spoke more words than these,
>   Fight on my merry men all;
> For why, my life is at an end,
>   Lord Percy sees my fall.

'Merry men', in the language of those times, is no more than a cheerful word for companions and fellow-soldiers. A passage in the eleventh book of Virgil's *Aeneid* is very much to be admired, where Camilla in her last agonies, instead of weeping over the wound she had received, as one might have expected from a warrior of her sex, considers only (like the hero of whom we are now speaking) how the battle should be continued after her death.

> Tum sic exspirans, etc.
> A gathering mist o'erclouds her cheerful eyes;
> And from her cheeks the rosy colour flies.
> Then, turns to her, whom, of her female train,
> She trusted most, and thus she speaks with pain.
> Acca, 'tis past! He swims before my sight,
> Inexorable death; and claims his right.
> Bear my last words to Turnus, fly with speed,
> And bid him timely to my charge succeed:
> Repel the Trojans, and the town relieve:
> Farewell. . . .

Turnus did not die in so heroic a manner; though our poet seems to have had his eye upon Turnus's speech in the last verse

> Lord Percy sees my fall.
> . . . Vicisti, et victum tendere palmas
> Ausonii videre . . . .

Earl Percy's lamentation over his enemy is generous, beautiful, and passionate; I must only caution the reader not to let the simplicity of the style, which one may well pardon in so old a poet, prejudice him against the greatness of the thought.

> Then leaving life Earl Percy took
> The dead man by the hand,
> And said Earl Douglas for thy life
> Would I had lost my land.

> O Christ! my very heart doth bleed
> With sorrow for thy sake;
> For sure a more renowned knight
> Mischance did never take.

That beautiful line *Taking the dead man by the hand*, will put the reader in mind of Aeneas's behaviour towards Lausus, whom he himself had slain as he came to the rescue of his aged father.

> At vero ut vultum vidit morientis, et ora,
> ora modis Anchisiades, pallentia miris:
> ingemuit, miserans graviter, dextramque tetendit, etc.

Tum sic exspirans: *Aeneid*, 11. 820. The English translation here, and below, is Dryden's.
Vicisti, et victum: *Aeneid*, 12. 936–7. Thou hast conquered, and the Ausonians have seen me stretch forth my hands.
At vero: *Aeneid*, 10. 821–3.

The pious prince beheld young Lausus dead;
He grieved, he wept; then grasped his hand, and said,
Poor hapless youth! What praises can be paid
To worth so great . . .!

I shall take another opportunity to consider the other parts of this
old song.

74   *Friday May 25 1711*

. . . Pendent opera interrupta . . . .   Virg.

In my last Monday's paper I gave some general instances of those
beautiful strokes which please the reader in the old song of *Chevy-
Chase*; I shall here, according to my promise, be more particular,
and show that the sentiments in that ballad are extremely natural
and poetical, and full of the majestic simplicity which we admire
in the greatest of the ancient poets: for which reason I shall quote
several passages of it, in which the thought is altogether the same
with what we meet in several passages of the *Aeneid*; not that I
would infer from thence, that the poet (whoever he was) proposed
to himself any imitation of those passages, but that he was directed
to them in general by the same kind of poetical genius, and by
the same copyings after nature.

  Had this old song been filled with epigrammatical turns and
points of wit, it might perhaps have pleased the wrong taste of
some readers; but it would never have become the delight of the
common people, nor have warmed the heart of Sir Philip Sidney
like the sound of a trumpet; it is only nature that can have this
effect, and please those tastes which are the most unprejudiced or
the most refined. I must however beg leave to dissent from so great
an authority as that of Sir Philip Sidney, in the judgement which
he has passed as to the rude style[n] and evil apparel of this antiquated song; for there are several parts in it where not only the
thought but the language is majestic, and the numbers sonorous;
at least, the apparel is much more gorgeous than many of the poets
made use of in Queen Elizabeth's time, as the reader will see in
several of the following quotations.

Motto: Virgil, *Aeneid*, 4. 88: The works are broken off.

What can be greater than either the thought or the expression in that stanza,

> To drive the deer with hound and horn
> Earl Percy took his way;
> The child may rue that was unborn
> The hunting of that day?

This way of considering the misfortunes which this battle would bring upon posterity, not only on those who were born immediately after the battle and lost their fathers in it, but on those also who perished in future battles which took their rise from this quarrel of the two earls, is wonderfully beautiful, and conformable to the way of thinking among the ancient poets.

> Audiet pugnas vitio parentum
> rara juventus.   Hor.[n]

What can be more sounding and poetical, or resemble more the majestic simplicity of the Ancients, than the following stanzas?

> The stout Earl of Northumberland
> A vow to God did make,
> His pleasure in the Scottish woods
> Three summer's days to take.
>
> With fifteen hundred bowmen bold,
> All chosen men of might,
> Who knew full well, in time of need,
> To aim their shafts aright.
>
> The hounds ran swiftly through the woods
> The nimble deer to take,
> And with their cries the hills and dales
> An echo shrill did make.

> . . . Vocat ingenti clamore Cithaeron
> Taygetique canes, domitrixque Epidaurus equorum:
> et vox assensu nemorum ingeminata remugit.[n]

> Lo, yonder doth Earl Douglas come,
> His men in armour bright;
> Full twenty hundred Scottish spears,
> All marching in our sight.
>
> All men of pleasant Tividale,
> Fast by the River Tweed, etc.

The country of the Scotch warriors described in these two last verses, has a fine romantic situation, and affords a couple of smooth words for verse. If the reader compares the foregoing six lines of the

song with the following Latin verses, he will see how much they are
written in the spirit of Virgil.

> Adversi campo apparent, hastasque reductis
> protendunt longe dextris; et spicula vibrant:
> quique altum Preneste viri, quique arva Gabinae
> Junonis, gelidumque Anienem, et roscida rivis
> Hernica saxa colunt: . . . qui rosea rura Velini,
> qui Tetricae horrentes rupes, montemque Severum,
> Casperiamque colunt, Forulosque et flumen Himellae:
> qui Tiberim Fabarimque bibunt. . . .[n]

But to proceed.

> Earl Douglas on a milk-white steed,
>   Most like a baron bold,
> Rode foremost of the company,
>   Whose armour shone like gold.

> Turnus ut antevolans tardum precesserat agmen, etc
> Vidisti, quo Turnus equo, quibus ibat in armis
> aureus. . . .[n]

> Our English archers bent their bows,
>   Their hearts were good and true;
> At the first flight of arrows sent,
>   Full threescore Scots they slew.

> They closed full fast on every side,
>   No slackness there was found;
> And many a gallant gentleman
>   Lay gasping on the ground.

> With that there came an arrow keen
>   Out of an English bow,
> Which struck Earl Douglas to the heart
>   A deep and deadly blow.

Aeneas was wounded after the same manner by an unknown hand
in the midst of a parley.

> Has inter voces, media inter talia verba,
> ecce viro stridens alis allapsa sagitta est,
> incertum qua pulsa manu. . . .[n]

But of all the descriptive parts of this song, there are none more
beautiful than the four following stanzas, which have a great force
and spirit in them, and are filled with very natural circumstances.
The thought in the third stanza was never touched by any other
poet, and is such an one as would have shined in Homer or in Virgil.

> So thus did both these nobles die
>   Whose courage none could stain;
> An English archer then perceived
>   The noble Earl was slain.
>
> He had a bow bent in his hand,
>   Made of a trusty tree,
> An arrow of a cloth-yard long
>   Unto the head drew he.
>
> Against Sir Hugh Montgomery
>   So right his shaft he set,
> The grey-goose wing that was thereon
>   In his heart-blood was wet.
>
> This fight did last from break of day
>   Till setting of the sun.
> For when they rung the evening bell
>   The battle scarce was done.

One may observe likewise, that in the catalogue of the slain the author has followed the example of the greatest ancient poets, not only in giving a long list of the dead, but by diversifying it with little characters of particular persons.

> And with Earl Douglas there was slain
>   Sir Hugh Montgomery,
> Sir Charles Carrel, that from the field
>   One foot would never fly:
>
> Sir Charles Murrel of Ratcliff too,
>   His sister's son was he,
> Sir David Lamb, so well esteemed,
>   Yet saved could not be.

The familiar sound in these names destroys the majesty of the description; for this reason I do not mention this part of the poem but to show the natural cast of thought which appears in it, as the two last verses look almost like a translation of Virgil.

> . . . Cadit et Ripheus justissimus unus
> qui fuit in Teucris et servantissimus aequi,
> diis aliter visum est. . . .[n]

In the catalogue of the English who fell, Witherington's behaviour is in the same manner particularized very artfully, as the reader is prepared for it by that account which is given of him in the beginning of the battle: though I am satisfied your little buffoon readers (who have seen that passage ridiculed in *Hudibras*)[n] will not be able to take the beauty of it: for which reason I dare not so much as quote it.

> Then stepped a gallant squire forth,
> Witherington was his name,
> Who said, I would not have it told
> To Henry our King for shame,
>
> That e'er my Captain fought on foot
> And I stood looking on.

We meet with the same heroic sentiment in Virgil.

> Non pudet, O Rutuli, cunctis pro talibus unam
> objectare animam? numerone an viribus aequi
> non sumus? . . .[n]

What can be more natural or more moving, than the circumstances in which he describes the behaviour of those women who had lost their husbands on this fatal day?

> Next day did many widows come
> Their husbands to bewail,
> They washed their wounds in brinish tears,
> But all would not prevail.
>
> Their bodies bathed in purple blood,
> They bore with them away;
> They kissed them dead a thousand times,
> When they were clad in clay.

Thus we see how the thoughts of this poem, which naturally arise from the subject, are always simple, and sometimes exquisitely noble; that the language is often very sounding, and that the whole is written with a true poetical spirit.

If this song had been written in the Gothic manner, which is the delight of all our little wits, whether writers or readers, it would not have hit the taste of so many ages, and have pleased the readers of all ranks and conditions. I shall only beg pardon for such a profusion of Latin quotations; which I should not have made use of, but that I feared my own judgement would have looked too singular on such a subject, had not I supported it by the practice and authority of Virgil.

85   *Thursday June 7 1711*

Interdum speciosa locis, morataque recte
fabula nullius Veneris, sine pondere et arte,
valdius oblectat populum, meliusque moratur,
quam versus inopes rerum, nugaeque canorae.   **Hor.**

It is the custom of the Mahometans, if they see any printed or written paper upon the ground, to take it up and lay it aside carefully, as not knowing but it may contain some piece of their Koran.[n] I must confess I have so much of the Mussulman in me, that I cannot forbear looking into every printed paper which comes in my way, under whatsoever despicable circumstances it may appear; for as no mortal author, in the ordinary fate and vicissitude of things, knows to what use his works may, some time or other, be applied, a man may often meet with very celebrated names in a paper of tobacco. I have lighted my pipe more than once with the writings of a prelate, and know a friend of mine who, for these several years, has converted the essays of a man of quality into a kind of fringe for his candlesticks. I remember, in particular, after having read over a poem of an eminent author on a victory, I met with several fragments of it upon the next rejoicing-day, which had been employed in squibs and crackers, and by that means celebrated its subject in a double capacity. I once met with a page of Mr. Baxter under a Christmas pie. Whether or no the pastrycook had made use of it through chance, or waggery, for the defence of that superstitious viand,[n] I know not; but, upon the perusal of it, I conceived so good an idea of the author's piety, that I bought the whole book. I have often profited by these accidental readings, and have sometimes found very curious pieces that are either out of print, or not to be met with in the shops of our London booksellers. For this reason, when my friends take a survey of my library, they are very much surprised to find, upon the shelf of folios, two long band-boxes

---

Motto: Horace, *Ars poetica*, 319–22.

> Sometimes in rough and undigested plays
> We meet with such a lucky character,
> As being humoured right and well pursued,
> Succeeds much better, than the shallow verse,
> And chiming trifles, of more studious pens.   ROSCOMMON

Baxter: Richard Baxter (1615–91), the Puritan divine and controversialist.

standing upright among my books, till I let them see that they are both of them lined with deep erudition and abstruse literature. I might likewise mention a paper kite, from which I have received great improvement; and a hat-case, which I would not exchange for all the beavers in Great Britain. This my inquisitive temper, or rather impertinent humour of prying into all sorts of writing, with my natural aversion to loquacity, give me a good deal of employment when I enter any house in the country; for I can't, for my heart, leave a room before I have thoroughly studied the walls of it, and examined the several printed papers[n] which are usually pasted upon them. The last piece that I met with upon this occasion, gave me a most exquisite pleasure. My reader will think I am not serious, when I acquaint him that the piece I am going to speak of was the old ballad of the 'Two Children in the Wood', which is one of the darling songs of the common people, and has been the delight of most Englishmen in some part of their age.[n]

This song is a plain simple copy of nature, destitute of all the helps and ornaments of art. The tale of it is a pretty tragical story, and pleases for no other reason, but because it is a copy of nature. There is even a despicable simplicity in the verse; and yet, because the sentiments appear genuine and unaffected, they are able to move the mind of the most polite reader with inward meltings of humanity and compassion. The incidents grow out of the subject, and are such as are the most proper to excite pity. For which reason the whole narration has something in it very moving; notwithstanding the author of it (whoever he was) has delivered it in such an abject phrase, and poorness of expression, that the quoting any part of it would look like a design of turning it into ridicule. But though the language is mean, the thoughts, as I have before said, from one end to the other are natural; and therefore cannot fail to please those who are not judges of language, or those who notwithstanding they are judges of language, have a true and unprejudiced taste of nature. The condition, speech and behaviour of the dying parents, with the age, innocence and distress of the children, are set forth in such tender circumstances, that it is impossible for a reader of common humanity not to be affected with them. As for the circumstance of the robin redbreast, it is indeed a little poetical ornament; and to show the genius of the author amidst all his simplicity, it is just the same kind of fiction which one of the greatest of the Latin poets has made use of upon a parallel occasion; I mean that passage in Horace, where he describes himself when he was a child, fallen asleep in a desert wood, and covered with leaves by the turtles that took pity on him.

Me fabulosae Vulture in Apulo,
altricis extra limen Apuliae
    ludo fatigatumque somno
        fronde nova puerum palumbes
    texere . . .[n]

I have heard that the late Lord Dorset,[n] who had the greatest wit tempered with the greatest candour, and was one of the finest critics as well as the best poets of his age, had a numerous collection of old English ballads, and took a particular pleasure in the reading of them. I can affirm the same of Mr. Dryden, and know several of the most refined writers of our present age, who are of the same humour.

I might likewise refer my reader to Molière's thoughts on this subject, as he has expressed them in the character of the Misanthrope[n]; but those only who are endowed with a true greatness of soul and genius, can divest themselves of the little images of ridicule, and admire nature in her simplicity and nakedness. As for the little conceited wits of the age, who can only show their judgment by finding fault, they cannot be supposed to admire these productions which have nothing to recommend them but the beauties of nature, when they do not know how to relish even those compositions that, with all the beauties of nature, have also the additional advantages of art.

candour: here used in the sense of 'freedom from malice'.

THE FABLE

"Ἴδμεν ψεύδεα πολλὰ λέγειν ἐτύμοισιν ὁμοῖα,
ἴδμεν δ᾽ εὖτ᾽ ἐθέλωμεν, ἀληθέα μυθήσασθαι.   Hes.

Fables were the first pieces of wit that made their appearance in the world, and have been still highly valued, not only in times of the greatest simplicity, but among the most polite ages of mankind.[n] Jotham's Fable of the Trees[n] is the oldest that is extant, and as beautiful as any which have been made since that time. Nathan's Fable of the Poor Man and his Lamb is likewise more ancient than any that is extant, besides the above-mentioned, and had so good an effect as to convey instruction to the ear of a king without offending it, and to bring the man after God's own heart to a right sense of his guilt and his duty. We find Aesop[n] in the most distant ages of Greece; and if we look into the very beginnings of the Commonwealth of Rome, we see a mutiny among the common people appeased by a Fable of the Belly and the Limbs,[n] which was indeed very proper to gain the attention of an incensed rabble, at a time when perhaps they would have torn to pieces any man who had preached the same doctrine to them in an open and direct manner. As fables took their birth in the very infancy of learning, they never flourished more than when learning was at its greatest height. To justify this assertion, I shall put my reader in mind of Horace,[n] the greatest wit and critic in the Augustan age; and of Boileau,[n] the most correct poet among the Moderns: not to mention La Fontaine, who by this way of writing is come more into vogue than any other author of our times.

The fables I have here mentioned are raised altogether upon brutes and vegetables, with some of our own species mixed among them, when the moral hath so required. But besides this kind of fable there is another in which the actors are passions, virtues, vices, and other imaginary persons of the like nature. Some of the ancient critics will have it that the *Iliad* and *Odyssey* of Homer are fables of this nature;[n] and that the several names of gods and heroes are

Motto: Hesiod, *Theogony*, 27–8. We know how to speak many false things as though they were true; but we know, when we will, to utter true things.
Poor Man and his Lamb: 2 Sam. 12: 1–4.

nothing else but the affections of the mind in a visible shape and
character. Thus they tell us, that Achilles, in the first *Iliad*, represents
anger, or the irascible part of human nature: that upon drawing his
sword against his superior in a full assembly, Pallas is only another
name for reason, which checks and advises him upon that occasion;
and at her first appearance touches him upon the head, that part of
the man being looked upon as the seat of reason. And thus of the
rest of the poem. As for the *Odyssey*, I think it is plain that Horace
considered it as one of these allegorical fables, by the moral which
he has given us of several parts of it. The greatest Italian wits have
applied themselves to the writing of this latter kind of fables:
as Spenser's *Faerie Queene* is one continued series of them from the
beginning to the end of that admirable work. If we look into the
finest prose authors of antiquity, such as Cicero, Plato, Xenophon,
and many others, we shall find that this was likewise their favourite
kind of fable. I shall only further observe upon it, that the first of this
sort that made any considerable figure in the world was that of
Hercules meeting with Pleasure and Virtue, which was invented by
Prodicus, who lived before Socrates, and in the first dawnings of
philosophy. He used to travel through Greece by virtue of this
fable, which procured him a kind reception in all the market towns,
where he never failed telling it as soon as he had gathered an audience
about him.

After this short preface, which I have made up of such materials
as my memory does at present suggest to me, before I present my
reader with a fable of this kind, which I design as the entertainment
of the present paper, I must in a few words open the occasion of it.

In the account which Plato gives us of the conversation and behaviour of Socrates the morning he was to die, he tells the following
circumstance.

When Socrates' fetters were knocked off (as was usual to be
done on the day that the condemned person was to be executed)
being seated in the midst of his disciples, and laying one of his
legs over the other, in a very unconcerned posture, he began to
rub it where it had been galled by the iron; and whether it was
to show the indifference with which he entertained the thoughts

Pallas: Pallas Athene, the goddess of wisdom.
Horace: *Epistles*, 1. 2. 17–31.
Virtue: Xenophon, *Memorabilia*, 2. 1. 21–34.
Prodicus: of Ceos, a contemporary of Socrates, devised the well-known fable,
  'The Choice of Hercules'.
Plato: *Phaedo*, 60.

of his approaching death, or after his usual manner, to take every occasion of philosophizing upon some useful subject, he observed the pleasure of that sensation which now arose in those very parts of his leg, that just before had been so much pained by the fetter. Upon this he reflected on the nature of pleasure and pain in general, and how constantly they succeed one another. To this he added, that if a man of a good genius for a fable were to represent the nature of pleasure and pain in that way of writing, he would probably join them together after such a manner, that it would be impossible for the one to come into any place, without being followed by the other.

It is possible, that if Plato had thought it proper at such a time to describe Socrates launching out into a discourse which was not of a piece with the business of the day, he would have enlarged upon this hint, and have drawn it out into some beautiful allegory or fable. But since he has not done it, I shall attempt to write one myself in the spirit of that divine author.

There were two families which from the beginning of the world were as opposite to each other as light and darkness. The one of them lived in Heaven, and the other in Hell. The youngest descendant of the first family was Pleasure, who was the daughter of Happiness, who was the child of Virtue, who was the offspring of the Gods. These, as I said before, had their habitation in Heaven. The youngest of the opposite family was Pain, who was the son of Misery, who was the child of Vice, who was the offspring of the Furies. The habitation of this race of beings was in Hell.

The middle station of nature between these two opposite extremes was the earth, which was inhabited by creatures of a middle kind, neither so virtuous as the one, nor so vicious as the other, but partaking of the good and bad qualities of these two opposite families. Jupiter considering that this species, commonly called man, was too virtuous to be miserable, and too vicious to be happy; that he might make a distinction between the good and the bad, ordered the two youngest of the above-mentioned families, Pleasure who was the daughter of Happiness, and Pain who was the son of Misery, to meet one another upon this part of nature which lay in the half way between them, having promised to settle it upon them both, provided they could agree upon the division of it, so as to share mankind between them.

Pleasure and Pain were no sooner met in their new habitation, but they immediately agreed upon this point, that Pleasure should take possession of the virtuous, and Pain of the vicious part of that species which was given up to them. But upon examining to which of them any individual they met with belonged, they found each of them had a right to him; for that, contrary to what they had seen in their old places of residence, there was no person so vicious who had not some good in him, nor any person so virtuous who had not in him some evil. The truth of it is, they generally found upon search, that in the most vicious man Pleasure might lay a claim to an hundredth part, and that in the most virtuous man Pain might come in for at least two thirds. This they saw would occasion endless disputes between them, unless they could come to some accommodation. To this end there was a marriage proposed between them, and at length concluded: by this means it is that we find Pleasure and Pain are such constant yoke-fellows, and that they either make their visits together, or are never far asunder. If Pain comes into an heart he is quickly followed by Pleasure; and if Pleasure enters, you may be sure Pain is not far off.

But notwithstanding this marriage was very convenient for the two parties, it did not seem to answer the intention of Jupiter in sending them among mankind. To remedy therefore this inconvenience, it was stipulated between them by article, and confirmed by the consent of each family, that notwithstanding they here possessed the species indifferently; upon the death of every single person, if he was found to have in him a certain proportion of evil, he should be dispatched into the infernal regions by a passport from Pain, there to dwell with Misery, Vice, and the Furies. Or on the contrary, if he had in him a certain proportion of good, he should be dispatched into Heaven by a passport from Pleasure, there to dwell with Happiness, Virtue and the Gods.

512   *Friday October 17 1712*

Lectorem delectando pariterque monendo.   Hor.

There is nothing which we receive with so much reluctance as advice. We look upon the man who gives it us as offering an affront to our understanding, and treating us like children or idiots. We consider the instruction as an implicit censure, and the zeal which any one shows for our good on such an occasion as a piece of presumption or impertinence. The truth of it is, the person who pretends to advise, does, in that particular, exercise a superiority over us, and can have no other reason for it, but that, in comparing us with himself, he thinks us defective either in our conduct or our understanding. For these reasons, there is nothing so difficult as the art of making advice agreeable; and indeed all the writers, both ancient and modern, have distinguished themselves among one another, according to the perfection at which they have arrived in this art. How many devices have been made use of, to render this bitter potion palatable? Some convey their instructions to us in the best chosen words, others

Motto: Horace, *Ars poetica*, 344.
                    That in one line instructs and pleases all.   CREECH

in the most harmonious numbers, some in points of wit, and others in short proverbs.

But among all the different ways of giving counsel, I think the finest, and that which pleases the most universally, is fable, in whatsoever shape it appears. If we consider this way of instructing or giving advice, it excels all others, because it is the least shocking, and the least subject to those exceptions which I have before mentioned.

This will appear to us, if we reflect, in the first place, that upon the reading of a fable we are made to believe we advise ourselves. We peruse the author for the sake of the story, and consider the precepts rather as our own conclusions, than his instructions. The moral insinuates itself imperceptibly, we are taught by surprise, and become wiser and better unawares. In short, by this method a man is so far overreached as to think he is directing himself, whilst he is following the dictates of another, and consequently is not sensible of that which is the most unpleasing circumstance in advice.

In the next place, if we look into human nature, we shall find that the mind is never so much pleased, as when she exerts herself in any action that gives her an idea of her own perfections and abilities. This natural pride and ambition of the soul is very much gratified in the reading of a fable; for in writings of this kind, the reader comes in for half of the performance; every thing appears to him like a discovery of his own; he is busied all the while in applying characters and circumstances, and is in this respect both a reader and a composer. It is no wonder therefore that on such occasions, when the mind is thus pleased with itself, and amused with its own discoveries, that it is highly delighted with the writing which is the occasion of it. For this reason the *Absalom and Achitophel* was one of the most popular poems that ever appeared in English.[n] The poetry is indeed very fine, but had it been much finer it would not have so much pleased, without a plan which gave the reader an opportunity of exerting his own talents.

This oblique manner of giving advice is so inoffensive, that if we look into ancient histories, we find the wise men of old very often chose to give counsel to their kings in fables. To omit many which will occur to every one's memory, there is a pretty instance of this nature in a Turkish tale, which I do not like the worse for that little oriental extravagance which is mixed with it.[n]

We are told that the Sultan Mahmoud, by his perpetual wars abroad, and his tyranny at home, had filled his dominions with

amused: i.e., engaged, occupied.

ruin and desolation, and half-unpeopled the Persian empire. The
Vizier to this great Sultan, (whether an humorist or an enthusiast
we are not informed) pretended to have learned of a certain Dervish
to understand the language of birds, so that there was not a bird
that could open his mouth but the Vizier knew what it was he said.
As he was one evening with the Emperor, in their return from
hunting, they saw a couple of owls upon a tree that grew near an
old wall out of an heap of rubbish. 'I would fain know,' says the
Sultan, 'what those two owls are saying to one another; listen to their
discourse, and give me an account of it.' The Vizier approached the
tree, pretending to be very attentive to the two owls. Upon his
return to the Sultan, 'Sir,' says he, 'I have heard part of their
conversation, but dare not tell you what it is.' The Sultan would not
be satisfied with such an answer, but forced him to repeat word for
word everything the owls had said. 'You must know then,' said the
Vizier, 'that one of these owls has a son, and the other a daughter,
between whom they are now upon a treaty of marriage. The father
of the son said to the father of the daughter, in my hearing, Brother,
I consent to this marriage, provided you will settle upon your
daughter fifty ruined villages for her portion. To which the father of
the daughter replied, Instead of fifty I will give her five hundred, if
you please. God grant a long life to Sultan Mahmoud! whilst he
reigns over us we shall never want ruined villages.'

The story says, the Sultan was so touched with the fable, that
he rebuilt the towns and villages which had been destroyed, and
from that time forward consulted the good of his people.

To fill up my paper, I shall add a most ridiculous piece of natural
magic, which was taught by no less a philosopher than Democritus,
namely, that if the blood of certain birds, which he mentioned,
were mixed together, it would produce a serpent of such a wonderful virtue that whoever did eat it should be skilled in the language
of birds, and understand every thing they said to one another.[n]
Whether the Dervish above-mentioned might not have eaten such a
serpent, I shall leave to the determinations of the learned.

---

humorist: a person subject to 'humours' or fancies; a fantastical or whimsical
person.
enthusiast: one who holds extravagant and visionary religious opinions.
Democritus: (*c.* 460 – *c.* 370 B.C.), the 'laughing philosopher'.

MODERN POETRY

. . . *nunc augur Apollo,*
nunc Lyciae sortes, nunc et Jove missus ab ipso
interpres divum fert horrida jussa per auras.
Scilicet is superis labor . . . . Virg.

I am always highly delighted with the discovery of any rising genius
among my countrymen. For this reason I have read over, with great
pleasure, the late Miscellany published by Mr. Pope, in which there
are many excellent compositions of that ingenious gentleman.[n] I
have had a pleasure, of the same kind, in perusing a poem that is just
published *On the Prospect of Peace,*[n] and which, I hope, will meet
with such a reward from its patrons, as so noble a performance
deserves. I was particularly well pleased to find that the author had
not amused himself with fables out of the pagan theology, and that
when he hints at any thing of this nature, he alludes to it only as to a
fable.

Many of our modern authors, whose learning very often extends
no farther than Ovid's *Metamorphoses,* do not know how to celebrate a great man, without mixing a parcel of schoolboy tales
with the recital of his actions. If you read a poem on a fine woman,
among the authors of this class, you shall see that it turns more upon
Venus or Helen, than on the party concerned. I have known a copy
of verses on a great hero highly commended, but upon asking to
hear some of the beautiful passages, the admirer of it has repeated
to me a speech of Apollo, or a description of Polypheme. At other
times when I have searched for the actions of a great man, who gave
a subject to the writer, I have been entertained with the exploits of a
river god, or have been forced to attend a Fury in her mischievous
progress, from one end of the poem to the other. When we are at
school it is necessary for us to be acquainted with the system of
pagan theology, and may be allowed to enliven a theme, or point an
epigram with an heathen god; but when we would write a manly

Motto: Virgil, *Aeneid*, 4. 376–9.
     Now Lycian lots, and now the Delian god;
     Now Hermes is employed from Jove's abode,
     To warn him hence; as if the peaceful state
     Of Heavenly powers were touched with human fate!   DRYDEN.

panegyric, that should carry in it all the colours of truth, nothing can be more ridiculous than to have recourse to our Jupiters and Junos.

No thought is beautiful which is not just, and no thought can be just which is not founded in truth, or at least in that which passes for such.[n]

In mock heroic poems, the use of the heathen mythology is not only excusable but graceful, because it is the design of such compositions to divert, by adapting the fabulous machines of the Ancients to low subjects, and at the same time by ridiculing such kinds of machinery in modern writers.[n] If any are of opinion, that there is a necessity of admitting these classical legends into our serious compositions, in order to give them a more poetical turn; I would recommend to their consideration the Pastorals of Mr. Philips.[n] One would have thought it impossible for this kind of poetry to have subsisted without fauns and satyrs, wood-nymphs and water-nymphs, with all the tribe of rural deities. But we see he has given a new life, and a more natural beauty to this way of writing, by substituting in the place of these antiquated fables, the superstitious mythology which prevails among the shepherds of our own country.

Virgil and Homer might compliment their heroes, by interweaving the actions of deities with their achievements; but for a Christian author to write in the pagan creed, to make Prince Eugene a favourite of Mars, or to carry on a correspondence between Bellona and the Marshal de Villars, would be downright puerility, and unpardonable in a poet that is past sixteen. It is want of sufficient elevation in a genius to describe realities, and place them in a shining light, that makes him have recourse to such trifling antiquated fables; as a man may write a fine description of Bacchus or Apollo, that does not know how to draw the character of any of his contemporaries.

In order, therefore, to put a stop to this absurd practice, I shall publish the following edict, by virtue of that Spectatorial Authority with which I stand invested.

'Whereas the time of a general peace is, in all appearance, drawing near; being informed that there are several ingenious persons who

Prince Eugene of Savoy: (1663–1736), general in the service of the Austrian Emperor, victor with Marlborough in the battles of Blenheim, Oudenarde, and Malplaquet, over the French forces.

Bellona: the Roman goddess of war.

Villars: Claude Louis Hector, duc de Villars (1653–1734), the best of the generals in the service of Louis XIV.

intend to show their talents on so happy an occasion, and being willing, as much as in me lies, to prevent that effusion of nonsense, which we have good cause to apprehend; I do hereby strictly require every person, who shall write on this subject, to remember that he is a Christian, and not to sacrifice his Catechism to his poetry. In order to it, I do expect of him in the first place, to make his own poem without depending upon Phoebus for any part of it, or calling out for aid upon any one of the Muses by name. I do like wise positively forbid the sending of Mercury with any particular message or dispatch relating to the peace, and shall by no means suffer Minerva to take upon her the shape of any plenipotentiary concerned in this great work. I do further declare, that I shall not allow the Destinies to have had an hand in the deaths of the several thousands who have been slain in the late war, being of opinion that all such deaths may be very well accounted for by the Christian system of powder and ball. I do therefore strictly forbid the Fates to cut the thread of man's life upon any pretence whatsoever, unless it be for the sake of the rhyme. And whereas I have good reason to fear, that Neptune will have a great deal of business on his hands, in several poems which we may now suppose are upon the anvil, I do also prohibit his appearance, unless it be done in metaphor, simile, or any very short allusion, and that even here he be not permitted to enter, but with great caution and circumspection. I desire that the same rule may be extended to his whole fraternity of heathen gods, it being my design to condemn every poem to the flames, in which Jupiter thunders, or exercises any other act of authority, which does not belong to him: in short, I expect that no pagan agent shall be introduced, or any fact related which a man cannot give credit to with a good conscience. Provided always, that nothing herein contained shall extend, or be construed to extend, to several of the female poets in this nation, who shall be still left in full possession of their gods and goddesses, in the same manner as if this paper had never been written.'

POPE'S *ESSAY ON CRITICISM*

253   *Thursday December 20 1711*

Indignor quicquam reprehendi, non quia crasse
compositum, illepideve putetur, sed quia nuper.   Hor.

There is nothing which more denotes a great mind, than the abhorrence of envy and detraction. This passion reigns more among bad poets, than among any other set of men.

As there are none more ambitious of fame, than those who are conversant in poetry, it is very natural for such as have not succeeded in it to depreciate the works of those who have. For since they cannot raise themselves to the reputation of their fellow writers, they must endeavour to sink it to their own pitch, if they would still keep themselves upon a level with them.

The greatest wits that ever were produced in one age, lived together in so good an understanding, and celebrated one another with so much generosity, that each of them receives an additional lustre from his contemporaries, and is more famous for having lived with men of so extraordinary a genius, than if he had himself been the sole wonder of the age. I need not tell my reader, that I here point at the reign of Augustus, and I believe he will be of my opinion, that neither Virgil nor Horace would have gained so great a reputation in the world, had they not been the friends and admirers of each other. Indeed all the great writers of that age, for whom singly we have so great an esteem, stand up together as vouchers for one another's reputation. But at the same time that Virgil was celebrated by Gallus, Propertius, Horace, Varius, Tucca and Ovid, we know that Bavius and Maevius were his declared foes and calumniators.[n]

In our own country a man seldom sets up for a poet, without attacking the reputation of all his brothers in the art. The ignorance of the Moderns, the scribblers of the age, the decay of poetry are the topics of detraction, with which he makes his entrance into the world: but how much more noble is the fame that is built on

Motto: Horace, *Epistles*, 2. 1. 76–77.
> I hate a fop should scorn a *faultless* page,
> Because 'tis new, nor yet approved by age.   CREECH.

candour and ingenuity, according to those beautiful lines of Sir
John Denham, in his poem on Fletcher's works.

> But whither am I strayed? I need not raise
> Trophies to thee from other men's dispraise;
> Nor is thy fame on lesser ruins built,
> Nor needs thy juster title the foul guilt
> Of eastern kings, who to secure their reign
> Must have their brothers, sons, and kindred slain.

I am sorry to find that an author, who is very justly esteemed
among the best judges, has admitted some strokes of this nature
into a very fine poem, I mean *The Art of Criticism*, which was published some months since, and is a masterpiece in its kind. The
observations follow one another like those in Horace's *Art of Poetry*,
without that methodical regularity which would have been requisite
in a prose author. They are some of them uncommon, but such as
the reader must assent to, when he sees them explained with that
elegance and perspicuity in which they are delivered. As for those
which are the most known, and the most received, they are placed in
so beautiful a light, and illustrated with such apt allusions, that they
have in them all the graces of novelty, and make the reader, who was
before acquainted with them, still more convinced of their truth and
solidity. And here give me leave to mention what Monsieur Boileau
has so very well enlarged upon in the preface to his works, that wit
and fine writing doth not consist so much in advancing things that
are new, as in giving things that are known an agreeable turn.[n]
It is impossible, for us who live in the later ages of the world, to make
observations in criticism, morality, or in any art or science, which
have not been touched upon by others. We have little else left us,
but to represent the common sense of mankind in more strong, more
beautiful, or more uncommon lights. If a reader examines Horace's
Art of Poetry, he will find but very few precepts in it, which he may
not meet with in Aristotle, and which were not commonly known by
all the poets of the Augustan Age. His way of expressing and applying
them, not his invention of them, is what we are chiefly to admire.

For this reason I think there is nothing in the world so tiresome
as the works of those critics, who write in a positive dogmatic way,
without either language, genius or imagination. If the reader would
see how the best of the Latin critics writ, he may find their manner

---

Candour: here and, as frequently in the *Spectator*, in the now obsolete sense of
'freedom from malice'. Johnson defines the word as 'sweetness of temper,
kindness'.

The Art of Criticism: Pope's *Essay on Criticism* had been advertised in *Spectator*
65 (15 May 1711) as 'this day' published.

very beautifully described in the characters of Horace, Petronius, Quintilian and Longinus, as they are drawn in the essay of which I am now speaking.

Since I have mentioned Longinus, who in his reflections has given us the same kind of sublime, which he observes in the several passages that occasioned them; I cannot but take notice, that our English author has after the same manner exemplified several of his precepts in the very precepts themselves. I shall produce two or three instances of this kind. Speaking of the insipid smoothness which some readers are so much in love with, he has the following verses.

> These equal syllables alone require,
> Though oft the ear the open vowels tire,
> While expletives their feeble aid do join,
> And ten low words oft creep in one dull line.

The gaping of the vowels in the second line, the expletive *do* in the third, and the ten monosyllables in the fourth, give such a beauty to this passage, as would have been very much admired in an ancient poet. The reader may observe the following lines in the same view.

> A needless Alexandrine ends the song,
> That like a wounded snake, drags its slow length along.

And afterwards,

> 'Tis not enough no harshness gives offence,
> The sound must seem an echo to the sense.
> Soft is the strain when Zephyr gently blows,
> And the smooth stream in smoother numbers flows
> But when loud surges lash the sounding shore,
> The hoarse, rough verse should like the torrent roar.
> When Ajax strives, some rock's vast weight to throw,
> The line too labours, and the words move slow;
> Not so, when swift Camilla scours the plain,
> Flies o'er th'unbending corn, and skims along the main.

The beautiful distich upon Ajax in the foregoing lines, puts me in mind of a description in Homer's *Odyssey*, which none of the critics have taken notice of.[n] It is where Sisyphus is represented lifting his stone up the hill, which is no sooner carried to the top of it, but it immediately tumbles to the bottom. This double motion

---

'*Tis not enough*: The three passages quoted from Pope's *Essay* are lines 344–7, 356–7, 364–73.
Odyssey: 11. 593–8.

of the stone is admirably described in the numbers of these verses. As in the four first it is heaved up by several spondees, intermixed with proper breathing-places, and at last trundles down in a continued line of dactyls.

Καὶ μὴν Σίσυφον εἰσεῖδον, κρατέρ' ἄλγε' ἔχοντα,
λᾶαν βαστάζοντα πελώριον ἀμφοτέρῃσιν.
Ἤτοι ὁ μέν, σκηριπτόμενος χερσίν τε ποσίν τε,
λᾶαν ἄνω ὤθεσκε ποτὶ λόφον. ἀλλ' ὅτε μέλλοι
ἄκρον ὑπερβαλέειν, τότ' ἀποστρέψασκε Κραταιίς,
αὖτις ἔπειτα πέδονδε κυλίνδετο λᾶας ἀναιδής.

It would be endless to quote verses out of Virgil which have this particular kind of beauty in the numbers; but I may take an occasion in a future paper to show several of them which have escaped the observation of others.

I cannot conclude this paper without taking notice that we have three poems in our tongue, which are of the same nature, and each of them a masterpiece in its kind; the *Essay on Translated Verse*, the *Essay on the Art of Poetry*, and the *Essay upon Criticism*.[n]

Paradise Lost

Cedite Romani scriptores, cedite Graii.   Propert.

There is nothing in nature more irksome than general discourses, especially when they turn chiefly upon words. For this reason I shall waive the discussion of that point which was started some years since, whether Milton's *Paradise Lost* may be called an heroic poem?[n] Those who will not give it that title, may call it (if they please) a divine poem. It will be sufficient to its perfection, if it has in it all the beauties of the highest kind of poetry; and as for those who allege it is not an heroic poem, they advance no more to the diminution of it, than if they should say Adam is not Aeneas, nor Eve Helen.

I shall therefore examine it by the rules of epic poetry, and see whether it falls short of the *Iliad* or *Aeneid* in the beauties which are essential to that kind of writing. The first thing to be considered in an epic poem, is the fable, which is perfect or imperfect, according as the action which it relates is more or less so.[n] This action should have three qualifications in it. First, it should be but one action.[n] Secondly, it should be an entire action; and thirdly, it should be a great action. To consider the action of the *Iliad*, *Aeneid*, and *Paradise Lost* in these three several lights. Homer to preserve the unity of his action hastens into the midst of things, as Horace has observed: had he gone up to Leda's egg, or begun much later, even at the rape of Helen, or the investing of Troy, it is manifest that the story of the poem would have been a series of several actions. He therefore opens his poem with the discord of his princes, and artfully interweaves in the several succeeding parts of it, an account of every thing material which relates to them, and had passed before this fatal dissension. After the same manner Aeneas makes his first appearance in the Tyrrhene seas, and within sight of Italy, because the action proposed to be celebrated was that of his settling himself in Latium. But because it was necessary for the reader to know what had happened to him in the taking of Troy, and in the preceding parts of his voyage, Virgil makes his hero relate it by way of episode in the

---

Motto: Propertius, *Elegies*, 2. 34. 65: Give place, ye bards of Rome and Grecian wits!

Horace: *Ars poetica*, 146–52.

Leda: in Greek mythology Helen was born of Leda and Zeus, who had courted her in the form of a swan.

second and third books of the *Aeneid*. The contents of both which books come before those of the first book in the thread of the story, though for preserving of this unity of action, they follow it in the disposition of the poem. Milton, in imitation of these two great poets, opens his *Paradise Lost* with an infernal council plotting the Fall of Man, which is the action he proposed to celebrate; and as for those great actions, the battle of the angels, and the creation of the world, (which preceded in point of time, and which, in my opinion, would have entirely destroyed the unity of his principal action, had he related them in the same order that they happened) he cast them into the fifth, sixth and seventh books, by way of episode to this noble poem.

Aristotle himself allows, that Homer has nothing to boast of as to the unity of his fable, though at the same time that great critic and philosopher endeavours to palliate this imperfection in the Greek poet, by imputing it in some measure to the very nature of an epic poem. Some have been of opinion, that the *Aeneid* also labours in this particular, and has episodes which may be looked upon as excrescences rather than as parts of the action. On the contrary, the poem which we have now under our consideration, hath no other episodes than such as naturally arise from the subject, and yet is filled with such a multitude of astonishing incidents, that it gives us at the same time a pleasure of the greatest variety, and of the greatest simplicity; uniform in its nature, though diversified in the execution.

I must observe also, that as Virgil in the poem which was designed to celebrate the original of the Roman Empire, has described the birth of its great rival, the Carthaginian Commonwealth: Milton with the like art in his poem on the Fall of Man, has related the fall of those angels who are his professed enemies. Besides the many other beauties in such an episode, its running parallel with the great action of the poem, hinders it from breaking the unity so much as another episode would have done, that had not so great an affinity with the principal subject. In short, this is the same kind of beauty which the critics admire in the *Spanish Fryar, or the Double Discovery*, where the two different plots look like counterparts and copies of one another.

The second qualification required in the action of an epic poem is, that it should be an entire action: an action is entire when it is

---

Aristotle: Poetics, 26. 6.
Carthaginian Commonwealth: see Le Bossu, Book ii, Ch. xi.
The Spanish Fryar, or the Double Discovery: by Dryden (1681).

complete in all its parts; or as Aristotle describes it, when it consists of a beginning, a middle, and an end. Nothing should go before it, be intermixed with it, or follow after it, that is not related to it. As on the contrary, no single step should be omitted in that just and regular progress which it must be supposed to take from its original to its consummation. Thus we see the anger of Achilles in its birth, its continuance and effects; and Aeneas's settlement in Italy, carried on through all the oppositions in his way to it both by sea and land. The action in Milton excels (I think) both the former in this particular; we see it contrived in Hell, executed upon Earth, and punished by Heaven. The parts of it are told in the most distinct manner, and grow out of one another in the most natural order.

The third qualification of an epic poem is its greatness. The anger of Achilles was of such consequence, that it embroiled the kings of Greece, destroyed the heroes of Asia, and engaged all the gods in factions. Aeneas's settlement in Italy produced the Caesars, and gave birth to the Roman Empire. Milton's subject was still greater than either of the former; it does not determine the fate of single persons or nations, but of a whole species. The united powers of Hell are joined together for the destruction of mankind, which they effected in part, and would have completed, had not Omnipotence itself interposed. The principal actors are Man in his greatest perfection, and Woman in her highest beauty. Their enemies are the fallen angels: the Messiah their friend, and the Almighty their protector. In short, every thing that is great in the whole circle of being, whether within the verge of nature, or out of it, has a proper part assigned it in this admirable poem.

In poetry, as in architecture, not only the whole, but the principal members, and every part of them, should be great. I will not presume to say, that the Book of Games in the *Aeneid*, or that in the *Iliad*, are not of this nature, nor to reprehend Virgil's simile of the top, and many other of the same kind in the *Iliad*, as liable to any censure in this particular; but I think we may say, without derogating from those wonderful performances, that there is an indisputable and unquestioned magnificence in every part of *Paradise Lost*, and indeed a much greater than could have been formed upon any pagan system.

But Aristotle, by the greatness of the action, does not only mean

---

Aristotle: *Poetics*, 23. 1.
Book of Games: *Aeneid*, 5; *Iliad*, 23.
simile of the top: *Aeneid*, 7. 378–84.
Aristotle: *Poetics*, 7. 4.

that it should be great in its nature, but also in its duration, or in other words, that it should have a due length in it, as well as what we properly call greatness. The just measure of this kind of magnitude, he explains by the following similitude. An animal, no bigger than a mite, cannot appear perfect to the eye, because the sight takes it in at once, and has only a confused idea of the whole, and not a distinct idea of all its parts; if on the contrary you should suppose an animal of ten thousand furlongs in length, the eye would be so filled with a single part of it, that it could not give the mind an idea of the whole. What these animals are to the eye, a very short or a very long action would be to the memory. The first would be, as it were, lost and swallowed up by it, and the other difficult to be contained in it. Homer and Virgil have shown their principal art in this particular; the action of the *Iliad*, and that of the *Aeneid*, were in themselves exceeding short, but are so beautifully extended and diversified by the invention of episodes[n], and the machinery of gods, with the like poetical ornaments, that they make up an agreeable story sufficient to employ the memory without overcharging it. Milton's action is enriched with such a variety of circumstances, that I have taken as much pleasure in reading the contents of his books, as in the best invented story I ever met with. It is possible, that the traditions on which the *Iliad* and *Aeneid* were built, had more circumstances in them than the history of the Fall of Man, as it is related in Scripture. Besides it was easier for Homer and Virgil to dash the truth with fiction, as they were in no danger of offending the religion of their country by it. But as for Milton, he had not only a very few circumstances upon which to raise his poem, but was also obliged to proceed with the greatest caution in everything that he added out of his own invention. And, indeed, notwithstanding all the restraints he was under, he has filled his story with so many surprising incidents, which bear so close analogy with what is delivered in Holy Writ, that it is capable of pleasing the most delicate reader, without giving offence to the most scrupulous.

The modern critics have collected from several hints in the *Iliad* and *Aeneid* the space of time, which is taken up by the action of each of those poems;[n] but as a great part of Milton's story was transacted in regions that lie out of the reach of the sun and the sphere of day, it is impossible to gratify the reader with such a calculation, which indeed would be more curious than instructive; none of the critics, either ancient or modern, having laid down rules to circumscribe the action of an epic poem with any determined number of years, days or hours.

But of this more particularly hereafter.

273   *Saturday January 12 1712*

. . . *Notandi sunt tibi mores.*   Hor.

Having examined the action of *Paradise Lost*, let us in the next place consider the actors. This is Aristotle's method of considering; first the fable, and secondly the manners, or, as we generally call them in English, the fable and the characters.[n]

Homer has excelled all the heroic poets that ever wrote, in the multitude and variety of his characters. Every god that is admitted into his poem, acts a part which would have been suitable to no other deity. His princes are as much distinguished by their manners as by their dominions; and even those among them, whose characters seem wholly made up of courage, differ from one another as to the particular kinds of courage in which they excel. In short, there is scarce a speech or action in the *Iliad*, which the reader may not ascribe to the person that speaks or acts, without seeing his name at the head of it.

Homer does not only outshine all other poets in the variety, but also in the novelty of his characters. He has introduced among his Grecian princes a person, who had lived in three Ages of Men, and conversed with Theseus, Hercules, Polyphemus, and the first race of heroes. His principal actor is the son of a goddess, not to mention the offspring of other deities, who have likewise a place in his poem, and the venerable Trojan prince, who was the father of so many kings and heroes. There is in these several characters of Homer, a

Motto: Horace, *Ars poetica*, 156: Note well the manners.

Ages of Men: Nestor, king of Pylos, the wise, aged statesman in the *Iliad* (1. 247–65).

Theseus: King of Attica, famous for slaying the Minotaur in Crete, as well as for other exploits. *Hercules*, the best known of the Greek legendary heroes, and personification of masculine strength. *Polyphemus*, one of the Cyclopes (*Odyssey*, Book ix).

son of a goddess: Achilles, leader of the Myrmidons and slayer of Hector. Thetis, a Nereid, married a mortal (Peleus) and became mother of Achilles.

Trojan prince: Priam, King of Troy, slain by Neoptolemus at the taking of the city (*Iliad*, Book xxiv), father of Hector and Paris.

certain dignity as well as novelty, which adapts them in a more peculiar manner to the nature of an heroic poem. Though, at the same time, to give them the greater variety, he has described a Vulcan, that is, a buffoon among his gods, and a Thersites among his mortals.

Virgil falls infinitely short of Homer in the characters of his poem, both as to their variety and novelty. Aeneas is indeed a perfect character, but as for Achates, though he is styled the hero's friend, he does nothing in the whole poem which may deserve that title. Gyas, Mnestheus, Sergetus and Cloanthus, are all of them men of the same stamp and character,

> ... Fortemque Gyan, fortemque Cloanthum.

There are indeed several very natural incidents in the part of Ascanius, as that of Dido cannot be sufficiently admired. I do not see anything new or particular in Turnus. Pallas and Evander are remote copies of Hector and Priam, as Lausus and Mezentius are almost parallels to Pallas and Evander. The characters of Nisus and Euryalus are beautiful, but common. We must not forget the parts of Sinon, Camilla, and some few others, which are fine improvements on the Greek poet. In short, there is neither that variety nor novelty in the persons of the *Aeneid*, which we meet with in those of the *Iliad*.

If we look into the characters of Milton, we shall find that he has introduced all the variety his fable was capable of receiving. The whole species of mankind was in two persons at the time to which the subject of his poem is confined. We have, however, four distinct characters in these two persons. We see Man and Woman in the

---

Vulcan: Hephaestus, god of fire (especially volcanic fire), depicted as lame and frequently in ridiculous situations. *Thersites*: Homer shows him as railing at Agamemnon (*Iliad*, 2. 211–77).

Virgil: *Aeneid*, 1. 222: (brave Gyas, brave Cloanthus).

persons of the Aeneid: of the persons in the *Aeneid* mentioned here, Ascanius was the son of Aeneas; Dido was the Queen of Carthage, who welcomed Aeneas and his men after their shipwreck and who took her own life when Aeneas left her (Book iv); Turnus, King of the Rutuli, opposed the invasion of the Trojans and the proposed marriage of Lavinia to Aeneas, and was slain by Aeneas; Pallas, the son of King Evander of Pallanteum (Book viii), would be a counterpart of Hector, son of Priam of Troy; Lausus and his father Mezentius were among the warriors who opposed the invasion of the Trojans (Book vii); Nisus and Euryalus, of all the companions of Aeneas, formed the closest friendship: they took part in the foot-race in Book v, and were both killed in a nocturnal raid on the Latian camp (Book ix); Sinon was the Greek spy who succeeded in getting the wooden horse into Troy (Book ii); and Camilla was the famous Volscian warrior described at the close of Book vii.

highest innocence and perfection, and in the most abject state of guilt and infirmity. The two last characters are, indeed, very common and obvious, but the two first are not only more magnificent, but more new than any characters either in Virgil or Homer, or indeed in the whole circle of nature.[n]

Milton was so sensible of this defect in the subject of his poem, and of the few characters it would afford him, that he has brought into it two actors of a shadowy and fictitious nature, in the persons of Sin and Death,[n] by which means he has wrought into the body of his fable a very beautiful and well invented allegory. But notwithstanding the fineness of this allegory may atone for it in some measure; I cannot think that persons of such a chimerical existence are proper actors in an epic poem; because there is not that measure of probability annexed to them, which is requisite in writings of this kind, as I shall show more at large hereafter.

Virgil has, indeed, admitted Fame as an actress in the *Aeneid*, but the part she acts is very short, and none of the most admired circumstances in that divine work. We find in mock-heroic poems, particularly in the *Dispensary* and the *Lutrin*,[n] several allegorical persons of this nature, which are very beautiful in those compositions, and may, perhaps, be used as an argument, that the authors of them were of opinion, such characters might have a place in an epic work. For my own part, I should be glad the reader would think so, for the sake of the poem I am now examining, and must further add, that if such empty unsubstantial beings may be ever made use of on this occasion, never were any more nicely imagined, and employed in more proper actions, than those of which I am now speaking.

Another principal actor in this poem is the great Enemy of Mankind. The part of Ulysses in Homer's *Odyssey* is very much admired by Aristotle, as perplexing that fable with very agreeable plots and intricacies, not only by the many adventures in his voyage, and the subtlety of his behaviour, but by the various concealments and discoveries of his person in several parts of that poem.[n] But the crafty being I have now mentioned, makes a much longer voyage than Ulysses, puts in practice many more wiles and stratagems, and hides himself under a greater variety of shapes and appearances, all of which are severally detected, to the great delight and surprise of the reader.

We may likewise observe with how much art the poet has varied several characters of the persons that speak in his infernal assembly.

Fame: *Aeneid*, 4. 173–97.
Aristotle: *Poetics*, 17. 5; 24. 10.

On the contrary, how has he represented the whole Godhead exerting itself towards man in its full benevolence under the threefold distinction of a Creator, a Redeemer, and a Comforter!

Nor must we omit the person of Raphael, who amidst his tenderness and friendship for man, shows such a dignity and condescension in all his speech and behaviour, as are suitable to a superior nature. The angels are indeed as much diversified in Milton, and distinguished by their proper parts, as the gods are in Homer or Virgil. The reader will find nothing ascribed to Uriel, Gabriel, Michael, or Raphael, which is not in a particular manner suitable to their respective characters.[n]

There is another circumstance in the principal actors of the *Iliad* and *Aeneid*, which gives a peculiar beauty to those two poems, and was therefore contrived with very great judgement.[n] I mean the authors' having chosen for their heroes persons who were so nearly related to the people for whom they wrote. Achilles was a Greek, and Aeneas the remote founder of Rome. By this means their countrymen (whom they principally proposed to themselves for their readers) were particularly attentive to all the parts of their story, and sympathized with their heroes in all their adventures. A Roman could not but rejoice in the escapes, successes and victories of Aeneas, and be grieved at any defeats, misfortunes or disappointments that befell him; as a Greek must have had the same regard for Achilles. And it is plain, that each of those poems have lost this great advantage, among those readers to whom their heroes are as strangers, or indifferent persons.

Milton's poem is admirable in this respect, since it is impossible for any of its readers, whatever nation, country or people he may belong to, not to be related to the persons who are the principal actors in it; but what is still infinitely more to its advantage, the principal actors in this poem are not only our progenitors, but our representatives. We have an actual interest in everything they do, and no less than our utmost happiness is concerned, and lies at stake in all their behaviour.

I shall subjoin as a corollary to the foregoing remark, an admirable observation out of Aristotle, which hath been very much misrepresented in the quotations of some modern critics. 'If a man of perfect and consummate virtue falls into a misfortune, it raises our pity, but not our terror, because we do not fear that it may be our own case, who do not resemble the suffering person.'[n] But as that great philosopher adds, 'If we see a man of virtue mixed with infirmities, fall into any misfortune, it does not only raise our pity but our terror; because we are afraid that the like misfortunes may happen to ourselves, who resemble the character of the suffering person.'

I shall only remark in this place, that the foregoing observation of Aristotle, though it may be true in other occasions, does not hold in this; because in the present case, though the persons who fall into misfortune are of the most perfect and consummate virtue, it is not to be considered as what may possibly be, but what actually is our own case; since we are embarked with them on the same bottom, and must be partakers of their happiness or misery.

In this, and some other very few instances, Aristotle's rules for epic poetry (which he had drawn from his reflections upon Homer) cannot be supposed to square exactly with the heroic poems which have been made since his time; since it is evident to every impartial judge his rules would still have been more perfect, could he have perused the *Aeneid* which was made some hundred years after his death.

In my next I shall go through other parts of Milton's poem; and hope that what I shall there advance, as well as what I have already written, will not only serve as a comment upon Milton, but upon Aristotle.

279   *Saturday January 19 1712*

Reddere personae scit convenientia cuique.   Hor.

We have already taken a general survey of the fable and characters in Milton's *Paradise Lost*: the parts which remain to be considered, according to Aristotle's method, are the sentiments and the language. Before I enter upon the first of these, I must advertise my reader, that it is my design as soon as I have finished my general reflections on these four several heads, to give particular instances out of the poem now before us of beauties and imperfections which may be observed under each of them, as also of such other particulars as may not properly fall under any of them. This I thought fit to premise, that the reader may not judge too hastily of this piece of criticism, or look upon it as imperfect, before he has seen the whole extent of it.

The sentiments in an epic poem are the thoughts and behaviour

Motto: Horace, *Ars poetica*, 316: He knows how to give each person a becoming part.

which the author ascribes to the persons whom he introduces, and are *just* when they are conformable to the characters of the several persons. The sentiments have likewise a relation to *things* as well as *persons*, and are then perfect when they are such as are adapted to the subject. If in either of these cases the poet endeavours to argue or explain, to magnify or diminish, to raise love or hatred, pity or terror, or any other passion, we ought to consider whether the sentiments he makes use of are proper for those ends. Homer is censured by the critics for his defect as to this particular in several parts of the *Iliad* and *Odyssey*, though at the same time those who have treated this great poet with candour, have attributed this defect to the times in which he lived.[n] It was the fault of the age, and not of Homer, if there wants that delicacy in some of his sentiments, which now appears in the works of men of a much inferior genius. Besides, if there are blemishes in any particular thoughts, there is an infinite beauty in the greatest part of them. In short, if there are many poets who would not have fallen into the meanness of some of his sentiments, there are none who could have risen up to the greatness of others. Virgil has excelled all others in the propriety of his sentiments. Milton shines likewise very much in this particular: nor must we omit one consideration which adds to his honour and reputation. Homer and Virgil introduced persons whose characters are commonly known among men, and such as are to be met with either in history, or in ordinary conversation. Milton's characters, most of them, lie out of nature, and were to be formed purely by his own invention. It shows a greater genius in Shakespeare, to have drawn his Caliban, than his Hotspur or Julius Caesar: the one was to be supplied out of his own imagination, whereas the other might have been formed upon tradition, history and observation.[n] It was much easier therefore for Homer to find proper sentiments for an assembly of Grecian generals, than for Milton to diversify his Infernal Council with proper characters, and inspire them with a variety of sentiments. The loves of Dido and Aeneas are only copies of what passed between other persons. Adam and Eve, before the Fall, are a different species from that of mankind, who are descended from them; and none but a poet of the most unbounded invention, and the most exquisite judgement, could have filled their conversation and behaviour with so many apt circumstances during their state of innocence.

Nor is it sufficient for an epic poem to be filled with such thoughts

---

candour: here used in the sense of 'openness of mind, fairness, impartiality, justice'.

as are natural, unless it abound also with such as are sublime. Virgil in this particular falls short of Homer.[n] He has not indeed so many thoughts that are low and vulgar; but at the same time has not so many thoughts that are sublime and noble. The truth of it is, Virgil seldom rises into very astonishing sentiments, where he is not fired by the *Iliad*. He everywhere charms and pleases us by the force of his own genius; but seldom elevates and transports us where he does not fetch his hints from Homer.

Milton's chief talent, and indeed his distinguishing excellence, lies in the sublimity of his thoughts. There are others of the moderns who rival him in every other part of poetry; but in the greatness of his sentiments he triumphs over all the poets both modern and ancient, Homer only excepted. It is impossible for the imagination of man to distend itself with greater ideas, than those which he has laid together in his first, second and sixth books. The seventh, which describes the Creation of the World, is likewise wonderfully sublime, though not so apt to stir up emotion in the mind of the reader, nor consequently so perfect in the epic way of writing, because it is filled with less action. Let the judicious reader compare what Longinus has observed on several passages in Homer, and he will find parallels for most of them in the *Paradise Lost*.

From what has been said we may infer, that as there are two kinds of sentiments, the natural and the sublime, which are always to be pursued in an heroic poem, there are also two kinds of thoughts which are carefully to be avoided. The first are such as are affected and unnatural; the second such as are mean and vulgar. As for the first kind of thoughts we meet with little or nothing that is like them in Virgil: he has none of those trifling points and puerilities that are so often to be met with in Ovid, none of the epigrammatic turns of Lucan, none of those swelling sentiments which are so frequent in Statius and Claudian, none of those mixed embellishments of Tasso.[n] Everything is just and natural. His sentiments show that he had a perfect insight into human nature, and that he knew everything which was the most proper to affect it.

Mr. Dryden has in some places, which I may hereafter take notice of, misrepresented Virgil's way of thinking as to this particular, in the translation he has given us of the *Aeneid*. I do not remember that Homer anywhere falls into the faults above-mentioned, which were indeed the false refinements of later ages. Milton, it must be confessed, has sometimes erred in this respect, as I shall show more

---

Longinus: *On the Sublime*, 9.
points: witty or ingenious turns of thought.

at large in another paper; though considering all the poets of the age in which he writ, were infected with this wrong way of thinking, he is rather to be admired that he did not give more into it, than that he did sometimes comply with the vicious taste which prevails so much among modern writers.

But since several thoughts may be natural which are low and grovelling, an epic poet should not only avoid such sentiments as are unnatural or affected, but also such as are mean and vulgar. Homer has opened a great field of raillery to men of more delicacy than greatness of genius, by the homeliness of some of his sentiments. But, as I have before said, these are rather to be imputed to the simplicity of the age in which he lived, to which I may also add, of that which he described, than to any imperfection in that divine poet. Zoilus, among the Ancients, and Monsieur Perrault, among the Moderns, pushed their ridicule very far upon him, on account of some such sentiments. There is no blemish to be observed in Virgil under this head, and but a very few in Milton.

I shall give but one instance of this impropriety of thought in Homer, and at the same time compare it with an instance of the same nature, both in Virgil and Milton. Sentiments which raise laughter, can very seldom be admitted with any decency into an heroic poem, whose business is to excite passions of a much nobler nature. Homer, however, in his characters of Vulcan and Thersites, in his story of Mars and Venus, in his behaviour of Irus, and in other passages, has been observed to have lapsed into the burlesque character, and to have departed from that serious air which seems essential to the magnificence of an epic poem. I remember but one laugh in the whole *Aeneid*, which rises in the fifth book upon Monoetes, where he is represented as thrown overboard, and drying

---

another paper: No. 297 (pp. 83–8 below).

Zoilus of Amphipolis: a rhetorician of the fourth century B.C., who wrote nine books against Homer, attacking the Homeric epics on aesthetic, grammatical, and moral grounds.

Charles Perrault: (1628–1703), in the *Parallèles des Anciens et des Modernes*, the first volume of which appeared in 1688, sought to prove the superiority of modern authors over the ancients. See also Boileau, *Critical Reflections on Longinus*, especially Reflection vi.

Vulcan and Thersites: described together in No. 273 (page 67) above, as buffoons, the first among Homer's gods, the second among his mortals. *Iliad*, 1. 595–600; 2. 211–77.

Mars and Venus: *Odyssey*, 8. 266–366.

Irus: the beggar with whom Odysseus fights on his return to Ithaca (*Odyssey*, 18. 1–107).

Monoetes: *Aeneid*, 5. 158–82.

himself upon a rock. But this piece of mirth is so well timed, that the severest critic can have nothing to say against it, for it is in the book of games and diversions, where the reader's mind may be supposed to be sufficiently relaxed for such an entertainment. The only piece of pleasantry in *Paradise Lost*, is where the evil spirits are described as rallying the angels upon the success of their new invented artillery. This passage I look upon to be the most exceptionable in the whole poem, as being nothing else but a string of puns, and those too very indifferent.

>   . . . Satan beheld their plight,
> And to his mates thus in derision called.
>   O friends, why come not on these victors proud!
> Erewhile they fierce were coming, and when we,
> To entertain them fair with open front,
> And breast, (what could we more) propounded terms
> Of composition, straight they changed their minds,
> Flew off, and into strange vagaries fell,
> As they would dance, yet for a dance they seemed
> Somewhat extravagant, and wild, perhaps
> For joy of offered peace: but I suppose
> If our proposals once again were heard,
> We should compel them to a quick result.
>   To whom thus Belial in like gamesome mood.
> Leader, the terms we sent, were terms of weight,
> Of hard contents, and full of force urged home,
> Such as we might perceive amused them all,
> And stumbled many; who receives them right,
> Had need, from head to foot, well understand;
> Not understood, this gift they have besides,
> They show us when our foes walk not upright.
>   Thus they among themselves in pleasant vein
> Stood scoffing . . .

Satan beheld: *PL*, vi. 607–29 ('So they', line 628).

285 *Saturday January 26 1712*

Ne quicunque deus, quicunque adhibebitur heros,
regali conspectus in auro nuper et ostro,
migret in obscuras humili sermone tabernas:
aut dum vitat humum, nubes et inania captet. Hor.

Having already treated of the fable, the characters, and sentiments in the *Paradise Lost*, we are in the last place to consider the language; and as the learned world is very much divided upon Milton as to this point, I hope they will excuse me if I appear particular in any of my opinions, and incline to those who judge the most advantageously of the author.[n]

It is requisite that the language of an heroic poem should be both perspicuous and sublime.[n] In proportion as either of these two qualities are wanting, the language is imperfect. Perspicuity is the first and most necessary qualification; insomuch, that a good-natured reader sometimes overlooks a little slip even in the grammar or syntax, where it is impossible for him to mistake the poet's sense. Of this kind is that passage in Milton, wherein he speaks of Satan.

> ... God and his Son except,
> Created thing nought valued he nor shunned.

And that in which he describes Adam and Eve.

> Adam the goodliest man of men since born
> His sons, the fairest of her daughters Eve.

It is plain, that in the former of these passages, according to the natural syntax, the divine persons mentioned in the first line are represented as created beings; and that in the other, Adam and Eve are confounded with their sons and daughters. Such little blemishes as these, when the thought is great and natural, we should, with Horace, impute to a pardonable inadvertency, or to the weakness

Motto: Horace, *Ars poetica*, 227–30:

> But then they did not wrong themselves so much
> To make a god, a hero, or a king,
> (Stripped of his golden crown and purple robe)
> Descend to a mechanic dialect,
> Nor (to avoid such meanness) soaring high
> With empty sound, and airy notions fly. ROSCOMMON.

Satan: *PL*, ii. 678–9.
Adam and Eve: *PL*, iv. 323–4.
Horace: *Ars poetica*, 351–3.

of human nature, which cannot attend to each minute particular, and give the last finishing to every circumstance in so long a work. The ancient critics therefore, who were acted by a spirit of candour, rather than that of cavilling, invented certain figures of speech, on purpose to palliate little errors of this nature in the writings of those authors, who had so many greater beauties to atone for them.

If clearness and perspicuity were only to be consulted, the poet would have nothing else to do but to clothe his thoughts in the most plain and natural expressions. But, since it often happens, that the most obvious phrases, and those which are used in ordinary conversation, become too familiar to the ear, and contract a kind of meanness by passing through the mouths of the vulgar, a poet should take particular care to guard himself against idiomatic ways of speaking. Ovid and Lucan have many poornesses of expression upon this account, as taking up with the first phrases that offered, without putting themselves to the trouble of looking after such as would not only be natural, but also elevated and sublime. Milton has but a few failings in this kind, of which, however, you may meet with some instances, as in the following passages.

> Embryos and idiots, eremites and friars
> White, black and grey, with all their trumpery,
> Here pilgrims roam . . .
> . . . A while discourse they hold,
> No fear lest dinner cool; when thus began
> Our author . . .
> Who of all ages to succeed, but feeling
> The evil on him brought by me, will curse
> My head. 'Ill fare our ancestor impure,
> For this we may thank Adam' . . .

The great masters in composition know very well that many an elegant phrase becomes improper for a poet or an orator, when it has been debased by common use. For this reason the works of ancient authors, which are written in dead languages, have a great advantage over those which are written in languages that are now spoken. Were there any mean phrases or idioms in Virgil and Homer, they would not shock the ear of the most delicate modern reader, so much as they would have done that of an old Greek or Roman,

---

candour: here used in the sense of 'fairness, impartiality, justice'.
idiomatic: this is the first quotation in *OED* to illustrate this sense of the word, i.e. vernacular, colloquial.
Embryos and idiots: *PL*, iii. 474–6.
. . . A while discourse: *PL*, v. 395–7.
Who of all ages: *PL*, x. 733–6.

because we never hear them pronounced in our streets, or in ordinary conversation.

It is not therefore sufficient, that the language of an epic poem be perspicuous, unless it be also sublime. To this end it ought to deviate from the common forms and ordinary phrases of speech. The judgement of a poet very much discovers itself in shunning the common roads of expression, without falling into such ways of speech as may seem stiff and unnatural; he must not swell into a false sublime, by endeavouring to avoid the other extreme. Among the Greeks, Aeschylus, and sometimes Sophocles, were guilty of this fault; among the Latins, Claudian and Statius; and among our own countrymen, Shakespeare and Lee. In these authors the affectation of greatness often hurts the perspicuity of the style, as in many others the endeavour after perspicuity prejudices its greatness.

Aristotle has observed, that the idiomatic style may be avoided, and the sublime formed, by the following methods. First, by the use of metaphors: such are those in Milton.

> Imparadised in one another's arms,
> . . . And in his hand a reed
> Stood waving tipped with fire; . . .
> The grassy clods now calved. . . .
> Spangled with eyes . . .

In these and innumerable other instances, the metaphors are very bold but just; I must however observe, that the metaphors are not thick sown in Milton, which always savours too much of wit; that they never clash with one another, which as Aristotle observes, turns a sentence into a kind of an enigma or riddle; and that he seldom has recourse to them where the proper and natural words will do as well.

Another way of raising the language, and giving it a poetical turn, is to make use of the idioms of other tongues. Virgil is full of the Greek forms of speech, which the critics call Hellenisms, as Horace

---

Aeschylus (525–456 B.C.) and *Sophocles* (496–406 B.C.): Greek dramatic poets.
Claudian: for Claudian and Statius, see No. 279 above (p. 72, and note).
Lee: Nathaniel Lee (1653 ?–92), bombastic writer of tragedies, was frequently linked with Shakespeare at this time.
Aristotle: *Poetics*, 22. 1.
Imparadised: *PL*, iv. 506.
. . . And in his hand: *PL*, vi. 579–80.
The grassy clods: *PL*, vii. 463.
Spangled with eyes: *PL*, xi. 130.
riddle: *Poetics*, 22. 2.
tongues: Ibid. 22. 2–3.

4*

in his Odes abounds with them much more than Virgil. I need not mention the several dialects which Homer has made use of for this end. Milton, in conformity with the practice of the ancient poets, and with Aristotle's rule has infused a great many Latinisms, as well as Grecisms, and sometimes Hebraisms, into the language of his poem, as towards the beginning of it.

> Nor did they not perceive the evil plight
> In which they were, or the fierce pains not feel.
> Yet to their Gen'ral's voice they soon obeyed.
> . . . Who shall tempt with wand'ring feet
> The dark unbottomed infinite abyss,
> And through the palpable obscure find out
> His uncouth way, or spread his airy flight
> Upborn with indefatigable wings
> Over the vast abrupt!
> . . . So both ascend
> In the visions of God . . .

Under this head may be reckoned the placing the adjective after the substantive, the transposition of words, the turning the adjective into a substantive, with several other foreign modes of speech, which this poet has naturalized to give his verse the greater sound, and throw it out of prose.

The third method mentioned by Aristotle, is what agrees with the genius of the Greek language more than with that of any other tongue, and is therefore more used by Homer than by any other poet. I mean the lengthening of a phrase by the addition of words, which may either be inserted or omitted, as also by the extending or contracting of particular words by the insertion or omission of certain syllables. Milton has put in practice this method of raising his language, as far as the nature of our tongue will permit, as in the passage above-mentioned, Eremite, for what is hermit, in common discourse. If you observe the measure of his verse, he has with great judgement suppressed a syllable in several words, and shortened those of two syllables into one, by which method, besides the above-mentioned advantage, he has given a greater variety to his numbers. But this practice is more particularly remarkable in the names of persons and of countries, as Beëlzebub, Hessebon,

---

Nor did they not perceive: *PL*, i. 335–7.
. . . *Who shall tempt*: *PL*, ii. 404–9.
. . . *So both ascend*: *PL*, xi. 376–7.
Aristotle: *Poetics*, 22. 4.
Beëlzebub: the Latin Vulgate form of the Hebrew *Baal-zebub*.
Hessebon: (*PL*, i. 408), the Greek form of the Hebrew *Heshbon*.

and in many other particulars, wherein he has either changed the name, or made use of that which is not the most commonly known, that he might the better depart from the language of the vulgar.

The same reason recommended to him several old words, which also makes his poem appear the more venerable, and gives it a greater air of antiquity.[n]

I must likewise take notice, that there are in Milton several words of his own coining, as Cerberean, miscreated, Hell-doomed, embryon atoms, and many others. If the reader is offended at this liberty in our English poet, I would recommend him to a discourse in Plutarch, which shows us how frequently Homer has made use of the same liberty.

Milton, by the above-mentioned helps, and by the choice of the noblest words and phrases which our tongue would afford him, has carried our language to a greater height than any of the English poets have ever done before or after him, and made the sublimity of his style equal to that of his sentiments.

I have been the more particular in these observations on Milton's style, because it is that part of him in which he appears the most singular. The remarks I have here made upon the practice of other poets, with my observations out of Aristotle, will perhaps alleviate the prejudice which some have taken to his poem upon this account; though after all, I must confess, that I think his style, though admirable in general, is in some places too much stiffened and obscured by the frequent use of those methods, which Aristotle has prescribed for the raising of it.

This redundancy of those several ways of speech which Aristotle calls 'foreign language', and with which Milton has so very much enriched, and in some places darkened the language of his poem, was the more proper for his use, because his poem is written in blank verse. Rhyme, without any other assistance, throws the language off from prose, and very often makes an indifferent phrase pass unregarded; but where the verse is not built upon rhymes, there pomp of sound, and energy of expression, are indispensably necessary to support the style, and keep it from falling into the flatness of prose.

Those who have not a taste for this elevation of style, and are

---

coining: *PL*, ii. 655, 683, 697, 900. J.D. (*Gentleman's Magazine*, April 1780, p. 175) pointed out that 'miscreated' was not coined by Milton, having been used by Spenser in *The Faerie Queene* (I. ii. 3. 1; II. vii. 42. 9). 'Cerberean' is also to be found earlier than Milton. 'Embryon': mod. 'embryo'.

Plutarch: *The Life and Poetry of Homer* (1. 16), formerly attributed to Plutarch.

foreign language: Aristotle, *Poetics*, 22. 1.

apt to ridicule a poet when he goes out of the common forms of expression, would do well to see how Aristotle has treated an ancient author, called Euclid, for his insipid mirth upon this occasion. Mr. Dryden used to call this sort of men his prose-critics.

I should, under this head of the language, consider Milton's numbers, in which he has made use of several elisions, that are not customary among other English poets, as may be particularly observed in his cutting off the letter Y when it precedes a vowel. This, and some other innovations in the measure of his verse, has varied his numbers in such a manner, as makes them incapable of satiating the ear and cloying the reader, which the same uniform measure would certainly have done, and which the perpetual returns of rhyme never fail to do in long narrative poems. I shall close these reflections upon the language of *Paradise Lost*, with observing that Milton has copied after Homer, rather than Virgil, in the length of his periods, the copiousness of his phrases, and the running of his verses into one another.

291   *Saturday February 2 1712*

. . . *Ubi plura nitent in carmine, non ego paucis*
offendar maculis, quas aut incuria fudit,
aut humana parum cavit natura . . . . Hor.

I have now considered Milton's *Paradise Lost* under those four great heads of the fable, the characters, the sentiments, and the language; and have shown that he excels, in general, under each of these heads. I hope that I have made several discoveries which may appear new, even to those who are versed in critical learning. Were I indeed to choose my readers, by whose judgement I would stand or fall, they should not be such as are acquainted only with the French and Italian critics, but also with the ancient and modern who have written in either of the learned languages. Above all, I would have them well versed in the Greek and Latin poets, without which a man

---

Euclid: Aristotle, *Poetics*, 22. 5.

Motto: Horace, *Ars poetica*, 351–3:
> If numerous graces shine in what he writes,
> I'll not condemn though some few faults appear,
> Which common frailty leaves, or want of care. CREECH.

very often fancies that he understands a critic, when in reality he does not comprehend his meaning.

It is in criticism, as in all other sciences and speculations; one who brings with him any implicit notions and observations which he has made in his reading of the poets, will find his own reflections methodized and explained, and perhaps several little hints that had passed in his mind, perfected and improved in the works of a good critic; whereas one who has not these previous lights, is very often an utter stranger to what he reads, and apt to put a wrong interpretation upon it.

Nor is it sufficient, that a man who sets up for a judge in criticism, should have perused the authors above-mentioned, unless he has also a clear and logical head. Without this talent he is perpetually puzzled and perplexed amidst his own blunders, mistakes the sense of those he would confute, or if he chances to think right, does not know how to convey his thoughts to another with clearness and perspicuity. Aristotle, who was the best critic, was also one of the best logicians that ever appeared in the world.

Mr. Locke's *Essay on Human Understanding* would be thought a very odd book for a man to make himself master of, who would get a reputation by critical writings; though at the same time it is very certain, that an author who has not learned the art of distinguishing between words and things, and of ranging his thoughts, and setting them in proper lights, whatever notions he may have, will lose himself in confusion and obscurity. I might further observe, that there is not a Greek or Latin critic who has not shown, even in the style of his criticisms, that he was a master of all the elegance and delicacy of his native tongue.

The truth of it is, there is nothing more absurd, than for a man to set up for a critic, without a good insight into all the parts of learning; whereas many of those who have endeavoured to signalize themselves by works of this nature among our English writers, are not only defective in the above-mentioned particulars, but plainly discover by the phrases which they make use of, and by their confused way of thinking, that they are not acquainted with the most common and ordinary systems of arts and sciences. A few general rules extracted out of the French authors, with a certain cant of words, has sometimes set up an illiterate heavy writer for a most judicious and formidable critic.

One great mark, by which you may discover a critic who has neither taste nor learning, is this, that he seldom ventures to praise any passage in an author which has not been before received and applauded by the public,[n] and that his criticism turns wholly upon little faults and errors. This part of a critic is so very easy to succeed in, that we find every ordinary reader, upon the publishing of a new poem, has wit and ill-nature enough to turn several passages of it into ridicule, and very often in the right place. This Mr. Dryden has very agreeably remarked in those two celebrated lines,

> Errors, like straws, upon the surface flow;
> He who would search for pearls must dive below.

A true critic ought to dwell rather upon excellencies than imperfections, to discover the concealed beauties of a writer, and communicate to the world such things as are worth their observation.[n] The most exquisite words and finest strokes of an author are those which very often appear the most doubtful and exceptionable, to a man who wants a relish for polite learning; and they are these, which a sour undistinguishing critic[n] generally attacks with the greatest violence. Tully observes, that it is very easy to brand or fix a mark upon what he calls *verbum ardens*, or, as it may be rendered into English, a glowing bold expression, and to turn it into ridicule by a cold ill-natured criticism. A little wit is equally capable of exposing a beauty, and of aggravating a fault; and though such a treatment of an author naturally produces indignation in the mind of an understanding reader, it has however its effect among the generality of those whose hands it falls into, the rabble of mankind being very apt to think that everything which is laughed at with any mixture of wit, is ridiculous in itself.

Such a mirth as this, is always unseasonable in a critic, as it rather prejudices the reader than convinces him, and is capable of making a beauty, as well as a blemish, the subject of derision. A man, who cannot write with wit on a proper subject, is dull and stupid, but one who shows it in an improper place, is as impertinent and absurd. Besides, a man who has the gift of ridicule is apt to find fault with anything that gives him an opportunity of exerting his beloved talent, and very often censures a passage, not because there is any fault in it, but because he can be merry upon it. Such kinds of pleasantry are very unfair and disingenuous in works of criticism, in which the greatest masters, both ancient and modern, have always appeared with a serious and instructive air.

As I intend in my next paper to show the defects in Milton's *Paradise Lost*, I thought fit to premise these few particulars, to the end that the reader may know I enter upon it, as on a very

Dryden: *All for Love, Prologue*, 25–6.
Tully: Cicero, *Ad Marcum Brutum Orator*, 8. 27.

ungrateful work, and that I shall just point at the imperfections, without endeavouring to inflame them with ridicule. I must also observe with Longinus, that the productions of a great genius, with many lapses and inadvertencies, are infinitely preferable to the works of an inferior kind of author, which are scrupulously exact and conformable to all the rules of correct writing.[n]

I shall conclude my paper with a story out of Boccalini, which sufficiently shows us the opinion that judicious author entertained of the sort of critics I have been here mentioning. A famous critic, says he, having gathered together all the faults of an eminent poet, made a present of them to Apollo, who received them very graciously, and resolved to make the author a suitable return for the trouble he had been at in collecting them. In order to this, he set before him a sack of wheat, as it had been just threshed out of the sheaf. He then bid him pick out the chaff from among the corn, and lay it aside by itself. The critic applied himself to the task with great industry and pleasure, and after having made the due separation, was presented by Apollo with the chaff for his pains.

297   *Saturday February 9 1712*

. . . velut si
egregio inspersos reprendas corpore naevos.   Hor.

After what I have said in my last Saturday's paper, I shall enter on the subject of this without farther preface, and remark the several defects which appear in the fable, the characters, the sentiments, and the language of Milton's *Paradise Lost*; not doubting but the reader will pardon me, if I allege at the same time whatever may be said for the extenuation of such defects. The first imperfection which I shall observe in the fable, is, that the event of it is unhappy.[n]

The fable of every poem is according to Aristotle's division either *simple* or *implex*. It is called simple when there is no change of

---

Longinus: *On the Sublime*, 33 (Ch. 27 in Boileau's translation).
Boccalini: Trajano Boccalini (1556–1613), the Italian satirist.
Advices from Parnassus (1706), pp. 184–5.
Motto: Horace, *Satires* 1. 6. 66–7: As perfect beauties often have a mole. CREECH.
implex: *Poetics*, 10. 1. Dacier (p. 159) translates: 'Fables are either Simple or Implex, for all those actions which fables imitate have either one or t'other of these qualities.'

fortune in it, implex when the fortune of the chief actor changes from bad to good, or from good to bad. The implex fable is thought the most perfect; I suppose, because it is more proper to stir up the passions of the reader, and to surprise him with a greater variety of accidents.

The implex fable is therefore of two kinds: in the first the chief actor makes his way through a long series of dangers and difficulties, till he arrives at honour and prosperity, as we see in the story of Ulysses. In the second, the chief actor in the poem falls from some eminent pitch of honour and prosperity, into misery and disgrace. Thus we see Adam and Eve sinking from a state of innocence and happiness, into the most abject condition of sin and sorrow.

The most taking tragedies among the Ancients were built on this last sort of implex fable, particularly the tragedy of *Oedipus*, which proceeds upon a story, if we may believe Aristotle, the most proper for tragedy that could be invented by the wit of man. I have taken some pains in a former paper to show, that this kind of implex fable, wherein the event is unhappy, is more apt to affect an audience than that of the first kind; notwithstanding many excellent pieces among the ancients, as well as most of those which have been written of late years in our own country, are raised upon contrary plans. I must however own, that I think this kind of fable, which is the most perfect in tragedy, is not so proper for an heroic poem.[n]

Milton seems to have been sensible of this imperfection in his fable, and has therefore endeavoured to cure it by several expedients; particularly by the mortification which the great adversary of mankind meets with upon his return to the assembly of infernal spirits, as it is described in a beautiful passage of the tenth book; and likewise by the vision, wherein Adam at the close of the poem sees his offspring triumphing over his great enemy, and himself restored to a happier Paradise than that from which he fell.

There is another objection against Milton's fable, which is indeed almost the same with the former, though placed in a different light, namely, that the hero in the *Paradise Lost* is unsuccessful, and by no means a match for his enemies. This gave occasion to Mr. Dryden's reflection, that the devil was in reality Milton's hero.[n]

implex fable: Aristotle, *Poetics*, 11. 2–3. Dacier has a long note elaborating this point (pp. 166–7).
Oedipus: the *Oedipus Tyrannus* of Sophocles.
former paper: No. 40 (pp. 213–15).
infernal spirits: *PL*, x. 504 ff.
Adam: *PL*, xii. 325 ff.
Milton's hero: Dedication of *Aeneis* (Watson, ii. 233).

I think I have obviated this objection in my first paper. The *Paradise Lost* is an epic, or a narrative poem, and he that looks for an hero in it, searches for that which Milton never intended; but if he will needs fix the name of an hero upon any person in it, 'tis certainly the Messiah who is the hero, both in the principal action, and in the chief episodes. Paganism could not furnish out a real action for a fable greater than that of the *Iliad* or *Aeneid*, and therefore an heathen could not form a higher notion of a poem than one of that kind, which they call an heroic. Whether Milton's is not of a sublimer nature I will not presume to determine: it is sufficient that I show there is in the *Paradise Lost* all the greatness of plan, regularity of design, and masterly beauties which we discover in Homer and Virgil.

I must in the next place observe, that Milton has interwoven in the texture of his fable some particulars which do not seem to have probability enough for an epic poem, particularly in the actions which he ascribes to Sin and Death, and the picture which he draws of the Limbo of Vanity, with other passages in the second book. Such allegories rather savour of the spirit of Spenser and Ariosto, than of Homer and Virgil.

In the structure of his poem he has likewise admitted of too many digressions. It is finely observed by Aristotle, that the author of an heroic poem should seldom speak himself, but throw as much of his work as he can into the mouths of those who are his principal actors. Aristotle has given no reason for this precept; but I presume it is because the mind of the reader is more awed and elevated when he hears Aeneas or Achilles speak, than when Virgil or Homer talk in their own persons. Besides that assuming the character of an eminent man is apt to fire the imagination, and raise the ideas of the author. Tully tells us, mentioning his dialogue *Of Old Age*, in which Cato is the chief speaker, that upon a review of it he was agreeably imposed upon, and fancied that it was Cato, and not he himself, who uttered his thoughts on that subject.

If the reader would be at the pains to see how the story of the *Iliad* and the *Aeneid* is delivered by those persons who act in it, he will be surprised to find how little in either of these poems proceeds from the authors. Milton has, in the general disposition of his fable, very finely observed this great rule, insomuch, that there is scarce

Death: *PL*, ii. 648–889.
Limbo of Vanity: *PL*, iii. 444–97.
Ariosto: Lodovico Ariosto (1474–1533), author of *Orlando Furioso* (1516).
Aristotle: *Poetics*, 24. 7.
Tully: Cicero, *De Amicitia*, 1. 4.

a third part of it which comes from the poet; the rest is spoken either by Adam and Eve, or by some good or evil spirit who is engaged either in their destruction or defence.

From what has been here observed it appears, that digressions are by no means to be allowed of in an epic poem. If the poet, even in the ordinary course of his narration, should speak as little as possible, he should certainly never let his narration sleep for the sake of any reflections of his own. I have often observed, with a secret admiration, that the longest reflection in the *Aeneid* is in that passage of the tenth book, where Turnus is represented as dressing himself in the spoils of Pallas, whom he had slain. Virgil here lets his fable stand still for the sake of the following remark. 'How is the mind of man ignorant of futurity, and unable to bear prosperous fortune with moderation? The time will come when Turnus shall wish that he had left the body of Pallas untouched, and curse the day on which he dressed himself in these spoils.' As the great event of the *Aeneid*, and the death of Turnus, whom Aeneas slew because he saw him adorned with the spoils of Pallas, turns upon this incident, Virgil went out of his way to make this reflection upon it, without which so small a circumstance might possibly have slipped out of his readers' memory. Lucan, who was an injudicious poet, lets drop his story very frequently for the sake of unnecessary digressions or his *diverticula*, as Scaliger calls them. If he gives us an account of the prodigies which preceded the civil war, he declaims upon the occasion, and shows how much happier it would be for man, if he did not feel his evil fortune before it comes to pass, and suffer not only by its real weight, but by the apprehension of it. Milton's complaint of his blindness, his panegyric on marriage, his reflections on Adam and Eve's going naked, of the angels eating, and several other passages in his poem, are liable to the same exception, though I must confess there is so great a beauty in these very digressions, that I would not wish them out of his poem.

I have, in a former paper, spoken of the characters of Milton's *Paradise Lost*, and declared my opinion, as to the allegorical persons who are introduced in it.

If we look into the sentiments, I think they are sometimes defective under the following heads; first, as there are several of them too

---

Turnus: *Aeneid*, 10. 501–5.
Scaliger: J. C. Scaliger, *Poetics*, 6. 6.
apprehension: Lucan, *Pharsalia*, 2. 1–15.
Milton's complaint: *PL*, iii. 1–55; his panegyric: *PL*, iv. 750–70; his reflections:
    PL, iv. 312–20; the angels eating: *PL*, v. 404–33.
former paper: No. 273 (pp. 66–70).

much pointed, and some that degenerate even into puns. Of this last kind I am afraid is that in the first book, where, speaking of the pygmies, he calls them

> . . . The small infantry
> Warred on by cranes . . .

Another blemish that appears in some of his thoughts, is his frequent allusion to heathen fables, which are not certainly of a piece with the divine subject, of which he treats. I do not find fault with these allusions, where the poet himself represents them as fabulous, as he does in some places, but where he mentions them as truths and matters of fact. The limits of my paper will not give me leave to be particular in instances of this kind: the reader will easily remark them in his perusal of the poem.

A third fault in his sentiments, is an unnecessary ostentation of learning, which likewise occurs very frequently.[n] It is certain that both Homer and Virgil were masters of all the learning of their times, but it shows itself in their works after an indirect and concealed manner. Milton seems ambitious of letting us know, by his excursions on free-will and predestination, and his many glances upon history, astronomy, geography and the like, as well as by the terms and phrases he sometimes makes use of, that he was acquainted with the whole circle of arts and sciences.

If, in the last place, we consider the language of this great poet, we must allow what I have hinted in a former paper, that it is often too much laboured, and sometimes obscured by old words, transpositions, and foreign idioms. Seneca's objection to the style of a great author, *Riget ejus oratio, nihil in ea placidum nihil lene*, is what many critics make to Milton: as I cannot wholly refute it, so I have already apologized for it in another paper; to which I may further add, that Milton's sentiments and ideas were so wonderfully sublime, that it would have been impossible for him to have represented them in their full strength and beauty, without having recourse to these foreign assistances. Our language sunk under him, and was unequal to that greatness of soul, which furnished him with such glorious conceptions.

---

pygmies: *PL*, i. 575–6 ('That small infantry').

Seneca: Seneca the Elder, *Controversies*, 7. 4. 8 (altered): His manner of speech is stiff; there is nothing gentle or easy in it. The 'great author' is Calvus, who waged with Cicero a very unequal contest for supremacy among Roman orators.

another paper: No. 285 (pp. 75–80).

A second fault in his language is, that he often affects a kind of jingle in his words,[n] as in the following passages, and many others:

> And brought into the *world* a *world* of woe.
> . . . Begirt the Almighty throne
> *Beseeching* or *besieging* . . .
> This *tempted* our *attempt* . . .
> At one slight *bound* high overleapt all *bound.*

I know there are figures for this kind of speech, that some of the greatest Ancients have been guilty of it, and that Aristotle himself has given it a place in his rhetoric among the beauties of that art. But as it is in itself poor and trifling, it is I think at present universally exploded by all the masters of polite writing.

The last fault which I shall take notice of in Milton's style, is the frequent use of what the learned call technical words, or terms of art.[n] It is one of the great beauties of poetry, to make hard things intelligible, and to deliver what is abstruse of itself in such easy language as may be understood by ordinary readers: besides that the knowledge of a poet should rather seem born with him, or inspired, than drawn from books and systems. I have often wondered how Mr. Dryden could translate a passage out of Virgil after the following manner.

> Tack to the larboard, and stand off to sea.
> Veer starboard sea and land . . .

Milton makes use of *larboard* in the same manner. When he is upon building he mentions *Doric pillars, pilasters, cornice, frieze, architrave.* When he talks of heavenly bodies, you meet with *ecliptick,* and *eccentric,* the *trepidation, stars dropping from the zenith, rays culminating from the equator.* To which might be added many instances of the like kind in several other arts and sciences.

I shall in my next papers give an account of the many particular beauties in Milton, which would have been too long to insert under those general heads I have already treated of, and with which I intend to conclude this piece of criticism.

jingle: *PL*, ix. 11; v. 868–9; i. 642; iv. 181.
Aristotle: *Rhetoric*, 3. 11. 7.
Dryden: *Aeneis*, iii. 526–7.
larboard: *PL*, ii. 1019.
architrave: *PL*, i. 713–16.
equator: *PL*, iii. 740; iii. 575; iii. 483; i. 745; iii. 616–17.

303   *Saturday   February 16 1712*

> ... *volet haec sub luce videri,*
> *judicis argutum quae non formidat acumen.*   Hor.

I have seen in the works of a modern philosopher, a map of the spots in the sun. My last paper of the faults and blemishes in Milton's *Paradise Lost*, may be considered as a piece of the same nature. To pursue the allusion: as it is observed, that among the bright parts of the luminous body above-mentioned, there are some which glow more intensely, and dart a stronger light than others; so, notwithstanding I have already shown Milton's poem to be very beautiful in general, I shall now proceed to take notice of such beauties as appear to me more exquisite than the rest. Milton has proposed the subject of his poem in the following verses.

> Of Man's first disobedience, and the fruit
> Of that forbidden tree, whose mortal taste
> Brought death into the world and all our woe,
> With loss of Eden, till one greater Man
> Restore us, and regain the blissful seat,
> Sing Heavenly Muse . . . .

These lines are perhaps as plain, simple and unadorned as any of the whole poem, in which particular the author has conformed himself to the example of Homer, and the precept of Horace.[n]

His invocation to a work which turns in a great measure upon the creation of the world, is very properly made to the muse who inspired Moses in those books from whence our author drew his subject, and to the Holy Spirit who is therein represented as operating after a particular manner in the first production of Nature. This whole exordium rises very happily into noble language and sentiment, as I think the transition to the fable is exquisitely beautiful and natural.

The nine days astonishment, in which the angels lay entranced after their dreadful overthrow and fall from Heaven, before they could recover either the use of thought or speech, is a noble circumstance, and very finely imagined. (Vid. Hesiod.) The division of Hell

---

Motto: Horace, *Ars poetica*, 363–4:
> Poems, like pictures, some when near delight,
> At distance some, some ask the clearest light.   CREECH

philosopher: here 'natural philosopher' or scientist.
Of Man's first disobedience: *PL*, i. 1–6.
days astonishment: *PL*, i. 50–3.
Hesiod: the early Greek poet (perhaps 8th century B.C.) recounted the early history of the gods in his *Theogony*.

into seas of fire, and into firm ground impregnated with the same furious element, with that particular circumstance of the exclusion of hope from those infernal regions, are instances of the same great and fruitful invention.

The thoughts in the first speech and description of Satan, who is one of the principal actors in this poem, are wonderfully proper to give us a full idea of him. His pride, envy and revenge, obstinacy, despair and impenitence, are all of them very artfully interwoven. In short, his first speech is a complication of all those passions which discover themselves separately in several other of his speeches in the poem. The whole part of this great enemy of mankind is filled with such incidents as are very apt to raise and terrify the reader's imagination. Of this nature, in the book now before us, is his being the first that awakens out of the general trance, with his posture on the burning lake, his rising from it, and the description of his shield and spear.

> Thus Satan talking to his nearest mate,
> With head up-lift above the wave, and eyes
> That sparkling blazed, his other parts beside
> Prone on the flood, extended long and large,
> Lay floating many a rood . . .
> Forthwith upright he rears from off the pool
> His mighty stature; on each hand the flames
> Driven backward slope their pointing spires, and rolled
> In billows, leave i'th'midst a horrid vale.
> Then with expanded wings he steers his flight
> Aloft, incumbent on the dusky air
> That felt unusual weight . . .
> . . . His ponderous shield,
> Ethereal temper, massy, large and round,
> Behind him cast; the broad circumference
> Hung on his shoulders like the moon, whose orb
> Through optic glass the Tuscan artist views
> At evening from the top of Fesole,
> Or in Valdarno, to descry new lands,
> Rivers or mountains on her spotty globe.
> His spear, to equal which the tallest pine
> Hewn on Norwegian hills to be the mast
> Of some great ammiral, were but a wand,
> He walked with to support uneasy steps
> Over the burning marl . . .

element: *PL*, i. 61–4, 228–9.
hope: *PL*, i. 66.
Satan: *PL*, i. 84–124.
artfully: 'artistically, skilfully'.
Thus Satan: *PL*, i. 192–6, 221–7, 284–96.

To which we may add his call to the fallen angels that lay plunged and stupefied in the sea of fire.

> He called so loud, that all the hollow deep
> Of Hell resounded . . .

But there is no single passage in the whole poem worked up to a greater sublimity, than that wherein his person is described in those celebrated lines:

> . . . He, above the rest
> In shape and gesture proudly eminent
> Stood like a tower, etc.

His sentiments are every way answerable to his character, and suitable to a created being of the most exalted and most depraved nature. Such is that in which he takes possession of his place of torments.

> . . . Hail horrors, hail
> Infernal world, and thou profoundest Hell
> Receive thy new possessor, one who brings
> A mind not to be changed by place or time.

And afterwards,

> . . . Here at least
> We shall be free; the Almighty hath not built
> Here for his envy, will not drive us hence:
> Here we may reign secure, and in my choice
> To reign is worth ambition, though in Hell:
> Better to reign in Hell, than serve in Heaven.

Amidst those impieties which this enraged spirit utters in other places of the poem, the author has taken care to introduce none that is not big with absurdity, and incapable of shocking a religious reader; his words, as the poet describes them, bearing only a 'semblance of worth, not substance'. He is likewise with great art described as owning his adversary to be Almighty. Whatever perverse interpretation he puts on the justice, mercy, and other attributes of the Supreme Being, he frequently confesses his omnipotence, that being the perfection he was forced to allow him, and the only consideration which could support his pride under the shame of his defeat.

He called: *PL*, i. 314–15.   . . . *He above*: *PL*, i. 589–91.
Hail horrors . . .: *PL*, i. 250–3.   . . . *Here at least . . .*: *PL*, i. 258–63.
substance: *PL*, i. 529.   *Almighty*: *PL*, i. 144.

Nor must I here omit that beautiful circumstance of his bursting
out in tears, upon his survey of those innumerable spirits whom he
had involved in the same guilt and ruin with himself.

> . . . He now prepared
> To speak; whereat their doubled ranks they bend
> From wing to wing, and half enclose him round
> With all his peers: attention held them mute.
> Thrice he assayed, and thrice in spite of scorn
> Tears, such as angels weep, burst forth . . .

The catalogue of evil spirits has abundance of learning in it, and a
very agreeable turn of poetry, which rises in a great measure from its
describing the places where they were worshipped, by those beautiful
marks of rivers so frequent among the ancient poets. The author had
doubtless in this place Homer's catalogue of ships, and Virgil's
list of warriors in his view.[n] The characters of Moloch and Belial
prepare the reader's mind for their respective speeches and behaviour
in the second and sixth book. The account of Thammuz is finely
romantic, and suitable to what we read among the Ancients of the
worship which was paid to that idol.

> . . . Thammuz came next behind,
> Whose annual wound in Lebanon allured
> The Syrian damsels to lament his fate,
> In amorous ditties all a summer's day,
> While smooth Adonis from his native rock
> Ran purple to the sea, supposed with blood
> Of Thammuz yearly wounded: the love-tale,
> Infected Sion's daughters with like heat,
> Whose wanton passions in the sacred porch
> Ezekiel saw, when by the vision led
> His eye surveyed the dark idolatries
> Of alienated Judah. . . .

The reader will pardon me if I insert as a note on this beautiful
passage, the account given us by the late ingenious Mr. Maundrell[n]
of this ancient piece of worship, and probably the first occasion of
such a superstition. 'We came to a fair large river—doubtless the
ancient river Adonis, so famous for the idolatrous rites performed
here in lamentation of Adonis. We had the fortune to see what may
be supposed to be the occasion of that opinion which Lucian

. . . *He now prepared*: *PL*, i. 615–20.   *evil spirits*: *PL*, i. 376–521.
Homer: *Iliad*, 2. 494 ff.   *Virgil*: *Aeneid*, 7. 647 ff.
Belial: *PL*, i. 392–405, 490–505.   . . . *Thammuz*: *PL*, i. 446–57.
Lucian: *De Dea Syria*, 8.

relates, concerning this river, *viz.* that this stream, at certain seasons of the year, especially about the feast of Adonis, is of a bloody colour; which the heathens looked upon as proceeding from a kind of sympathy in the river for the death of Adonis, who was killed by a wild boar in the mountains, out of which this stream rises. Something like this we saw actually come to pass; for the water was stained to a surprising redness; and, as we observed in travelling, had discoloured the sea a great way into a reddish hue, occasioned doubtless by a sort of minium, or red earth, washed into the river by the violence of the rain, and not by any stain from Adonis's blood.'

The passage in the catalogue, explaining the manner how spirits transform themselves by contraction, or enlargement of their dimensions, is introduced with great judgement, to make way for several surprising accidents in the sequel of the poem. There follows one, at the very end of the first book, which is what the French critics call marvellous, but at the same time probable by reason of the passage last mentioned. As soon as the infernal palace is finished, we are told the multitude and rabble of spirits immediately shrunk themselves into a small compass, that there might be room for such a numberless assembly in this capacious hall. But it is the poet's refinement upon this thought, which I most admire, and which is indeed very noble in itself. For he tells us, that notwithstanding the vulgar, among the fallen spirits, contracted their forms, those of the first rank and dignity still preserved their natural dimensions.

> Thus incorporeal spirits to smallest forms
> Reduced their shapes immense, and were at large,
> Though without number still amidst the hall
> Of that infernal court. But far within,
> And in their own dimensions like themselves,
> The great Seraphic Lords and Cherubim,
> In close recess and secret conclave sate,
> A thousand demi-gods on golden seats,
> Frequent and full . . .

The character of Mammon, and the description of the Pandemonium, are full of beauties.

There are several other strokes in the first book wonderfully poetical, and instances of that sublime genius so peculiar to the author. Such is the description of Azazel's stature, and of the

The passage: *PL*, i. 423–31.   *Thus incorporeal*: *PL*, i. 789–97.
Mammon: *PL*, i. 678–88.   *Pandemonium*: *PL*, i. 710–30.
Azazel: *PL*, i. 533–9.

infernal standard, which he unfurls; as also of that ghastly light,
by which the fiends appear to one another in their place of torments.

> The seat of desolation, void of light,
> Save what the glimmering of those livid flames
> Casts pale and dreadful . . .

The shout of the whole host of fallen angels when drawn up in
battle array:

> . . . The universal host up sent
> A shout that tore Hell's concave, and beyond
> Frighted the reign of Chaos and old Night.

The review, which the leader makes of his infernal army:

> . . . He through the armed files
> Darts his experienced eye, and soon traverse
> The whole battalion views, their order due,
> Their visages and stature as of gods,
> Their number last he sums. And now his heart
> Distends with pride, and hardening in his strength
> Glories . . .

The flash of light, which appeared upon the drawing of their
swords;

> He spake: and to confirm his words outflew
> Millions of flaming swords, drawn from the thighs
> Of mighty Cherubim; the sudden blaze
> Far round illumined Hell . . .

The sudden production of the Pandemonium;

> Anon out of the earth a fabric huge
> Rose like an exhalation, with the sound
> Of dulcet symphonies and voices sweet.

The artificial illuminations made in it;

> . . . From the arched roof
> Pendent by subtle magic, many a row
> Of starry lamps and blazing cressets, fed
> With naphtha and asphaltus yielded light
> As from a sky . . .

The seat of desolation: *PL*, i. 181–3 ('these vivid flames').
. . . *The universal host*: *PL*, i. 541–3.
. . . *He through the armed files*: *PL*, i. 567–73.   *He spake*: *PL*, i. 663–6.
Anon: *PL*, i. 710–12.
. . . *From the arched roof*: *PL*, i. 726–30.

There are also several noble similes and allusions in the first book of *Paradise Lost*. And here I must observe, that when Milton alludes either to things or persons, he never quits his simile till it rises to some very great idea, which is often foreign to the occasion that gave birth to it. The resemblance does not, perhaps, last above a line or two, but the poet runs on with the hint, till he has raised out of it some glorious image or sentiment, proper to inflame the mind of the reader, and to give it that sublime kind of entertainment, which is suitable to the nature of an heroic poem. Those, who are acquainted with Homer's and Virgil's way of writing, cannot but be pleased with this kind of structure in Milton's similitudes. I am the more particular on this head, because ignorant readers, who have formed their taste upon the quaint similes, and little turns of wit, which are so much in vogue among modern poets, cannot relish these beauties which are of a much higher nature, and are therefore apt to censure Milton's comparisons, in which they do not see any surprising points of likeness. Monsieur Perrault was a man of this vitiated relish, and for that very reason has endeavoured to turn into ridicule several of Homer's similitudes, which he calls *comparaisons à longue queue*, long-tailed comparisons. I shall conclude this paper on the first book of Milton with the answer which Monsieur Boileau makes to Perrault on this occasion:

Comparisons, says he, in odes and epic poems are not introduced only to illustrate and embellish the discourse, but to amuse and relax the mind of the reader, by frequently disengaging him from too painful an attention to the principal subject, and by leading him into other agreeable images. Homer, says he, excelled in this particular, whose comparisons abound with such images of nature as are proper to relieve and diversify his subjects. He continually instructs the reader, and makes him take notice, even in objects which are every day before our eyes, of such circumstances as we should not otherwise have observed. To this he adds, as a maxim universally acknowledged, that it is not necessary in poetry for the points of the comparison to correspond with one another exactly, but that a general resemblance is sufficient, and that too much nicety in this particular savours of the rhetorician and epigrammatist.

In short, if we look into the conduct of Homer, Virgil, and Milton, as the great fable is the soul of each poem, so to give their works an agreeable variety, their episodes are so many short fables, and their

---

Perrault: Charles Perrault, *Parallèle des Anciens et des Modernes*, Quatrième Dialogue (Amsterdam, 1693), ii. 41–2.

epigrammatist: see Boileau's 'Critical Reflections on Longinus', Reflection V (Boileau's *Works*, 1711–12, ii. 103). Addison's quotation from Boileau is from Reflection VI (pp. 110–13).

similes so many short episodes; to which you may add, if you please, that their metaphors are so many short similes. If the reader considers the comparisons in the first book of Milton, of the sun in an eclipse, of the sleeping Leviathan, of the bees swarming about their hive, of the fairy dance, in the view wherein I have here placed them, he will easily discover the great beauties that are in each of those passages.

309   *Saturday February 23 1712*

Di, quibus imperium est animarum, umbraeque silentes,
et Chaos, et Phlegethon, loca nocte silentia late;
sit mihi fas audita loqui: sit numine vestro
pandere res alta terra et caligine mersas.   Virg.

I have before observed in general, that the persons whom Milton introduces into his poem always discover such sentiments and behaviour, as are in a peculiar manner conformable to their respective characters. Every circumstance in their speeches and actions, is with great justness and delicacy adapted to the persons who speak and act. As the poet very much excels in this consistency of his characters, I shall beg leave to consider several passages of the second book in this light. That superior greatness and mock-majesty, which is ascribed to the prince of the fallen angels, is admirably preserved in the beginning of this book. His opening and closing the debate; his taking on himself that great enterprise at the thought of which the whole infernal assembly trembled; his encountering the hideous phantom who guarded the gates of Hell, and appeared to him in all his terrors, are instances of that proud and daring mind which could not brook submission even to Omnipotence.

fairy dance: *PL*, i. 594–9, 200–8, 768–75, 781–8.

Motto: Virgil, *Aeneid*, 6. 264–7 (altered):

> Ye realms, yet unrevealed to human sight,
> Ye gods, who rule the regions of the night,
> Ye gliding ghosts, permit me to relate
> The mystic wonders of your silent state.   DRYDEN

before observed: No. 279 (pp. 70–1).
Omnipotence: *PL*, ii. 11 ff., 465–7, 629 ff., 666 ff.

> Satan was now at hand, and from his seat
> The monster moving onward came as fast
> With horrid strides, Hell trembled as he strode.
> The undaunted Fiend what this might be admired,
> Admired, not feared . . .

The same boldness and intrepidity of behaviour discovers itself in the several adventures which he meets with during his passage through the regions of unformed matter, and particularly in his address to those tremendous powers who are described as presiding over it.

The part of Moloch is likewise in all its circumstances full of that fire and fury which distinguish this spirit from the rest of the fallen angels. He is described in the first book as besmeared with the blood of human sacrifices, and delighted with the tears of parents, and the cries of children. In the second book he is marked out as the fiercest spirit that fought in Heaven; and if we consider the figure which he makes in the sixth book, where the battle of the angels is described, we find it every way answerable to the same furious enraged character.

> . . . Where the might of Gabriel fought,
> And with fierce ensigns pierced the deep array
> Of Moloch, furious king, who him defied,
> And at his chariot wheels to drag him bound
> Threatened, nor from the Holy One of Heaven
> Refrained his tongue blasphemous; but anon
> Down cloven to the waist, with shattered arms
> And uncouth pain fled bellowing. . . .

It may be worth while to observe, that Milton has represented this violent impetuous spirit, who is hurried on by such precipitate passions, as the first that rises in the assembly, to give his opinion upon their present posture of affairs. Accordingly he declares himself abruptly for war, and appears incensed at his companions, for losing so much time as even to deliberate upon it. All his sentiments are rash, audacious and desperate. Such is that of arming themselves with their tortures, and turning their punishments upon him who inflicted them.

> . . . No, let us rather choose,
> Armed with Hell flames and fury, all at once

Satan: *PL*, ii. 674–8.   *powers*: *PL*, ii. 968–87.
fallen angels: *PL*, ii. 43–108.   *children*: *PL*, i. 392–3.
Heaven: *PL*, ii. 44–5.   *. . . Where the might*: *PL*, vi. 355–62.
war: *PL*, ii. 51.   *. . . No, let us*: *PL*, ii. 60–70.

O'er Heaven's high towers to force resistless way,
Turning our tortures into horrid arms
Against the Torturer; when to meet the noise
Of his almighty engine he shall hear
Infernal thunder, and for lightning see
Black fire and horror shot with equal rage
Among his angels; and his throne itself
Mixed with Tartarean sulphur, and strange fire,
His own invented torments . . .

His preferring annihilation to shame or misery, is also highly suitable to his character; as the comfort he draws from their disturbing the peace of Heaven, that if it be not victory it is revenge, is a sentiment truly diabolical and becoming the bitterness of this implacable spirit.

Belial is described, in the first book, as the idol of the lewd and luxurious. He is in the second book, pursuant to that description, characterized as timorous and slothful; and if we look into the sixth book, we find him celebrated in the battle of angels for nothing but that scoffing speech which he makes to Satan, on their supposed advantage over the enemy. As his appearance is uniform, and of a piece, in these three several views, we find his sentiments in the infernal assembly every way conformable to his character. Such are his apprehensions of a second battle, his horrors of annihilation, his preferring to be miserable rather than *not to be*. I need not observe, that the contrast of thought in this speech, and that which precedes it, gives an agreeable variety to the debate.

Mammon's character is so fully drawn in the first book, that the poet adds nothing to it in the second. We were before told, that he was the first who taught mankind to ransack the earth for gold and silver, and that he was the architect of Pandemonium, or the infernal palace, where the evil spirits were to meet in council. His speech in this book is every way suitable to so depraved a character. How proper is that reflection, of their being unable to taste the happiness of Heaven were they actually there, in the mouth of one, who while he was in Heaven, is said to have had his mind dazzled with the outward pomps and glories of the place, and to have been more intent on the riches of the pavement, than on the beatific vision. I shall also leave the reader to judge how agreeable the following sentiments are to the same character.

annihilation: *PL*, ii. 92–8.
slothful: *PL*, ii. 117.
not to be: *PL*, ii. 143–51.
reflection: *PL*, ii. 237–49.

peace of Heaven: *PL*, ii. 101–5.
scoffing speech: *PL*, vi. 620–7.
Mammon: *PL*, i. 678–88, 732–51.

> . . . This deep world
> Of darkness do we dread? How oft amidst
> Thick cloud and dark doth Heaven's all-ruling Sire
> Choose to reside, his glory unobscured,
> And with the majesty of darkness round
> Covers his throne; from whence deep thunders roar
> Mustering their rage, and Heaven resembles Hell?
> As he our darkness, cannot we his light
> Imitate when we please? This desert soil,
> Wants not her hidden lustre, gems and gold;
> Nor want we skill or art, from whence to raise
> Magnificence; and what can Heaven show more?

Beëlzebub, who is reckoned the second in dignity that fell, and is in the first book, the second that awakens out of the trance, and confers with Satan upon the situation of their affairs, maintains his rank in the book now before us. There is a wonderful majesty described in his rising up to speak. He acts as a kind of moderator between the two opposite parties, and proposes a third undertaking, which the whole assembly gives into. The motion he makes of detaching one of their body in search of a new world is grounded upon a project devised by Satan, and cursorily proposed by him in the following lines of the first book.

> Space may produce new worlds, whereof so rife
> There went a fame in Heaven, that he ere long
> Intended to create, and therein plant
> A generation, whom his choice regard
> Should favour equal to the Sons of Heaven:
> Thither, if but to pry, shall be perhaps
> Our first eruption, thither or elsewhere:
> For this infernal pit shall never hold
> Celestial spirits in bondage, nor the abyss
> Long under darkness cover. But these thoughts
> Full counsel must mature.

It is on this project that Beëlzebub grounds his proposal.

> . . . What if we find
> Some easier enterprise? There is a place
> (If ancient and prophetic fame in Heaven
> Err not) another world, the happy seat
> Of some new race called Man, about this time
> To be created like to us, though less
> In power and excellence, but favoured more

. . . *This deep world*: *PL*, ii. 262–73 ('Thick clouds', line 264).
Beëlzebub: *PL*, i. 79–191.   *assembly*: *PL*, ii. 299–416.
Space may produce: *PL*, i. 650–60.   . . . *What if we find*: *PL*, ii. 344–53.

> Of him who rules above; so was his will
> Pronounced among the gods, and by an oath,
> That shook Heaven's whole circumference, confirmed.

The reader may observe how just it was, not to omit in the first book the project upon which the whole poem turns: as also that the prince of the fallen angels was the only proper person to give it birth, and that the next to him in dignity was the fittest to second and support it.

There is besides, I think, something wonderfully beautiful, and very apt to affect the reader's imagination in this ancient prophecy or report in Heaven, concerning the creation of man. Nothing could show more the dignity of the species, than this tradition which ran of them before their existence. They are represented to have been the talk of Heaven, before they were created. Virgil, in compliment to the Roman Commonwealth, makes the heroes of it appear in their state of pre-existence; but Milton does a far greater honour to mankind in general, as he gives us a glimpse of them even before they are in being.

The rising of this great assembly is described in a very sublime and poetical manner.

> Their rising all at once was as the sound
> Of thunder heard remote . . . .

The diversions of the fallen angels, with the particular account of their place of habitation, are described with great pregnancy of thought, and copiousness of invention. The diversions are every way suitable to beings who had nothing left them but strength and knowledge misapplied. Such are their contentions at the race, and in feats of arms, with their entertainment in the following lines.

> Others with vast Typhoean rage more fell
> Rend up both rocks and hills, and ride the air
> In whirlwind; Hell scarce holds the wild uproar.

Their music is employed in celebrating their own criminal exploits, and their discourse in sounding the unfathomable depths of fate, freewill and foreknowledge.[n]

The several circumstances in the description of Hell are finely imagined; as the four rivers which disgorge themselves into the sea of

Virgil: *Aeneid*, 6. 752–886.   *Their rising all*: *PL*, ii. 476–7.
invention: *PL*, ii. 528 ff.   *Others with vast*: *PL*, ii. 539–41.
music: *PL*, ii. 546–55.   *foreknowledge*: *PL*, ii. 555–69.
circumstances: *PL*, ii. 575–81, 596–603, 583–6.

fire, the extremes of cold and heat, and the River of Oblivion. The monstrous animals produced in that infernal world are represented by a single line, which gives us a more horrid idea of them, than a much longer description would have done.

> . . . Nature breeds,
> Perverse, all monstrous, all prodigious things,
> Abominable, inutterable, and worse
> Than fables yet have feigned, or fear conceived,
> Gorgons, and Hydras, and Chimeras dire.

This episode of the fallen spirits, and their place of habitation, comes in very happily to unbend the mind of the reader from its attention to the debate. An ordinary poet would indeed have spun out so many circumstances to a great length, and by that means have weakened, instead of illustrated, the principal fable.

The flight of Satan to the gates of Hell is finely imaged.

I have already declared my opinion of the allegory concerning Sin and Death, which is however a very finished piece in its kind, when it is not considered as a part of an epic poem. The genealogy of the several persons is contrived with great delicacy. Sin is the daughter of Satan, and Death the offspring of Sin. The incestuous mixture between Sin and Death produces those monsters and hell-hounds which from time to time enter into their mother, and tear the bowels of her who gave them birth. These are the terrors of an evil conscience, and the proper fruits of Sin, which naturally rise from the apprehensions of Death. This last beautiful moral is, I think, clearly intimated in the speech of Sin, where complaining of this her dreadful issue, she adds,

> Before mine eyes in opposition sits
> Grim Death my son and foe, who sets them on.
> And me his parent would full soon devour
> For want of other prey, but that he knows
> His end with mine involved . . .

I need not mention to the reader the beautiful circumstance in the last part of this quotation. He will likewise observe how naturally the three persons concerned in this allegory are tempted by one common interest to enter into a confederacy together, and how properly Sin is made the portress of Hell, and the only being that can open the gates to that world of tortures.

. . . *Nature breeds*: *PL*, ii. 624–8.
flight of Satan: *PL*, ii. 629–43.
delicacy: *PL*, ii. 746–814.
tortures: *PL*, ii. 746, 774–7.

fallen spirits: *PL*, ii. 614–28.
allegory: No. 273 (p. 68).
Before mine eyes: *PL*, ii. 803–7.

The descriptive part of this allegory is likewise very strong, and full of sublime ideas. The figure of Death, the regal crown upon his head, his menace of Satan, his advancing to the combat, the outcry at his birth, are circumstances too noble to be passed over in silence, and extremely suitable to this King of Terrors. I need not mention the justness of thought which is observed in the generation of these several symbolical persons; that Sin was produced upon the first revolt of Satan, that Death appeared soon after he was cast into Hell, and that the terrors of conscience were conceived at the gate of this place of torments. The description of the gates is very poetical, as the opening of them is full of Milton's spirit.

> ... On a sudden open fly
> With impetuous recoil and jarring sound
> The infernal doors, and on their hinges grate
> Harsh thunder, that the lowest bottom shook
> Of Erebus. She opened, but to shut
> Excelled her power; the gates wide open stood,
> That with extended wings a bannered host
> Under spread ensigns marching might pass through
> With horse and chariots ranked in loose array;
> So wide they stood, and like a furnace mouth
> Cast forth redounding smoke and ruddy flame.

In Satan's voyage through the Chaos there are several imaginary persons described, as residing in that immense waste of matter. This may perhaps be conformable to the taste of those critics who are pleased with nothing in a poet which has not life and manners ascribed to it; but for my own part, I am pleased most with those passages in this description which carry in them a greater measure of probability, and are such as might possibly have happened. Of this kind is his first mounting in the smoke that rises from the infernal pit, his falling into a cloud of nitre, and the like combustible materials, that by their explosion still hurried him forward in his voyage; his springing upward like a pyramid of fire, with his laborious passage through that confusion of elements, which the poet calls

> The womb of Nature and perhaps her grave.

The glimmering light which shot into the chaos from the utmost

combat: *PL*, ii. 666–76.   *outcry*: *PL*, ii. 787–9.
... *On a sudden*: *PL*, ii. 879–89.   *voyage*: *PL*, ii. 927–1055.
imaginary persons: Addison returns to this in No. 315 (p. 107).
Of this kind: *PL*, ii. 928–38, 1013.   *The womb of Nature*: *PL*, ii. 911.
light: *PL*, ii. 1034–7.

verge of the creation, with the distant discovery of the Earth that
hung close by the Moon, are wonderfully beautiful and poetical.

315   *Saturday March 1 1712*

Nec deus intersit, nisi dignus vindice nodus
inciderit .... Hor.

Horace advises a poet to consider thoroughly the nature and force
of his genius. Milton seems to have known, perfectly well, wherein
his strength lay, and has therefore chosen a subject entirely conformable to those talents, of which he was master. As his genius was
wonderfully turned to the sublime, his subject is the noblest that
could have entered into the thoughts of man. Every thing that is
truly great and astonishing, has a place in it. The whole system of the
intellectual world; the Chaos, and the Creation; Heaven, Earth and
Hell, enter into the constitution of his poem.

Having in the first and second book represented the infernal
world with all its horrors, the thread of his fable naturally leads him
into the opposite regions of bliss and glory.

If Milton's majesty forsakes him anywhere, it is in those parts of
his poem, where the divine persons are introduced as speakers.[n]
One may, I think, observe that the author proceeds with a kind of
fear and trembling, whilst he describes the sentiments of the Almighty. He dares not give his imagination its full play, but chooses
to confine himself to such thoughts as are drawn from the books of
the most orthodox divines, and to [such expressions as may be met
with in Scripture. The beauties, therefore, which we are to look for in
these speeches, are not of a poetical nature, nor so proper to fill the
mind with sentiments of grandeur, as with thoughts of devotion. The
passions, which they are designed to raise, are a divine love and
religious fear. The particular beauty of the speeches in the third
book, consists in that shortness and perspicuity of style, in which the
poet has couched the greatest mysteries of Christianity, and drawn

Earth: *PL*, ii. 1051–3. Thomas Newton, in his edition of *Paradise Lost* (1749),
 notes that it is not the earth which Satan discovers, but rather the universe.

Motto: Horace, *Ars poetica*, 191–2:
           Never presume to make a god appear,
           But for a business worthy of a god. ROSCOMMON

Horace: *Ars poetica*, 38–40.

together, in a regular scheme, the whole dispensation of Providence, with respect to Man. He has represented all the abstruse doctrines of predestination, free-will and grace, as also the great points of Incarnation and Redemption (which naturally grow up in a poem that treats of the Fall of Man) with great energy of expression, and in a clearer and stronger light than I ever met with in any other writer. As these points are dry in themselves to the generality of readers, the concise and clear manner in which he has treated them, is very much to be admired, as is likewise that particular art which he has made use of in the interspersing of all those graces of poetry, which the subject was capable of receiving.

The survey of the whole Creation, and of everything that is transacted in it, is a prospect worthy of Omniscience; and as much above that, in which Virgil has drawn his Jupiter, as the Christian idea of the Supreme Being is more rational and sublime than that of the heathens. The particular objects on which he is described to have cast his eye, are represented in the most beautiful and lively manner.

> Now had the Almighty Father from above,
> From the pure Empyrean where he sits
> High throned above all height, bent down his eye
> His own works and their works at once to view.
> About him all the sanctities of Heaven
> Stood thick as stars, and from his sight received
> Beatitude past utterance: on his right
> The radiant image of his glory sat,
> His only Son; on earth he first beheld
> Our two first parents, yet the only two
> Of mankind, in the happy garden placed,
> Reaping immortal fruits of joy and love,
> Uninterrupted joy, unrivalled love
> In blissful solitude; he then surveyed
> Hell and the gulf between, and Satan there
> Coasting the wall of Heaven on this side night
> In the dun air sublime, and ready now
> To stoop with wearied wings, and willing feet
> On the bare outside of this world, that seemed
> Firm land imbosomed without firmament,
> Uncertain which, in ocean or in air.
> Him God beholding from his prospect high,
> Wherein past, present, future he beholds,
> Thus to his only Son foreseeing spake.

Satan's approach to the confines of the Creation, is finely imaged in the beginning of the speech, which immediately follows. The

---

Jupiter: *Aeneid*, 1. 223–6.   *Now had*: *PL*, iii. 56–79.
Satan's approach: *PL*, iii. 80–9.

effects of this speech in the blessed spirits, and in the divine Person, to whom it was addressed, cannot but fill the mind of the reader with a secret pleasure and complacency.

> Thus while God spake, ambrosial fragrance filled
> All Heaven, and in the blessed spirits elect
> Sense of new joy ineffable diffused:
> Beyond compare the Son of God was seen
> Most glorious, in him all his Father shone
> Substantially expressed, and in his face
> Divine compassion visibly appeared,
> Love without end, and without measure grace.

I need not point out the beauty of that circumstance, wherein the whole host of angels are represented as standing mute; nor show how proper the occasion was to produce such a silence in Heaven. The close of this divine colloquy, with the hymn of angels that follows upon it, are so wonderfully beautiful and poetical, that I should not forbear inserting the whole passage, if the bounds of my paper would give me leave.

> No sooner had the Almighty ceased, but all
> The multitude of angels with a shout
> Loud as from numbers without number, sweet
> As from blest voices, uttering joy, Heaven rung
> With jubilee, and loud hosannas filled
> The eternal regions; etc., etc., . . .

Satan's walk upon the outside of the universe, which, at a distance, appeared to him of a globular form, but, upon his nearer approach, looked like an unbounded plain, is natural and noble: as his roaming upon the frontiers of the Creation, between that mass of matter, which was wrought into a world, and that shapeless unformed heap of materials, which still lay in chaos and confusion, strikes the imagination with something astonishingly great and wild. I have before spoken of the Limbo of Vanity, which the poet places upon this outermost surface of the universe, and shall here explain myself more at large on that, and other parts of the poem, which are of the same shadowy nature.

Aristotle observes, that the fable of an epic poem should abound in circumstances that are both credible and astonishing; or as the French critics choose to phrase it, the fable should be filled with the

---

complacency: here used in the obsolete sense of 'delight'.
Thus while God: *PL*, iii. 135–42.   *mute*: *PL*, iii. 217–18.
hymn: *PL*, iii. 274–415.   *No sooner had*: *PL*, iii. 344–9.
universe: *PL*, iii. 418–41.   *Limbo of Vanity*: No. 297 (p. 85).
Aristotle: *Poetics*, 24. 8, 10.

probable and the marvellous. This rule is as fine and just as any in
Aristotle's whole art of poetry.

If the fable is only probable, it differs nothing from a true history;
if it is only marvellous, it is no better than a romance. The great
secret therefore of heroic poetry is to relate such circumstances, as
may produce in the reader at the same time both belief and astonishment. This is brought to pass in a *well chosen* fable, by the account of
such things as have really happened, or at least of such things as have
happened according to the received opinions of mankind. Milton's
fable is a masterpiece of this nature; as the war in Heaven, the
condition of the fallen angels, the state of innocence, the temptation
of the serpent, and the Fall of Man, though they are very astonishing
in themselves, are not only credible, but actual points of faith.

The next method of reconciling miracles with credibility, is by a
happy invention of the poet; as in particular, when he introduces
agents of a superior nature, who are capable of effecting what is
wonderful, and what is not to be met with in the ordinary course of
things. Ulysses' ship being turned into a rock, and Aeneas's fleet
into a shoal of water-nymphs; though they are very surprising
accidents, are nevertheless probable, when we are told that they
were the gods who thus transformed them. It is this kind of machinery
which fills the poems both of Homer and Virgil with such circumstances as are wonderful, but not impossible, and so frequently
produce in the reader the most pleasing passion that can rise in the
mind of man, which is admiration.[n] If there be any instance in the
Aeneid liable to exception upon this account, it is in the beginning
of the third book, where Aeneas is represented as tearing up the
myrtle that dropped blood. To qualify this wonderful circumstance,
Polydorus tells a story from the root of the myrtle, that the
barbarous inhabitants of the country having pierced him with spears
and arrows, the wood which was left in his body took root in his
wounds, and gave birth to that bleeding tree. This circumstance
seems to have the marvellous without the probable, because it is
represented as proceeding from natural causes, without the inter-
position of any god, or other supernatural power capable of producing it. The spears and arrows grow of themselves, without so much as
the modern help of an enchantment. If we look into the fiction of
Milton's fable, though we find it full of surprising incidents, they are

Ulysses: *Odyssey*, 13. 146–83. *Aeneas*: *Aeneid*, 9. 107–22. These are cited together
   in Le Bossu (Book v, Ch. iii).
blood: *Aeneid*, 3. 19–68.
Polydorus: the son of Priam, he had been slain in Thrace by Polymnestor, the
   Thracian king. According to Homer, slain by Achilles.

generally suited to our notions of the things and persons described, and tempered with a due measure of probability. I must only make an exception to the Limbo of Vanity, with his episode of Sin and Death, and some of the imaginary persons in his Chaos. These passages are astonishing, but not credible; the reader cannot so far impose upon himself as to see a possibility in them, they are the description of dreams and shadows, not of things or persons. I know that many critics[n] look upon the stories of Circe, Polypheme, the Sirens, nay the whole *Odyssey* and *Iliad*, to be allegories; but allowing this to be true, they are fables, which considering the opinions of mankind that prevailed in the age of the poet, might possibly have been according to the letter. The persons are such as might have acted what is ascribed to them, as the circumstances in which they are represented, might possibly have been truths and realities. This appearance of probability is so absolutely requisite in the greater kinds of poetry, that Aristotle observes the ancient tragic writers made use of the names of such great men as had actually lived in the world, though the tragedy proceeded upon adventures they were never engaged in, on purpose to make the subject more credible. In a word, besides the hidden meaning of an epic allegory, the plain literal sense ought to appear probable. The story should be such as an ordinary reader may acquiesce in, whatever natural, moral, or political truth may be discovered in it by men of greater penetration.

Satan, after having long wandered upon the surface, or outmost wall of the universe, discovers at last a wide gap in it, which led into the Creation, and is described as the opening through which the angels pass to and fro into the lower world, upon their errands to mankind. His sitting upon the brink of this passage, and taking a survey of the whole face of nature that appeared to him new and fresh in all its beauties, with the simile illustrating this circumstance, fills the mind of the reader with as surprising and glorious an idea as any that arises in the whole poem. He looks down into that vast hollow of the universe with the eye, or (as Milton calls it in his first book) with the ken of an angel. He surveys all the wonders in this immense amphitheatre that lie between both the poles of Heaven, and takes in at one view the whole round of the Creation.

His flight between the several worlds that shined on every side of him, with the particular description of the sun, are set forth in all the

Chaos: Cf. Nos. 297, 273, 309 (pp. 85, 68, 101-2).   *Sirens*: *Odyssey*, Books 10–12.
Aristotle: *Poetics*, 9. 6.   *mankind*: *PL*, iii. 498–561.
simile: *PL*, iii. 543–51.   *first book*: *PL*, i. 59.

wantonness of a luxuriant imagination. His shape, speech and behaviour upon his transforming himself into an angel of light, are touched with exquisite beauty. The poet's thought of directing Satan to the sun, which in the vulgar opinion of mankind is the most conspicuous part of the Creation, and the placing in it an angel, is a circumstance very finely contrived, and the more adjusted to a poetical probability, as it was a received doctrine among the most famous philosophers, that every orb had its intelligence;[n] and as an apostle in Sacred Writ is said to have seen such an angel in the sun. In the answer which this angel returns to the disguised Evil Spirit, there is such a becoming majesty as is altogether suitable to a superior being. The part of it in which he represents himself as present at the Creation, is very noble in itself, and not only proper where it is introduced, but requisite to prepare the reader for what follows in the seventh book.

> I saw when at his word the formless mass,
> This world's material mould, came to a heap:
> Confusion heard his voice, and wild uproar
> Stood ruled, stood vast infinitude confined;
> Till at his second bidding darkness fled,
> Light shone, etc.

In the following part of the speech he points out the earth with such circumstances, that the reader can scarce forbear fancying himself employed on the same distant view of it.

> Look downward on that globe whose hither side
> With light from hence, though but reflected, shines;
> That place is Earth the seat of man, that light
> His day, etc.

I must not conclude my reflections upon this third book of *Paradise Lost*, without taking notice of that celebrated complaint of Milton with which it opens, and which certainly deserves all the praises that have been given it; though as I have before hinted, it may rather be looked upon as an excrescence, than as an essential part of the poem. The same observation might be applied to that beautiful digression upon hypocrisy, in the same book.

imagination: *PL*, iii. 561–633.
angel in the sun: Rev. 19. 17.
I saw when: *PL*, iii. 708–13.
complaint: *PL*, iii. 1–55.

angel of light: *PL*, iii. 634–44.
superior being: *PL*, iii. 694–736.
Look downward: *PL*, iii. 722–5.
hypocrisy: *PL*, iii. 682–9.

321 *Saturday March 8 1712*

Non satis est pulchra esse poemata, dulcia sunto. Hor.

Those, who know how many volumes have been written on the poems of Homer and Virgil, will easily pardon the length of my discourse upon Milton. The *Paradise Lost* is looked upon, by the best judges, as the greatest production, or at least the noblest work of genius, in our language, and therefore deserves to be set before an English reader in its full beauty. For this reason, though I have endeavoured to give a general idea of its graces and imperfections in my six first papers, I thought myself obliged to bestow one upon every book in particular. The three first books I have already dispatched, and am now entering upon the fourth. I need not acquaint my reader, that there are multitudes of beauties in this great author, especially in the descriptive parts of his poem, which I have not touched upon, it being my intention to point out those only, which appear to me the most exquisite, or those which are not so obvious to ordinary readers. Everyone that has read the critics, who have written upon the *Odyssey*, the *Iliad* and the *Aeneid*, knows very well, that though they agree in their opinions of the great beauties in those poems, they have nevertheless each of them discovered several master-strokes, which have escaped the observation of the rest. In the same manner, I question not, but any writer, who shall treat of this subject after me, may find several beauties in Milton, which I have not taken notice of. I must likewise observe, that as the greatest masters of critical learning differ among one another, as to some particular points in an epic poem, I have not bound myself scrupulously to the rules, which any one of them has laid down upon that art, but have taken the liberty sometimes to join with one, and sometimes with another, and sometimes to differ from all of them, when I have thought that the reason of the thing was on my side.

We may consider the beauties of the fourth book under three heads. In the first are those pictures of still life, which we meet with in the descriptions of Eden, Paradise, Adam's bower, etc. In the next are the machines, which comprehend the speeches and behaviour of the good and bad angels. In the last is the conduct of Adam and Eve, who are the principal actors in the poem.

In the description of Paradise,[n] the poet has observed Aristotle's rule of lavishing all the ornaments of diction on the weak unactive

---

Motto: Horace, *Ars poetica*, 99: It is not enough for poems to be beautiful, they must also be delightful.

5*

parts of the fable, which are not supported by the beauty of sentiments and characters.[n] Accordingly the reader may observe, that the expressions are more florid and elaborate in these descriptions, than in most other parts of the poem. I must further add, that though the drawings of gardens, rivers, rainbows, and the like dead pieces of nature, are justly censured in an heroic poem, when they run out into an unnecessary length; the description of Paradise would have been faulty, had not the poet been very particular in it, not only as it is the scene of the principal action, but as it is requisite to give us an idea of that happiness from which our first parents fell. The plan of it is wonderfully beautiful, and formed upon the short sketch which we have of it, in Holy Writ. Milton's exuberance of imagination, has poured forth such a redundancy of ornaments on this seat of happiness and innocence, that it would be endless to point out each particular.

I must not quit this head, without further observing, that there is scarce a speech of Adam or Eve in the whole poem, wherein the sentiments and allusions are not taken from this their delightful habitation. The reader, during their whole course of action, always finds himself in the walks of Paradise. In short, as the critics have remarked, that in those poems, wherein shepherds are actors, the thoughts ought always to take a tincture from the woods, fields and rivers; so we may observe, that our first parents seldom lose sight of their happy station in anything they speak or do; and, if the reader will give me leave to use the expression, that their thoughts are always *Paradisiacal*.

We are in the next place to consider the machines of the fourth book. Satan being now within prospect of Eden, and looking round upon the glories of the Creation, is filled with sentiments different from those which he discovered whilst he was in Hell. The place inspires him with thoughts more adapted to it: he reflects upon the happy condition from whence he fell, and breaks forth into a speech that is softened with several transient touches of remorse and self-accusation: but at length he confirms himself in impenitence, and in his design of drawing man into his own state of guilt and misery. This conflict of passions is raised with a great deal of art, as the opening of his speech to the sun is very bold and noble.

> O thou that with surpassing glory crowned
> Look'st from thy sole dominion like the god

Paradisiacal: actually not a new 'expression'. Examples are given in *OED* from 1649.

self-accusation: *PL*, iv. 18–113.   *O thou that with*: *PL*, iv. 32–9.

> Of this new world, at whose sight all the stars
> Hide their diminished heads, to thee I call
> But with no friendly voice, and add thy name
> O sun, to tell thee how I hate thy beams
> That bring to my remembrance from what state
> I fell, how glorious once above thy sphere.

This speech is, I think, the finest that is ascribed to Satan in the whole poem. The Evil Spirit afterwards proceeds to make his discoveries concerning our first parents, and to learn after what manner they may be best attacked. His bounding over the walls of Paradise; his sitting in the shape of a cormorant upon the Tree of Life, which stood in the centre of it, and overtopped all the other trees of the garden; his alighting among the herd of animals, which are so beautifully represented as playing about Adam and Eve, together with his transforming himself into different shapes, in order to hear their conversation, are circumstances that give an agreeable surprise to the reader, and are devised with great art, to connect that series of adventures in which the poet has engaged this great artificer of fraud.

The thought of Satan's transformation into a cormorant, and placing himself on the Tree of Life, seems raised upon that passage in the *Iliad*, where two deities are described, as perching on the top of an oak in the shape of vultures.

His planting himself at the ear of Eve under the form of a toad, in order to produce vain dreams and imaginations, is a circumstance of the same nature; as his starting up in his own form is wonderfully fine, both in the literal description, and in the moral which is concealed under it. His answer upon his being discovered, and demanded to give an account of himself, is conformable to the pride and intrepidity of his character.

> Know ye not then, said Satan, filled with scorn,
> Know ye not me? ye knew me once no mate
> For you, there sitting where you durst not soar;
> Not to know me argues yourselves unknown,
> The lowest of your throng; . . .

Zephon's rebuke, with the influence it had on Satan, is exquisitely graceful and moral. Satan is afterwards led away to Gabriel, the chief of the guardian angels, who kept watch in Paradise. His disdainful behaviour on this occasion is so remarkable a beauty, that

conversation: *PL*, iv. 179–83, 194–6, 395–7, 340–50, 397–408.
Iliad: 7. 58–60.   *imaginations*: *PL*, iv. 799–819.
Know ye not: *PL*, iv. 827–31.   *Zephon's rebuke*: *PL*, iv. 834–50.

the most ordinary reader cannot but take notice of it. Gabriel's
discovering his approach at a distance, is drawn with great strength
and liveliness of imagination.

> O friends, I hear the tread of nimble feet
> Hastening this way, and now by glimpse discern
> Ithuriel and Zephon through the shade;
> And with them comes a third of regal port,
> But faded splendour wan; who by his gait
> And fierce demeanour seems the Prince of Hell,
> Not likely to part hence without contest;
> Stand firm, for in his look defiance lours.

The conference between Gabriel and Satan abounds with sentiments proper for the occasion, and suitable to the persons of the
two speakers. Satan's clothing himself with terror when he prepares
for the combat is truly sublime, and at least equal to Homer's
description of Discord celebrated by Longinus, or to that of Fame in
Virgil, who are both represented with their feet standing upon the
earth, and their heads reaching above the clouds.

> While thus he spake, the angelic squadron bright
> Turned fiery red, sharpening in mooned horns
> Their phalanx, and began to hem him round
> With ported spears, etc.
> . . . On the other side, Satan alarmed,
> Collecting all his might dilated stood
> Like Teneriffe or Atlas unremoved.
> His stature reached the sky, and on his crest
> Sat horror plumed; . . .

I must here take notice, that Milton is everywhere full of hints,
and sometimes literal translations, taken from the greatest of the
Greek and Latin poets. But this I may reserve for a discourse by itself,
because I would not break the thread of these speculations that are
designed for English readers, with such reflections as would be of no
use but to the learned.

I must however observe in this place, that the breaking off the
combat between Gabriel and Satan, by the hanging out of the
golden scales in Heaven, is a refinement upon Homer's thought,
who tells us, that before the battle between Hector and Achilles,
Jupiter weighed the event of it in a pair of scales. The reader may
see the whole passage in the 22nd *Iliad*.

O friends: *PL*, iv. 866–73.   *speakers*: *PL*, iv. 877–976.
Homer: Iliad, 4. 441–5.
Longinus: *On the Sublime*, 9. 4 (Boileau's trans., Ch. vii).
Virgil: *Aeneid*, 4. 176–7.   *While thus*: *PL*, iv. 977–80, 985–9.
golden scales: *PL*, iv. 996–1004.   *Iliad*: 22. 208 ff.; *Aeneid*, 12. 725–7.

Virgil, before the last decisive combat, describes Jupiter in the same manner, as weighing the fates of Turnus and Aeneas. Milton, though he fetched this beautiful circumstance from the *Iliad* and *Aeneid*, does not only insert it as a poetical embellishment, like the authors above-mentioned; but makes an artful use of it, for the proper carrying on of his fable, and for the breaking off the combat between the two warriors, who were upon the point of engaging. To this we may further add, that Milton is the more justified in this passage, as we find the same noble allegory in Holy Writ, where a wicked prince, some few hours before he was assaulted and slain, is said to have been 'weighed in the scales, and to have been found wanting'.

I must here take notice under the head of the machines, that Uriel's gliding down to the earth upon a sunbeam, with the poet's device to make him *descend*, as well in his return to the sun, as in his coming from it, is a prettiness that might have been admired in a little fanciful poet, but seems below the genius of Milton. The description of the host of armed angels walking their nightly round in Paradise, is of another spirit.

> So saying, on he led his radiant files,
> Dazzling the moon; . . .

as that account of the hymns which our first parents used to hear them sing in these their midnight walks, is altogether divine, and inexpressibly amusing to the imagination.

We are, in the last place, to consider the parts which Adam and Eve act in the fourth book. The description of them as they first appeared to Satan, is exquisitely drawn, and sufficient to make the fallen angel gaze upon them with all that astonishment, and those emotions of envy, in which he is represented.

> Two of far nobler shape erect and tall
> God-like erect, with native honour clad
> In naked majesty seemed lords of all,
> And worthy seemed, for in their looks divine
> The image of their glorious Maker shone,
> Truth, wisdom, sanctitude severe and pure;
> Severe, but in true filial freedom placed:
> For contemplation he and valour formed,

---

wicked prince: Dan. 5: 27.   *sunbeam*: *PL*, iv. 555–6, 589–92.
So saying . . . *PL*, iv. 797–8.   *hymns*: *PL*, iv. 680–8.
amusing: *OED* defines 'amusing' in this sense as 'engaging the mind or attention
    in a pleasing way; interesting' and quotes from No. 463 as the earliest example.
Two of far nobler . . . *PL*, iv. 288–94, 297–306, 319–22.

> For softness she and sweet attractive grace;
> He for God only, she for God in him:
> His fair large front, and eye sublime declared
> Absolute rule; and hyacinthine locks
> Round from his parted forelock manly hung
> Clustering, but not beneath his shoulders broad:
> She as a veil down to her slender waist
> Her unadorned golden tresses wore
> Dishevelled, but in wanton ringlets waved.
> So passed they naked on, nor shunned the sight
> Of God or angel, for they thought no ill:
> So hand in hand they passed, the loveliest pair
> That ever since in love's embraces met.

There is a fine spirit of poetry in the lines which follow, wherein they are described as sitting on a bed of flowers by the side of a fountain, amidst a mixed assembly of animals.

The speeches of these two first lovers flow equally from passion and sincerity. The professions they make to one another are full of warmth; but at the same time founded on truth. In a word, they are the gallantries of Paradise.

> ... When Adam first of men, ...
>   Sole partner and sole part of all these joys
> Dearer thyself than all; ...
> But let us ever praise him, and extol
> His bounty, following our delightful task,
> To prune those growing plants, and tend these flowers,
> Which were it toilsome, yet with thee were sweet.
> To whom thus Eve replied, O thou for whom
> And from whom I was formed, flesh of thy flesh,
> And without whom am to no end, my guide
> And head, what thou hast said is just and right.
> For we to him indeed all praises owe,
> And daily thanks, I chiefly who enjoy
> So far the happier lot, enjoying thee
> Preeminent by so much odds, while thou
> Like consort to thyself canst nowhere find, etc.

The remaining part of Eve's speech, in which she gives an account of herself upon her first creation, and the manner in which she was brought to Adam, is I think as beautiful a passage as any in Milton, or perhaps in any other poet whatsoever. These passages are all worked off with so much art, that they are capable of pleasing the most delicate reader, without offending the most severe.

> That day I oft remember, when from sleep, etc.

animals: *PL*, iv. 325–52.   *... When Adam*: *PL*, iv. 408, 411–12, 436–48.
Eve's speech: *PL*, iv. 449–91.   *That day*: *PL*, iv. 449.

A poet of less judgement and invention than this great author, would have found it very difficult to have filled these tender parts of the poem with sentiments proper for a state of innocence; to have described the warmth of love, and the professions of it, without artifice or hyperbole; to have made the man speak the most endearing things, without descending from his natural dignity, and the woman receiving them without departing from the modesty of her character; in a word, to adjust the prerogatives of wisdom and beauty, and make each appear to the other in its proper force and loveliness. This mutual subordination of the two sexes is wonderfully kept up in the whole poem, as particularly in the speech of Eve I have before mentioned, and upon the conclusion of it in the following lines.

> So spake our general mother, and with eyes
> Of conjugal attraction unreproved,
> And meek surrender, half embracing leaned
> On our first father, half her swelling breast
> Naked met his under the flowing gold
> Of her loose tresses hid; he in delight
> Both of her beauty and submissive charms
> Smiled with superior love, . . .

The poet adds, that the Devil turned away with envy at the sight of so much happiness.

We have another view of our first parents in their evening discourses, which is full of pleasing images and sentiments suitable to their condition and characters. The speech of Eve, in particular, is dressed up in such a soft and natural turn of words and sentiments, as cannot be sufficiently admired.

I shall close my reflections upon this book, with observing the masterly transition which the poet makes to their evening worship, in the following lines.

> Thus at their shady lodge arrived, both stood,
> Both turned, and under open sky adored
> The God that made both sky, air, earth and Heaven,
> Which they beheld, the moon's resplendent globe
> And starry pole: Thou also mad'st the night,
> Maker omnipotent, and thou the day, etc.

Most of the modern heroic poets have imitated the Ancients, in beginning a speech without premising, that the person said thus or thus; but as it is easy to imitate the Ancients in the omission of

---

So spake: PL, iv. 492–9.　　　　　　*characters*: PL, iv. 610–88.
speech of Eve: PL, iv. 635–58.　　　*Thus at their shady*: PL, iv. 720–5.

two or three words, it requires judgement to do it in such a manner as they shall not be missed, and that the speech may begin naturally without them. There is a fine instance of this kind out of Homer, in the twenty-third chapter of Longinus.[n]

327   *Saturday March 15 1712*

... *major rerum mihi nascitur ordo.*   Virg.

We were told in the foregoing book how the evil spirit practised upon Eve as she lay asleep, in order to inspire her with thoughts of vanity, pride and ambition. The author, who shows a wonderful art throughout his whole poem, in preparing the reader for the several occurrences that arise in it, founds upon the above-mentioned circumstance the first part of the fifth book. Adam upon his awaking finds Eve still asleep with an unusual discomposure in her looks. The posture in which he regards her, is described with a wonderful tenderness, as the whisper with which he awakens her, is the softest that ever was conveyed to a lover's ear.

> His wonder was to find unwakened Eve
> With tresses discomposed, and glowing cheek
> As through unquiet rest: he on his side
> Leaning half raised, with looks of cordial love
> Hung over her enamoured, and beheld
> Beauty, which whether waking or asleep,
> Shot forth peculiar graces; then with voice
> Mild, as when Zephyrus on Flora breathes,
> Her hand soft touching, whispered thus. Awake
> My fairest, my espoused, my latest found,
> Heaven's last best gift, my ever new delight,
> Awake, the morning shines, and the fresh field
> Calls us, we lose the prime, to mark how spring
> Our tended plants, how blows the citron grove,
> What drops the myrrh, and what the balmy reed,
> How nature paints her colours, how the bee
> Sits on the bloom, extracting liquid sweet.
> Such whispering waked her, but with startled eye
> On Adam, whom embracing, thus she spake.

Motto: Virgil, *Aeneid*, 7. 44:
>   A larger scene of action is display'd,
>   And, rising hence, a greater work is weigh'd.   DRYDEN

ambition: *PL*, iv. 799–819.   *His wonder was*: *PL*, v. 9–30.

> O sole in whom my thoughts find all repose,
> My glory, my perfection, glad I see
> Thy face, and morn returned . . .

I cannot but take notice that Milton, in the conferences between Adam and Eve, had his eye very frequently upon the book of Canticles, in which there is a noble spirit of eastern poetry, and very often not unlike what we meet with in Homer, who is generally placed near the age of Solomon. I think there is no question but the poet in the preceding speech remembered those two passages which are spoken on the like occasion, and filled with the same pleasing images of nature.

My beloved spake, and said unto me, Rise up, my love, my fair one, and come away; for lo, the winter is past, the rain is over and gone; the flowers appear on the earth; the time of the singing of birds is come, and the voice of the turtle is heard in our land. The fig-tree putteth forth her green figs, and the vines with the tender grape give a good smell. Arise, my love, my fair one, and come away.

Come, my beloved, let us go forth into the field; let us get up early to the vineyards, let us see if the vine flourish, whether the tender grape appear, and the pomegranates bud forth.

His preferring the Garden of Eden to that

> . . . Where the sapient king
> Held dalliance with his fair Egyptian spouse,

shows that the poet had this delightful scene in his mind.

Eve's dream is full of those 'high conceits engendering pride,' which we are told the Devil endeavoured to instil into her. Of this kind is that part of it where she fancies herself awakened by Adam in the following beautiful lines.

> Why sleep'st thou Eve? now is the pleasant time,
> The cool, the silent, save where silence yields
> To the night-warbling bird, that now awake
> Tunes sweetest his love-laboured song; now reigns
> Full orbed the moon, and with more pleasing light
> Shadowy sets off the face of things; in vain
> If none regard; Heaven wakes with all his eyes
> Whom to behold but thee, Nature's desire,
> In whose sight all things joy, with ravishment
> Attracted by thy beauty still to gaze.

An injudicious poet would have made Adam talk through the whole work, in such sentiments as these. But flattery and falsehood

are not the courtship of Milton's Adam, and could not be heard by
Eve in her state of innocence, excepting only in a dream produced
on purpose to taint her imagination. Other vain sentiments of the
same kind in this relation of her dream, will be obvious to every
reader. Though the catastrophe of the poem is finely presaged on this
occasion, the particulars of it are so artfully shadowed, that they
do not anticipate the story which follows in the ninth book. I shall
only add, that though the vision itself is founded upon truth, the
circumstances of it are full of that wildness and inconsistency
which are natural to a dream. Adam, conformable to his superior
character for wisdom, instructs and comforts Eve upon this occasion.

> So cheered he his fair spouse, and she was cheered,
> But silently a gentle tear let fall
> From either eye, and wiped them with her hair;
> Two other precious drops that ready stood,
> Each in their crystal sluice, he ere they fell
> Kissed as the gracious signs of sweet remorse
> And pious awe, that feared to have offended.

The morning hymn is written in imitation of one of those Psalms,
where, in the overflowings of gratitude and praise, the psalmist
calls not only upon the angels, but upon the most conspicuous
parts of the inanimate creation, to join with him in extolling their
common Maker. Invocations of this nature fill the mind with
glorious ideas of God's works, and awaken that divine enthusiasm,
which is so natural to devotion. But if this calling upon the dead
parts of nature, is at all times a proper kind of worship, it was in a
particular manner suitable to our first parents, who had the Creation
fresh upon their minds, and had not seen the various dispensations
of Providence, nor consequently could be acquainted with those
many topics of praise which might afford matter to the devotions of
their posterity. I need not remark the beautiful spirit of poetry
which runs through this whole hymn, nor the holiness of that
resolution with which it concludes.

Having already mentioned those speeches which are assigned to
the persons in this poem, I proceed to the description which the
poet gives of Raphael. His departure from before the throne, and
his flight through the choirs of angels, is finely imaged. As Milton
everywhere fills his poem with circumstances that are marvellous
and astonishing, he describes the Gate of Heaven as framed after

---

artfully: skilfully.   *So cheered he*: *PL*, v. 129–35.
morning hymn: *PL*, v. 153–208.   *Psalms*: e.g. Ps. 148.
choirs of angels: *PL*, v. 247–53.

such a manner, that it opened of itself upon the approach of the angel who was to pass through it.

> . . . till at the gate
> Of Heaven arrived, the gate self-opened wide,
> On golden hinges turning, as by work
> Divine the Sovereign Architect had framed.

The poet here seems to have regarded two or three passages in the eighteenth *Iliad*, as that in particular where, speaking of Vulcan, Homer says, that he had made twenty tripods running on golden wheels, which, upon occasion, might go of themselves to the assembly of the gods, and, when there was no more use for them, return again after the same manner.[n] Scaliger has rallied Homer very severely upon this point, as Mons. Dacier has endeavoured to defend it.[n] I will not pretend to determine, whether in this particular of Homer, the marvellous does not lose sight of the probable. As the miraculous workmanship of Milton's gates is not so extraordinary as this of the tripods, so I am persuaded he would not have mentioned it, had not he been supported in it by a passage in the Scripture, which speaks of wheels in Heaven that had life in them, and moved of themselves, or stood still, in conformity with the Cherubims, whom they accompanied.

There is no question but Milton had this circumstance in his thoughts, because in the following book he describes the chariot of the Messiah with *living* wheels, according to the plan in Ezekiel's vision.

> . . . Forth rushed with whirlwind sound
> The chariot of Paternal Deity
> Flashing thick flames, wheel within wheel undrawn,
> Itself instinct with spirit . . .

I question not but Bossu, and the two Daciers, who are for vindicating everything that is censured in Homer, by something parallel in Holy Writ, would have been very well pleased had they thought of confronting Vulcan's tripods with Ezekiel's wheels.

Raphael's descent to the earth, with the figure of his person, is represented in very lively colours. Several of the French, Italian and English poets have given a loose to their imaginations in the description of angels: but I do not remember to have met with any, so finely drawn and so conformable to the notions which are given of them in Scripture, as this in Milton. After having set him forth in

till at the gate: PL, v. 253–6. *tripods*: *Iliad*, 18. 372–7.
Scripture: Ezek. 1: 21, 10: 17. *Forth rushed*: PL, vi. 749–52.
Raphael: PL, v. 266–87.

all his heavenly plumage, and represented him as alighting upon
the earth, the poet concludes his description with a circumstance,
which is altogether new, and imagined with the greatest strength of
fancy.

> . . . Like Maia's son he stood,
> And shook his plumes, that heavenly fragrance filled
> The circuit wide. . . .

Raphael's reception by the guardian angels; his passing through
the wilderness of sweets; his distant appearance to Adam, have all
the graces that poetry is capable of bestowing. The author afterwards gives us a particular description of Eve in her domestic
employments.

> So saying, with dispatchful looks in haste
> She turns, on hospitable thoughts intent,
> What choice to choose for delicacy best,
> What order, so contrived as not to mix
> Tastes, not well joined, inelegant, but bring
> Taste after taste, upheld with kindliest change;
> Bestirs her then etc.

Though in this, and other parts of the same book, the subject is
only the housewifery of our first parent, it is set off with so many
pleasing images and strong expressions, as make it none of the
least agreeable parts in this divine work.

The natural majesty of Adam, and at the same time his sub-
missive behaviour to the superior being, who had vouchsafed to be
his guest; the solemn hail which the angel bestows upon the mother
of mankind, with the figure of Eve ministering at the table, are
circumstances which deserve to be admired.

Raphael's behaviour is every way suitable to the dignity of his
nature, and to that character of a sociable spirit, with which the
author has so judiciously introduced him. He had received instructions to converse with Adam, as one friend converses with another,
and to warn him of the enemy, who was contriving his destruction:
accordingly he is represented as sitting down at table with Adam,
and eating of the fruits of Paradise. The occasion naturally leads
him to his discourse on the food of angels. After having thus
entered into conversation with man upon more indifferent subjects,

---

Like Maia's son: *PL*, v. 285–7. Maia's son was Hermes.
graces: *PL*, v. 287–300.
Adam: *PL*, v. 350–60.   *So saying*: *PL*, v. 331–7.
Eve: *PL*, v. 443–5.   *hail*: *PL*, v. 388.
conversation: *PL*, v. 404–33.   *Paradise*: *PL*, v. 433.

he warns him of his obedience, and makes a natural transition to the history of that fallen angel, who was employed in the circumvention of our first parents.

Had I followed Monsieur Bossu's method in my first paper on Milton, I should have dated the action of *Paradise Lost* from the beginning of Raphael's speech in this book, as he supposes the action of the *Aeneid* to begin in the second book of that poem. I could allege many reasons for my drawing the action of the *Aeneid*, rather from its immediate beginning in the first book, than from its remote beginning in the second, and show why I have considered the sacking of Troy as an episode, according to the common acceptation of that word. But as this would be a dry unentertaining piece of criticism, and perhaps unnecessary to those who have read my first paper, I shall not enlarge upon it. Whichever of the notions be true, the unity of Milton's action is preserved according to either of them: whether we consider the Fall of Man in its immediate beginning, as proceeding from the resolutions taken in the Infernal Council, or in its more remote beginning, as proceeding from the first revolt of the angels in Heaven. The occasion which Milton assigns for this revolt, as it is founded on hints in Holy Writ, and on the opinion of some great writers, so it was the most proper that the poet could have made use of.

The revolt in Heaven is described with great force of imagination, and a fine variety of circumstances. The learned reader cannot but be pleased with the poet's imitation of Homer in the last of the following lines.

> At length into the limits of the North
> They came, and Satan took his royal seat
> High on a hill, far blazing, as a mount
> Raised on a mount, with pyramids and towers
> From diamond quarries hewn, and rocks of gold
> The palace of great Lucifer, (so call
> That structure in the dialect of men
> Interpreted) . . .

Homer mentions persons and things, which he tells us in the language of the gods are called by different names from those they go by in the language of men. Milton has imitated him with his usual judgement in this particular place, wherein he has likewise the authority of Scripture to justify him. The part of Abdiel, who was the only spirit that in this infinite host of angels preserved his

obedience: *PL*, v. 519–43.   *Bossu*: Book ii, Ch. xi.
At length: *PL*, v. 755–62.   *Homer*: *Iliad*, i. 403; 2. 813; 14. 291; 20. 74.

allegiance to his Maker, exhibits to us a noble moral of religious singularity. The zeal of the seraph breaks forth in a becoming warmth of sentiments and expressions, as the character which is given us of him denotes that generous scorn and intrepidity which attends heroic virtue. The author, doubtless, designed it as a pattern to those who live among mankind in their present state of degeneracy and corruption.

> So spake the seraph Abdiel faithful found,
> Among the faithless, faithful only he;
> Among innumerable false, unmoved,
> Unshaken, unseduced, unterrified;
> His loyalty he kept, his love, his zeal:
> Nor number, nor example with him wrought
> To swerve from truth, or change his constant mind
> Though single. From amidst them forth he passed,
> Long way through hostile scorn, which he sustained
> Superior, nor of violence feared aught;
> And with retorted scorn his back he turned
> On those proud towers to swift destruction doomed.

333   *Saturday March 22 1712*

. . . vocat in certamina divos.   Virg.

We are now entering upon the sixth book of *Paradise Lost*, in which the poet describes the battle of angels; having raised his reader's expectation, and prepared him for it by several passages in the preceding books. I omitted quoting these passages in my observations on the former books, having purposely reserved them for the opening of this, the subject of which gave occasion to them. The author's imagination was so inflamed with this great scene of action, that wherever he speaks of it, he rises, if possible, above himself. Thus where he mentions Satan in the beginning of his poem,

> Him the Almighty power
> Hurled headlong flaming from the ethereal sky,
> With hideous ruin and combustion down

---

singularity: *PL*, v. 805–907.   *So spake*: *PL*, v. 896–907.
Motto: Virgil, *Aeneid*, 6. 172: And to contention calls the gods.
Him the Almighty: *PL*, i. 44–9.

To bottomless perdition, there to dwell
In adamantine chains and penal fire,
Who durst defy the Omnipotent to arms.

We have likewise several noble hints of it in the infernal conference.

O Prince, O chief of many throned powers
That led the imbattled Seraphim to war,
Too well I see and rue the dire event,
That with sad overthrow and foul defeat
Hath lost us Heaven, and all this mighty host
In horrible destruction laid thus low.
But see the angry victor hath recalled
His ministers of vengeance and pursuit
Back to the Gates of Heaven: the sulphurous hail
Shot after us in storm, o'erblown hath laid
The fiery surge, that from the precipice
Of Heaven received us falling, and the thunder
Winged with red lightning and impetuous rage,
Perhaps hath spent his shafts, and ceases now
To bellow through the vast and boundless deep.

There are several other very sublime images on the same subject in the first book, as also in the second.

What when we fled amain, pursued and strook
With Heaven's afflicting thunder, and besought
The deep to shelter us; this Hell then seemed
A refuge from those wounds . . . .

In short, the poet never mentions anything of this battle but in such images of greatness and terror, as are suitable to the subject. Among several others, I cannot forbear quoting that passage where the power, who is described as presiding over the Chaos, speaks in the third book.

Thus Satan; and him thus the anarch old
With faltering speech and visage incomposed
Answered. I know thee, stranger, who thou art,
That mighty leading angel, who of late
Made head against Heaven's King, though overthrown.
I saw and heard, for such a numerous host
Fled not in silence through the frighted deep
With ruin upon ruin, rout on rout,
Confusion worse confounded; and Heaven Gates
Poured out by millions her victorious bands
Pursuing. . . .

O Prince: PL, i. 128–9, 134–7, 169–77.   *What when we fled*: PL, ii. 165–8.
third book: actually Book II.   *Thus Satan*: PL, ii. 988–98.

It required great pregnancy of invention, and strength of imagination, to fill this battle with such circumstances as should raise and astonish the mind of the reader; and, at the same time, an exactness of judgement to avoid everything that might appear light or trivial. Those who look into Homer, are surprised to find his battles still rising one above another, and improving in horror, to the conclusion of the *Iliad*. Milton's fight of angels is wrought up with the same beauty. It is ushered in with such signs of wrath as are suitable to Omnipotence incensed. The first engagement is carried on under a cope of fire, occasioned by the flights of innumerable burning darts and arrows, which are discharged from either host. The second onset is still more terrible, as it is filled with those artificial thunders, which seem to make the victory doubtful, and produce a kind of consternation, even in the good angels. This is followed by the tearing up of mountains and promontories; till, in the last place, Messiah comes forth in the fulness of majesty and terror. The pomp of his appearance, amidst the roarings of his thunders, the flashes of his lightnings, and the noise of his chariot wheels, is described with the utmost flights of human imagination.

There is nothing in the first and last day's engagement, which does not appear natural and agreeable enough to the ideas most readers would conceive of a fight between two armies of angels.

The second day's engagement is apt to startle an imagination, which has not been raised and qualified for such a description, by the reading of the ancient poets, and of Homer in particular. It was certainly a very bold thought in our author, to ascribe the first use of artillery to the rebel angels. But as such a pernicious invention may be well supposed to have proceeded from such authors, so it enters very properly into the thoughts of that being, who is all along described as aspiring to the majesty of his Maker. Such engines were the only instruments he could have made use of to imitate those thunders, that in all poetry, both sacred and profane, are represented as the arms of the Almighty. The tearing up the hills was not altogether so daring a thought as the former. We are, in some measure, prepared for such an incident by the description of the giants' war, which we meet with among the ancient poets. What still made this circumstance the more proper for the poet's use, is the opinion of many learned men, that the fable of the giants' war, which makes so great a noise in antiquity, and gave birth to the sublimest description

Omnipotence: *PL*, vi. 56–60.   *host*: *PL*, vi. 212–17.
good angels: *PL*, vi. 582–90.   *promontories*: *PL*, vi. 639–69.
imagination: *PL*, vi. 749–72.

in Hesiod's works, was an allegory founded upon this very tradition of a fight between the good and bad angels.

It may, perhaps, be worth while to consider with what judgement Milton, in this narration, has avoided everything that is mean and trivial in the descriptions of the Latin and Greek poets; and, at the same time, improved every great hint which he met with in their works upon this subject. Homer in that passage, which Longinus has celebrated for its sublimeness, and which Virgil and Ovid have copied after him, tells us, that the giants threw Ossa upon Olympus, and Pelion upon Ossa. He adds an epithet to Pelion (εἰνοσίφυλλον) which very much swells the idea, by bringing up to the reader's imagination all the woods that grew upon it. There is further a great beauty in his singling out by name these three remarkable mountains so well known to the Greeks.[n] This last is such a beauty as the scene of Milton's war could not possibly furnish him with. Claudian in his fragment upon the giants' war, has given full scope to that wildness of imagination which was natural to him. He tells us, that the giants tore up whole islands by the roots, and threw them at the gods. He describes one of them in particular taking up Lemnos in his arms, and whirling it to the skies, with all Vulcan's shop in the midst of it. Another tears up Mount Ida, with the river Enipeus which ran down the sides of it; but the poet, not content to describe him with this mountain upon his shoulders, tells us that the river flowed down his back, as he held it up in that posture. It is visible to every judicious reader, that such ideas savour more of burlesque than of the sublime. They proceed from a wantonness of imagination, and rather divert the mind than astonish it. Milton has taken everything that is sublime in these several passages, and composes out of them the following great image.

> From their foundations loosening to and fro
> They plucked the seated hills with all their load,
> Rocks, waters, woods, and by the shaggy tops
> Uplifting bore them in their hands: . . .

We have the full majesty of Homer in this short description, improved by the imagination of Claudian, without its puerilities.

Hesiod: *Theogony*, 664–745.
Homer: *Odyssey*, 11. 315–16.
sublimeness: *On the Sublime*, 8. 2 (Boileau's trans., Ch. vi).
εἰνοσίφυλλον: leaf-shaking.
posture: Claudian, *Gigantomachia*, 62–91. In Nos. 279 and 285 Claudian is mentioned in illustration of the false sublime (pp. 72, 77).
From their foundations: *PL*, vi. 643–6.

I need not point out the description of the fallen angels, seeing the promontories hanging over their heads in such a dreadful manner, with the other numberless beauties in this book, which are so conspicuous, that they cannot escape the notice of the most ordinary reader.

There are indeed so many wonderful strokes of poetry in this book, and such a variety of sublime ideas, that it would have been impossible to have given them a place within the bounds of this paper. Besides that, I find it in a great measure done to my hand, at the end of my Lord Roscommon's Essay on Translated Poetry. I shall refer my reader thither for some of the master-strokes in the sixth book of *Paradise Lost*, though at the same time there are many others which that noble author has not taken notice of.

Milton, notwithstanding the sublime genius he was master of, has in this book drawn to his assistance all the helps he could meet with among the ancient poets. The sword of Michael, which makes so great an havoc among the bad angels, was given him, we are told, out of the armoury of God.

> . . . But the sword
> Of Michael from the armoury of God
> Was given him tempered so, that neither keen
> Nor solid might resist that edge: it met
> The sword of Satan with steep force to smite
> Descending, and in half cut sheer . . .

This passage is a copy of that in Virgil, wherein the poet tells us, that the sword of Aeneas, which was given him by a deity, broke into pieces the sword of Turnus, which came from a mortal forge: as the moral in this place is divine, so by the way we may observe, that the bestowing on a man who is favoured by Heaven such an allegorical weapon, is very conformable to the old eastern way of thinking. Not only Homer has made use of it, but we find the Jewish hero in the book of Maccabees, who had fought the battles of the chosen people with so much glory and success, receiving in his dream a sword from the hand of the prophet Jeremiah. The follow-

Roscommon: near the end of the Earl of Roscommon's *Essay on Translated Verse* (1684) is a passage of 27 lines added to the 2nd edition (1685) headed in the margin, 'An Essay on blank verse out of the 6th Book of *Paradise Lost*' (for text see Spingarn, ii. 308–9).

But the sword: *PL*, vi. 320–5.

forge: *Aeneid*, 12. 728–41. It is the armour of Aeneas, not his sword, which shatters the weapon of Turnus.

Maccabees: 2 Macc. 15:15.

ing passage, wherein Satan is described as wounded by the sword of Michael, is in imitation of Homer.

> The griding sword with discontinuous wound
> Passed through him, but the ethereal substance closed
> Not long divisible, and from the gash
> A stream of nectarous humour issuing flowed
> Sanguine, such as celestial spirits may bleed,
> And all his armour stained . . .

Homer tells us in the same manner, that upon Diomedes wounding the gods, there flowed from the wound an 'ichor', or pure kind of blood, which was not bred from mortal viands; and that though the pain was exquisitely great, the wound soon closed up and healed in those beings who are vested with immortality.

I question not but Milton in his description of his furious Moloch flying from the battle, and bellowing with the wound he had received, had his eye on Mars in the *Iliad*, who upon his being wounded, is represented as retiring out of the fight, and making an outcry louder than that of a whole army when it begins the charge. Homer adds, that the Greeks and Trojans, who were engaged in a general battle, were terrified on each side with the bellowing of this wounded deity. The reader will easily observe how Milton has kept all the horror of this image without running into the ridicule of it.

> . . . Where the might of Gabriel fought,
> And with fierce ensigns pierced the deep array
> Of Moloch furious king, who him defied,
> And at his chariot wheels to drag him bound
> Threatened, nor from the Holy One of Heaven
> Refrained his tongue blasphemous; but anon
> Down cloven to the waist, with shattered arms
> And uncouth pain fled bellowing. . . .

Milton has likewise raised his description in this book with many images taken out of the poetical parts of Scripture. The Messiah's chariot, as I have before taken notice, is formed upon a vision of Ezekiel, who, as Grotius observes, has very much in him of Homer's spirit in the poetical parts of his prophecy.

The following lines in that glorious commission which is given the Messiah to extirpate the host of rebel angels, is drawn from a sublime passage in the Psalms.

The griding sword: *PL*, vi. 329–34. *immortality*: *Iliad*, 5. 334–42.
Moloch: *PL*, vi. 360–2. *charge*: *Iliad*, 5. 855–63.
Where the might: *PL*, vi. 355–62. *Ezekiel*: Ezek. 1:19 ff.
Hugo Grotius: *Opera Omnia Theologica* (1679), i. 401.
Psalms: Ps. 45:3.

> Go then thou mightiest in thy Father's might
> Ascend my chariot, guide the rapid wheels
> That shake Heaven's basis, bring forth all my war,
> My bow, my thunder, my almighty arms,
> Gird on thy sword on thy puissant thigh.

The reader will easily discover many other strokes of the same nature.

There is no question but Milton had heated his imagination with the fight of the gods in Homer, before he entered upon this engagement of the angels. Homer there gives us a scene of men, heroes and gods mixed together in battle. Mars animates the contending armies, and lifts up his voice in such a manner, that it is heard distinctly amidst all the shouts and confusion of the fight. Jupiter at the same time thunders over their heads; while Neptune raises such a tempest, that the whole field of battle, and all the tops of the mountains shake about them. The poet tells us, that Pluto himself, whose habitation was in the very centre of the earth, was so affrighted at the shock, that he leapt from his throne. Homer afterwards describes Vulcan as pouring down a storm of fire upon the River Xanthus, and Minerva as throwing a rock at Mars; who, he tells us, covered seven acres in his fall.

As Homer has introduced into his battle of the gods everything that is great and terrible in nature, Milton has filled his fight of good and bad angels with all the like circumstances of horror. The shout of armies, the rattling of brazen chariots, the hurling of rocks and mountains, the earthquake, the fire, the thunder, are all of them employed to lift up the reader's imagination, and give him a suitable idea of so great an action. With what art has the poet represented the whole body of the earth trembling, even before it was created.

> All Heaven resounded, and had Earth been then
> All Earth had to its centre shook . . . .

In how sublime and just a manner does he afterwards describe the whole Heaven shaking under the wheels of the Messiah's chariot, with that exception to the Throne of God?

Go then: *PL*, vi. 710–14. In Milton the last two lines read:

> My bow and thunder, my almighty arms
> Gird on, and sword upon thy puissant thigh.

fight: *Iliad*, 20. 51–66.
fall: *Iliad*, 21. 328–82, 403–14 ('seven roods').
All Heaven: *PL*, vi. 217–19:

> all Heaven
> Resounded, and had Earth been then, all Earth
> Had to her centre shook.

> ... Under his burning wheels
> The steadfast Empyrean shook throughout,
> All but the throne itself of God ....

Notwithstanding the Messiah appears clothed with so much terror and majesty, the poet has still found means to make his readers conceive an idea of him, beyond what he himself was able to describe.

> Yet half his strength he put not forth, but checked
> His thunder in mid volley, for he meant
> Not to destroy, but root them out of Heaven.

In a word, Milton's genius which was so great in itself, and so strengthened by all the helps of learning, appears in this book every way equal to his subject, which was the most sublime that could enter into the thoughts of a poet. As he knew all the arts of affecting the mind, he knew it was necessary to give it certain resting-places and opportunities of recovering itself from time to time: he has therefore with great address interspersed several speeches, reflections, similitudes, and the like reliefs, to diversify his narration, and ease the attention of the reader, that he might come fresh to his great action; and by such a contrast of ideas, have a more lively taste of the nobler parts of his description.

339   *Saturday March 29 1712*

> *... Ut his exordia primis*
> *omnia et ipse tener mundi concreverit orbis.*
> *Tum durare solum et discludere Nerea ponto*
> *coeperit, et rerum paullatim sumere formas.* Virg.

Longinus has observed, that there may be a loftiness in sentiments, where there is no passion, and brings instances out of ancient authors to support this his opinion. The pathetic, as that great critic

---

... *Under his burning*: *PL*, vi. 832–4.   *Yet half*: *PL*, vi. 853–5.

Motto: Virgil, *Eclogues*, 6. 33–6:
> He sung the secret seeds of nature's frame;
> How seas, and earth, and air, and active flame,
> Fell through the mighty void; and in their fall
> Were blindly gathered in this goodly ball. DRYDEN

Longinus: *On the Sublime*, 8 (Boileau's trans., Ch. vi).

observes, may animate and inflame the sublime, but is not essential
to it. Accordingly, as he further remarks, we very often find that
those, who excel most in stirring up the passions, very often want the
talent of writing in the great and sublime manner; and so on the
contrary. Milton has shown himself a master in both these ways of
writing. The seventh book, which we are now entering upon, is an
instance of that sublime, which is not mixed and worked up with
passion. The author appears in a kind of composed and sedate
majesty; and though the sentiments do not give so great an emotion
as those in the former book, they abound with as magnificent ideas.
The sixth book, like a troubled ocean, represents greatness in confusion; the seventh affects the imagination like the ocean in a calm,
and fills the mind of the reader without producing in it anything like
tumult or agitation.

The critic above-mentioned, among the rules which he lays down
for succeeding in the sublime way of writing, proposes to his reader,
that he should imitate the most celebrated authors who have gone
before him, and have been engaged in works of the same nature;
as in particular that if he writes on a poetical subject, he should consider how Homer would have spoken on such an occasion. By this
means one great genius often catches the flame from another, and
writes in his spirit, without copying servilely after him. There are a
thousand shining passages in Virgil, which have been lighted up by
Homer.

Milton, though his own natural strength of genius was capable of
furnishing out a perfect work, has doubtless very much raised and
ennobled his conceptions, by such an imitation as that which
Longinus has recommended.

In this book, which gives us an account of the six days' works, the
poet received but very few assistances from heathen writers, who
were strangers to the wonders of Creation. But as there are many
glorious strokes of poetry upon this subject in Holy Writ, the
author has numberless allusions to them through the whole course
of this book. The great critic I have before mentioned, though an
heathen, has taken notice of the sublime manner in which the law-
giver of the Jews has described the Creation in the first chapter of
Genesis; and there are many other passages in Scripture, which rise
up to the same majesty, where this subject is touched upon. Milton
has shown his judgement very remarkably, in making use of such of
these as were proper for his poem, and in duly qualifying those high

---

occasion: Longinus, 14. 1 (Boileau, Ch. xii).
critic: Longinus, 9. 9 (Boileau, Ch. vii).

strains of eastern poetry, which were suited to readers whose imaginations were set to an higher pitch than those of colder climates.

Adam's speech to the angel, wherein he desires an account of what had passed within the regions of nature before the Creation, is very great and solemn. The following lines, in which he tells him that the day is not too far spent for him to enter upon such a subject, are exquisite in their kind.

> And the great light of day yet wants to run
> Much of his race though steep, suspense in Heaven
> Held by thy voice, thy potent voice he hears,
> And longer will delay to hear thee tell
> His generation, etc. . . .

The angel's encouraging our first parents in a modest pursuit after knowledge, with the causes which he assigns for the Creation of the world, are very just and beautiful. The Messiah, by whom, as we are told in Scripture, the worlds were made, comes forth in the power of his Father, surrounded with an host of angels, and clothed with such a majesty as becomes his entering upon a work, which, according to our conceptions, appears the utmost exertion of Omnipotence. What a beautiful description has our author raised upon that hint in one of the prophets; 'And behold there came four chariots out from between two mountains, and the mountains were mountains of brass'?

> About his chariot numberless were poured
> Cherub and Seraph, Potentates and Thrones,
> And Virtues, winged Spirits, and chariots winged,
> From the armoury of God, where stand of old
> Myriads between two brazen mountains lodged
> Against a solemn day, harnessed at hand;
> Celestial equipage, and now came forth
> Spontaneous, for within them spirit lived
> Attendant on their lord: Heaven opened wide
> Her ever-during gates, harmonious sound
> On golden hinges moving . . .

I have before taken notice of these chariots of God, and of these Gates of Heaven, and shall here only add, that Homer gives us the same idea of the latter as opening of themselves, though he afterwards takes off from it, by telling us, that the hours first of all

---

Adam's speech: *PL*, vii. 70–108.   *And the great*: *PL*, vii. 98–102.
Scripture: John 1:3; Ephes. 3:9; Heb. 1:2, &c.
prophets: Zech. 6:1.   *About his chariot*: *PL*, vii. 197–207.
Gates of Heaven: See Nos. 327, 333.   *Homer*: *Iliad*, 5. 748–51; 8. 393–5.

removed those prodigious heaps of clouds which lay as a barrier before them.

I do not know anything in the whole poem more sublime than the description which follows, where the Messiah is represented at the head of his angels, as looking down into the Chaos, calming its confusion, riding into the midst of it, and drawing the first outline of the Creation.

> On Heavenly ground they stood, and from the shore
> They viewed the vast immeasurable abyss
> Outrageous as a sea, dark, wasteful, wild,
> Up from the bottom turned by furious winds
> And surging waves, as mountains to assault
> Heaven's height, and with the centre mix the pole.
>   Silence ye troubled waves, and thou deep, peace,
> Said then the Omnific Word, your discord end:
>   Nor stayed, but on the wings of Cherubim
> Uplifted, in paternal glory rode
> Far into Chaos, and the world unborn;
> For Chaos heard his voice; him all his train
> Followed in bright procession to behold
> Creation, and the wonders of his might.
> Then stayed the fervid wheels, and in his hand
> He took the golden compasses, prepared
> In God's eternal store, to circumscribe
> This Universe, and all created things:
> One foot he centered, and the other turned,
> Round through the vast profundity obscure,
> And said, thus far extend, thus far thy bounds,
> This be thy just circumference, O World.

The thought of the golden compasses is conceived altogether in Homer's spirit, and is a very noble incident in this wonderful description. Homer, when he speaks of the gods, ascribes to them several arms and instruments with the same greatness of imagination. Let the reader only peruse the description of Minerva's aegis, or buckler, in the fifth book of the *Iliad*, with her spear, which would overturn whole squadrons, and her helmet, that was sufficient to cover an army, drawn out of an hundred cities: the golden compasses, in the above-mentioned passage appear a very natural instrument in the hand of him, whom Plato somewhere calls the Divine Geometrician. As poetry delights in clothing abstracted ideas in allegories and sensible images,[n] we find a magnificent description of the Creation formed after the same manner in one of the prophets,

On Heavenly ground: *PL*, vii. 210–31.
Minerva's aegis: *Iliad*, 5. 738–47.
Divine Geometrician: Plutarch, *Symposiaca*, 8. 2 [718 C].

wherein he describes the Almighty Architect as measuring the waters in the hollow of his hand, meting out the Heavens with his span, comprehending the dust of the earth in a measure, weighing the mountains in scales, and the hills in a balance. Another of them describing the Supreme Being in this great work of Creation, represents him as laying the foundations of the earth, and stretching a line upon it. And in another place as garnishing the heavens, stretching out the north over the empty place, and hanging the earth upon nothing. This last noble thought Milton has expressed in the following verse.

> And Earth self-balanced on her centre hung.

The beauties of description in this book lie so very thick, that it is impossible to enumerate them in this paper. The poet has employed on them the whole energy of our tongue. The several great scenes of the Creation rise up to view one after another, in such a manner that the reader seems present at this wonderful work, and to assist among the choirs of angels, who are the spectators of it. How glorious is the conclusion of the first day.

> ... Thus was the first day even and morn.
> Nor past uncelebrated, nor unsung
> By the celestial choirs when orient light
> Exhaling first from darkness they beheld;
> Birth-day of Heaven and Earth; with joy and shout
> The hollow universal orb they filled.

We have the same elevation of thought in the third day, when the mountains were brought forth, and the deep was made.

> Immediately the mountains huge appear
> Emergent, and their broad bare backs up heave
> Into the clouds, their tops ascend the sky.
> So high as heaved the tumid hills, so low
> Down sunk a hollow bottom broad and deep,
> Capacious bed of waters . . . .

We have also the rising of the whole vegetable world described in this day's work, which is filled with all the graces that other poets have lavished on their descriptions of the spring, and leads the reader's imagination into a theatre equally surprising and beautiful.

The several glories of the Heavens make their appearance on the fourth day.

---

balance: Isa. 40:12.
hanging the earth: Job 26:7.
Thus was: *PL*, vii. 252–7.
theatre: *PL*, vii. 309–38.

Supreme Being: Job 38:4, 5.
And Earth: *PL*, vii. 242.
Immediately: *PL*, vii. 285–90.

First in his east the glorious lamp was seen
Regent of day, and all the horizon round
Invested with bright rays, jocund to run
His longitude through Heaven's high road: the gray
Dawn, and the Pleiades before him danced
Shedding sweet influence: less bright the moon,
But opposite in levelled west was set,
His mirror, with full face borrowing her light
From him, for other light she needed none
In that aspect, and still that distance keeps
Till night; then in the east her turn she shines
Revolved on Heaven's great axle, and her reign
With thousand lesser lights dividual holds,
With thousand thousand stars, that then appeared
Spangling the hemisphere . . . .

One would wonder how the poet could be so concise in his description of the six days' works, as to comprehend them within the bounds of an episode, and at the same time so particular, as to give us a lively idea of them. This is still more remarkable in his account of the fifth and sixth days, in which he has drawn out to our view the whole animal creation, from the reptile to the Behemoth. As the lion and the Leviathan are two of the noblest productions in the world of living creatures, the reader will find a most exquisite spirit of poetry, in the account which our author gives us of them. The sixth day concludes with the formation of man, upon which the angel takes occasion, as he did after the battle in Heaven, to remind Adam of his obedience, which was the principal design of this his visit.

The poet afterwards represents the Messiah returning into Heaven, and taking a survey of his great work. There is something inexpressibly sublime in this part of the poem, where the author describes that great period of time, filled with so many glorious circumstances; when the Heavens and Earth were finished; when the Messiah ascended up in triumph through the Everlasting Gates; when he looked down with pleasure upon his new Creation; when every part of Nature seemed to rejoice in its existence; when the morning stars sang together, and all the sons of God shouted for joy.

So even and morn accomplished the sixth day:
Yet not till the Creator from his work
Desisting, though unwearied, up returned,

First in his east: *PL*, vii. 370–84.   *Behemoth*: *PL*, vii. 387–504.
lion and Leviathan: *PL*, vii. 463–6, 412–16.   *formation of man*: *PL*, vii. 505–47.
joy: Job 38:7.
So even and morn: *PL*, vii. 550–68 (line 563, 'stations').

Up to the Heaven of Heavens his high abode,
Thence to behold this new created world
The addition of his empire; how it showed
In prospect from his throne, how good, how fair
Answering his great idea. Up he rode
Followed with acclamation and the sound
Symphonious of ten thousand harps that tuned
Angelic harmonies: the earth, the air
Resounded, (thou remember'st, for thou heard'st)
The Heavens and all the constellations rung,
The planets in their station listening stood,
While the bright pomp ascended jubilant.
Open, ye everlasting gates, they sung,
Open, ye Heavens, your living doors, let in
The great Creator from his work returned
Magnificent, his six days' work, a World.

I cannot conclude this book upon the Creation, without mentioning a poem which has lately appeared under that title.[n] The work was undertaken with so good an intention, and is executed with so great a mastery, that it deserves to be looked upon as one of the most useful and noble productions in our English verse. The reader cannot but be pleased to find the depths of philosophy enlivened with all the charms of poetry, and to see so great a strength of reason, amidst so beautiful a redundancy of imagination. The author has shown us that design in all the works of nature, which necessarily leads us to the knowledge of its first cause. In short, he has illustrated, by numberless and incontestable instances, that divine wisdom, which the son of Sirach has so nobly ascribed to the Supreme Being in his formation of the World, when he tells us, that 'He created her, and saw her, and numbered her, and poured her out upon all his works.'[n]

redundancy: superabundance.
He created her: Ecclus. 1:9.

345   *Saturday April 5 1712*

Sanctius his animal, mentisque capacius altae
Deerat adhuc, et quod dominari in caetera posset.
Natus homo est . . . .   Ov. Met.

The accounts which Raphael gives of the battle of angels, and the
Creation of the world, have in them those qualifications which the
critics judge requisite to an episode.[n] They are nearly related to the
principal action, and have a just connection with the fable.

The eighth book opens with a beautiful description of the impression which this discourse of the archangel made on our first
parents. Adam afterwards, by a very natural curiosity, enquires concerning the motions of those celestial bodies which make the most
glorious appearance among the six days' works. The poet here, with a
great deal of art, represents Eve as withdrawing from this part of
their conversation to amusements more suitable to her sex. He well
knew, that the episode in this book, which is filled with Adam's
account of his passion and esteem for Eve, would have been improper for her hearing, and has therefore devised very just and
beautiful reasons for her retiring.

> So spake our sire, and by his countenance seemed
> Entering on studious thoughts abstruse, which Eve
> Perceiving where she sat retired in sight,
> With lowliness majestic from her seat
> And grace that won who saw to wish her stay,
> Rose, and went forth among her fruits and flowers
> To visit how they prospered, bud and bloom,
> Her nursery; they at her coming sprung,
> And touched by her fair tendance gladlier grew.
> Yet went she not, as not with such discourse
> Delighted, or not capable her ear
> Of what was high: such pleasure she reserved
> Adam relating, she sole auditress;
> Her husband the relater she preferred
> Before the angel, and of him to ask
> Chose rather: he, she knew, would intermix
> Grateful digressions, and solve high dispute

Motto: Ovid, *Metamorphoses*, 1. 76–8:

> A creature of a more exalted kind
> Was wanting yet, and then was man designed;
> Conscious of thought, of more capacious breast,
> For empire formed and fit to rule the rest.   DRYDEN

So spake our sire: *PL*, viii. 39–58.

With conjugal caresses, from his lip
Not words alone pleased her. O when meet now
Such pairs in love, and mutual honour joined?

The angel's returning a doubtful answer to Adam's enquiries, was
not only proper for the moral reason which the poet assigns, but
because it would have been highly absurd to have given the sanction
of an archangel to any particular system of philosophy. The chief
points in the Ptolemaic and Copernican hypotheses are described
with great conciseness and perspicuity, and at the same time dressed
in very pleasing and poetical images.

Adam, to detain the angel, enters afterwards upon his own history,
and relates to him the circumstances in which he found himself upon
his creation; as also his conversation with his Maker, and his first
meeting with Eve. There is no part of the poem more apt to raise the
attention of the reader, than this discourse of our great ancestor;
as nothing can be more surprising and delightful to us, than to hear
the sentiments that arose in the first man while he was yet new and
fresh from the hands of his Creator. The poet has interwoven everything which is delivered upon this subject in Holy Writ with so
many beautiful imaginations of his own, that nothing can be conceived more just and natural than this whole episode. As our author
knew this subject could not but be agreeable to his reader, he would
not throw it into the relation of the six days' works, but reserved it
for a distinct episode, that he might have an opportunity of expatiat-
ing upon it more at large. Before I enter on this part of the poem, I
cannot but take notice of two shining passages in the dialogue between Adam and the angel. The first is that wherein our ancestor
gives an account of the pleasure he took in conversing with him,
which contains a very noble moral.

For while I sit with thee, I seem in Heaven,
And sweeter thy discourse is to my ear
Than fruits of palm-tree pleasantest to thirst
And hunger both, from labour, at the hour
Of sweet repast; they satiate, and soon fill,
Though pleasant, but thy words with grace divine
Imbued, bring to their sweetness no satiety.

The other I shall mention is that in which the angel gives a reason
why he should be glad to hear the story Adam was about to relate.

For I that day was absent, as befell,
Bound on a voyage uncouth and obscure,

dialogue: *PL*, viii. 250–520.   *For while I sit*: *PL*, viii. 210–16.
For I that day: *PL*, viii. 229–36.

> Far on excursion towards the Gates of Hell;
> Squared in full legion (such command we had)
> To see that none thence issued forth a spy,
> Or enemy, while God was in his work,
> Lest he incensed at such eruption bold,
> Destruction with Creation might have mixed.

There is no question but our poet drew the image in what follows from that in Virgil's sixth book, where Aeneas and the sybil stand before the adamantine gates which are there described as shut upon the place of torments, and listen to the groans, the clank of chains, and the noise of iron whips that were heard in those regions of pain and sorrow.

> Fast we found, fast shut
> The dismal gates, and barricadoed strong;
> But long ere our approaching heard within
> Noise, other than the sound of dance or song,
> Torment, and loud lament, and furious rage.

Adam then proceeds to give an account of his condition and sentiments immediately after his creation. How agreeably does he represent the posture in which he found himself, the delightful landscape that surrounded him, and the gladness of heart which grew up in him on that occasion.

> ... As new waked from soundest sleep
> Soft on the flowery herb I found me laid
> In balmy sweat, which with his beams the sun
> Soon dried, and on the reeking moisture fed.
> Straight toward Heaven my wondering eyes I turned,
> And gazed a while the ample sky, till raised
> By quick instinctive motion up I sprung
> As thitherward endeavouring, and upright
> Stood on my feet; about me round I saw
> Hill, dale, and shady woods and sunny plains,
> And liquid lapse of murmuring streams; by these
> Creatures that lived, and moved, and walked, or flew,
> Birds on the branches warbling; all things smiled:
> With fragrance, and with joy my heart o'erflowed.

Adam is afterwards described as surprised at his own existence, and taking a survey of himself, and of all the works of Nature. He likewise is represented as discovering by the light of reason, that he and everything about him must have been the effect of some Being infinitely good and powerful, and that this Being had a right to his worship and adoration. His first address to the sun, and to those

---

sorrow: *Aeneid*, 6. 552–8.   *Fast we found*: *PL*, viii. 240–4.
... *As new waked*: *PL*, viii. 253–66.   *adoration*: *PL*, viii. 267–77; 278–82.

parts of the Creation which made the most distinguished figure, is very natural and amusing to the imagination.

> Thou Sun, said I, fair light,
> And thou enlightened earth, so fresh and gay,
> Ye hills and dales, ye rivers, woods and plains,
> And ye that live and move, fair creatures tell,
> Tell if you saw, how came I thus, how here?

His next sentiment, when upon his first going to sleep he fancies himself losing his existence, and falling away into nothing, can never be sufficiently admired. His dream, in which he still preserves the consciousness of his existence, together with his removal into the garden which was prepared for his reception, are also circumstances finely imagined, and grounded upon what is delivered in Sacred Story.

These and the like wonderful incidents, in this part of the work, have in them all the beauties of novelty, at the same time that they have all the graces of nature. They are such as none but a great genius could have thought of, though, upon the perusal of them, they seem to rise of themselves from the subject of which he treats. In a word, though they are natural they are not obvious, which is the true character of all fine writing.

The impression which the interdiction of the Tree of Life left in the mind of our first parent, is described with great strength and judgement, as the image of the several beasts and birds passing in review before him is very beautiful and lively.

> Each bird and beast behold
> Approaching two and two, these cowering low
> With blandishment, each bird stooped on his wing:
> I named them as they passed . . .

Adam, in the next place, describes a conference which he held with his Maker upon the subject of solitude. The poet here represents the Supreme Being, as making an essay of his own work, and putting to the trial that reasoning faculty, with which he had endued his creature. Adam urges, in this divine colloquy, the impossibility of his being happy, though he was the inhabitant of Paradise, and Lord of the whole Creation, without the conversation and society of some rational creature, who should partake those blessings with him. This

---

imagination: See No. 321 (above, p. 113). In No. 351 (below, p. 146) and elsewhere 'amusement' is used in the modern sense of 'diversion'.

Thou Sun: *PL*, viii. 273–7.   *Sacred Story*: *PL*, viii. 292–451.
judgement: *PL*, viii. 333–6.   *Each bird*: *PL*, viii. 349–52.
solitude: *PL*, viii. 357–451.

dialogue, which is supported chiefly by the beauty of the thoughts, without other poetical ornaments, is as fine a part as any in the whole poem: the more the reader examines the justness and delicacy of its sentiments, the more he will find himself pleased with it. The poet has wonderfully preserved the character of majesty and condescension in the Creator, and at the same time that of humility and adoration in the creature, as particularly in the following lines,

> Thus I presumptuous; and the vision bright,
> As with a smile more brightened, thus replied, etc.
> . . . I with leave of speech implored
> And humble deprecation thus replied,
> Let not my words offend thee, Heavenly Power,
> My Maker, be propitious while I speak.

Adam then proceeds to give an account of his second sleep, and of the dream in which he beheld the formation of Eve. The new passion that was awakened in him at the sight of her is touched very finely.

> Under his forming hands a creature grew,
> Manlike, but different sex; so lovely fair,
> That what seemed fair in all the world seemed now
> Mean, or in her summed up, in her contained,
> And in her looks, which from that time infused
> Sweetness into my heart, unfelt before,
> And into all things from her air inspired
> The spirit of love and amorous delight.

Adam's distress upon losing sight of this beautiful phantom, with his exclamations of joy and gratitude at the discovery of a real creature, who resembled the apparition which had been presented to him in his dream; the approaches he makes to her, and his manner of courtship, are all laid together in a most exquisite propriety of sentiments.

Though this part of the poem is worked up with great warmth and spirit, the love, which is described in it, is every way suitable to a state of innocence. If the reader compares the description which Adam here gives of his leading Eve to the nuptial bower, with that which Mr. Dryden has made on the same occasion in a scene of his *Fall of Man*, he will be sensible of the great care which Milton took to avoid all thoughts on so delicate a subject, that might be offensive

---

Thus I presumptous: *PL*, viii. 367–8, 377–80.
formation of Eve: *PL*, viii. 452–77.
Under his forming hands: *PL*, viii. 470–7.
sentiments: *PL*, viii. 478–520.
Dryden: *The State of Innocence, and Fall of Man* (1678), III. i.

to religion or good manners. The sentiments are chaste, but not cold, and convey to the mind ideas of the most transporting passion, and of the greatest purity. What a noble mixture of rapture and innocence has the author joined together, in the reflection which Adam makes on the pleasures of love, compared to those of sense.

> Thus have I told thee all my state, and brought
> My story to the sum of earthly bliss
> Which I enjoy, and must confess to find
> In all things else delight indeed, but such
> As used or not, works in the mind no change,
> Nor vehement desire, these delicacies
> I mean of taste, sight, smell, herbs, fruits and flowers,
> Walks, and the melody of birds; but here
> Far otherwise, transported I behold,
> Transported touch; here passion first I felt,
> Commotion strange, in all enjoyments else
> Superior and unmoved, here only weak
> Against the charm of beauty's powerful glance.
> Or nature failed in me, and left some part
> Not proof enough such object to sustain,
> Or from my side subducting, took perhaps
> More than enough; at least on her bestowed
> Too much of ornament, in outward show
> Elaborate, of inward less exact.
>   . . . When I approach
> Her loveliness, so absolute she seems
> And in herself complete, so well to know
> Her own, that what she wills to do or say,
> Seems wisest, virtuousest, discreetest, best:
> All higher knowledge in her presence falls
> Degraded: wisdom in discourse with her
> Loses discountenanced, and like folly shows;
> Authority and reason on her wait,
> As one intended first, not after made
> Occasionally; and to consummate all,
> Greatness of mind and nobleness their seat
> Build in her loveliest, and create an awe
> About her, as a guard angelic placed.[n]

These sentiments of love, in our first parent, gave the angel such an insight into human nature, that he seems apprehensive of the evils which might befall the species in general, as well as Adam in particular, from the excess of this passion. He therefore fortifies him against it by timely admonitions; which very *artfully* prepare the mind of the reader for the occurrences of the next book, where the

Thus have I told thee: *PL*, viii. 521–39, 546–59.
admonitions: *PL*, viii. 561–94.
artfully: skilfully.

weakness of which Adam here gives such distant discoveries,
brings about that fatal event which is the subject of the poem. His
discourse, which follows the gentle rebuke he received from the
angel, shows that his love, however violent it might appear, was still
founded in reason, and consequently not improper for Paradise.

> Neither her outside form so fair, nor aught
> In procreation common to all kinds
> (Though higher of the genial bed by far,
> And with mysterious reverence I deem)
> So much delights me as those graceful acts,
> Those thousand decencies that daily flow
> From all her words and actions mixed with love
> And sweet compliance, which declare unfeigned
> Union of mind, or in us both one soul;
> Harmony to behold in wedded pair.

Adam's speech, at parting with the angel, has in it a deference and
gratitude agreeable to an inferior nature, and at the same time a
certain dignity and greatness, suitable to the father of mankind in his
state of innocence.

351   *Saturday April 12 1712*

. . . In te omnis domus inclinata recumbit.   Virg.

If we look into the three great heroic poems which have appeared in
the world, we may observe that they are built upon very slight
foundations. Homer lived near 300 years after the Trojan War, and,
as the writing of history was not then in use among the Greeks, we
may very well suppose, that the tradition of Achilles and Ulysses had
brought down but very few particulars to his knowledge, though
there is no question but he has wrought into his two poems such of
their remarkable adventures as were still talked of among his
contemporaries.

The story of Aeneas, on which Virgil founded his poem, was likewise very bare of circumstances, and by that means afforded him an
opportunity of embellishing it with fiction, and giving a full range to

Neither her outside form: *PL*, viii. 596–605 ('Neither her outside found so fair').
innocence: *PL*, viii. 645–51.
Motto: Virgil, *Aeneid*. 12. 59: On thee rests all our sinking house.

his own invention. We find, however, that he has interwoven, in the course of his fable, the principal particulars, which were generally believed among the Romans, of Aeneas his voyage and settlement in Italy.

The reader may find an abridgment of the whole story as collected out of the ancient historians, and as it was received among the Romans, in Dionysius Halicarnasseus.

Since none of the critics have considered Virgil's fable, with relation to this history of Aeneas, it may not, perhaps, be amiss to examine it in this light, so far as regards my present purpose. Whoever looks into the abridgment above-mentioned, will find that the character of Aeneas is filled with piety to the gods, and a superstitious observation of prodigies, oracles, and predictions. Virgil has not only preserved this character in the person of Aeneas, but has given a place in his poem to those particular prophecies which he found recorded of him in history and tradition. The poet took the matters of fact as they came down to him, and circumstanced them after his own manner, to make them appear the more natural, agreeable or surprising. I believe very many readers have been shocked at that ludicrous prophecy, which one of the harpies pronounces to the Trojans in the third book, namely, that before they had built their intended city, they should be reduced by hunger to eat their very tables. But, when they hear that this was one of the circumstances that had been transmitted to the Romans in the history of Aeneas, they will think the poet did very well in taking notice of it. The historian above-mentioned, acquaints us, a prophetess had foretold Aeneas, that he should take his voyage westward, till his companions should eat their tables, and that accordingly, upon his landing in Italy, as they were eating their flesh upon cakes of bread, for want of other conveniences, they afterwards fed on the cakes themselves, upon which one of the company said merrily, 'We are eating our tables.' They immediately took the hint, says the historian, and concluded the prophecy to be fulfilled. As Virgil did not think it proper to omit so material a particular in the history of Aeneas, it may be worth while to consider with how much judgement he has qualified it, and taken off everything that might have appeared improper for a passage in an heroic poem. The prophetess who foretells it is an hungry harpy, as the person who discovers it is young Ascanius.

Heus etiam mensas consumimus inquit Iulus!

Dionysius Halicarnasseus: Roman Antiquities, I. 45–64.
circumstanced: furnished with details. The last quotation in *OED* is dated 1774.
tables: *Aeneid*, 3. 255–7.   *Heus etiam*: *Aeneid*, 7. 116.

Such an observation, which is beautiful in the mouth of a boy, would have been ridiculous from any other of the company. I am apt to think that the changing of the Trojan fleet into water-nymphs, which is the most violent machine in the whole *Aeneid*, and has given offence to several critics, may be accounted for the same way. Virgil himself, before he begins that relation, premises that what he was going to tell appeared incredible, but that it was justified by tradition. What further confirms me that this change of the fleet was a celebrated circumstance in the history of Aeneas, is, that Ovid has given a place to the same metamorphosis in his account of the heathen mythology.

None of the critics I have met with, having considered the fable of the *Aeneid* in this light, and taken notice how the tradition, on which it was founded, authorizes those parts in it which appear the most exceptionable; I hope the length of this reflection will not make it unacceptable to the curious part of my readers.

The history, which was the basis of Milton's poem, is still shorter than either that of the *Iliad* or *Aeneid*. The poet has likewise taken care to insert every circumstance of it in the body of his fable. The ninth book, which we are here to consider, is raised upon that brief account in Scripture, wherein we are told that the serpent was more subtle than any beast of the field, that he tempted the woman to eat of the forbidden fruit, that she was overcome by this temptation, and that Adam followed her example. From these few particulars Milton has formed one of the most entertaining fables that invention ever produced. He has disposed of these several circumstances among so many agreeable and natural fictions of his own, that his whole story looks only like a comment upon Sacred Writ, or rather seems to be a full and complete relation of what the other is only an epitome. I have insisted the longer on this consideration, as I look upon the disposition and contrivance of the fable to be the principal beauty of the ninth book, which has more story in it, and is fuller of incidents, than any other in the whole poem. Satan's traversing the globe, and still keeping within the shadow of the night, as fearing to be dis-covered by the angel of the sun, who had before detected him, is one of those beautiful imaginations which introduces this his second series of adventures. Having examined the nature of every creature, and found out one which was the most proper for his purpose, he again returns to Paradise; and, to avoid discovery, sinks by night

---

water-nymphs: *Aeneid*, 9. 107–22. Addison refers to this also in No. 315 (p. 106) and No. 589.

mythology: *Metamorphoses*, 14. 530–65.

example: Gen. 3.   *adventures*: *PL*, ix. 58–69.

with a river that ran under the garden, and rises up again through a
fountain that issued from it by the Tree of Life. The poet, who, as we
have before taken notice, speaks as little as possible in his own
person, and, after the example of Homer, fills every part of his work
with manners and characters, introduces a soliloquy of this infernal
agent, who was thus restless in the destruction of man. He is then
described as gliding through the garden under the resemblance of a
mist, in order to find out that creature in which he designed to tempt
our first parents. This description has something in it very poetical
and surprising.

> So saying, through each thicket dank or dry
> Like a black mist, low creeping, he held on
> His midnight search, where soonest he might find
> The serpent: him fast sleeping soon he found
> In labyrinth of many a round self-rolled,
> His head the midst, well-stored with subtle wiles.

The author afterwards gives us a description of the morning,
which is wonderfully suitable to a divine poem, and peculiar to that
first season of nature: he represents the earth before it was cursed,
as a great altar breathing out its incense from all parts, and sending
up a pleasant savour to the nostrils of its Creator; to which he adds a
noble idea of Adam and Eve, as offering their morning worship, and
filling up the universal concert of praise and adoration.

> Now when as sacred light began to dawn
> In Eden on the humid flowers, that breathed
> Their morning incense, when all things that breathe
> From the earth's great altar send up silent praise
> To the Creator, and his nostrils fill
> With grateful smell, forth came the human pair
> And joined their vocal worship to the choir
> Of creatures wanting voice . . .

The dispute which follows between our two first parents is represented with great art: it proceeds from a difference of judgement,
not of passion, and is managed with reason, not with heat: it is such
a dispute as we may suppose might have happened in Paradise, had
man continued happy and innocent. There is a great delicacy in the
moralities which are interspersed in Adam's discourse, and which the
most ordinary reader cannot but take notice of. That force of love
which the father of mankind so finely describes in the eighth book,

Tree of Life: *PL*, ix. 69–96.   *destruction of man*: *PL*, ix. 99–178.
So saying: *PL*, ix. 179–84.   *Now when*: *PL*, ix. 192–9.
art: *PL*, ix. 205–384.

and which is inserted in the foregoing paper, shows itself here in
many fine instances: as in those fond regards he casts towards Eve
at her parting from him.

> Her long with ardent look his eye pursued
> Delighted, but desiring more her stay.
> Oft he to her his charge of quick return
> Repeated, she to him as oft engaged
> To be returned by noon amid the bower.

In his impatience and amusement during her absence.

> . . . Adam the while
> Waiting desirous her return, had wove
> Of choicest flowers a garland to adorn
> Her tresses, and her rural labours crown,
> As reapers oft are wont their Harvest Queen.
> Great joy he promised to his thoughts, and new
> Solace in her return, so long delayed;

But particularly in that passionate speech, where seeing her
irrecoverably lost, he resolves to perish with her, rather than to live
without her.

> . . . Some cursed fraud
> Or enemy hath beguiled thee, yet unknown,
> And me with thee hath ruined, for with thee
> Certain my resolution is to die;
> How can I live without thee, how forego
> Thy sweet converse and love so dearly joined,
> To live again in these wild woods forlorn?
> Should God create another Eve, and I
> Another rib afford, yet loss of thee
> Would never from my heart; no, no, I feel
> The link of nature draw me: flesh of flesh,
> Bone of my bone thou art, and from thy state
> Mine never shall be parted bliss or woe.

The beginning of this speech, and the preparation to it, are
animated with the same spirit as the conclusion, which I have here
quoted.

The several wiles which are put in practice by the tempter, when he
found Eve separated from her husband, the many pleasing images of
nature, which are intermixed in this part of the story, with its
gradual and regular progress to the fatal catastrophe, are so very
remarkable, that it would be superfluous to point out their respective
beauties.

Her long: *PL*, ix. 397–401.   *Adam the while*: *PL*, ix. 838–44.
Some cursed fraud: *PL*, ix. 904–16 ('fraud of enemy').
preparation: *PL*, ix. 888–904.

I have avoided mentioning any particular similitudes in my remarks on this great work, because I have given a general account of them in my paper on the first book. There is one, however, in this part of the poem which I shall here quote, as it is not only very beautiful, but the closest of any in the whole poem; I mean that where the serpent is described as rolling forward in all his pride, animated by the evil spirit, and conducting Eve to her destruction, while Adam was at too great a distance from her, to give her his assistance. These several particulars are all of them wrought into the following similitude.

> . . . Hope elevates, and joy
> Brightens his crest, as when a wandering fire
> Compact of unctuous vapour, which the night
> Condenses, and the cold environs round,
> Kindled through agitation to a flame,
> (Which oft, they say, some evil spirit attends)
> Hovering and blazing with delusive light,
> Misleads the amazed night-wanderer from his way
> To bogs and mires, and oft through pond or pool,
> There swallowed up and lost, from succour far.

That secret intoxication of pleasure, with all those transient flushings of guilt and joy which the poet represents in our first parents upon their eating the forbidden fruit, to those flaggings of spirit, damps of sorrow and mutual accusations which succeed it, are conceived with a wonderful imagination, and described in very natural sentiments.

When Dido in the fourth *Aeneid* yielded to that fatal temptation which ruined her, Virgil tells us, the earth trembled, the heavens were filled with flashes of lightning, and the nymphs howled upon the mountain tops. Milton, in the same poetical spirit, has described all nature as disturbed upon Eve's eating the forbidden fruit.

> So saying, her rash hand in evil hour
> Forth reaching to the fruit, she plucked, she eat:
> Earth felt the wound, and Nature from her seat
> Sighing through all her works gave signs of woe
> That all was lost . . . .

Upon Adam's falling into the same guilt, the whole Creation appears a second time in convulsions.

> . . . He scrupled not to eat
> Against his better knowledge, not deceived,

Hope elevates: *PL*, ix. 633–42.
mountain tops: *Aeneid*, 4. 166–8.
He scrupled: *PL*, ix. 997–1003.

fruit: *PL*, ix. 1007–189.
So saying: *PL*, ix. 780–4.

> But fondly overcome with female charm.
> Earth trembled from her entrails, as again
> In pangs, and Nature gave a second groan,
> Sky loured and muttering thunder some sad drops
> Wept at completing of the mortal sin . . .

As all Nature suffered by the guilt of our first parents, these symptoms of trouble and consternation are wonderfully imagined, not only as prodigies, but as marks of her sympathising in the Fall of Man.

Adam's converse with Eve, after having eaten the forbidden fruit, is an exact copy of that between Jupiter and Juno, in the fourteenth *Iliad*. Juno there approaches Jupiter with the girdle which she had received from Venus, upon which he tells her, that she appeared more charming and desirable than she had ever done before, even when their loves were at the highest. The poet afterwards describes them as reposing on a summit of Mount Ida, which produced under them a bed of flowers, the lotus, the crocus, and the hyacinth, and concludes his description with their falling asleep.

Let the reader compare this with the following passage in Milton, which begins with Adam's speech to Eve.

> For never did thy beauty since the day
> I saw thee first and wedded thee, adorned
> With all perfections so inflame my sense
> With ardour to enjoy thee, fairer now
> Than ever, bounty of this virtuous tree.
>   So said he, and forebore not glance or toy
> Of amorous intent, well understood
> Of Eve, whose eye darted contagious fire.
> Her hand he seized, and to a shady bank
> Thick overhead with verdant roof embowered
> He led her nothing loth: flowers were the couch,
> Pansies, and violets, and asphodel,
> And hyacinth, earth's freshest softest lap.
> There they their fill of love, and love's disport
> Took largely, of their mutual guilt the seal,
> The solace of their sin, till dewy sleep
> Oppressed them . . .

As no poet seems ever to have studied Homer more, or to have more resembled him in the greatness of genius than Milton, I think I should have given but a very imperfect account of his beauties, if I had not observed the most remarkable passages which look like parallels in these two great authors. I might, in the course of these criticisms, have taken notice of many particular lines and expressions

The poet: *Iliad*, 14. 292–353.   *For never*: *PL*, ix. 1029–45.

which are translated from the Greek poet, but as I thought this would have appeared too minute and over-curious, I have purposely omitted them. The greater incidents, however, are not only set off by being shown in the same light, with several of the same nature in Homer, but by that means may be also guarded against the cavils of the tasteless or ignorant.

357　*Saturday April 19 1712*

. . . quis talia fando . . .
temperet a lacrymis?　Virg.

The tenth book of *Paradise Lost* has a greater variety of persons in it than any other in the whole poem. The author upon the winding up of his action introduces all those who had any concern in it, and shows with great beauty the influence which it had upon each of them. It is like the last act of a well-written tragedy, in which all who had a part in it are generally drawn up before the audience, and represented under those circumstances in which the determination of the action places them.

I shall therefore consider this book under four heads, in relation to the Celestial, the Infernal, the Human, and the Imaginary Persons, who have their respective parts allotted in it.

To begin with the Celestial Persons: the guardian angels of Paradise are described as returning to Heaven upon the Fall of Man, in order to approve their vigilance; their arrival, their manner of reception, with the sorrow which appeared in themselves, and in those spirits who are said to rejoice at the conversion of a sinner, are very finely laid together in the following lines.

> Up into Heaven from Paradise in haste
> The angelic guards ascended, mute and sad
> For man, for of his state by this they knew
> Much wondering how the subtle fiend had stolen
> Entrance unseen. Soon as the unwelcome news
> From earth arrived at Heaven Gate, displeased
> All were who heard, dim sadness did not spare
> That time celestial visages, yet mixed
> With pity, violated not their bliss.

Motto: Virgil, *Aeneid*, 2. 6, 8: At such a tale who can forbear to weep?
Up into Heaven: *PL*, x. 17–33.

About the new-arrived, in multitudes
The ethereal people ran, to hear and know
How all befell: they towards the throne supreme
Accountable made haste to make appear
With righteous plea, their utmost vigilance,
And easily approved; when the Most High
Eternal Father from his secret cloud,
Amidst in thunder uttered thus his voice.

The same Divine Person who in the foregoing parts of this poem interceded for our first parents before their Fall, overthrew the rebel angels, and created the world, is now represented as descending to Paradise, and pronouncing sentence upon the three offenders. The cool of the evening, being a circumstance with which Holy Writ introduces this great scene, it is poetically described by our author, who has also kept religiously to the form of words, in which the three several sentences were passed upon Adam, Eve and the serpent. He has rather chosen to neglect the numerousness of his verse, than to deviate from those speeches which are recorded on this great occasion. The guilt and confusion of our first parents standing naked before their Judge, is touched with great beauty. Upon the arrival of Sin and Death into the works of the Creation, the Almighty is again introduced as speaking to his angels that surrounded him.

See with what heat these dogs of Hell advance
To waste and havoc yonder world, which I
So fair and good created, etc.

The following passage is formed upon that glorious image in Holy Writ which compares the voice of an innumerable host of angels, uttering Hallelujahs, to the voice of mighty thunderings, or of many waters.

He ended, and the heavenly audience loud
Sung Hallelujah, as the sound of seas,
Through multitude that sung: just are thy ways,
Righteous are thy decrees in all thy works,
Who can extenuate thee?

Though the author in the whole course of his poem, and particularly in the book we are now examining, has infinite allusions to places of Scripture, I have only taken notice in my remarks of such

---

offenders: *PL*, x. 85–102.
numerousness: here used in the sense of 'regularity in measure or rhythm'. This is the earliest example of the word in this sense in *OED*.
See with what: *PL*, x. 616–18.　　　　　*Holy Writ*: Rev. 19:6.
He ended: *PL*, x. 641–5 ('on all thy works').

as are of a poetical nature, and which are woven with great beauty
into the body of his fable. Of this kind is that passage in the present
book, where describing Sin as marching through the works of
Nature, he adds,

> Behind her Death
> Close following pace for pace, not mounted yet
> On his pale horse: . . .

Which alludes to that passage in Scripture so wonderfully poetical,
and terrifying to the imagination.

And I looked, and behold, a pale horse, and his name that sat on him was
Death, and Hell followed with him: and power was given unto them over
the fourth part of the earth, to kill with sword, and with hunger, and with
sickness, and with the beasts of the earth.

Under this first head of Celestial Persons we must likewise take notice
of the command which the angels received, to produce several
changes in Nature, and sully the beauty of the Creation. Accordingly
they are represented as infecting the stars and planets with malignant
influences, weakening the light of the sun, bringing down the winter
into the milder regions of Nature, planting winds and storms in
several quarters of the sky, storing the clouds with thunder, and in
short, perverting the whole frame of the universe to the condition of
its criminal inhabitants. As this is a noble incident in the poem, the
following lines, in which we see the angels heaving up the earth, and
placing it in a different posture to the sun from what it had before the
Fall of Man, is conceived with that sublime imagination which was
so peculiar to this great author.

> Some say he bid his angels turn askance
> The poles of earth twice ten degrees and more
> From the sun's axle; they with labour pushed
> Oblique the centric globe . . .

We are in the second place to consider the Infernal Agents under
the view which Milton has given us of them in this book. It is
observed by those who would set forth the greatness of Virgil's plan,
that he conducts his reader through all the parts of the earth which
were discovered in his time. Asia, Africa and Europe are the several
scenes of his fable. The plan of Milton's poem is of an infinitely
greater extent, and fills the mind with many more astonishing

---

Behind her Death: *PL*, x. 588–90
And I looked: Rev. 6:8 (the text reads 'with death' rather than 'with sickness'
beauty of the creation: *PL*, x. 649–67.
Some say he bid: *PL*, x. 668–71.

circumstances. Satan, having surrounded the earth seven times, departs at length from Paradise. We then see him steering his course among the constellations, and after having traversed the whole Creation, pursuing his voyage through the Chaos, and entering into his own infernal dominions.

His first appearance in the assembly of fallen angels is worked up with circumstances which give a delightful surprise to the reader; but there is no incident in the whole poem which does this more than the transformation of the whole audience, that follows the account their leader gives them of his expedition. The gradual change of Satan himself is described after Ovid's manner, and may vie with any of those celebrated transformations which are looked upon as the most beautiful parts in that poet's works. Milton never fails of improving his own hints, and bestowing the last finishing touches to every incident which is admitted into his poem. The unexpected hiss which rises in this episode, the dimensions and bulk of Satan so much superior to those of the infernal spirits who lay under the same transformation, with the annual change which they are supposed to suffer, are instances of this kind. The beauty of the diction is very remarkable in this whole episode, as I have observed in the sixth paper of these remarks the great judgement with which it was contrived.

The parts of Adam and Eve, or the Human Persons, come next under our consideration. Milton's art is nowhere more shown than in his conducting the parts of these our first parents. The representation he gives of them, without falsifying the story, is wonderfully contrived to influence the reader with pity and compassion towards them. Though Adam involves the whole species in misery, his crime proceeds from a weakness which every man is inclined to pardon and commiserate, as it seems rather the frailty of human nature, than of the person who offended. Everyone is apt to excuse a fault which he himself might have fallen into. It was the excess of love for Eve that ruined Adam and his posterity. I need not add, that the author is justified in this particular by many of the Fathers, and the most orthodox writers. Milton has by this means filled a great part of his poem with that kind of writing which the French critics call the *tender*, and which is in a particular manner engaging to all sorts of readers.

Adam and Eve, in the book we are now considering, are likewise

seven times. Pl. ix. 63–9.
infernal dominions: *PL*, x. 325–49, 414–20.   *assembly*: *PL*, x. 441–59.
expedition: *PL*, x. 504–47.   *annual change*: *PL*, x. 575–7.
sixth paper: No. 297 (p. 84).

drawn with such sentiments as do not only interest the reader in their afflictions; but raise in him the most melting passions of humanity and commiseration. When Adam sees the several changes in Nature produced about him, he appears in a disorder of mind suitable to one who had forfeited both his innocence and his happiness. He is filled with horror, remorse, despair; in the anguish of his heart he expostulates with his Creator for having given him an unasked existence.

> Did I request thee, Maker, from my clay
> To mould me man, did I solicit thee
> From darkness to promote me, or here place
> In this delicious garden? As my will
> Concurred not to my being, 'twere but right
> And equal to reduce me to my dust,
> Desirous to resign, and render back
> All I received . . .

He immediately after recovers from his presumption, owns his doom to be just, and begs that the death which is threatened him may be inflicted on him.

> . . . Why delays
> His hand to execute what his decree
> Fixed on this day? Why do I overlive,
> Why am I mocked with death, and lengthened out
> To deathless pain? How gladly would I meet
> Mortality my sentence, and be earth
> Insensible, how glad would lay me down
> As in my mother's lap? There should I rest
> And sleep secure; his dreadful voice no more
> Would thunder in my ears, no fear of worse
> To me and to my offspring, would torment me
> With cruel expectation . . . .

This whole speech is full of the like emotion, and varied with all those sentiments which we may suppose natural to a mind so broken and disturbed. I must not omit that generous concern which our first father shows in it for his posterity, and which is so proper to affect the reader.

> . . . Hide me from the face
> Of God, whom to behold was then my height
> Of happiness: yet well if here would end
> The misery, I deserved it, and would bear
> My own deservings; but this will not serve;
> All that I eat, or drink, or shall beget,
> Is propagated curse. O voice once heard

Did I request: *PL*, x. 743–50.
Why delays: *PL*, x. 771–82 (in line 778 'I should').   *Hide me*: *PL*, x. 723–31.

> Delightfully, increase and multiply,
> Now death to hear! ...
>   ... In me all
> Posterity stands cursed: fair patrimony
> That I must leave you, sons; O were I able
> To waste it all myself, and leave you none!
> So disinherited how would you bless
> Me now your curse! Ah, why should all mankind
> For one man's fault thus guiltless be condemned
> If guiltless? But from me what can proceed
> But all corrupt ...

Who can afterwards behold the father of mankind extended upon the earth, uttering his midnight complaints, bewailing his existence, and wishing for death, without sympathizing with him in his distress?

> Thus Adam to himself lamented loud
> Through the still night, not now, as ere man fell
> Wholesome and cool and mild, but with black air
> Accompanied, with damps and dreadful gloom
> Which to his evil conscience represented
> All things with double terror: on the ground
> Outstretched he lay, on the cold ground, and oft
> Cursed his creation, death as oft accused
> Of tardy execution. ...

The part of Eve in this book is no less passionate, and apt to sway the reader in her favour. She is represented with great tenderness as approaching Adam, but is spurned from him with a spirit of up-braiding and indignation conformable to the nature of man, whose passions had now gained the dominion over him. The following passage, wherein she is described as renewing her addresses to him, with the whole speech that follows it, have something in them exquisitely moving and pathetic.

> He added not, and from her turned: but Eve
> Not so repulsed, with tears that ceased not flowing
> And tresses all disordered, at his feet
> Fell humble, and enbracing them, besought
> His peace, and thus proceeded in her plaint.
>   Forsake me not thus Adam, witness Heaven
> What love sincere and reverence in my heart
> I bear thee, and unweeting have offended,
> Unhappily deceived; thy suppliant
> I beg, and clasp thy knees; bereave me not,
> Whereon I live, thy gentle looks, thy aid,
> Thy counsel in this uttermost distress,

In me all: PL, x. 817–25.   *Thus Adam*: PL, x. 845–53.
dominion: PL, x. 863–908.   *He added not*: PL, x. 909–24.

My only strength and stay: forlorn of thee
Whither shall I betake me, where subsist?
While yet we live, scarce one short hour perhaps,
Between us two let there be peace, etc.

Adam's reconcilement to her is worked up in the same spirit of
tenderness. Eve afterwards proposes to her husband, in the blindness of her despair, that to prevent their guilt from descending upon
posterity they should resolve to live childless; or, if that could not be
done, they should seek their own deaths by violent methods. As
those sentiments naturally engage the reader to regard the mother of
mankind with more than ordinary commiseration, they likewise
contain a very fine moral. The resolution of dying to end our miseries
does not show such a degree of magnanimity as a resolution to bear
them, and submit to the dispensations of Providence. Our author has
therefore, with great delicacy, represented Eve as entertaining this
thought, and Adam as disapproving it.

We are, in the last place, to consider the Imaginary Persons, or
Death and Sin, who act a large part in this book.[n] Such beautiful
extended allegories are certainly some of the finest compositions of
genius; but, as I have before observed, are not agreeable to the
nature of an heroic poem. This of Sin and Death is very exquisite in
its kind, if not considered as a part of such a work. The truths contained in it are so clear and open that I shall not lose time in explaining them, but shall only observe, that a reader who knows the
strength of the English tongue will be amazed to think how the
poet could find such apt words and phrases to describe the actions
of those two imaginary persons, and particularly in that part where
Death is exhibited as forming a bridge over the Chaos: a work
suitable to the genius of Milton.

Since the subject I am upon gives me an opportunity of speaking
more at large of such shadowy and imaginary persons as may be
introduced into heroic poems, I shall beg leave to explain myself
in a matter which is curious in its kind, and which none of the
critics have treated of. It is certain Homer and Virgil are full of
imaginary persons, who are very beautiful in poetry when they are
just shown, without being engaged in any series of action. Homer
indeed represents Sleep as a person, and ascribes a short part to him
in his *Iliad*; but we must consider that though we now regard such
a person as entirely shadowy and unsubstantial, the heathens made
statues of him, placed him in their temples, and looked upon him

methods: *PL*, x. 979–1006.   *Chaos*: *PL*, x. 282–324.
Sleep: *Iliad*, 14. 231–91.

as a real deity. When Homer makes use of other such allegorical persons it is only in short expressions, which convey an ordinary thought to the mind in the most pleasing manner, and may rather be looked upon as poetical phrases than allegorical descriptions.[n] Instead of telling us that men naturally fly when they are terrified, he introduces the persons of Flight and Fear, who he tells us are inseparable companions. Instead of saying that the time was come when Apollo ought to have received his recompence, he tells us that the Hours brought him his reward. Instead of describing the effects which minerva's aegis produced in battle, he tells us that the brims of it were encompassed by Terror, Rout, Discord, Fury, Pursuit, Massacre and Death. In the same figure of speaking he represents Victory as following Diomedes,[n] Discord as the mother of funerals and mourning, Venus as dressed by the Graces, Bellona as wearing Terror and Consternation like a garment. I might give several other instances out of Homer, as well as a great many out of Virgil. Milton has likewise very often made use of the same way of speaking, as where he tells us that Victory sat on the right hand of the Messiah, when he marched forth against the rebel angels; that at the rising of the sun the Hours unbarred the gates of light; that Discord was the daughter of Sin. Of the same nature are those expressions where describing the singing of the nightingale he adds, Silence was pleased; and upon the Messiah's bidding peace to the Chaos, Confusion heard his voice. I might add innumerable instances of our poet's writing in this beautiful figure. It is plain that these I have mentioned, in which persons of an imaginary nature are introduced, are such short allegories as are not designed to be taken in the literal sense, but only to convey particular circumstances to the reader after an unusual and entertaining manner. But when such persons are introduced as principal actors, and engaged in a series of adventures, they take too much upon them, and are by no means proper for an heroic poem, which ought to appear credible in its principal parts. I cannot forbear therefore thinking that Sin and Death are as improper agents in a work of this nature, as Strength and Necessity in one of the tragedies of Aeschylus,[n] who represented those two persons nailing down Prometheus to a rock, for which he has been justly censured by the greatest critics.[n] I do not know any

---

companions: *Iliad*, 9. 1–3.
aegis: *Iliad*: 5. 738–42 (cf. also 4. 439–40).
Bellona: the Roman goddess of war.
rebel angels: *PL*, vi. 762.
Sin: *PL*, x. 707–8.
Confusion: *PL*, iii. 710.

reward: *Iliad*, 21. 450.
Discord: *Iliad*, 4. 440; 11. 73.
garment: *Iliad*, 5. 338.
gates of light: *PL*, vi. 4.
Silence: *PL*, iv. 604.

imaginary person made use of in a more sublime manner of thinking than that in one of the prophets, who describing God as descending from Heaven, and visiting the sins of mankind, adds that dreadful circumstance; 'Before him went the Pestilence'. It is certain this imaginary person might have been described in all her purple spots. The Fever might have marched before her, Pain might have stood at her right hand, Frenzy on her left, and Death in her rear. She might have been introduced as gliding down from the tail of a comet, or darted upon the earth in a flash of lightning: she might have tainted the atmosphere with her breath; the very glaring of her eyes might have scattered infection. But I believe every reader will think that in such sublime writings the mentioning of her as it is done in Scripture has something in it more just, as well as great, than all that the most fanciful poet could have bestowed upon her in the richness of his imagination.

363   *Saturday April 26 1712*

> *. . . Crudelis ubique*
> *luctus, ubique pavor, et plurima mortis imago.*   Virg.

Milton has shown a wonderful art in describing that variety of passions which arise in our first parents upon the breach of the commandment that had been given them. We see them gradually passing from the triumph of their guilt through remorse, shame, despair, contrition, prayer, and hope, to a perfect and complete repentance. At the end of the tenth book they are represented as prostrating themselves upon the ground, and watering the earth with their tears: to which the poet joins this beautiful circumstance, that they offered up their penitential prayers on the very place where their Judge appeared to them when he pronounced their sentence.

> . . . They forthwith to the place
> Repairing, where he judged them, prostrate fell
> Before him reverent, and both confessed
> Humbly their faults, and pardon begged, with tears
> Watering the ground . . .

one of the prophets: Hab. 3:5.
Motto: Virgil, *Aeneid*, 2. 368–9:
> All parts resound with tumults, plaints, and fears,
> And grisly Death in sundry shapes appears.   DRYDEN
They forthwith: *PL*, x. 1098–102.

There is a beauty of the same kind in a tragedy of Sophocles, where Oedipus, after having put out his own eyes, instead of breaking his neck from the palace battlements (which furnishes so elegant an entertainment for our English audience)[n] desires that he may be conducted to Mount Cithaeron, in order to end his life in that very place where he was exposed in his infancy, and where he should then have died, had the will of his parents been executed.

As the author never fails to give a poetical turn to his sentiments, he describes in the beginning of this book the acceptance which these their prayers met with, in a short allegory formed upon that beautiful passage in Holy Writ. 'And another angel came and stood at the altar, having a golden censer; and there was given unto him much incense, that he should offer it with the prayers of all saints upon the golden altar, which was before the throne: and the smoke of the incense which came with the prayers of the saints, ascended up before God.'

> . . . To Heaven their prayers
> Flew up, nor missed the way, by envious winds
> Blown vagabond or frustrate: in they passed
> Dimensionless through heavenly doors, then clad
> With incense, where the golden altar fumed,
> By their great Intercessor, came in sight
> Before the Father's throne . . . .

We have the same thought expressed a second time in the intercession of the Messiah, which is conceived in very emphatic sentiments and expressions.

Among the poetical parts of Scripture which Milton has so finely wrought into this part of his narration, I must not omit that wherein Ezekiel speaking of the angels who appeared to him in a vision, adds that 'every one had four faces' and that 'their whole bodies, and their backs, and their hands, and their wings were full of eyes round about.'

> . . . The cohort bright
> Of watchful Cherubim; four faces each
> Had, like a double Janus, all their shape
> Spangled with eyes . . .

The assembling of all the angels of Heaven to hear the solemn decree passed upon man is represented in very lively ideas. The

---

Sophocles: *Oedipus Tyrannus*, 1452–7.   *Holy Writ*: Rev. 8:3, 4.
To Heaven: *PL*, xi. 14–20.   *expressions*: *PL*, xi. 20–44.
Ezekiel: Ezek. 1:6; 10:12.   *The cohort*: *PL*, xi. 127–30.
ideas: *PL*, xi. 72–83.

Almighty is here described as remembering mercy in the midst of
judgement, and commanding Michael to deliver his message in the
mildest terms, lest the spirit of man, which was already broken with
the sense of his guilt and misery, should fail before him.

> . . . Yet lest they faint
> At the sad sentence rigorously urged,
> For I behold them softened and with tears
> Bewailing their excess, all terror hide.

The conference of Adam and Eve is full of moving sentiments.
Upon their going abroad after the melancholy night which they had
passed together, they discover the lion and the eagle pursuing each
of them their prey towards the eastern gates of Paradise. There is a
double beauty in this incident, not only as it presents great and just
omens which are always agreeable in poetry; but as it expresses
that enmity which was now produced in the animal creation. The
poet, to show the like changes in Nature, as well as to grace his fable
with a noble prodigy, represents the sun in an eclipse. This particular
incident has likewise a fine effect upon the imagination of the reader,
in regard to what follows; for at the same time that the sun is under
an eclipse, a bright cloud descends in the western quarter of the
heavens, filled with an host of angels, and more luminous than the
sun itself. The whole theatre of Nature is darkened, that this glorious
machine may appear in all its lustre and magnificence.

> . . . Why in the east
> Darkness ere day's mid-course, and morning light
> More orient in that western cloud that draws
> O'er the blue firmament a radiant white,
> And slow descends, with something heavenly fraught?
> He erred not, for by this the Heavenly bands
> Down from a sky of jasper lighted now
> In Paradise, and on a hill made halt;
> A glorious apparition . . .

I need not observe how properly this author, who always suits
his parts to the actors whom he introduces, has employed Michael
in the expulsion of our first parents from Paradise. The archangel
on this occasion neither appears in his proper shape, nor in that
familiar manner with which Raphael the sociable spirit entertained
the father of mankind before the Fall. His person, his port and

---

Yet lest they faint: *PL*, xi. 108–11.   *sentiments*: *PL*, xi. 141–80.
Paradise: *PL*, xi. 184–90.
Why in the east: *PL*, xi. 203–11 (line 205: in yon western cloud).

behaviour are suitable to a spirit of the highest rank, and exquisitely
described in the following passage.

> . . . The archangel soon drew nigh
> Not in his shape celestial, but as man
> Clad to meet man; over his lucid arms
> A military vest of purple flowed
> Livelier than Meliboean, or the grain
> Of Sarra, worn by kings and heroes old
> In time of truce; Iris had dipt the woof;
> His starry helm, unbuckled, showed him prime
> In manhood where youth ended; by his side
> As in a glistering zodiac hung the sword,
> Satan's dire dread, and in his hand the spear.
> Adam bowed low, he kingly from his state
> Inclined not, but his coming thus declared.

Eve's complaint upon hearing that she was to be removed from
the Garden of Paradise is wonderfully beautiful. The sentiments are
not only proper to the subject; but have something in them particularly soft and womanish.

> Must I then leave thee, Paradise? thus leave
> Thee, native soil, these happy walks and shades,
> Fit haunt of gods? Where I had hope to spend
> Quiet though sad the respite of that day
> That must be mortal to us both. O flowers
> That never will in other climate grow,
> My early visitation, and my last
> At even, which I bred up with tender hand
> From the first opening bud, and gave you names;
> Who now shall rear you to the sun, or rank
> Your tribes, and water from the ambrosial fount?
> Thee lastly, nuptial bower, by me adorned
> With what to sight or smell was sweet; from thee
> How shall I part, and whither wander down
> Into a lower world, to this obscure
> And wild, how shall we breathe in other air
> Less pure, accustomed to immortal fruits?

Adam's speech abounds with thoughts which are equally moving,
but of a more masculine and elevated turn. Nothing can be conceived more sublime and poetical, than the following passage in it.

> This most afflicts me, that departing hence
> As from his face I shall be hid, deprived
> His blessed countenance; here I could frequent,

The archangel: *PL*, xi. 238–50.
Must I then: *PL*, xi. 269–85 (Must I thus leave thee).
This most afflicts me: *PL*, xi. 315–33 (line 329: footstep).

> With worship, place by place where he vouchsafed
> Presence divine, and to my sons relate;
> On this mount he appeared, under this tree
> Stood visible, among these pines his voice
> I heard, here with him at this fountain talked:
> So many grateful altars I would rear
> Of grassy turf, and pile up every stone
> Of lustre from the brook, in memory,
> Or monument to ages, and thereon
> Offer sweet smelling gums and fruits and flowers:
> In yonder nether world where shall I seek
> His bright appearances, or footsteps trace?
> For though I fled him angry, yet recalled
> To life prolonged and promised race, I now
> Gladly behold though but his utmost skirts
> Of glory, and far off his steps adore.

The angel afterwards leads Adam to the highest mount of Paradise, and lays before him a whole hemisphere, as a proper stage for those visions which were to be represented on it. I have before observed how the plan of Milton's poem is in many particulars greater than that of the *Iliad* or *Aeneid*. Virgil's hero, in the last of these poems, is entertained with a sight of all those who are to descend from him, but though that episode is justly admired as one of the noblest designs in the whole *Aeneid*, every one must allow that this of Milton is of a much higher nature. Adam's vision is not confined to any particular tribe of mankind, but extends to the whole species.

In this great review, which Adam takes of all his sons and daughters, the first objects he is presented with exhibit to him the story of Cain, and Abel, which is drawn together with much closeness and propriety of expression. That curiosity and natural horror which arises in Adam at the sight of the first dying man is touched with great beauty.

> But have I now seen death, is this the way
> I must return to native dust? O sight
> Of terror foul and ugly to behold,
> Horrid to think, how horrible to feel!

The second vision sets before him the image of death in a great variety of appearances. The angel, to give him a general idea of those effects, which his guilt had brought upon his posterity, places before him a large hospital, or lazar-house, filled with persons lying under all kinds of mortal diseases. How finely has the poet told us

visions: *PL*, xi. 376–411.   *Virgil's hero*: *Aeneid*, 6. 756–885.
propriety of expression: *PL*, xi. 429–47.   *But have I now*: *PL*, xi. 462–5.
image of death: *PL*, xi. 477–93.

that the sick persons languished under lingering and incurable
distempers by an apt and judicious use of such imaginary beings, as
those I mentioned in my last paper.

> Dire was the tossing, deep the groans, Despair
> Tended the sick, busy from couch to couch;
> And over them triumphant Death his dart
> Shook, but delayed to strike, though oft invoked
> With vows as their chief good and final hope.

The passion which likewise rises in Adam on this occasion is very
natural.

> Sight so deform what heart of rock could long
> Dry-eyed behold? Adam could not, but wept
> Though not of woman born; compassion quelled
> His best of man, and gave him up to tears.

The discourse between the angel and Adam which follows,
abounds with noble morals.

As there is nothing more delightful in poetry, than a contrast and
opposition of incidents, the author, after this melancholy prospect
of death and sickness, raises up a scene of mirth, love and jollity.
The secret pleasure that steals into Adam's heart, as he is intent upon
this vision, is imagined with great delicacy. I must not omit the
description of the loose female troupe, who seduced the sons of God
as they are called in Scripture.

> For that fair female troupe thou saw'st that seemed
> Of goddesses, so blithe, so smooth, so gay,
> Yet empty of all good wherein consists
> Woman's domestic honour and chief praise;
> Bred only and completed to the taste
> Of lustful appetence, to sing, to dance,
> To dress, and troll the tongue, and roll the eye.
> To these that sober race of men, whose lives
> Religious titled them the sons of God,
> Shall yield up all their virtue, all their fame
> Ignobly, to the trains and to the smiles
> Of these fair atheists . . .

The next vision is of a quite contrary nature, and filled with the
horrors of war. Adam at the sight of it, melts into tears, and breaks
out in that passionate speech;

Dire was the tossing: *PL*, xi. 489–93 (line 490: busiest).
Sight so deform: *PL*, xi. 494–7.   *morals*: *PL*, xi. 500–55.
jollity: *PL*, xi. 580–97.   *For that fair*: *PL*, xi. 614–25.
war: *PL*, xi. 638–73.

> ... O what are these,
> Death's ministers not men, who thus deal death
> Inhumanly to men, and multiply
> Ten thousand fold the sin of him who slew
> His brother: for of whom such massacre
> Make they but of their brethren, men of men?

Milton, to keep up an agreeable variety in his visions, after having raised in the mind of his reader the several ideas of terror which are conformable to the description of war, passes on to those softer images of triumphs and festivals, in that vision of lewdness and luxury, which ushers in the Flood.

As it is visible, that the poet had his eye upon Ovid's account of the universal deluge, the reader may observe with how much judgement he has avoided everything that is redundant or puerile in the Latin poet. We do not here see the wolf swimming among the sheep, nor any of those wanton imaginations which Seneca found fault with, as unbecoming the great catastrophe of Nature. If our poet has imitated that verse in which Ovid tells us, that there was nothing but sea, and that this sea had no shore to it, he has not set the thought in such a light as to incur the censure which critics have passed upon it. The latter part of that verse in Ovid is idle and superfluous;[n] but just and beautiful in Milton.

> Jamque mare et tellus nullum discrimen habebant,
> nil nisi pontus erat deerant quoque littora ponto.   OVID.

> ... Sea covered sea,
> Sea without shore .... MILTON.

In Milton the former part of the description does not forestall the latter. How much more great and solemn on this occasion is that which follows in our English poet,

> ... And in their palaces
> Where luxury late reigned, sea monsters whelped
> And stabled ...

than that in Ovid, where we are told, that the sea-calves lay in those places where the goats were used to browse? The reader may find several other parallel passages in the Latin and English description

O what are these: *PL*, xi. 675–80.   *Flood*: *PL*, xi. 712–18.
Ovid: *Metamorphoses*, 1. 260–312.   *sheep*: *Metamorphoses*, 1. 304.
Seneca: *Natural Questions*, 3. 27.
Ovid: *Metamorphoses*, 1. 291–2. (And now there is no difference between sea and
    land; there was nothing but sea, and that sea had no shore.)
Sea covered sea: *PL*, xi. 749–50.   *And in their palaces*: *PL*, xi. 750–2.
sea-calves:: *Metamorphoses* ,1. 299–300.

of the Deluge, wherein our poet has visibly the advantage. The sky's being overcharged with clouds, the descending of the rains, the rising of the seas, and the appearance of the rainbow, are such descriptions as everyone must take notice of. The circumstance relating to Paradise is so finely imagined and suitable to the opinions of many learned authors, that I cannot forbear giving it a place in this paper.

> . . . Then shall this mount
> Of Paradise by might of waves be moved
> Out of his place, pushed by the horned flood,
> With all his verdure spoiled, and trees adrift
> Down the great river to the opening gulf,
> And there take root an island salt and bare,
> The haunt of seals and orcs, and sea-mews' clang.

The transition which the poet makes from the vision of the Deluge, to the concern it occasioned in Adam, is exquisitely graceful, and copied after Virgil, though the first thought it introduces is rather in the spirit of Ovid.

> How didst thou grieve, then Adam, to behold
> The end of all thy offspring, end so sad,
> Depopulation; thee another flood,
> Of tears and sorrow, a flood thee also drowned,
> And sunk thee as thy sons: till gently reared
> By the angel, on thy feet thou stood'st at last,
> Though comfortless, as when a father mourns
> His children, all in view destroyed at once.

I have been the more particular in my quotations out of the eleventh book of *Paradise Lost*, because it is not generally reckoned among the most shining books of this poem;[n] for which reason, the reader might be apt to overlook those many passages in it, which deserve our admiration. The eleventh and twelfth are indeed built upon that single circumstance of the removal of our first parents from Paradise, but though this is not in itself so great a subject as that in most of the foregoing books, it is extended and diversified with so many surprising incidents and pleasing episodes, that these two last books can by no means be looked upon as unequal parts of this divine poem. I must further add, that had not Milton represented our first parents as driven out of Paradise, his Fall of Man would not have been complete, and consequently his action would have been imperfect.

seas: *PL*, xi. 738–50. *rainbow*: *PL*, xi. 865–7.
Then shall this mount: *PL*, xi. 829–35.
How didst thou grieve: *PL*, xi. 754–61.

369 *Saturday May 3 1712*

Segnius irritant animos demissa per aures
quam quae sunt oculis subjecta fidelibus . . . . Hor.

Milton, after having represented in vision the history of mankind to
the first great period of Nature, dispatches the remaining part of it in
narration. He has devised a very handsome reason for the angel's
proceeding with Adam after this manner; though doubtless, the true
reason was the difficulty which the poet would have found to have
shadowed out so mixed and complicated a story in visible objects.
I could wish, however, that the author had done it, whatever pains it
might have cost him. To give my opinion freely, I think that the
exhibiting part of the history of mankind in vision, and part in
narrative, is as if an history painter should put in colours one half of
his subject, and write down the remaining part of it. If Milton's
poem flags anywhere it is in this narration, where in some places the
author has been so attentive to his divinity, that he has neglected his
poetry. The narration, however, rises very happily on several
occasions, where the subject is capable of poetical ornaments, as
particularly in the confusion which he describes among the builders
of Babel, and in his short sketch of the plagues of Egypt. The storm
of hail and fire, with the darkness that overspread the land for three
days, are described with great strength. The beautiful passage, which
follows, is raised upon noble hints in Scripture.

> . . . Thus with ten wounds
> The river-dragon tamed at length submits
> To let his sojourners depart, and oft
> Humbles his stubborn heart, but still as ice
> More hardened after thaw, till in his rage
> Pursuing whom he late dismissed, the sea
> Swallows him with his host, but them lets pass
> As on dry land between two crystal walls,
> Awed by the rod of Moses so to stand
> Divided . . .

The river-dragon is an allusion to the crocodile, which inhabits

Motto: Horace, *Ars poetica*, 180–1 (altered):
> Things only *told*, though of the same degree,
> Do raise our passions less than what we *see*.   CREECH

Adam: *PL*, xii. 8–10.
history painter: a painter of 'histories', pictorial representations of events or
incidents.
Babel: *PL*, xii. 52–62.   *Egypt*: *PL*, xii. 181–8.
Thus with ten wounds: *PL*, xii. 190–9.

the Nile, from whence Egypt derives her plenty. This allusion is taken from that sublime passage in *Ezekiel*. 'Thus saith the Lord God, behold, I am against thee Pharaoh King of Egypt, the great dragon that lieth in the midst of his rivers, which hath said, My river is mine own, and I have made it for myself.' Milton has given us another very noble and poetical image in the same description, which is copied almost word for word out of the history of Moses.

> All night he will pursue, but his approach
> Darkness defends between till morning watch;
> Then through the fiery pillar and the cloud
> God looking forth, will trouble all his host,
> And craze their chariot wheels: when by command
> Moses once more his potent rod extends
> Over the sea; the sea his rod obeys;
> On their embattled ranks the waves return
> And overwhelm their war: . . .

As the principal design of this episode was to give Adam an idea of the Holy Person, who was to reinstate human nature in that happiness and perfection from which it had fallen, the poet confines himself to the line of Abraham, from whence the Messiah was to descend. The angel is described as seeing the patriarch actually travelling towards the Land of Promise, which gives a particular liveliness to this part of the narration.

> I see him, but thou canst not, with what faith
> He leaves his gods, his friends, and native soil
> Ur of Chaldea, passing now the ford,
> To Haran, after him a cumbrous train
> Of herds and flocks, and numerous servitude;
> Not wandering poor, but trusting all his wealth
> With God, who called him, in a land unknown.
> Canaan he now attains, I see his tents
> Pitched about Shechem, and the neighbouring plain
> Of Moreh, there by promise he receives
> Gift to his progeny of all that land;
> From Hamath northward to the desert south
> (Things by their names I call, though yet unnamed).

As Virgil's vision in the sixth *Aeneid* probably gave Milton the hint of this whole episode, the last line is a translation of that verse, where Anchises mentions the names of places, which they were to bear hereafter.

> Haec tum nomina erunt, nunc sunt sine nomine terrae.

Ezekiel: Ezek. 29:3.   *Moses*: Exod. 14:19–31.
All night: *PL*, xii. 206–14.   *I see him*: *PL*, xii. 128–40.
Anchises: *Aeneid*, 6. 776. (These shall then be names that now are lands without name.)

The poet has very finely represented the joy and gladness of heart, which rises in Adam upon his discovery of the Messiah. As he sees his day at a distance through types and shadows, he rejoices in it; but when he finds the Redemption of man completed, and Paradise again renewed, he breaks forth in rapture and transport,

> O goodness infinite, goodness immense!
> That all this good of evil shall produce, etc.

I have hinted, in my sixth paper on Milton, that an heroic poem, according to the opinion of the best critics, ought to end happily, and leave the mind of the reader, after having conducted it through many doubts and fears, sorrows and disquietudes, in a state of tranquillity and satisfaction. Milton's fable, which had so many other qualifications to recommend it, was deficient in this particular. It is here therefore, that the poet has shown a most exquisite judgement, as well as the finest invention, by finding out a method to supply this natural defect in his subject. Accordingly he leaves the Adversary of Mankind, in the last view which he gives us of him, under the lowest state of mortification and disappointment. We see him chewing ashes, grovelling in the dust, and loaden with supernumerary pains and torments. On the contrary, our two first parents are comforted by dreams and visions, cheered with promises of salvation, and, in a manner, raised to a greater happiness than that which they had forfeited: in short, Satan is represented miserable in the height of his triumphs, and Adam triumphant in the height of misery.

Milton's poem ends very nobly. The last speeches of Adam and the archangel are full of moral and instructive sentiments. The sleep that fell upon Eve, and the effects it had in quieting the disorders of her mind, produces the same kind of consolation in the reader, who cannot peruse the last beautiful speech which is ascribed to the mother of mankind, without a secret pleasure and satisfaction.

> Whence thou return'st, and whither went'st, I know;
> For God is also in sleep, and dreams advise,
> Which he hath sent propitious, some great good
> Presaging, since with sorrow and heart's distress
> Wearied I fell asleep: but now lead on;
> In me is no delay: with thee to go
> Is to stay here; without thee here to stay
> Is to go hence unwilling; thou to me

Messiah: *PL*, xii. 372–85.
sixth paper: see No. 297 (p. 83).
sentiments: *PL*, xii. 552–605.

O goodness infinite: *PL*, xii. 469–70.
torments: *PL*, x. 566.
Whence thou return'st: *PL*, xii. 610–23.

Art all things under Heaven, all places thou
Who for my wilful crime art banished hence.
This farther consolation yet secure
I carry hence; though all by me is lost,
Such favour, I unworthy, am vouchsafed,
By me the promised seed shall all restore.

The following lines which conclude the poem rise in a most glorious
blaze of poetical images and expressions.

Heliodorus in his *Aethiopica* acquaints us that the motion of the
gods differs from that of mortals, as the former do not stir their
feet, nor proceed step by step, but slide over the surface of the earth
by an uniform swimming of the whole body.[n] The reader may
observe with how poetical a description Milton has attributed the
same kind of motion to the angels who were to take possession of
Paradise.

So spake our mother Eve, and Adam heard
Well pleased, but answered not; for now too nigh
The archangel stood, and from the other hill
To their fixed station, all in bright array
The Cherubim descended; on the ground
Gliding meteorous, as evening mist
Risen from a river, o'er the marish glides,
And gathers ground fast at the labourer's heel
Homeward returning. High in front advanced,
The brandished sword of God before them blazed
Fierce as a comet . . .

The author helped his invention in the following passage, by
reflecting on the behaviour of the angel, who, in Holy Writ, has the
conduct of Lot and his family. The circumstances drawn from that
relation are very gracefully made use of on this occasion.

In either hand the hastening angel caught
Our lingering parents, and to the eastern gate
Led them direct; and down the cliff as fast
To the subjected plain; then disappeared.
They looking back, etc. . . .

The scene which our first parents are surprised with upon their
looking back on Paradise, wonderfully strikes the reader's imagination, as nothing can be more natural than the tears they shed on that
occasion.

They looking back, all the eastern side behold
Of Paradise, so late their happy seat,

So spake: *PL*, xii. 624–34.   *Lot*: Gen. 19:16.
In either hand: *PL*, xii. 637–71.   *They looking back*: *PL*, xii. 641–7.

> Waved over by that flaming brand, the gate
> With dreadful faces thronged and fiery arms:
> Some natural tears they dropped, but wiped them soon;
> The world was all before them, where to choose
> Their place of rest, and Providence their guide.

If I might presume to offer at the smallest alteration in this divine work, I should think the poem would end better with the passage here quoted, than with the two verses which follow.

> They hand in hand with wandering steps and slow,
> Through Eden took their solitary way.

These two verses, though they have their beauty, fall very much below the foregoing passage, and renew in the mind of the reader that anguish which was pretty well laid by that consideration,

> The world was all before them, where to choose
> Their place of rest, and Providence their guide.

The number of books in *Paradise Lost* is equal to those of the *Aeneid*. Our author in his first edition had divided his poem into ten books, but afterwards broke the seventh and the eleventh each of them into two different books, by the help of some small additions.[n] This second division was made with great judgement, as any one may see who will be at the pains of examining it. It was not done for the sake of such a chimerical beauty as that of resembling Virgil in this particular, but for the more just and regular disposition of this great work.

Those who have read Bossu,[n] and many of the critics who have written since his time, will not pardon me if I do not find out the particular moral which is inculcated in *Paradise Lost*. Though I can by no means think with the last-mentioned French author, that an epic writer first of all pitches upon a certain moral, as the ground-work and foundation of his poem, and afterwards finds out a story to it: I am, however, of opinion, that no just heroic poem ever was, or can be made, from whence one great moral may not be deduced. That which reigns in Milton is the most universal and most useful that can be imagined; it is in short this: that obedience to the will of God makes men happy, and that disobedience makes them miserable. This is visibly the moral of the principal fable which turns upon Adam and Eve, who continued in Paradise while they kept the command that was given them, and were driven out of it as soon as they had transgressed. This is likewise the moral of the principal

They hand in hand: *PL*, xii. 648–9.

episode, which shows us how an innumerable multitude of angels fell from their state of bliss, and were cast into Hell upon their disobedience. Besides this great moral, which may be looked upon as the soul of the fable, there are an infinity of under-morals which are to be drawn from the several parts of the poem, and which make this work more useful and instructive than any other poem in any language.

Those who have criticized on the *Odyssey*, the *Iliad*, and *Aeneid*, have taken a great deal of pains to fix the number of months or days contained in the action of each of those poems.[n] If anyone thinks it worth his while to examine this particular in Milton, he will find that from Adam's first appearance in the fourth book, to his expulsion from Paradise in the twelfth, the author reckons ten days. As for that part of the action which is described in the three first books, as it does not pass within the regions of Nature, I have before observed that it is not subject to any calculations of time.

I have now finished my observations on a work which does an honour to the English nation. I have taken a general view of it under those four heads, the Fable, the Characters, the Sentiments and the Language, and made each of them the subject of a particular paper. I have in the next place spoken of the censures which our author may incur under each of these heads, which I have confined to two papers, though I might have enlarged the number, if I had been disposed to dwell on so ungrateful a subject. I believe, however, that the severest reader will not find any little fault in heroic poetry, which this author has fallen into, that does not come under one of those heads among which I have distributed his several blemishes. After having thus treated at large of *Paradise Lost*, I could not think it sufficient to have celebrated this poem in the whole, without descending to particulars. I have therefore bestowed a paper upon each book, and endeavoured not only to prove that the poem is beautiful in general, but to point out its particular beauties, and to determine wherein they consist. I have endeavoured to show how some passages are beautiful by being sublime, others by being soft, others by being natural; which of them are recommended by the passion, which by the moral, which by the sentiment, and which by the expression. I have likewise endeavoured to show how the genius of the poet shines by a happy invention, a distant allusion, or a judicious imitation; how he has copied or improved Homer or Virgil, and raised his own imaginations by the use which he has made of several poetical passages in Scripture. I might have inserted also several passages of Tasso, which our author has imitated; but as I do not look upon Tasso to be a sufficient voucher, I would not perplex my reader with such quotations, as might do more honour to the Italian than the English poet.[n] In short, I have endeavoured to particularize those innumerable kinds of beauty, which it would be tedious to recapitulate, but which are essential to poetry, and which may be met with in the works of this great author. Had I thought, at my first engaging in this design, that it would have led me to so great a length, I believe I should never have entered upon it; but the kind reception which it has met with among those whose judgements I have a value for, as well as the uncommon demand which my bookseller tells me has been made for these particular discourses, give me no reason to repent of the pains I have been at in composing them.

Taste and the Pleasures of the Imagination

. . . Musaeo contingere cuncta lepore.   Lucr.

Gratian very often recommended the fine taste, as the utmost perfection of an accomplished man. As this word arises very often in conversation, I shall endeavour to give some account of it, and to lay down rules how we may know whether we are possessed of it, and how we may acquire that fine taste of writing, which is so much talked of among the polite world.

Most languages make use of this metaphor, to express that faculty of the mind, which distinguishes all the most concealed faults and nicest perfections in writing. We may be sure this metaphor would not have been so general in all tongues, had there not been a very great conformity between that mental taste, which is the subject of this paper, and that sensitive taste which gives us a relish of every different flavour that affects the palate. Accordingly we find, there are as many degrees of refinement in the intellectual faculty, as in the sense, which is marked out by this common denomination.

I knew a person who possessed the one in so great a perfection, that after having tasted ten different kinds of tea, he would distinguish, without seeing the colour of it, the particular sort which was offered him; and not only so, but any two sorts of them that were mixed together in an equal proportion; nay, he has carried the experiment so far, as upon tasting the composition of three different sorts, to name the parcels from whence the three several ingredients were taken. A man of a fine taste in writing will discern, after the same manner, not only the general beauties and imperfections of an author, but discover the several ways of thinking and expressing himself, which diversify him from all other authors, with the several foreign infusions of thought and language, and the particular authors from whom they were borrowed.

After having thus far explained what is generally meant by a fine

---

Motto: Lucretius, *De reram natura*, 1. 934 (altered): To grace each subject with wit.

Gratian: Baltasar Gracián (1601–58), the Spanish Jesuit, is best known for his popular *Oráculo Manual y arte de prudencia* (1647). The reference here is to his *Arte de ingenio* (1642), in which he praises the taste for conceits. An English translation appeared in 1681.

taste in writing, and shown the propriety of the metaphor which is used on this occasion, I think I may define it to be *that faculty of the soul, which discerns the beauties of an author with pleasure, and the imperfections with dislike.* If a man would know whether he is possessed of this faculty, I would have him read over the celebrated works of antiquity, which have stood the test of so many different ages and countries; or those works among the Moderns, which have the sanction of the politer part of our contemporaries. If upon the perusal of such writings he does not find himself delighted in an extraordinary manner, or, if upon reading the admired passages in such authors, he finds a coldness and indifference in his thoughts, he ought to conclude, not (as is too usual among tasteless readers) that the author wants those perfections which have been admired in him, but that he himself wants the faculty of discovering them.

He should, in the second place, be very careful to observe, whether he tastes the distinguishing perfections, or, if I may be allowed to call them so, the specific qualities of the author whom he peruses; whether he is particularly pleased with Livy for his manner of telling a story, with Sallust for his entering into those internal principles of action which arise from the characters and manners of the persons he describes, or with Tacitus for his displaying those outward motives of safety and interest, which give birth to the whole series of trans-actions which he relates.[n]

He may likewise consider, how differently he is affected by the same thought, which presents itself in a great writer, from what he is when he finds it delivered by a person of an ordinary genius. For there is as much difference in apprehending a thought clothed in Cicero's language, and that of a common author, as in seeing an object by the light of a taper, or by the light of the sun.

It is very difficult to lay down rules for the acquirement of such a taste as that I am here speaking of. The faculty must in some degree be born with us, and it very often happens, that those who have other qualities in perfection are wholly void of this. One of the most eminent mathematicians of the age[n] has assured me, that the greatest pleasure he took in reading Virgil, was in examining Aeneas' voyage by the map, as I question not but many a modern compiler of history would be delighted with little more in that divine author, than in the bare matters of fact.

But notwithstanding this faculty must in some measure be born with us, there are several methods for cultivating and improving it, and without which it will be very uncertain, and of little use to the person that possesses it. The most natural method for this purpose is to be conversant among the writings of the most polite authors.

A man who has any relish for fine writing, either discovers new beauties, or receives stronger impressions from the masterly strokes of a great author every time he peruses him: besides that he naturally wears himself into the same manner of speaking and thinking.

Conversation with men of a polite genius is another method for improving our natural taste. It is impossible for a man of the greatest parts to consider anything in its whole extent, and in all its variety of lights. Every man, besides those general observations which are to be made upon an author, forms several reflections that are peculiar to his own manner of thinking; so that conversation will naturally furnish us with hints which we did not attend to, and make us enjoy other men's parts and reflections as well as our own. This is the best reason I can give for the observation which several have made, that men of great genius in the same way of writing seldom rise up singly, but at certain periods of time appear together, and in a body; as they did at Rome in the reign of Augustus, and in Greece about the age of Socrates. I cannot think that Corneille, Racine, Molière, Boileau, La Fontaine, Bruyère, Bossu, or the Daciers, would have written so well as they have done, had they not been friends and contemporaries.[n]

It is likewise necessary for a man who would form to himself a finished taste of good writing, to be well versed in the works of the best critics both ancient and modern. I must confess that I could wish there were authors of this kind, who, beside the mechanical rules which a man of very little taste may discourse upon, would enter into the very spirit and soul of fine writing, and show us the several sources of that pleasure which rises in the mind upon the perusal of a noble work. Thus although in poetry it be absolutely necessary that the unities of time, place and action, with other points of the same nature should be thoroughly explained and understood; there is still something more essential, to the art, something that elevates and astonishes the fancy, and gives a greatness of mind to the reader, which few of the critics besides Longinus have considered.[n]

Our general taste in England is for epigram, turns of wit, and forced conceits, which have no manner of influence, either for the bettering or enlarging the mind of him who reads them, and have been carefully avoided by the greatest writers, both among the Ancients and Moderns. I have endeavoured in several of my speculations to banish this Gothic taste which has taken possession among us.[n] I entertained the Town for a week together with an essay upon wit, in which I endeavoured to detect several of those false kinds which have been admired in the different ages of the world; and at the same time to show wherein the nature of true wit consists. I afterwards gave an instance of the great force which lies in a natural simplicity of thought to affect the mind of the reader, from such vulgar pieces as have little else besides this single qualification to recommend them. I have likewise examined the works of the greatest poet which our nation or perhaps any other has produced, and particularized most of those rational and manly beauties[n] which give a value to that divine work. I shall next Saturday enter upon an essay on the Pleasures of the Imagination, which though it shall consider that subject at large, will perhaps suggest to the reader what it is that gives a beauty to many passages of the finest writers both in prose and verse. As an undertaking of this nature is entirely new, I question not but it will be received with candour.

411   *Saturday June 21 1712*

Avia Pieridum peragro loca, nullius ante
trita solo; juvat integros accedere fonteis;
atque haurire: . . . Lucr.

Our sight is the most perfect and most delightful of all our senses. It fills the mind with the largest variety of ideas, converses with its objects at the greatest distance, and continues the longest in action without being tired or satiated with its proper enjoyments. The sense of feeling can indeed give us a notion of extension, shape, and all other ideas that enter at the eye, except colours; but at the same time it is very much straitened and confined in its operations, to the number, bulk, and distance of its particular objects. Our sight seems designed to supply all these defects, and may be considered as a more delicate and diffusive kind of touch, that spreads itself over an infinite multitude of bodies, comprehends the largest figures, and brings into our reach some of the most remote parts of the universe.

It is this sense which furnishes the imagination with its ideas; so that by the pleasures of the imagination or fancy (which I shall

---

candour: here used, as frequently in the eighteenth century, to signify 'freedom from malice, favourable disposition, kindliness' (*OED*). Johnson's *Dictionary* (1755) defines it as 'sweetness of temper, kindness'.

Motto: Lucretius, *De rerum natura*, 1. 926–8:

> The Muses' close retreat I wander o'er,
> Their unacquainted solitudes explore,
> At the spring-head it charms me to be first,
> And in the untainted stream to quench my thirst. BROUGHTON

use promiscuously) I here mean such as arise from visible objects, either when we have them actually in our view, or when we call up their ideas into our minds by paintings, statues, descriptions, or any the like occasion. We cannot indeed have a single image in the fancy that did not make its first entrance through the sight; but we have the power of retaining, altering and compounding those images, which we have once received, into all the varieties of picture and vision that are most agreeable to the imagination; for by this faculty a man in a dungeon is capable of entertaining himself with scenes and landscapes more beautiful than any that can be found in the whole compass of nature.

There are few words in the English language which are employed in a more loose and uncircumscribed sense than those of the fancy and the imagination. I therefore thought it necessary to fix and determine the notion of these two words, as I intend to make use of them in the thread of my following speculations, that the reader may conceive rightly what is the subject which I proceed upon. I must therefore desire him to remember, that by the pleasures of the imagination, I mean only such pleasures as arise originally from sight, and that I divide these pleasures into two kinds: my design being first of all to discourse of those primary pleasures of the imagination, which entirely proceed from such objects as are before our eyes; and in the next place to speak of those secondary pleasures of the imagination which flow from the ideas of visible objects, when the objects are not actually before the eye, but are called up into our memories, or formed into agreeable visions of things that are either absent or fictitious.[n]

The pleasures of the imagination, taken in their full extent, are not so gross as those of sense, nor so refined as those of the understanding. The last are, indeed, more preferable, because they are founded on some new knowledge or improvement in the mind of man; yet it must be confessed, that those of the imagination are as great and as transporting as the other. A beautiful prospect delights the soul, as much as a demonstration; and a description in Homer has charmed more readers than a chapter in Aristotle. Besides, the pleasures of the imagination have this advantage, above those of the understanding, that they are more obvious, and more easy to be acquired. It is but opening the eye, and the scene enters. The colours paint themselves on the fancy, with very little attention of thought or application of mind in the beholder. We are struck, we know not how, with the symmetry of any thing we see, and immediately assent to the beauty of an object, without enquiring into the particular causes and occasions of it.

A man of a polite imagination, is let into a great many pleasures that the vulgar are not capable of receiving.[n] He can converse with a picture, and find an agreeable companion in a statue. He meets with a secret refreshment in a description, and often feels a greater satisfaction in the prospect of fields and meadows, than another does in the possession. It gives him, indeed, a kind of property in everything he sees, and makes the most rude uncultivated parts of nature administer to his pleasures: so that he looks upon the world, as it were, in another light, and discovers in it a multitude of charms, that conceal themselves from the generality of mankind.

There are, indeed, but very few who know how to be idle and innocent, or have a relish of any pleasures that are not criminal; every diversion they take is at the expense of some one virtue or another, and their very first step out of business is into vice or folly. A man should endeavour, therefore, to make the sphere of his innocent pleasures as wide as possible, that he may retire into them with safety, and find in them such a satisfaction as a wise man would not blush to take. Of this nature are those of the imagination, which do not require such a bent of thought as is necessary to our more serious employments, nor, at the same time, suffer the mind to sink into that negligence and remissness, which are apt to accompany our more sensual delights, but, like a gentle exercise to the faculties, awaken them from sloth and idleness, without putting them upon any labour or difficulty.

We might here add, that the pleasures of the fancy are more conducive to health, than those of the understanding, which are worked out by dint of thinking, and attended with too violent a labour of the brain. Delightful scenes, whether in nature, painting, or poetry, have a kindly influence on the body, as well as the mind, and not only serve to clear and brighten the imagination, but are able to disperse grief and melancholy, and to set the animal spirits in pleasing and agreeable motions. For this reason Sir Francis Bacon, in his essay upon health, has not thought it improper to prescribe to his reader a poem or a prospect, where he particularly dissuades him from knotty and subtle disquisitions, and advises him to pursue studies, that fill the mind with splendid and illustrious objects, as histories, fables, and contemplations of nature.[n]

I have in this paper, by way of introduction, settled the notion of those pleasures of the imagination, which are the subject of my present undertaking, and endeavoured, by several considerations, to recommend to my reader the pursuit of those pleasures. I shall, in my next paper, examine the several sources from whence these pleasures are derived.

412   *Monday   June 23   1712*

... *Divisum sic breve fiet opus.*   Mart.

I shall first consider those pleasures of the imagination, which arise
from the actual view and survey of outward objects: and these, I
think, all proceed from the sight of what is great, uncommon, or
beautiful. There may, indeed, be something so terrible or offensive,
that the horror or loathsomeness of an object may overbear the
pleasure which results from its greatness, novelty, or beauty, but
still there will be such a mixture of delight in the very disgust it gives
us, as any of these three qualifications are most conspicuous and
prevailing.

By greatness, I do not only mean the bulk of any single object,
but the largeness of a whole view, considered as one entire piece.
Such are the prospects of an open champaign country, a vast uncultivated desert, of huge heaps of mountains, high rocks and
precipices, or a wide expanse of waters, where we are not struck with
the novelty or beauty of the sight, but with that rude kind of magnificence which appears in many of these stupendous works of
nature. Our imagination loves to be filled with an object, or to
grasp at anything that is too big for its capacity. We are flung into a
pleasing astonishment at such unbounded views, and feel a delightful
stillness and amazement in the soul at the apprehension of them.
The mind of man naturally hates everything that looks like a
restraint upon it, and is apt to fancy itself under a sort of confinement, when the sight is pent up in a narrow compass, and shortened
on every side by the neighbourhood of walls or mountains. On the
contrary, a spacious horizon is an image of liberty, where the eye has
room to range abroad, to expatiate at large on the immensity of its
views, and to lose itself amidst the variety of objects that offer
themselves to its observation. Such wide and undetermined prospects
are as pleasing to the fancy, as the speculations of eternity or
infinitude are to the understanding. But if there be a beauty or un-
commonness joined with this grandeur, as in a troubled ocean, a
heaven adorned with stars and meteors, or a spacious landscape cut
out into rivers, woods, rocks, and meadows, the pleasure still grows
upon us, as it arises from more than a single principle.

Everything that is new or uncommon raises a pleasure in the

Motto: Martial, *Epigrams*, 4. 82. 8: The work thus divided will become brief.

overbear: i.e. outweigh. This is the earliest example in *OED* of the word in this
sense.

imagination, because it fills the soul with an agreeable surprise, gratifies its curiosity, and gives it an idea of which it was not before possessed. We are, indeed, so often conversant with one set of objects, and tired out with so many repeated shows of the same things, that whatever is new or uncommon contributes a little to vary human life, and to divert our minds, for a while, with the strangeness of its appearance: it serves us for a kind of refreshment, and takes off from that satiety we are apt to complain of in our usual and ordinary entertainments.[n] It is this that bestows charms on a monster, and makes even the imperfections of nature please us. It is this that recommends variety, where the mind is every instant called off to something new, and the attention not suffered to dwell too long, and waste itself on any particular object. It is this, likewise, that improves what is great or beautiful, and makes it afford the mind a double entertainment. Groves, fields, and meadows, are at any season of the year pleasant to look upon, but never so much as in the opening of the spring, when they are all new and fresh, with their first gloss upon them, and not yet too much accustomed and familiar to the eye. For this reason there is nothing that more enlivens a prospect than rivers, jetteaus, or falls of water, where the scene is perpetually shifting, and entertaining the sight every moment with something that is new. We are quickly tired with looking upon hills and valleys, where everything continues fixed and settled in the same place and posture, but find our thoughts a little agitated and relieved at the sight of such objects as are ever in motion, and sliding away from beneath the eye of the beholder.

But there is nothing that makes its way more directly to the soul than beauty,[n] which immediately diffuses a secret satisfaction and complacency through the imagination, and gives a finishing to anything that is great or uncommon. The very first discovery of it strikes the mind with an inward joy, and spreads a cheerfulness and delight through all its faculties. There is not perhaps any real beauty or deformity more in one piece of matter than another, because we might have been so made, that whatsoever now appears loathsome to us, might have shown itself agreeable; but we find by experience, that there are several modifications of matter which the mind, without any previous consideration, pronounces at first sight beautiful or deformed. Thus we see that every different species of sensible

---

jetteau: *jet d'eau*, an ornamental jet of water ascending from a fountain or pipe. This obsolete form apparently arose from a confusion of Italian *getto* (*d'acqua*) and French *jet d'eau* (*OED*).

complacency: here used, as commonly in the eighteenth century, to mean 'pleasure' or 'delight', with no connotation of 'self-satisfaction'.

creatures has its different notions of beauty, and that each of them is most affected with the beauties of its own kind. This is nowhere more remarkable than in birds of the same shape and proportion, where we often see the male determined in his courtship by the single grain or tincture of a feather, and never discovering any charms but in the colour of its species.

> Scit thalamo servare fidem, sanctasque veretur
> connubii leges, non illum in pectore candor
> sollicitat niveus; neque pravum accendit amorem
> splendida lanugo, vel honesta in vertice crista,
> purpureusve nitor pennarum; ast agmina late
> foeminea explorat cautus, maculasque requirit
> cognatas, paribusque interlita corpora guttis:
> ni faceret, pictis sylvam circum undique monstris
> confusam aspiceres vulgo, partusque biformes,
> et genus ambiguum, et Veneris monumenta nefandae.
>   Hinc merula in nigro se oblectat nigra marito,
> hinc socium lasciva petit philomela canorum,
> agnoscitque pares sonitus, hinc noctua tetram
> canitiem alarum, et glaucos miratur ocellos.
> Nempe sibi semper constat, crescitque quotannis
> lucida progenies, castos confessa parentes;
> dum virides inter saltus lucosque sonoros
> vere novo exultat plumasque decora juventus
> explicat ad solem, patriisque coloribus ardet.[n]

There is a second kind of beauty that we find in the several products of art and nature, which does not work in the imagination with that warmth and violence as the beauty that appears in our proper species, but is apt however to raise in us a secret delight, and a kind of fondness for the places or objects in which we discover it. This consists either in the gaiety or variety of colours, in the symmetry and proportion of parts, in the arrangement and disposition of bodies, or in a just mixture and concurrence of all together. Among these several kinds of beauty the eye takes most delight in colours. We nowhere meet with a more glorious or pleasing show in Nature, than what appears in the heavens at the rising and setting of the sun, which is wholly made up of those different stains of light that show themselves in clouds of a different situation. For this reason we find the poets, who are always addressing themselves to the imagination, borrowing more of their epithets from colours than from any other topic.

As the fancy delights in everything that is great, strange, or beautiful, and is still more pleased the more it finds of these perfec-

---

sensible creatures: here simply 'creatures endowed with the faculty of sensation'.

tions in the same object, so is it capable of receiving a new satisfaction by the assistance of another sense. Thus any continued sound, as the music of birds, or a fall of water, awakens every moment the mind of the beholder, and makes him more attentive to the several beauties of the place that lie before him. Thus if there arises a fragrancy of smells or perfumes, they heighten the pleasures of the imagination, and make even the colours and verdure of the landscape appear more agreeable; for the ideas of both senses recommend each other, and are pleasanter together than when they enter the mind separately: as the different colours of a picture, when they are well disposed, set off one another, and receive an additional beauty from the advantage of their situation.

413 *Tuesday June 24 1712*

. . . Causa latet, vis est notissima . . . . Ovid.

Though in yesterday's paper we considered how everything that is great, new, or beautiful, is apt to affect the imagination with pleasure, we must own that it is impossible for us to assign the necessary cause of this pleasure, because we know neither the nature of an idea, nor the substance of a human soul, which might help us to discover the conformity or disagreeableness of the one to the other; and therefore, for want of such a light, all that we can do in speculations of this kind, is to reflect on those operations of the soul that are most agreeable, and to range, under their proper heads, what is pleasing or displeasing to the mind, without being able to trace out the several necessary and efficient causes from whence the pleasure or displeasure arises.[n]

Final causes lie more bare and open to our observation, as there are often a great variety that belong to the same effect; and these, though they are not altogether so satisfactory, are generally more useful than the other, as they give us greater occasion of admiring the goodness and wisdom of the First Contriver.

One of the final causes of our delight, in anything that is great, may be this. The Supreme Author of our being has so formed the soul of man, that nothing but himself can be its last, adequate, and proper happiness. Because, therefore, a great part of our happiness

---

Motto: Ovid, *Metamorphoses*, 4. 287: The cause is secret, but the effect is known.

must arise from the contemplation of his being, that he might give our souls a just relish of such a contemplation, he has made them naturally delight in the apprehension of what is great or unlimited. Our admiration, which is a very pleasing motion of the mind, immediately rises at the consideration of any object that takes up a great deal of room in the fancy, and, by consequence, will improve into the highest pitch of astonishment and devotion when we contemplate his nature, that is neither circumscribed by time nor place, nor to be comprehended by the largest capacity of a created being.

He has annexed a secret pleasure to the idea of anything that is new or uncommon, that he might encourage us in the pursuit after knowledge,[n] and engage us to search into the wonders of his Creation; for every new idea brings such a pleasure along with it, as rewards any pains we have taken in its acquisition, and consequently serves as a motive to put us upon fresh discoveries.

He has made everything that is beautiful in our own species pleasant, that all creatures might be tempted to multiply their kind, and fill the world, with inhabitants; for 'tis very remarkable that wherever Nature is crossed in the production of a monster (the result of any unnatural mixture) the breed is incapable of propagating its likeness, and of founding a new order of creatures; so that unless all animals were allured by the beauty of their own species, generation would be at an end, and the earth unpeopled.

In the last place, he has made everything that is beautiful in all other objects pleasant, or rather has made so many objects appear beautiful, that he might render the whole Creation more gay and delightful. He has given almost everything about us the power of raising an agreeable idea in the imagination: so that it is impossible for us to behold his works with coldness or indifference, and to survey so many beauties without a secret satisfaction and complacency. Things would make but a poor appearance to the eye, if we saw them only in their proper figures and motions: and what reason can we assign for their exciting in us many of those ideas which are different from anything that exists in the objects themselves, (for such are light and colours) were it not to add supernumerary ornaments to the universe, and make it more agreeable to the imagination? We are everywhere entertained with pleasing shows and apparitions, we discover imaginary glories in the heavens, and in the earth, and see some of this visionary beauty poured out upon the whole Creation; but what a rough unsightly sketch of Nature should we be entertained with, did all her colouring disappear, and the several distinctions of light and shade vanish? In short, our souls are at present delightfully lost and bewildered in a pleasing delusion, and we walk about like the enchanted hero of a romance, who sees beautiful castles, woods and meadows; and at the same time hears the warbling of birds, and the purling of streams; but upon the finishing of some secret spell, the fantastic scene breaks up, and the disconsolate knight finds himself on a barren heath, or in a solitary desert. It is not improbable that something like this may be the state of the soul after its first separation, in respect of the images it will receive from matter; though indeed the ideas of colours are so pleasing and beautiful in the imagination, that it is possible the soul will not be deprived of them, but perhaps find them excited by some other occasional cause, as they are at present by the different impressions of the subtle matter on the organ of sight.

I have here supposed that my reader is acquainted with that great modern discovery, which is at present universally acknowledged by all the enquirers into natural philosophy; namely, that light and colours, as apprehended by the imagination, are only ideas in the mind, and not qualities that have any existence in matter. As this is a truth which has been proved incontestably by many modern philosophers, and is indeed one of the finest speculations in that science, if the English reader would see the notion explained at large, he may find it in the eighth chapter of the second book of Mr. Locke's *Essay on Human Understanding.*[n]

414   *Wednesday June 25 1712*

> *. . . Alterius sic*
> *altera poscit opem res et conjurat amice.*   Hor.

If we consider the works of Nature and Art, as they are qualified to entertain the imagination, we shall find the last very defective, in comparison of the former; for though they may sometimes appear as beautiful or strange, they can have nothing in them of that vastness and immensity, which afford so great an entertainment to the mind of the beholder. The one may be as polite and delicate as the other, but can never show herself so august and magnificent in the design. There is something more bold and masterly in the rough

---

Motto: Horace, *Ars poetica*, 410–11:
> Each by itself is vain, I'm sure, but joined,
> Their force is strong, each proves the other's friend.   CREECH

careless strokes of Nature,[n] than in the nice touches and embellishments of art.[n] The beauties of the most stately garden or palace lie in
a narrow compass, the imagination immediately runs them over, and
requires something else to gratify her; but, in the wide fields of
Nature, the sight wanders up and down without confinement, and is
fed with an infinite variety of images, without any certain stint or
number. For this reason we always find the poet in love with a
country life, where Nature appears in the greatest perfection, and
furnishes out all those scenes that are most apt to delight the
imagination.

> Scriptorum chorus omnis amat nemus et fugit urbes.   HOR.[n]

> Hic secura quies, et nescia fallere vita,
> dives opum variarum; hic latis otia fundis,
> speluncae, vivique lacus, hic frigida Tempe,
> mugitusque boum, mollesque sub arbore somni.   VIR.[n]

But though there are several of these wild scenes, that are more
delightful than any artificial shows; yet we find the works of Nature
still more pleasant, the more they resemble those of art: for in this
case our pleasure arises from a double principle; from the agreeable-
ness of the objects to the eye, and from their similitude to other
objects: we are pleased as well with comparing their beauties, as
with surveying them, and can represent them to our minds, either as
copies or originals. Hence it is that we take delight in a prospect
which is well laid out, and diversified with fields and meadows,
woods and rivers, in those accidental landscapes of trees, clouds and
cities, that are sometimes found in the veins of marble, in the curious
fretwork of rocks and grottos, and, in a word, in anything that hath
such a variety or regularity as may seem the effect of design, in what
we call the works of chance.

If the products of Nature rise in value, according as they more or
less resemble those of art, we may be sure that artificial works
receive a greater advantage from their resemblance of such as are
natural; because here the similitude is not only pleasant, but the
pattern more perfect. The prettiest landscape I ever saw, was one
drawn on the walls of a dark room, which stood opposite on one
side to a navigable river, and on the other to a park. The experiment
is very common in optics. Here you might discover the waves and
fluctuations of the water in strong and proper colours, with the
picture of a ship entering at one end, and sailing by degrees through
the whole piece. On another there appeared the green shadows of
trees, waving to and fro with the wind, and herds of deer among
them in miniature, leaping about upon the wall. I must confess, the

novelty of such a sight may be one occasion of its pleasantness to the imagination, but certainly the chief reason is its near resemblance to nature, as it does not only, like other pictures, give the colour and figure, but the motion of the things it represents.[n]

We have before observed, that there is generally in Nature something more grand and august, than what we meet with in the curiosities of art. When, therefore, we see this imitated in any measure, it gives us a nobler and more exalted kind of pleasure than what we receive from the nicer and more accurate productions of art. On this account our English gardens are not so entertaining to the fancy as those in France and Italy,[n] where we see a large extent of ground covered over with an agreeable mixture of garden and forest, which represent everywhere an artificial rudeness, much more charming than that neatness and elegancy which we meet with in those of our own country. It might, indeed, be of ill consequence to the public, as well as unprofitable to private persons, to alienate so much ground from pasturage, and the plough, in many parts of a country that is so well peopled, and cultivated to a far greater advantage. But why may not a whole estate be thrown into a kind of garden by frequent plantations, that may turn as much to the profit, as the pleasure of the owner? A marsh overgrown with willows, or a mountain shaded with oaks, are not only more beautiful, but more beneficial, than when they lie bare and unadorned. Fields of corn make a pleasant prospect, and if the walks were a little taken care of that lie between them, if the natural embroidery of the meadows were helped and improved by some small additions of art, and the several rows of hedges set off by trees and flowers, that the soil was capable of receiving, a man might make a pretty landscape of his own possessions.[n]

Writers, who have given us an account of China, tell us, the inhabitants of that country laugh at the plantations of our Europeans, which are laid out by the rule and line; because, they say, anyone may place trees in equal rows and uniform figures. They choose rather to show a genius in works of this nature, and therefore always conceal the art by which they direct themselves. They have a word, it seems, in their language, by which they express the particular beauty of a plantation that thus strikes the imagination at first sight, without discovering what it is that has so agreeable an effect.[n] Our British gardeners, on the contrary, instead of humouring nature, love to deviate from it as much as possible. Our trees rise in cones, globes, and pyramids. We see the marks of the scissors upon every plant and bush. I do not know whether I am singular in my opinion, but, for my own part, I would rather look upon a tree in all its luxuriancy and diffusion of boughs and branches, than when it is thus cut and trimmed into a mathematical figure; and cannot but fancy that an orchard in flower looks infinitely more delightful, than all the little labyrinths of the most finished parterre. But as our great modellers of gardens have their magazines of plants to dispose of, it is very natural for them to tear up all the beautiful plantations of fruit trees, and contrive a plan that may most turn to their own profit, in taking off their evergreens, and the like movable plants, with which their shops are plentifully stocked.

415   *Thursday June 26 1712*

Adde tot egregias urbes, operumque laborem.   Virg.

Having already shown how the fancy is affected by the works of Nature, and afterwards considered in general both the works of Nature and of Art, how they mutually assist and complete each other, in forming such scenes and prospects as are most apt to delight the mind of the beholder, I shall in this paper throw together some reflections on that particular art, which has a more immediate tendency, than any other, to produce those primary pleasures of the imagination, which have hitherto been the subject of this discourse. The art I mean is that of architecture, which I shall consider only with regard to the light in which the foregoing speculations have placed it, without entering into those rules and maxims which the great masters of architecture have laid down, and explained at large in numberless treatises upon that subject.

Greatness, in the works of architecture, may be considered as relating to the bulk and body of the structure, or the manner in which it is built. As for the first, we find the Ancients, especially among the eastern nations of the world, infinitely superior to the Moderns.

Not to mention the Tower of Babel, of which an old author says, there were the foundations to be seen in his time, which looked like a

---

Motto: Virgil, *Georgics*, 2. 155:
> Next add our cities of illustrious name,
> Their costly labour and stupendous frame.   DRYDEN

Babel: Gen. 11:1–9.

spacious mountain; what could be more noble than the walls of Babylon,[n] its hanging gardens, and its temple to Jupiter Belus, that rose a mile high by eight several stories, each storey a furlong in height, and on the top of which was the Babylonian observatory? I might here, likewise, take notice of the huge rock that was cut into the figure of Semiramis, with the smaller rocks that lay by it in the shape of tributary kings; the prodigious basin, or artificial lake, which took in the whole Euphrates, till such time as a new canal was formed for its reception, with the several trenches through which that river was conveyed.[n] I know there are persons who look upon some of these wonders of art as fabulous, but I cannot find any grounds for such a suspicion, unless it be that we have no such works among us at present. There were indeed many greater advantages for building in those times, and in that part of the world, than have been met with ever since. The earth was extremely fruitful, men lived generally on pasturage, which requires a much smaller number of hands than agriculture: there were few trades to employ the busy part of mankind, and fewer arts and sciences to give work to men of speculative tempers; and what is more than all the rest, the prince was absolute; so that when he went to war, he put himself at the head of a whole people: as we find Semiramis leading her three millions[n] to the field, and yet overpowered by the number of her enemies. 'Tis no wonder, therefore, when she was at peace, and turned her thoughts on building, that she could accomplish so great works, with such a prodigious multitude of labourers: besides that, in her climate, there was small interruption of frosts and winters, which make the northern workmen lie half the year idle. I might mention too, among the benefits of the climate, what historians say of the earth, that it sweated out a bitumen[n] or natural kind of mortar, which is doubtless the same with that mentioned in Holy Writ, as contributing to the structure of Babel. 'Slime they used instead of mortar.'

In Egypt we still see their pyramids, which answer to the descriptions that have been made of them; and I question not but a traveller might find out some remains of the labyrinth that covered a whole province, and had a hundred temples disposed among its several quarters and divisions.

Jupiter Belus: i.e. Zeus, whom the Babylonians called Belus, to whom Semiramis built a temple in the city. (Diodorus Siculus, 2. 9. 4; cf. Herodatus 1. 181).

Semiramis: in Assyrian legend the wife of Ninus, the founder of Nineveh. After securing her husband's death she assumed the government of Assyria and built the city of Babylon.

Holy Writ: Gen. 11: 3.

divisions: Diodorus Siculus, 1. 61. 2; 1. 66. 3–6.

The Wall of China is one of these eastern pieces of magnificence, which makes a figure even in the map of the world, although an account of it would have been thought fabulous, were not the wall itself still extant.

We are obliged to devotion for the noblest buildings, that have adorned the several countries of the world. It is this which has set men at work on temples and public places of worship, not only that they might, by the magnificence of the building, invite the deity to reside within it, but that such stupendous works might, at the same time, open the mind to vast conceptions, and fit it to converse with the divinity of the place. For everything that is majestic, imprints an awfulness and reverence on the mind of the beholder, and strikes in with the natural greatness of the soul.

In the second place we are to consider greatness of manner in architecture, which has such force upon the imagination, that a small building, where it appears, shall give the mind nobler ideas than one of twenty times the bulk, where the manner is ordinary or little. Thus, perhaps, a man would have been more astonished with the majestic air that appeared in one of Lysippus's statues of Alexander, though no bigger than the life, than he might have been with Mount Athos, had it been cut into the figure of the hero, according to the proposal of Phidias,[n] with a river in one hand, and a city in the other.

Let any one reflect on the disposition of mind he finds in himself, at his first entrance into the Pantheon[n] at Rome, and how his imagination is filled with something great and amazing; and, at the same time, consider how little, in proportion, he is affected with the inside of a Gothic cathedral, though it be five times larger than the other; which can arise from nothing else, but the greatness of the manner in the one, and the meanness in the other.[n]

I have seen an observation upon this subject in a French author, which very much pleased me. It is in Monsieur Fréart's *Parallel of the Ancient and Modern Architecture*.[n] I shall give it the reader with the same terms of art which he has made use of.

I am observing [says he] a thing which, in my opinion, is very curious, whence it proceeds, that in the same quantity of superficies, the one *manner* seems great and magnificent, and the other poor and trifling;

Wall of China: Sir William Temple, 'Of Heroick Virtue', *Miscellanea*, Part ii (*Works*, 1720, i. 198); Louis le Comte, *Memoirs and Observvations* . . . (1697), pp. 75–6.

strike in with: i.e. fit in with, agree with. *OED* gives quotations from 1704 to 1714.

Lysippus: (*fl.* 372–316 B.C.). The favourite sculptor of Alexander the Great. According to Plutarch (*Life of Alexander*, 4, 1) his statues gave the best likeness of Alexander's person.

the reason is fine and uncommon. I say then, that to introduce into architecture this grandeur of manner, we ought so to proceed, that the division of the principal members of the order may consist but of few parts, that they be all great and of a bold and ample relievo, and swelling; and that the eye, beholding nothing little and mean, the imagination may be more vigorously touched and affected with the work that stands before it. For example; in a cornice, if the gola or cymatium of the corona, the coping, the modillions or dentelli, make a noble show by their graceful projections, if we see none of that ordinary confusion which is the result of those little cavities, quarter rounds of the astragal, and I know not how many other intermingled particulars, which produce no effect in great and massy works, and which very unprofitably take up place to the prejudice of the principal member, it is most certain that this manner will appear solemn and great; as on the contrary, that will have but a poor amd mean effect, where there is a redundancy of those smaller ornaments, which divide and scatter the angles of the sight into such a multitude of rays, so pressed together that the whole will appear but a confusion.

Among all the figures in architecture, there are none that have a greater air than the concave and the convex; and we find in all the ancient and modern architecture, as well in the remote parts of China, as in countries nearer home, that round pillars and vaulted roofs make a great part of those buildings which are designed for pomp and magnificence. The reason I take to be, because in these figures we generally see more of the body, than in those of other kinds. There are, indeed, figures of bodies, where the eye may take in two thirds of the surface; but as in such bodies the sight must split upon several angles, it does not take in one uniform idea, but several ideas of the same kind. Look upon the outside of a dome, your eye half surrounds it; look up into the inside,[n] and at one glance you have all the prospect of it; the entire concavity falls into your eye at once, the sight being as the centre that collects and gathers into it the lines of the whole circumference: in a square pillar, the sight often takes in but a fourth part of the surface, and, in a square concave, must move up and down to the different sides, before it is master of all the inward surface. For this reason, the fancy is infinitely more struck with the view of the open air, and skies, that passes through an arch, than what comes through a square, or any other figure. The figure of the rainbow does not contribute less to its magnificence, than the colours to its beauty, as it is very

---

gola (gula) *or cymatium* (cyma), defined in *OED* as 'a moulding of the cornice; the outline of which consists of a concave and a convex line.'

astragal: a small moulding placed round the top or bottom of columns and used to separate the different parts of the architrave in ornamental entablatures (*OED*).

poetically described by the son of Sirach: 'Look upon the rainbow, and praise him that made it; very beautiful it is in its brightness: it encompasses the heavens with a glorious circle, and the hands of the Most High have bended it.'

Having thus spoken of that greatness which affects the mind in architecture, I might next show the pleasure that arises in the imagination from what appears new and beautiful in this art; but as every beholder has naturally a greater taste of these two perfections in every building which offers itself to his view, than of that which I have hitherto considered, I shall not trouble my reader with any reflections upon it. It is sufficient for my present purpose, to observe, that there is nothing in this whole art which pleases the imagination, but as it is great, uncommon, or beautiful.

416   *Friday June 27 1712*

Quatenus hoc simile est oculis, quod mente videmus.   Lucr.

I at first divided the pleasures of the imagination, into such as arise from objects that are actually before our eyes, or that once entered in at our eyes, and are afterwards called up into the mind, either barely by its own operations, or on occasion of something without us, as statues or descriptions. We have already considered the first division, and shall therefore enter on the other, which, for distinction sake, I have called the secondary pleasures of the imagination. When I say the ideas we receive from statues, descriptions, or such like occasions, are the same that were once actually in our view, it must not be understood that we had once seen the very place, action, or person which are carved or described. It is sufficient, that we have seen places, persons, or actions, in general, which bear a resemblance, or at least some remote analogy with what we find represented. Since it is in the power of the imagination, when it is once stocked with particular ideas, to enlarge, compound, and vary them at her own pleasure.[n]

Among the different kinds of representation, statuary is the most

---

Son of Sirach: Ecclus. 43:11 (altered).
Motto: Lucretius, *De rerum natura*, 4. 750: For this reason what we fancy in our mind resembles what we see with the eyes.

natural, and shows us something *likest* the object that is represented. To make use of a common instance, let one who is born blind take an image in his hands, and trace out with his fingers the different furrows and impressions of the chisel, and he will easily conceive how the shape of a man, or beast, may be represented by it; but should he draw his hand over a picture, where all is smooth and uniform, he would never be able to imagine how the several prominencies and depressions of a human body could be shown on a plain piece of canvas, that has in it no unevenness or irregularity. Description runs yet further from the things it represents than painting; for a picture bears a real resemblance to its original, which letters and syllables are wholly void of. Colours speak all languages, but words are understood only by such a people or nation. For this reason, though men's necessities quickly put them on finding out speech, writing is probably of a later invention than painting; particularly we are told, that in America when the Spaniards first arrived there, expresses were sent to the Emperor of Mexico in paint, and the news of his country delineated by the strokes of a pencil, which was a more natural way than that of writing, though at the same time much more imperfect, because it is impossible to draw the little connexions of speech, or to give the picture of a conjunction or an adverb. It would be yet more strange, to represent visible objects by sounds that have no ideas annexed to them, and to make something like description in music. Yet it is certain, there may be confused, imperfect notions of this nature raised in the imagination by an artificial composition of notes; and we find that great masters in the art are able, sometimes, to set their hearers in the heat and hurry of a battle, to overcast their minds with melancholy scenes and apprehensions of deaths and funerals, or to lull them into pleasing dreams of groves and Elysiums.

In all these instances, this secondary pleasure of the imagination proceeds from that action of the mind, which compares the ideas arising from the original objects, with the ideas we receive from the statue, picture, description, or sound that represents them. It is impossible for us to give the necessary reason, why this operation of the mind is attended with so much pleasure, as I have before observed on the same occasion; but we find a great variety of entertainments derived from this single principle; for it is this that not only gives us a relish of statuary, painting and description, but makes us delight in all the actions and arts of mimicry. It is this that makes the several kinds of wit pleasant, which consists, as I

expresses: special messengers.   *before observed*: No. 413 (p. 181).

have formerly shown, in the affinity of ideas: and we may add, it is this also that raises the little satisfaction we sometimes find in the different sorts of false wit; whether it consist in the affinity of letters, as in anagram, acrostic; or of syllables, as in doggerel rhymes, echoes; or of words, as in puns, quibbles; or of a whole sentence or poem, to wings, and altars. The final cause, probably, of annexing pleasure to this operation of the mind, was to quicken and encourage us in our searches after truth, since the distinguishing one thing from another, and the right discerning betwixt our ideas, depends wholly upon our comparing them together, and observing the congruity or disagreement that appears among the several works of Nature.

But I shall here confine myself to those pleasures of the imagination, which proceed from ideas raised by words, because most of the observations that agree with descriptions, are equally applicable to painting and statuary.

Words, when well chosen, have so great a force in them, that a description often gives us more lively ideas than the sight of things themselves. The reader finds a scene drawn in stronger colours, and painted more to the life in his imagination, by the help of words, than by an actual survey of the scene which they describe.[n] In this case the poet seems to get the better of Nature; he takes, indeed, the landscape after her, but gives it more vigorous touches, heightens its beauty, and so enlivens the whole piece, that the images, which flow from the objects themselves, appear weak and faint, in comparison of those that come from the expressions. The reason, probably, may be, because in the survey of any object we have only so much of it painted on the imagination, as comes in at the eye; but in its description, the poet gives us as free a view of it as he pleases, and discovers to us several parts, that either we did not attend to, or that lay out of our sight when we first beheld it. As we look on any object, our idea of it is, perhaps, made up of two or three simple ideas; but when the poet represents it, he may either give us a more complex idea of it, or only raise in us such ideas as are most apt to affect the imagination.

It may be here worth our while to examine, how it comes to pass that several readers, who are all acquainted with the same language, and know the meaning of the words they read, should nevertheless have a different relish of the same descriptions. We find one transported with a passage, which another runs over with coldness and indifference, or finding the representation extremely natural, where

formerly shown: No. 62 (p. 16).

another can perceive nothing of likeness and conformity. This different taste must proceed, either from the perfection of imagination in one more than in another, or from the different ideas that several readers affix to the same words. For, to have a true relish, and form a right judgement of a description, a man should be born with a good imagination, and must have well weighed the force and energy that lie in the several words of a language, so as to be able to distinguish which are most significant and expressive of their proper ideas, and what additional strength and beauty they are capable of receiving from conjunction with others. The fancy must be warm, to retain the print of those images it hath received from outward objects; and the judgement discerning, to know what expressions are most proper to clothe and adorn them to the best advantage. A man who is deficient in either of these respects, though he may receive the general notion of a description, can never see distinctly all its particular beauties: as a person, with a weak sight, may have the confused prospect of a place that lies before him, without entering into its several parts, or discerning the variety of its colours in their full glory and perfection.

417   *Saturday June 28 1712*

*Quem tu Melpomene semel
nascentem placido lumine videris,
   illum non labor Isthmius
clarabit pugilem, non equus impiger, etc.
Sed quae Tibur aquae fertile perfluunt,
   et spissae nemorum comae
fingent Aeolio carmine nobilem.*   Hor.

We may observe, that any single circumstance of what we have formerly seen often raises up a whole scene of imagery, and awakens numberless ideas that before slept in the imagination; such a

Motto: Horace, *Odes*, 4. 3. 1–4, 10–12:
> The youth, whose birth the kindly muse
> With an indulgent aspect views,
> Shall neither at the barrier shine,
> Nor the Olympic garland win.
> But Tibur's streams, and verdant glades,
> The limpid spring and gloomy shades,
> Shall fill his never dying lays,
> And crown him with immortal praise.   BROUGHTON

particular smell or colour is able to fill the mind, on a sudden, with
the picture of the fields or gardens where we first met with it, and to
bring up into view all the variety of images that once attended it.
Our imagination takes the hint, and leads us unexpectedly into
cities or theatres, plains or meadows. We may further observe, when
the fancy thus reflects on the scenes that have passed in it formerly,
those, which were at first pleasant to behold, appear more so upon
reflection, and that the memory heightens the delightfulness of the
original. A Cartesian[n] would account for both these instances in the
following manner.

The set of ideas, which we received from such a prospect or
garden, having entered the mind at the same time, have a set of
traces belonging to them in the brain, bordering very near upon one
another; when, therefore, any one of these ideas arises in the
imagination, and consequently dispatches a flow of animal spirits
to its proper trace, these spirits, in the violence of their motion, run
not only into the trace, to which they were more particularly
directed, but into several of those that lie about it: by this means
they awaken other ideas of the same set, which immediately determine a new dispatch of spirits, that in the same manner open other
neighbouring traces, till at last the whole set of them is blown up,
and the whole prospect or garden flourishes in the imagination.
But because the pleasure we received from these places far surmount-
ed, and overcame the little disagreeableness we found in them, for
this reason there was at first a wider passage worn in the pleasure
traces, and, on the contrary, so narrow a one in those which belonged to the disagreeable ideas, that they were quickly stopped up,
and rendered incapable of receiving any animal spirits, and consequently of exciting any unpleasant ideas in the memory.

It would be in vain to enquire, whether the power of imagining
things strongly proceeds from any greater perfection in the soul,
or from any nicer texture in the brain of one man than of another.
But this is certain, that a noble writer should be born with this
faculty in its full strength and vigour, so as to be able to receive
lively ideas from outward objects, to retain them long, and to range
them together, upon occasion, in such figures and representations
as are most likely to hit the fancy of the reader. A poet should take as
much pains in forming his imagination, as a philosopher in cultivating his understanding. He must gain a due relish of the works of
Nature, and be thoroughly conversant in the various scenery of a
country life.

When he is stored with country images, if he would go beyond
pastoral, and the lower kinds of poetry, he ought to acquaint him-

self with the pomp and magnificence of courts. He should be very well versed in everything that is noble and stately in the productions of art, whether it appear in painting or statuary, in the great works of architecture which are in their present glory, or in the ruins of those which flourished in former ages.

Such advantages as these help to open a man's thoughts, and to enlarge his imagination, and will therefore have their influence on all kinds of writing, if the author knows how to make right use of them. And among those of the learned languages who excel in this talent, the most perfect in their several kinds, are perhaps Homer, Virgil, and Ovid. The first strikes the imagination wonderfully with what is great, the second with what is beautiful, and the last with what is strange. Reading the *Iliad* is like travelling through a country uninhabited, where the fancy is entertained with a thousand savage prospects of vast deserts, wide uncultivated marshes, huge forests, misshapen rocks and precipices. On the contrary, the *Aeneid* is like a well-ordered garden, where it is impossible to find out any part unadorned, or to cast our eyes upon a single spot, that does not produce some beautiful plant or flower. But when we are in the *Metamorphoses*, we are walking on enchanted ground, and see nothing but scenes of magic lying round us.

Homer is in his province, when he is describing a battle or a multitude, a hero or a god. Virgil is never better pleased, than when he is in his Elysium, or copying out an entertaining picture. Homer's epithets generally mark out what is great, Virgil's what is agreeable. Nothing can be more magnificent than the figure Jupiter makes in the first *Iliad*, nor more charming than that of Venus in the first *Aeneid*.

> Ἦ, καὶ κυανέῃσιν ἐπ' ὀφρύσι νεῦσε Κρονίων·
> ἀμβρόσιαι δ' ἄρα χαῖται ἐπερρώσαντο ἄνακτος,
> κρατὸς ἀπ' Ἀθανάτοιο· μέγαν δ' ἐλέλιξεν Ὄλυμπον.[n]

> Dixit, et avertens rosea cervice refulsit:
> ambrosiaeque comae divinum vertice odorem
> spiravere: pedes vestis defluxit ad imos:
> et vera incessu patuit dea . . .[n]

Homer's persons are most of them godlike and terrible: Virgil has scarce admitted any into his poem, who are not beautiful, and has taken particular care to make his hero so.

> . . . lumenque juventae
> purpureum, et laetos oculis afflavit honores.[n]

In a word, Homer fills his readers with sublime ideas, and, I believe, has raised the imagination of all the good poets that have come after him. I shall only instance Horace, who immediately takes fire at the first hint of any passage in the *Iliad* or *Odyssey*, and always rises above himself, when he has Homer in his view. Virgil has drawn together, into his *Aeneid*, all the pleasing scenes his subject is capable of admitting, and in his *Georgics* has given us a collection of the most delightful landscapes that can be made out of fields and woods, herds of cattle, and swarms of bees.

Ovid, in his *Metamorphoses*, has shown us how the imagination may be affected by what is strange. He describes a miracle in every story, and always gives us the sight of some new creature at the end of it. His art consists chiefly in well-timing his description, before the first shape is quite worn off, and the new one perfectly finished; so that he everywhere entertains us with something we never saw before, and shows monster after monster, to the end of the *Metamorphoses*.

If I were to name a poet that is a perfect master in all these arts of working on the imagination, I think Milton may pass for one: and if his *Paradise Lost* falls short of the *Aeneid* or *Iliad* in this respect, it proceeds rather from the fault of the language in which it is written, than from any defect of genius in the author. So divine a poem in English, is like a stately palace built of brick, where one may see architecture in as great a perfection as in one of marble, though the materials are of a coarser nature. But to consider it only as it regards our present subject: what can be conceived greater than the battle of angels, the majesty of Messiah, the stature and behaviour of Satan and his peers? what more beautiful than Pandemonium, Paradise, Heaven, angels, Adam and Eve? what more strange, than the Creation of the world, the several metamorphoses of the fallen angels, and the surprising adventures their leader meets with in his search after Paradise? No other subject could have furnished a poet with scenes so proper to strike the imagination, as no other poet could have painted those scenes in more strong and lively colours.

418   *Monday June 30 1712*

. . . ferat et rubus asper amomum.   Virg.

The pleasures of these secondary views of the imagination, are of a wider and more universal nature than those it has, when joined with

Motto: Virgil, *Eclogues*, 3. 89: And myrrh instead of thorns shall grow.
BROUGHTON

sight; for not only what is great, strange or beautiful, but anything that is disagreeable when looked upon, pleases us in an apt description. Here, therefore, we must enquire after a new principle of pleasure, which is nothing else but the action of the mind, which *compares* the ideas that arise from words, with the ideas that arise from the objects themselves; and why this operation of the mind is attended with so much pleasure, we have before considered. For this reason therefore, the description of a dunghill is pleasing to the imagination, if the image be represented to our minds by suitable expressions; though, perhaps, this may be more properly called the pleasure of the understanding than of the fancy, because we are not so much delighted with the image that is contained in the description, as with the aptness of the description to excite the image.

But if the description of what is little, common or deformed, be acceptable to the imagination, the description of what is great, surprising or beautiful, is much more so; because here we are not only delighted with *comparing* the representation with the original, but are highly pleased with the original itself. Most readers, I believe, are more charmed with Milton's description of Paradise, than of Hell; they are both, perhaps, equally perfect in their kind, but in the one the brimstone and sulphur are not so refreshing to the imagination, as the beds of flowers, and the wilderness of sweets in the other.

There is yet another circumstance which recommends a description more than all the rest, and that is, if it represents to us such objects as are apt to raise a secret ferment in the mind of the reader, and to work, with violence, upon his passions. For, in this case, we are at once warmed and enlightened, so that the pleasure becomes more universal, and is several ways qualified to entertain us. Thus, in painting, it is pleasant to look on the picture of any face, where the resemblance is hit, but the pleasure increases, if it be the picture of a face that is beautiful, and is still greater, if the beauty be softened with an air of melancholy or sorrow. The two leading passions which the more serious parts of poetry endeavour to stir up in us, are terror and pity. And here, by the way, one would wonder how it comes to pass, that such passions as are very unpleasant at all other times, are very agreeable when excited by proper descriptions. It is not strange, that we should take delight in such passages as are apt to produce hope, joy, admiration, love, or the like emotions in us, because they never rise in the mind without an inward pleasure which attends them. But how comes it to pass, that we should take delight in being terrified or dejected by a description, when we find so much uneasiness in the fear or grief which we receive from any other occasion?

If we consider, therefore, the nature of this pleasure, we shall find that it does not arise so properly from the description of what is terrible, as from the reflection we make on ourselves at the time of reading it. When we look on such hideous objects, we are not a little pleased to think we are in no danger of them. We consider them at the same time, as dreadful and harmless; so that the more frightful appearance they make, the greater is the pleasure we receive from the sense of our own safety. In short, we look upon the terrors of a description, with the same curiosity and satisfaction that we survey a dead monster.

> ... Informe cadaver
> protrahitur, nequeunt expleri corda tuendo
> terribiles oculos: vultum, villosaque setis
> pectora semiferi, atque extinctos faucibus ignes.   VIRG.[n]

It is for the same reason that we are delighted with the reflecting upon dangers that are past, or in looking on a precipice at a distance, which would fill us with a different kind of horror, if we saw it hanging over our heads.

In the like manner, when we read of torments, wounds, deaths, and the like dismal accidents, our pleasure does not flow so properly from the grief which such melancholy descriptions give us, as from the secret comparison which we make between ourselves and the person who suffers. Such representations teach us to set a just value upon our own condition, and make us prize our good fortune which exempts us from the like calamities.[n] This is, however, such a kind of pleasure as we are not capable of receiving, when we see a person actually lying under the tortures that we meet with in a description; because, in this case, the object presses too close upon our senses, and bears so hard upon us, that it does not give us time or leisure to reflect on ourselves. Our thoughts are so intent upon the miseries of the sufferer, that we cannot turn them upon our own happiness. Whereas, on the contrary, we consider the misfortunes we read in history or poetry, either as past, or as fictitious, so that the reflection upon ourselves rises in us insensibly, and overbears the sorrow we conceive for the sufferings of the afflicted.

But because the mind of man requires something more perfect in matter, than what it finds there, and can never meet with any sight in nature which sufficiently answers its highest ideas of pleasantness; or, in other words, because the imagination can fancy to itself things more great, strange, or beautiful, than the eye ever saw, and is still sensible of some defect in what it has seen; on this account it is the part of a poet to humour the imagination in its own notions, by mending and perfecting nature where he describes a reality, and by adding greater beauties than are put together in nature, where he describes a fiction.

He is not obliged to attend her in the slow advances which she makes from one season to another, or to observe her conduct, in the successive production of plants and flowers. He may draw into his description all the beauties of the spring and autumn, and make the whole year contribute something to render it the more agreeable. His rose-trees, woodbines, and jasmines, may flower together, and his beds be covered at the same time with lilies, violets, and amaranths. His soil is not restrained to any particular set of plants, but is proper either for oaks or myrtles, and adapts itself to the products of every climate. Oranges may grow wild in it; myrrh may be met with in every hedge, and if he thinks it proper to have a grove of spices, he can quickly command sun enough to raise it. If all this will not furnish out an agreeable scene, he can make several new species of flowers, with richer scents and higher colours, than any that grow in the gardens of nature. His concerts of birds may be as full and harmonious, and his woods as thick and gloomy as he pleases. He is at no more expense in a long vista, than a short one, and can as easily throw his cascades from a precipice of half a mile high, as from one of twenty yards. He has his choice of the winds, and can turn the course of his rivers in all the variety of meanders, that are most delightful to the reader's imagination. In a word, he has the modelling of nature in his own hands, and may give her what charms he pleases, provided he does not reform her too much, and run into absurdities, by endeavouring to excel.

419   *Tuesday July 1 1712*

... *mentis gratissimus error*.   Hor.

There is a kind of writing, wherein the poet quite loses sight of nature, and entertains his reader's imagination with the characters and actions of such persons as have many of them no existence, but what he bestows on them.[n] Such are fairies, witches, magicians, demons, and departed spirits. This Mr. Dryden calls 'the fairy way of writing',[n] which is, indeed, more difficult than any other that

Motto: Horace, *Epistles* 2. 2. 140: A most pleasant delusion.

depends on the poet's fancy, because he has no pattern to follow in it, and must work altogether out of his own invention.

There is a very odd turn of thought required for this sort of writing, and it is impossible for a poet to succeed in it, who has not a particular cast of fancy, and an imagination naturally fruitful and superstitious. Besides this, he ought to be very well versed in legends and fables, antiquated romances, and the traditions of nurses and old women, that he may fall in with our natural prejudices, and humour those notions which we have imbibed in our infancy. For, otherwise, he will be apt to make his fairies talk like people of his own species, and not like other sets of beings, who converse with different objects, and think in a different manner from that of mankind;

> Sylvis deducti caveant, me judice, Fauni
> ne velut innati triviis ac paene forenses
> aut nimium teneris juvenentur versibus ... HOR.[n]

I do not say with Mr. Bayes in *The Rehearsal*, that spirits must not be confined to speak sense, but it is certain their sense ought to be a little discoloured, that it may seem particular, and proper to the person and the condition of the speaker.

These descriptions raise a pleasing kind of horror in the mind of the reader, and amuse his imagination with the strangeness and novelty of the persons who are represented in them. They bring up into our memory the stories we have heard in our childhood, and favour those secret terrors and apprehensions to which the mind of man is naturally subject. We are pleased with surveying the different habits and behaviours of foreign countries, how much more must we be delighted and surprised when we are led, as it were, into a new creation, and see the persons and manners of another species? Men of cold fancies, and philosophical dispositions, object to this kind of poetry, that it has not probability enough to affect the imagination. But to this it may be answered, that we are sure, in general, there are many intellectual beings in the world besides ourselves, and several species of spirits, who are subject to different laws and economies from those of mankind;[n] when we see, therefore, any of these represented naturally, we cannot look upon the representation as altogether impossible; nay, many are prepossessed with such false opinions, as dispose them to believe these particular delusions; at

---

The Rehearsal: (by the Duke of Buckingham and others, 1671) Act V, scene i.
amuse: here used almost in the obsolete sense 'to bewilder, puzzle' (*OED*), but with 'a pleasing kind of horror'. In the next paragraph ('to amuse mankind') the word is used in the ordinary eighteenth-century meaning, 'to beguile, delude, cheat'. The last quotation in *OED* in this sense is dated 1817.

least, we have all heard so many pleasing relations in favour of them, that we do not care for seeing through the falsehood, and willingly give ourselves up to so agreeable an imposture.

The Ancients have not much of this poetry among them, for, indeed, almost the whole substance of it owes its original to the darkness and superstition of later ages, when pious frauds were made use of to amuse mankind, and frighten them into a sense of their duty. Our forefathers looked upon Nature with more reverence and horror, before the world was enlightened by learning and philosophy, and loved to astonish themselves with the apprehensions of witchcraft, prodigies, charms and enchantments. There was not a village in England that had not a ghost in it, the churchyards were all haunted, every large common had a circle of fairies[n] belonging to it, and there was scarce a shepherd to be met with who had not seen a spirit.

Among all the poets of this kind our English are much the best, by what I have yet seen, whether it be that we abound with more stories of this nature, or that the genius of our country is fitter for this sort of poetry. For the English are naturally fanciful, and very often disposed by that gloominess and melancholy of temper, which is so frequent in our nation, to many wild notions and visions, to which others are not so liable.

Among the English, Shakespeare has incomparably excelled all others.[n] That noble extravagance of fancy, which he had in so great perfection, thoroughly qualified him to touch this weak superstitious part of his reader's imagination; and made him capable of succeeding, where he had nothing to support him besides the strength of his own genius. There is something so wild and yet so solemn in the speeches of his ghosts, fairies, witches, and the like imaginary persons, that we cannot forbear thinking them natural, though we have no rule by which to judge of them, and must confess, if there are such beings in the world, it looks highly probable they should talk and act as he has represented them.

There is another sort of imaginary beings, that we sometimes meet with among the poets, when the author represents any passion, appetite, virtue or vice, under a visible shape, and makes it a person or an actor in his poem. Of this nature are the descriptions of Hunger and Envy in Ovid, of Fame in Virgil, and of Sin and Death in Milton. We find a whole creation of the like shadowy persons in

---

Ovid: *Metamorphoses*, 2. 768–82.   *Virgil*: *Aeneid*, 4. 173–88.
Milton: Cf. No. 357 (pp. 155–7), where Addison criticizes particularly these 'extended allegories'.

Spenser, who had an admirable talent in representations of this kind. I have discoursed of these emblematical persons in former papers, and shall therefore only mention them in this place. Thus we see how many ways poetry addresses itself to the imagination, as it has not only the whole circle of Nature for its province, but makes new worlds of its own, shows us persons who are not to be found in being, and represents even the faculties of the soul, with her several virtues and vices, in a sensible shape and character.

I shall, in my two following papers, consider in general, how other kinds of writing are qualified to please the imagination, with which I intend to conclude this essay.

420   *Wednesday July 2 1712*

. . . Quocunque volunt mentem auditoris agunto.   Hor.

As the writers in poetry and fiction borrow their several materials from outward objects, and join them together at their own pleasure, there are others who are obliged to follow Nature more closely, and to take entire scenes out of her. Such are historians, natural philosophers, travellers, geographers, and, in a word, all who describe visible objects of a real existence.

It is the most agreeable talent of an historian, to be able to draw up his armies and fight his battles in proper expressions, to set before our eyes the divisions, cabals, and jealousies of great men, and to lead us step by step into the several actions and events of his history. We love to see the subject unfolding itself by just degrees, and breaking upon us insensibly, that so we may be kept in a pleasing suspense, and have time given us to raise our expectations, and to side with one of the parties concerned in the relation. I confess this shows more the art than the veracity of the historian, but I am only to speak of him as he is qualified to please the imagination. And in this respect Livy has, perhaps, excelled all who ever went before him, or have written since his time.[n] He describes everything in so lively a manner, that his whole history is an admirable picture, and touches

Spenser: in No. 297 (p. 85), Addison had coupled Spenser with Ariosto as a
   writer of allegories, contrasting them with Homer and Virgil.

Motto: Horace, *Ars poetica*, 100 (altered):
     And raise men's passions to what height they will.   ROSCOMMON

on such proper circumstances in every story, that his reader becomes a kind of spectator, and feels in himself all the variety of passions, which are correspondent to the several parts of the relation.

But among this set of writers, there are none who more gratify and enlarge the imagination, than the authors of the new philosophy, whether we consider their theories of the earth or heavens, the discoveries they have made by glasses, or any other of their contemplations on Nature. We are not a little pleased to find every green leaf swarm with millions of animals, that at their largest growth are not visible to the naked eye. There is something very engaging to the fancy, as well as to our reason, in the treatises of metals, minerals, plants and meteors. But when we survey the whole earth at once, and the several planets that lie within its neighbourhood, we are filled with a pleasing astonishment, to see so many worlds hanging one above another, and sliding round their axles in such an amazing pomp and solemnity. If, after this, we contemplate those wide fields of ether, that reach in height as far as from Saturn to the fixed stars, and run abroad almost to an infinitude, our imagination finds its capacity filled with so immense a prospect, and puts itself upon the stretch to comprehend it. But if we yet rise higher, and consider the fixed stars as so many vast oceans of flame, that are each of them attended with a different set of planets, and still discover new firmaments, and new lights, that are sunk farther in those unfathomable depths of ether, so as not to be seen by the strongest of our telescopes, we are lost in such a labyrinth of suns and worlds, and confounded with the immensity and magnificence of Nature.

Nothing is more pleasant to the fancy, than to enlarge itself, by degrees, in its contemplation of the various proportions which its several objects bear to each other, when it compares the body of man to the bulk of the whole earth, the earth to the circle it describes round the sun, that circle to the sphere of the fixed stars, the sphere of the fixed stars to the circuit of the whole Creation, the whole Creation itself to the infinite space that is everywhere diffused about it; or when the imagination works downward, and considers the bulk of a human body, in respect of an animal, a hundred times less than a mite, the particular limbs of such an animal, the different springs which actuate the limbs, the spirits which set these springs a-going, and the proportionable minuteness of these several parts, before they have arrived at their full growth and perfection. But if, after all this, we take the least particle of these animal spirits, and consider its capacity of being wrought into a world, that shall contain within those narrow dimensions a heaven and earth, stars and planets, and every different species of living creatures, in the same analogy and proportion they bear to each other in our own universe; such a speculation, by reason of its nicety, appears ridiculous to those who have not turned their thoughts that way, though, at the same time, it is founded on no less than the evidence of a demonstration. Nay, we might yet carry it farther, and discover in the smallest particle of this little world, a new inexhausted fund of matter, capable of being spun out into another universe.

I have dwelt the longer on this subject, because I think it may show us the proper limits, as well as the defectiveness, of our imagination; how it is confined to a very small quantity of space, and immediately stopped in its operations, when it endeavours to take in anything that is very great, or very little. Let a man try to conceive the different bulk of an animal, which is twenty, from another which is a hundred times less than a mite, or to compare, in his thoughts, a length of a thousand diameters of the earth, with that of a million, and he will quickly find that he has no different measures in his mind, adjusted to such extraordinary degrees of grandeur or minuteness. The understanding, indeed, opens an infinite space on every side of us, but the imagination, after a few faint efforts, is immediately at a stand,[n] and finds herself swallowed up in the immensity of the void that surrounds it: our reason can pursue a particle of matter through an infinite variety of divisions, but the fancy soon loses sight of it, and feels in itself a kind of chasm, that wants to be filled with matter of a more sensible bulk. We can neither widen nor contract the faculty to the dimensions of either extreme: the object is too big for our capacity, when we would comprehend the circumference of a world, and dwindles into nothing, when we endeavour after the idea of an atom.

It is possible this defect of imagination may not be in the soul itself, but as it acts in conjunction with the body. Perhaps there may not be room in the brain for such a variety of impressions, or the animal spirits may be incapable of figuring them in such a manner, as is necessary to excite so very large or very minute ideas. However it be, we may well suppose that beings of a higher nature very much excel us in this respect, as it is probable the soul of man will be infinitely more perfect hereafter in this faculty, as well as in all the rest; insomuch that, perhaps, the imagination will be able to keep pace with the understanding, and to form in itself distinct ideas of all the different modes and quantities of space.

421   *Thursday July 3 1712*

Ignotis errare locis, ignota videre
flumina gaudebat; studio minuente laborem.   Ov.

The pleasures of the imagination are not wholly confined to such particular authors as are conversant in material objects, but are often to be met with among the polite masters of morality, criticism, and other speculations abstracted from matter; who, though they do not directly treat of the visible parts of nature, often draw from them their similitudes, metaphors, and allegories. By these allusions a truth in the understanding is as it were reflected by the imagination; we are able to see something like colour and shape in a notion, and to discover a scheme of thoughts traced out upon matter. And here the mind receives a great deal of satisfaction, and has two of its faculties gratified at the same time, while the fancy is busy in copying after the understanding, and transcribing ideas out of the intellectual world into the material.

The great art of a writer shows itself in the choice of pleasing allusions, which are generally to be taken from the *great* or *beautiful* works of Art or Nature; for though whatever is new or uncommon is apt to delight the imagination, the chief design of an allusion being to illustrate and explain the passages of an author, it should be always borrowed from what is more known and common, than the passages which are to be explained.

Allegories, when well chosen, are like so many tracks of light in a discourse, that make everything about them clear and beautiful. A noble metaphor, when it is placed to an advantage, casts a kind of glory round it, and darts a lustre through a whole sentence: these different kinds of allusion are but so many different manners of similitude, and, that they may please the imagination, the likeness ought to be very exact, or very agreeable, as we love to see a picture where the resemblance is just, or the posture and air graceful. But we often find eminent writers very faulty in this respect; great scholars are apt to fetch their comparisons and allusions from the sciences in which they are most conversant, so that a man may see the compass of their learning in a treatise on the most indifferent subject. I have read a discourse upon love, which none but a profound chemist could understand, and have heard many a sermon

Motto: Ovid, *Metamorphoses*, 4. 294–5:

He sought fresh fountains in a foreign soil;
The pleasure lessened the attending toil.   BROUGHTON

that should only have been preached before a congregation of Cartesians. On the contrary, your men of business usually have recourse to such instances as are too mean and familiar. They are for drawing the reader into a game of chess or tennis, or for leading him from shop to shop, in the cant of particular trades and employments. It is certain, there may be found an infinite variety of very agreeable allusions in both these kinds, but, for the generality, the most entertaining ones lie in the works of Nature, which are obvious to all capacities, and more delightful than what is to be found in arts and sciences.

It is this talent of affecting the imagination, that gives an embellishment to good sense, and makes one man's compositions more agreeable than another's. It sets off all writings in general, but is the very life and highest perfection of poetry. Where it shines in an eminent degree, it has preserved several poems for many ages, that have nothing else to recommend them; and where all the other beauties are present, the work appears dry and insipid, if this single one be wanting. It has something in it like creation; it bestows a kind of existence, and draws up to the reader's view, several objects which are not to be found in being. It makes additions to nature, and gives a greater variety to God's works. In a word, it is able to beautify and adorn the most illustrious scenes in the universe, or to fill the mind with more glorious shows and apparitions, than can be found in any part of it.

We have now discovered the several originals of those pleasures that gratify the fancy; and here, perhaps, it would not be very difficult to cast under their proper heads those contrary objects, which are apt to fill it with distaste and terror; for the imagination is as liable to pain as pleasure. When the brain is hurt by any accident, or the mind disordered by dreams or sickness, the fancy is overrun with wild dismal ideas, and terrified with a thousand hideous monsters of its own framing.

> Eumenidum veluti demens videt agmina Pentheus,
> et solem geminum, et duplices se ostendere Thebas.
> Aut Agamemnonius scenis agitatus Orestes,
> armatam facibus matrem et serpentibus atris
> cum videt, ultricesque sedent in limine Dirae.   VIR.[n]

There is not a sight in nature so mortifying as that of a distracted person, when his imagination is troubled, and his whole soul disordered and confused. Babylon in ruins is not so melancholy a

---

employments: cf. No. 297 (p. 88), for criticism of the use of 'terms of art' in poetry.

spectacle. But to quit so disagreeable a subject, I shall only consider, by way of conclusion, what an infinite advantage this faculty gives an Almighty Being over the soul of man, and how great a measure of happiness or misery we are capable of receiving from the imagination only.

We have already seen the influence that one man has over the fancy of another, and with what ease he conveys into it a variety of imagery; how great a power then may we suppose lodged in him, who knows all the ways of affecting the imagination, who can infuse what ideas he pleases, and fill those ideas with terror and delight to what degree he thinks fit? He can excite images in the mind, without the help of words, and make scenes rise up before us and seem present to the eye, without the assistance of bodies or exterior objects. He can transport the imagination with such beautiful and glorious visions, as cannot possibly enter into our present conceptions, or haunt it with such ghastly spectres and apparitions, as would make us hope for annihilation, and think existence no better than a curse. In short, he can so exquisitely ravish or torture the soul through this single faculty, as might suffice to make up the whole heaven or hell of any finite being.

This essay on the pleasures of the imagination having been published in separate papers, I shall conclude it with a table of the principal contents in each paper.

THE CONTENTS

PAPER I

The perfection of our sight above our other senses. The pleasures of the imagination arise originally from sight. The pleasures of the imagination divided under two heads. The pleasures of the imagination in some respects equal to those of the understanding. The extent of the pleasures of the imagination. The advantages a man receives from a relish of these pleasures. In what respect they are preferable to those of the understanding.

PAPER II

Three sources of all the pleasures of the imagination, in our survey of outward objects. How what is great pleases the imagination. How what is new pleases the imagination. How what is beautiful, in our own species, pleases the imagination. How what is beautiful in general pleases the imagination. What other accidental causes may contribute to the heightening of these pleasures.

PAPER III

Why the necessary cause of our being pleased with what is great, new or beautiful, unknown. Why the final cause more known and more useful. The final cause of our being pleased with what is great. The final cause of our being pleased with what is new. The final cause of our being pleased with what is beautiful in our own species. The final cause of our being pleased with what is beautiful in general.

PAPER IV

The works of Nature more pleasant to the imagination than those of art. The works of Nature still more pleasant, the more they resemble those of art. The works of art more pleasant, the more they resemble those of Nature. Our English plantations and gardens considered in the foregoing light.

PAPER V

Of architecture as it affects the imagination. Greatness in architecture relates either to the bulk or to the manner. Greatness of bulk in the ancient Oriental buildings. The ancient accounts of these buildings confirmed, 1. From the advantages, for raising such works, in the first ages of the world and in the eastern climates: 2. From several of them which are still extant. Instances how greatness of manner affects the imagination. A French author's observations on this subject. Why concave and convex figures give a greatness of manner to works of architecture. Everything that pleases the imagination in architecture is either great, beautiful or new.

PAPER VI

The secondary pleasures of the imagination. The several sources of these pleasures (statuary, painting, description and music) compared together. The final cause of our receiving pleasure from these several sources. Of descriptions in particular. The power of words over the imagination. Why one reader more pleased with descriptions than another.

PAPER VII

How a whole set of ideas hang together, etc. A natural cause assigned for it. How to perfect the imagination of a writer. Who among the ancient poets had this faculty in its greatest perfection. Homer excelled in imagining what is great; Virgil in imagining what is beautiful; Ovid in imagining what is new. Our own countryman Milton, very perfect in all three respects.

PAPER VIII

Why anything that is unpleasant to behold, pleases the imagination when well described. Why the imagination receives a more exquisite pleasure from the description of what is great, new, or beautiful. This pleasure still heightened, if what is described raises passion in the mind. Disagreeable passions pleasing when raised by apt descriptions. Why terror and grief are pleasing to the mind, when excited by descriptions. A particular advantage the writers in poetry and fiction have to please the imagination. What liberties are allowed them.

PAPER IX

Of that kind of poetry which Mr. Dryden calls the fairy way of writing. How a poet should be qualified for it. The pleasures of the imagination that arise from it. In this respect, why the Moderns excel the Ancients. Why the English excel the Moderns. Who the best among the English. Of emblematical persons.

PAPER X

What authors please the imagination who have nothing to do with fiction. How history pleases the imagination. How the authors of the new philosophy please the imagination. The bounds and defects of the imagination. Whether these defects are essential to the imagination.

PAPER XI

How those please the imagination who treat of subjects abstracted from matter, by allusions taken from it. What allusions most pleasing to the imagination. Great writers how faulty in this respect. Of the art of imagining in general. The imagination capable of pain as well as pleasure. In what degree the imagination is capable either of pain or pleasure.

Drama

ENGLISH TRAGEDY

Multa fero, ut placem genus irritabile vatum,
cum scribo . . . . Hor.

As a perfect tragedy[n] is the noblest production of human nature, so it is capable of giving the mind one of the most delightful and most improving entertainments. A virtuous man (says Seneca) struggling with misfortunes, is such a spectacle as gods might look upon with pleasure: and such a pleasure it is which one meets with in the representation of a well-written tragedy. Diversions of this kind wear out of our thoughts everything that is mean and little. They cherish and cultivate that humanity which is the ornament of our nature. They soften insolence, soothe affliction, and subdue the mind to the dispensations of Providence.

It is no wonder therefore that in all the polite nations of the world, this part of the drama has met with public encouragement.

The modern tragedy excels that of Greece and Rome, in the intricacy and disposition of the fable; but, what a Christian writer would be ashamed to own, falls infinitely short of it in the moral part of the performance.

This I may show more at large hereafter; and in the meantime, that I may contribute something towards the improvement of the English tragedy, I shall take notice, in this and in other following papers, of some particular parts in it that seem liable to exception.

Aristotle observes,[n] that the iambic verse in the Greek tongue was the most proper for tragedy: because at the same time that it lifted up the discourse from prose, it was that which approached nearer to it than any other kind of verse. For, says he, we may observe that men in ordinary discourse very often speak iambics, without taking notice of it. We may make the same observation of our English blank verse,[n] which often enters into our common discourse, though we do not attend to it, and is such a due medium between rhyme and

Motto: Horace, *Epistles*, 2. 2. 102–3:

> A thousand things I suffer to assuage
> The waspish poets, and to cool their rage;
> Because I write myself. CREECH

Seneca: i.e. the younger Seneca, 'Seneca the Philosopher' (c. 4 B.C.–A.D. 65), the Roman Stoic philosopher, author of moral treatises and dialogues, and tragedies. *De Providentia*. 2.8.9.

prose, that it seems wonderfully adapted to tragedy. I am therefore very much offended when I see a play in rhyme, which is as absurd in English, as a tragedy of hexameters would have been in Greek or Latin. The solecism is, I think, still greater, in those plays that have some scenes in rhyme and some in blank verse, which are to be looked upon as two several languages; or where we see some particular similes dignified with rhyme, at the same time that everything about them lies in blank verse. I would not however debar the poet from concluding his tragedy, or, if he pleases, every act of it, with two or three couplets, which may have the same effect as an air in the Italian opera after a long recitativo, and give the actor a graceful exit. Besides that we see a diversity of numbers in some parts of the old tragedy, in order to hinder the ear from being tired with the same continued modulation of voice. For the same reason I do not dislike the speeches in our English tragedy that close with an hemistich, or half verse, notwithstanding the person who speaks after it begins a new verse, without filling up the preceding one; nor with abrupt pauses and breakings-off in the middle of a verse, when they humour any passion that is expressed by it.

Since I am upon this subject, I must observe that our English poets have succeeded much better in the style, than in the sentiments of their tragedies. Their language is very often noble and sonorous, but the sense either very trifling or very common. On the contrary, in the ancient tragedies, and indeed in those of Corneille and Racine,[n] though the expressions are very great, it is the thought that bears them up and swells them. For my own part, I prefer a noble sentiment that is depressed with homely language, infinitely before a vulgar one that is blown up with all the sound and energy of expression. Whether this defect in our tragedies may arise from want of genius, knowledge, or experience in the writers, or from their compliance with the vicious taste of their readers, who are better judges of the language than of the sentiments, and consequently relish the one more than the other, I cannot determine. But I believe it might rectify the conduct both of the one and of the other, if the writer laid down the whole contexture of his dialogue in plain English, before he turned it into blank verse; and if the reader, after the perusal of a scene, would consider the naked thought of every speech in it, when divested of all its tragic ornaments; by this means, without being imposed upon by words, we may judge impartially of the thought, and consider whether it be natural or great enough for the person that utters it, whether it deserves to shine in such a blaze of eloquence, or show itself in such a variety of lights as are generally made use of by the writers of our English tragedy.

I must in the next place observe, that when our thoughts are great and just, they are often obscured by the sounding phrases, hard metaphors,[n] and forced expressions in which they are clothed. Shakespeare is often very faulty in this particular. There is a fine observation in Aristotle[n] to this purpose, which I have never seen quoted. The expression, says he, ought to be very much laboured in the unactive parts of the fable, as in descriptions, similitudes, narrations, and the like; in which the opinions, manners and passions of men are not represented; for these (namely the opinions, manners and passions) are apt to be obscured by pompous phrases, and elaborate expressions. Horace, who copied most of his criticisms after Aristotle, seems to have had his eye on the foregoing rule, in the following verses:

> Et tragicus plerumque dolet sermone pedestri,
> Telephus et Peleus, cum pauper et exul uterque,
> projicit ampullas et sesquipedalia verba,
> si curat cor spectantis tetigisse querela.

> Tragedians too lay by their state, to grieve.
> Peleus and Telephus, exiled and poor,
> Forget their swelling and gigantic words.

LD. ROSCOMMON

Among our modern English poets, there is none who was better turned for tragedy than Lee; if instead of favouring the impetuosity of his genius, he had restrained it, and kept it within its proper bounds. His thoughts are wonderfully suited to tragedy, but frequently lost in such a cloud of words, that it is hard to see the beauty of them: there is an infinite fire in his works, but so involved in smoke, that it does not appear in half its lustre. He frequently succeeds in the passionate parts of the tragedy, but more particularly where he slackens his efforts, and eases the style of those epithets and metaphors, in which he so much abounds. What can be more natural, more soft, or more passionate, than that line in Statira's

---

Et tragicus plerumque: *Ars poetica*, 95–8.

Peleus and Telephus: subjects of tragedies by Sophocles and Euripides. 'These two princes having been driven out of their dominions, came to beg assistance in Greece, and went up and down dressed like beggars.' (Roscommon's note.)

Roscommon: Wentworth Dillon, 4th Earl of Roscommon (*c.* 1633–85). His translation of Horace's *Ars Poetica* was published in 1680.

Lee: Nathaniel Lee (*c.* 1649–92), one of the most influential writers of tragedy in his day, and at this time commonly ranked with Dryden.

Statira: *The Rival Queens*, I. i: Then he will talk, good gods how he will talk!

speech, where she describes the charms of Alexander's conversation?

Then he would talk, good gods! How he would talk!

That unexpected break in the line, and turning the description of his manner of talking into an admiration of it, is inexpressibly beautiful, and wonderfully suited to the fond character of the person that speaks it. There is a simplicity in the words, that outshines the utmost pride of expression.

Otway[n] has followed nature in the language of his tragedy, and therefore shines in the passionate parts, more than any of our English poets. As there is something familiar and domestic in the fable of his tragedy, more than in those of any other poet, he has little pomp, but great force in his expressions. For which reason, though he has admirably succeeded in the tender and melting part of his tragedies, he sometimes falls into too great a familiarity of phrase in those parts, which, by Aristotle's rule, ought to have been raised and supported by the dignity of expression.

It has been observed by others, that this poet has founded his tragedy of *Venice Preserved*[n] on so wrong a plot, that the greatest characters in it are those of rebels and traitors. Had the hero of his play discovered the same good qualities in the defence of his country, that he showed for its ruin and subversion, the audience could not enough pity and admire him: but as he is now represented we can only say of him, what the Roman historian says of Catiline, that his fall would have been glorious (si pro patria sic concidisset) had he so fallen in the service of his country.

40   *Monday, April* 16, 1711

Ac ne forte putes me, quae facere ipse recusem,
cum recte tractent alii, laudare maligne;
ille per extentum funem mihi posse videtur
ire poeta, meum qui pectus inaniter angit,
irritat, mulcet, falsis terroribus implet,
ut magus, et modo me Thebis, modo ponit Athenis.   Hor.

The English writers of tragedy are possessed with a notion, that when they represent a virtuous or innocent person in distress, they

the Roman historian: Lucius Annaeus Florus, *Epitome*, 2. 12.
Motto: Horace, *Epistles*, 2. 1. 208–13: But lest I may seem unwilling to praise others who are doing well what I refuse to attempt, that poet seems to me to be able to walk a tight rope, who with imagined woes can move me to pity, anger, or imaginary fears, like a magician, and bear my spirit to Thebes or Athens, and fix it there.

ought not to leave him till they have delivered him out of his
troubles, or made him triumph over his enemies. This error they
have been led into by a ridiculous doctrine in modern criticism, that
they are obliged to an equal distribution of rewards and punishments,
and an impartial execution of poetical justice. Who were the first that
established this rule I know not; but I am sure it has no foundation
in nature, in reason, or in the practice of the Ancients. We find that
good and evil happen alike to all men on this side the grave; and as
the principal design of tragedy is to raise commiseration and terror
in the minds of the audience, we shall defeat this great end, if we
always make virtue and innocence happy and successful. Whatever
crosses and disappointments a good man suffers in the body of the
tragedy, they will make but small impression on our minds, when
we know that in the last act he is to arrive at the end of his wishes and
desires. When we see him engaged in the depth of his afflictions, we
are apt to comfort ourselves, because we are sure he will find his
way out of them; and that his grief, how great soever it may be at
present, will soon terminate in gladness. For this reason the ancient
writers of tragedy treated men in their plays, as they are dealt with in
the world, by making virtue sometimes happy and sometimes
miserable, as they found it in the fable which they made choice of, or
as it might affect their audience in the most agreeable manner.
Aristotle considers the tragedies that were written in either of these
kinds, and observes, that those which ended unhappily, had always
pleased the people, and carried away the prize in the public disputes
of the stage, from those that ended happily. Terror and commiseration leave a pleasing anguish in the mind; and fix the audience
in such a serious composure of thought, as is much more lasting and
delightful than any little transient starts of joy and satisfaction.
Accordingly we find, that more of our English tragedies have
succeeded, in which the favourites of the audience sink under their
calamities, than those in which they recover themselves out of them.
The best plays of this kind are *The Orphan, Venice Preserved,
Alexander the Great, Theodosius, All for Love, Oedipus, Oroonoko,
Othello*, etc.[n] *King Lear* is an admirable tragedy of the same kind, as
Shakespeare wrote it; but as it is reformed according to the chimerical
notion of poetical justice, in my humble opinion it has lost half its
beauty.[n] At the same time I must allow, that there are very noble
tragedies which have been framed upon the other plan, and have
ended happily; as indeed most of the good tragedies, which have
been written since the starting of the above-mentioned criticism,
have taken this turn: as *The Mourning Bride*,[n] *Tamerlane, Ulysses,*

Aristotle: Poetics 13. 4–6.

Phaedra and Hippolitus, with most of Mr. Dryden's. I must also allow, that many of Shakespeare's, and several of the celebrated tragedies of antiquity, are cast in the same form. I do not therefore dispute against this way of writing tragedies, but against the criticism that would establish this as the only method; and by that means would very much cramp the English tragedy, and perhaps give a wrong bent to the genius of our writers.

The tragicomedy,[n] which is the product of the English theatre, is one of the most monstrous inventions that ever entered into a poet's thoughts. An author might as well think of weaving the adventures of Aeneas and Hudibras into one poem, as of writing such a motley piece of mirth and sorrow. But the absurdity of these performances is so very visible, that I shall not insist upon it.

The same objections which are made to tragicomedy, may in some measure be applied to all tragedies that have a double plot in them; which are likewise more frequent upon the English stage, than upon any other: for though the grief of the audience, in such performances, be not changed into another passion, as in tragi-comedies; it is diverted upon another object, which weakens their concern for the principal action, and breaks the tide of sorrow, by throwing it into different channels. This inconvenience, however, may in a great measure be cured, if not wholly removed, by the skilful choice of an underplot, which may bear such a near relation to the principal design, as to contribute towards the completion of it, and be concluded by the same catastrophe.[n]

There is also another particular, which may be reckoned among the blemishes, or rather the false beauties, of our English tragedy: I mean those particular speeches, which are commonly known by the name of rants.[n] The warm and passionate parts of a tragedy, are always the most taking with the audience; for which reason we often see the players pronouncing, in all the violence of action, several parts of the tragedy which the author writ with great temper, and designed that they should have been so acted. I have seen Powell[n] very often raise himself a loud clap by this artifice. The poets that were acquainted with this secret, have given frequent occasion for such emotions in the actor, by adding vehemence to words where there was no passion, or inflaming a real passion into fustian. This hath filled the mouths of our heroes with bombast; and given them such sentiments, as proceed rather from a swelling than a greatness of mind. Unnatural exclamations, curses, vows, blasphemies, a defiance of mankind, and an outraging of the gods, frequently pass upon the audience for towering thoughts, and have accordingly met with infinite applause.

I shall here add a remark, which I am afraid our tragic writers may make an ill use of. As our heroes are generally lovers, their swelling and blustering upon the stage very much recommends them to the fair part of their audience. The ladies are wonderfully pleased to see a man insulting kings, or affronting the gods, in one scene, and throwing himself at the feet of his mistress in another. Let him behave himself insolently towards the men, and abjectly towards the fair one, and it is ten to one but he proves a favourite of the boxes. Dryden and Lee, in several of their tragedies, have practised this secret with good success.

But to show how a rant pleases beyond the most just and natural thought that is not pronounced with vehemence, I would desire the reader, when he sees the tragedy of *Oedipus*,[n] to observe how quietly the hero is dismissed at the end of the third act, after having pronounced the following lines, in which the thought is very natural, and apt to move compassion.

> To you, good gods, I make my last appeal,
> Or clear my virtues, or my crimes reveal.
> If in the maze of Fate I blindly run,
> And backward trod those paths I sought to shun;
> Impute my errors to your own decree,
> My hands are guilty, but my heart is free.

Let us then observe with what thunder-claps of applause he leaves the stage, after the impieties and execrations at the end of the fourth act; and you will wonder to see an audience so cursed and so pleased at the same time.

> O that as oft I have at Athens seen,
> [Where, by the way, there was no stage till many
>   years after Oedipus.]
> The stage arise, and the big clouds descend;
> So now, in very deed, I might behold,
> This ponderous globe, and all yon marble roof,
> Meet, like the hands of Jove, and crush mankind.
> For all elements, etc.

ADVERTISEMENT

Having spoken of Mr. Powell, as sometimes raising himself applause from the ill taste of an audience; I must do him the justice to own, that he is excellently formed for a tragedian, and, when he pleases, deserves the admiration of the best judges; as I doubt not but he will in the *Conquest of Mexico*, which is acted for his own benefit tomorrow night.[n]

42 *Wednesday April 18 1711*

Garganum mugire putes nemus aut mare Thuscum,
tanto cum strepitu ludi spectantur, et artes,
divitiaeque peregrinae; quibus oblitus actor
cum stetit in scena, concurrit dextera laevae.
Dixit adhuc aliquid? Nil sane. Quid placet ergo?
Lana Tarentino violas imitata veneno. Hor.

Aristotle has observed, that ordinary writers in tragedy endeavour to raise terror and pity in their audience, not by proper sentiments and expressions, but by the dresses and decorations of the stage. There is something of this kind very ridiculous in the English theatre. When the author has a mind to terrify us, it thunders; when he would make us melancholy, the stage is darkened. But among all our tragic artifices, I am the most offended at those which are made use of to inspire us with magnificent ideas of the persons that speak. The ordinary method of making an hero, is to clap a huge plume of feathers upon his head, which rises so very high, that there is often a greater length from his chin to the top of his head, than to the sole of his foot.[n] One would believe, that we thought a great man and a tall man the same thing. This very much embarrasses the actor, who is forced to hold his neck extremely stiff and steady all the while he speaks; and notwithstanding any anxieties which he pretends for his mistress, his country, or his friends, one may see by his action, that his greatest care and concern is to keep the plume of feathers from falling off his head. For my own part, when I see a man uttering his complaints under such a mountain of feathers, I am apt to look upon him rather as an unfortunate lunatic, than a distressed hero. As these superfluous ornaments upon the head make a great man, a princess generally receives her grandeur from those additional incumbrances that fall into her tail: I mean the broad sweeping train that follows her in all her motions, and finds constant employment for a boy who stands behind her to open and spread it to advantage. I do not know how others are affected at this sight, but, I must confess, my

Motto: Horace, *Epistles*, 2. 1. 202–7:
> As when the winds dash waves against the shore,
> Or lash the woods, and all the monsters roar;
> So great the shout when rich and strangely drest,
> The player comes, they clap his gaudy vest.
> Well hath the actor spoken? *Not a line*:
> Why then d'ye clap? *Oh, sir, his clothes are fine.* CREECH

eyes are wholly taken up with the page's part; and as for the queen, I am not so attentive to anything she speaks, as to the right adjusting of her train, lest it should chance to trip up her heels, or incommode her, as she walks to and fro upon the stage. It is, in my opinion, a very odd spectacle, to see a queen venting her passion in a disordered motion, and a little boy taking care all the while that they do not ruffle the tail of her gown. The parts that the two persons act on the stage at the same time, are very different: the princess is afraid lest she should incur the displeasure of the king her father, or lose the hero her lover, whilst her attendant is only concerned lest she should entangle her feet in her petticoat.

We are told, that an ancient tragic poet,[n] to move the pity of his audience for his exiled kings and distressed heroes, used to make the actors represent them in dresses and clothes that were threadbare and decayed. This artifice for moving pity, seems as ill contrived, as that we have been speaking of to inspire us with a great idea of the persons introduced upon the stage. In short, I would have our conceptions raised by the dignity of thought and sublimity of expression, rather than by a train of robes or a plume of feathers.

Another mechanical method of making great men, and adding dignity to kings and queens, is to accompany them with halberts and battle-axes.[n] Two or three shifters of scenes, with the two candle-snuffers, make up a complete body of guards upon the English stage; and by the addition of a few porters dressed in red coats, can represent above a dozen legions.[n] I have sometimes seen a couple of armies drawn up together upon the stage, when the poet has been disposed to do honour to his generals. It is impossible for the reader's imagination to multiply twenty men into such prodigious multitudes, or to fancy that two or three hundred thousand soldiers are fighting in a room of forty or fifty yards in compass. Incidents of such nature should be told, not represented.

> ... Non tamen intus
> digna geri promes in scenam: multaque tolles
> ex oculis, quae mox narret facundia praesens.   HOR.

> Yet there are things improper for a scene,
> Which men of judgement only will relate.   L. ROSCOMMON

I should therefore, in this particular, recommend to my country-men the example of the French stage, where the kings and queens always appear unattended, and leave their guards behind the scenes. I should likewise be glad if we imitated the French in banishing from our stage the noise of drums, trumpets, and huzzas; which is sometimes so very great, that when there is a battle in the Haymarket Theatre,[n] one may hear it as far as Charing-Cross.

I have here only touched upon those particulars which are made use of to raise and aggrandize the persons of a tragedy; and shall show in another paper the several expedients which are practised by authors of a vulgar genius to move terror, pity, or admiration, in their hearers.

The tailor and the painter often contribute to the success of a tragedy more than the poet. Scenes affect ordinary minds as much as speeches; and our actors are very sensible, that a well-dressed play has sometimes brought them as full audiences, as a well-written one. The Italians have a very good phrase to express this art of imposing upon the spectators by appearances: they call it the *fourberia della scena*, the knavery or trickish part of the drama. But however the show and outside of the tragedy may work upon the vulgar, the more understanding part of the audience immediately see through it and despise it.

A good poet will give the reader a more lively idea of an army or a battle in a description, than if he actually saw them drawn up in squadrons and batallions, or engaged in the confusion of a fight. Our minds should be opened to great conceptions and inflamed with glorious sentiments by what the actor speaks, more than by what he appears. Can all the trappings or equipage of a king or hero, give Brutus half that pomp and majesty which he receives from a few lines in Shakespeare?

44   *Friday April 20 1711*

Tu quid ego et populus mecum desideret audi.   Hor.

Among the several artifices which are put in practice by the poets to fill the minds of an audience with terror, the first place is due to thunder and lightning, which are often made use of at the descending of a god or the rising of a ghost, at the vanishing of a devil, or at the death of a tyrant.[n] I have known a bell introduced into several tragedies with good effect; and have seen the whole assembly in a very great alarm all the while it has been ringing.[n] But there is

Motto: Horace, *Ars poetica*, 153: Now hear what every auditor expects.
ROSCOMMON

nothing which delights and terrifies our English theatre so much as a ghost, especially when he appears in a bloody shirt. A spectre has very often saved a play, though he has done nothing but stalked across the stage, or rose through a cleft of it, and sunk again without speaking one word. There may be a proper season for these several terrors; and when they only come in as aids and assistances to the poet, they are not only to be excused, but to be applauded. Thus the sounding of the clock in *Venice Preserved*,[n] makes the hearts of the whole audience quake; and conveys a stronger terror to the mind, than it is possible for words to do. The appearance of the ghost in *Hamlet* is a masterpiece in its kind, and wrought up with all the circumstances that can create either attention or horror. The mind of the reader is wonderfully prepared for his reception by the discourses that precede it: his dumb behaviour at his first entrance, strikes the imagination very strongly; but every time he enters, he is still more terrifying. Who can read the speech with which young Hamlet accosts him, without trembling?

> *Hor.*   Look, my lord, it comes.
> *Ham.*   Angels and ministers of grace defend us.
> Be thou a spirit of health, or goblin damned;
> Bring with thee airs from Heaven, or blasts from Hell;
> Be thy events wicked or charitable;
> Thou com'st in such a questionable shape
> That I will speak to thee. I'll call thee Hamlet,
> King, Father, Royal Dane: Oh! Oh! Answer me,
> Let me not burst in ignorance; but tell
> Why thy canonized bones, hearsed in death,
> Have burst their cerements? Why the sepulchre
> Wherein we saw thee quietly inurned,
> Hath oped his ponderous and marble jaws
> To cast thee up again? What may this mean?
> That thou dead corse again in complete steel,
> Revisit'st thus the glimpses of the moon,
> Making night hideous?

I do not therefore find fault with the artifices above-mentioned when they are introduced with skill, and accompanied by proportionable sentiments and expressions in the writing.

For the moving of pity, our principal machine is the handkerchief; and indeed in our common tragedies, we should not know very often that the persons are in distress by anything they say, if they did not from time to time apply their handkerchiefs to their eyes. Far be it from me to think of banishing this instrument of sorrow from the stage; I know a tragedy could not subsist without it: all that I would

Hamlet, I. iv. 38–54.

contend for, is, to keep it from being misapplied. In a word, I would have the actor's tongue sympathize with his eyes.

A disconsolate mother with a child in her hand, has frequently drawn compassion from the audience, and has therefore gained a place in several tragedies.[n] A modern writer that observed how this had took in other plays, being resolved to double the distress, and melt his audience twice as much as those before him had done, brought a princess upon the stage with a little boy in one hand and a girl in the other. This too had a very good effect. A third poet, being resolved to outwrite all his predecessors, a few years ago introduced three children, with great success: and as I am informed, a young gentleman who is fully determined to break the most obdurate hearts, has a tragedy by him, where the first person that appears upon the stage, is an afflicted widow in her mourning-weeds, with half a dozen fatherless children attending her, like those that usually hang about the figure of Charity. Thus several incidents that are beautiful in a good writer, become ridiculous by falling into the hands of a bad one.

But among all our methods of moving pity or terror, there is none so absurd and barbarous, and what more exposes us to the contempt and ridicule of our neighbours, than that dreadful butchering of one another which is so very frequent upon the English stage. To delight in seeing men stabbed, poisoned, racked, or impaled, is certainly the sign of a cruel temper: and as this is often practised before the British audience, several French critics, who think these are grateful spectacles to us, take occasion from them to represent us as a people that delight in blood.[n] It is indeed very odd, to see our stage strewed with carcasses in the last scene of a tragedy; and to observe in the wardrobe of the playhouse several daggers, poniards, wheels, bowls for poison, and many other instruments of death. Murders and executions are always transacted behind the scenes in the French theatre; which in general is very agreeable to the manners of a polite and civilized people: but as there are no exceptions to this rule on the French stage, it leads them into absurdities almost as ridiculous as that which falls under our present censure. I remember in the famous play of Corneille, written upon the subject of the Horatii and Curiatii; the fierce young hero who had overcome the Curiatii one after another, (instead of being congratulated by his sister for his victory, being upbraided by her for having slain her lover) in the height of his passion and resentment kills her. If anything could

instruments: this recalls the 'Inventory' described in *Tatler* 42.
Corneille: *Horace* (1640). The incident occurs in Act IV, scene v.

extenuate so brutal an action, it would be the doing of it on a sudden, before the sentiments of nature, reason, or manhood could take place in him. However, to avoid public bloodshed, as soon as his passion is wrought to its height, he follows his sister the whole length of the stage, and forbears killing her till they are both withdrawn behind the scenes. I must confess, had he murdered her before the audience, the indecency might have been greater; but as it is, it appears very unnatural, and looks like killing in cold blood. To give my opinion upon this case; the fact ought not to have been represented, but to have been told if there was any occasion for it.

It may not be unacceptable to the reader, to see how Sophocles has conducted a tragedy under the like delicate circumstances. Orestes was in the same condition with Hamlet in Shakespeare, his mother having murdered his father, and taken possession of his kingdom in conspiracy with her adulterer. That young prince therefore, being determined to revenge his father's death upon those who filled his throne, conveys himself by a beautiful stratagem into his mother's apartment with a resolution to kill her. But because such a spectacle would have been too shocking to the audience, this dreadful resolution is executed behind the scenes: the mother is heard calling out to her son for mercy; and the son answering her, that she showed no mercy to his father: after which she shrieks out that she is wounded, and by what follows we find that she is slain. I don't remember that in any of our plays there are speeches made behind the scenes, though there are other instances of this nature to be met with in those of the Ancients: and I believe my reader will agree with me, that there is something infinitely more affecting in this dreadful dialogue between the mother and her son behind the scenes, than could have been in anything transacted before the audience. Orestes immediately after meets the usurper at the entrance of his palace; and by a very happy thought of the poet avoids killing him before the audience, by telling him that he should live some time in his present bitterness of soul before he would dispatch him, and by ordering him to retire into that part of the palace where he had slain his father, whose murder he would revenge in the very same place where it was committed.[n] By this means the poet observes that decency, which Horace afterwards established by a rule, of forbearing to commit parricides or unnatural murders before the audience.

> Nec coram populo natos Medea trucidet.

> Let not Medea draw her murdering knife,
> And spill her children's blood upon the stage;

Let not Medea: Horace, *Ars poetica*, 185.

The French have therefore refined too much upon Horace's rule, who never designed to banish all kinds of death from the stage, but only such as had too much horror in them, and which would have a better effect upon the audience when transacted behind the scenes. I would therefore recommend to my countrymen the practice of the ancient poets, who were very sparing of their public executions, and rather chose to perform them behind the scenes, if it could be done with as great an effect upon the audience. At the same time I must observe, that though the devoted persons of the tragedy were seldom slain before the audience, which has generally something ridiculous in it, their bodies were often produced after their death, which has always in it something melancholy or terrifying; so that the killing on the stage does not seem to have been avoided only as an indecency, but also as an improbability.[n]

> Nec pueros coram populo Medea trucidet;
> aut humana palam coquat exta nefarius Atreus;
> aut in avem Progne vertatur, Cadmus in anguem,
> quodcunque ostendis mihi sic, incredulus odi. HOR.

> Medea must not draw her murdering knife,
> Nor Atreus there his horrid feast prepare.
> Cadmus and Progne's metamorphosis,
> (She to a swallow turned, he to a snake,)
> And whatsoever contradicts my sense,
> I hate to see, and never can believe. L. ROSCOMMON

I have now gone through the several dramatic inventions which are made use of by the ignorant poets to supply the place of tragedy, and by the skilful to improve it; some of which I could wish entirely rejected, and the rest to be used with caution. It would be an endless task to consider comedy in the same light, and to mention the innumerable shifts that small wits put in practice to raise a laugh. Bullock in a short coat, and Norris in a long one, seldom fail of this effect.[n] In ordinary comedies, a broad and a narrow brimmed hat are different characters. Sometimes the wit of the scene lies in a shoulder belt, and sometimes in a pair of whiskers. A lover running about the stage, with his head peeping out of a barrel,[n] was thought a very good jest in King Charles the Second's time; and invented by one of the first wits of that age. But because ridicule is not so delicate as compassion, and because the objects that make us laugh are infinitely

Medea must not draw: in the play of Euripides.
Atreus: in Greek legend, murdered the children of his brother Thyestes and served them as a feast to their father.
Progne: see Ovid, *Metamorphoses*, 4. 576; 6. 668.

more numerous than those that make us weep, there is a much
greater latitude for comic than tragic artifices, and by consequence a
much greater indulgence to be allowed them.

548ⁿ   *Friday November 28 1712*

... Vitiis nemo sine nascitur, optimus ille
qui minimis urgetur .... Hor.

Mr. Spectator,   *Nov.* 27, 1712
'I have read this day's paper with a great deal of pleasure, and
could send you an account of several elixirs and antidotes in your
third volume, which your correspondents have not taken notice of
in their advertisements; and at the same time must own to you,
that I have seldom seen a shop furnished with such a variety of
medicaments, and in which there are fewer soporifics.ⁿ The several
vehicles you have invented for conveying your unacceptable truths
to us, are what I most particularly admire, as I am afraid they are
secrets which will die with you. I do not find that any of your critical
essays are taken notice of in this paper, notwithstanding I look upon
them to be excellent cleansers of the brain, and could venture to
superscribe them with an advertisement which I have lately seen in
one of our newspapers, wherein there is an account given of a
sovereign remedy for restoring the taste to all such persons whose
palates have been vitiated by distempers, unwholesome food, or any
the like occasions.ⁿ But to let fall the allusion, notwithstanding your
criticisms, and particularly the candour which you have discovered in
them, are not the least taking part of your works, I find your opinion
concerning Poetical Justice, as it is expressed in the first part of your
fortieth *Spectator*, is controverted by some eminent critics; and as
you now seem, to our great grief of heart, to be winding up your
bottoms, I hoped you would have enlarged a little upon that subject.
It is indeed but a single paragraph in your works, and I believe those

Motto: Horace, *Satires*, 1. 3. 68–9 (altered):
        There's none but hath some fault, and he's the best,
        Most virtuous he, that's spotted with the least. CREECH

critics: John Dennis is undoubtedly the chief of the 'eminent critics' referred to
    here.

winding up your bottoms: bottom is defined in *OED* as 'a clew or nucleus on
    which to wind thread; also a skein or ball of thread'.

who have read it with the same attention I have done, will think there is nothing to be objected against it. I have however drawn up some additional arguments to strengthen the opinion which you have there delivered, having endeavoured to go to the bottom of that matter, which you may either publish or suppress as you think fit.

'Horace in my motto says, that all men are vicious, and that they differ from one another, only as they are more or less so. Boileau has given the same account of our wisdom, as Horace has of our virtue.

> Tous les hommes sont fous et, malgré tous leurs soins,
> Ne diffèrent entre eux, que du plus et du moins.

All men, says he, are fools, and in spite of their endeavours to the contrary, differ from one another only as they are more or less so.

'Two or three of the old Greek poets have given the same turn to a sentence which describes the happiness of man in this life;

> Τὸ ζῆν ἀλύπως, ἀνδρός ἐστιν εὐτυχοῦς.
> That man is most happy who is the least miserable.

It will not perhaps be unentertaining to the polite reader, to observe how these three beautiful sentences are formed upon different subjects by the same way of thinking; but I shall return to the first of them.

'Our goodness being of a comparative, and not an absolute nature, there is none who in strictness can be called a virtuous man. Everyone has in him a natural alloy, though one may be fuller of dross than another: for this reason I cannot think it right to introduce a perfect or a faultless man upon the stage; not only because such a character is improper to move compassion, but because there is no such a thing in Nature. This might probably be one reason why the *Spectator* in one of his papers took notice of that late invented term called Poetical Justice, and the wrong notions into which it has led some tragic writers. The most perfect man has vices enough to draw down punishments upon his head, and to justify Providence in regard to any miseries that may befall him. For this reason I cannot think, but that the instruction and moral are much finer, where a man who is virtuous in the main of his character falls into distress, and sinks under the blows of fortune at the end of a tragedy, than when he is represented as happy and triumphant. Such an example corrects the insolence of human nature, softens the mind of the beholder with sentiments of pity and compassion, comforts

---

Boileau, Satires, iv. 39–40 ('du plus ou du moins').
Greek Poets: Menander, *Gnomai Monostichoi*, 509 (Meineke, *Fragmenta Comicorum Graecorum*, iv (1841), 354).

him under his own private affliction, and teaches him not to judge of men's virtues by their successes. I cannot think of one real hero in all antiquity so far raised above human infirmities, that he might not be very naturally represented in a tragedy as plunged in misfortunes and calamities. The poet may still find out some prevailing passion or indiscretion in his character, and show it in such a manner, as will sufficiently acquit the gods of any injustice in his sufferings. For as Horace observes in my text, the best man is faulty, though not in so great a degree as those whom we generally call vicious men.

'If such a strict poetical justice, as some gentlemen insist upon, were to be observed in this art, there is no manner of reason why it should not extend to heroic poetry, as well as tragedy. But we find it so little observed in Homer, that his Achilles is placed in the greatest point of glory and success, though his character is morally vicious, and only poetically good, if I may use the phrase of our modern critics.[n] The *Aeneid* is filled with innocent unhappy persons. Nisus and Euryalus, Lausus and Pallas come all to unfortunate ends. The poet takes notice in particular, that in the sacking of Troy, Ripheus fell, who was the most just man among the Trojans,

> . . . cadit et Ripheus justissimus unus
> qui fuit in Teucris et servantissimus aequi.
> Dis aliter visum est . . .[n]

and that Panthus could neither be preserved by his transcendent piety, nor by the holy fillets of Apollo, whose priest he was,

> . . . nec te tua plurima Panthu
> labentem pietas, nec Apollinis infula texit.   *Aen.* l. 2.[n]

I might here mention the practice of ancient tragic poets, both Greek and Latin, but as this particular is touched upon in the paper above-mentioned, I shall pass it over in silence. I could produce passages out of Aristotle in favour of my opinion, and if in one place he says that an absolutely virtuous man should not be represented as unhappy, this does not justify anyone who shall think fit to bring in an absolutely virtuous man upon the stage. Those who are acquainted with that author's way of writing know very well, that to take the whole extent of his subject into his divisions of it, he often makes use of such cases as are imaginary, and not reducible to

Nisus and Euryalus: for these characters see note on No. 273 (p. 67).
Panthus: son of Othryas, priest of Apollo. When Troy was burned he followed Aeneas and was killed.
Aristotle: *Poetics*, 13. 2.

practice: he himself declares that such tragedies as ended unhappily bore away the prize in theatrical contentions, from those which ended happily; and for the fortieth speculation, which I am now considering, as it has given reasons why these are more apt to please an audience, so it only proves that these are generally preferable to the other, though at the same time it affirms that many excellent tragedies have and may be written in both kinds.

'I shall conclude with observing, that though the *Spectator* above-mentioned is so far against the rule of Poetical Justice as to affirm that good men may meet with an unhappy catastrophe in tragedy, it does not say that ill men may go off unpunished. The reason for this distinction is very plain, namely, because the best of men are vicious enough to justify Providence for any misfortunes and afflictions which may befall them, but there are many men so criminal that they can have no claim or pretence to happiness. The best of men may deserve punishment, but the worst of men cannot deserve happiness.'

prize: Aristotle, *Poetics*, 13. 6.

CRITIQUES ON PLAYS BY *RICHARD STEELE*

The Man of Mode or Sir Fopling Flutter

65   *Tuesday   May 15 1711*

. . . *Demetri, teque, Tigelli,*
discipularum inter jubeo plorare cathedras.   HOR.

After having at large explained what wit is, and described the false
appearances of it, all that labour seems but an useless enquiry,
without some time be spent in considering the application of it. The
seat of wit, when one speaks as a man of the town and the world, is
the playhouse; I shall therefore fill this paper with reflections upon
the use of it in that place. The application of wit in the theatre has as
strong an effect upon the manners of our gentlemen, as the taste of it
has upon the writings of our authors. It may, perhaps, look like a
very presumptuous work, though not foreign from the duty of a
SPECTATOR, to tax the writings of such as have long had the general
applause of a nation: but I shall always make reason, truth, and
nature the measures of praise and dispraise; if those are for me, the
generality of opinion is of no consequence against me; if they are
against me, the general opinion cannot long support me.

Without further preface, I am going to look into some of our most
applauded plays, and see whether they deserve the figure they at
present bear in the imaginations of men, or not.

In reflecting upon these works, I shall chiefly dwell upon that for
which each respective play is most celebrated. The present paper
shall be employed upon *Sir Fopling Flutter*.[n] The received character
of this play is, that it is the pattern of genteel comedy. Dorimant and
Harriet are the characters of greatest consequence, and if these are
low and mean, the reputation of the play is very unjust.

I will take for granted, that a fine gentleman should be honest in
his actions, and refined in his language. Instead of this, our hero,
in this piece, is a direct knave in his designs, and a clown in his
language. Bellair is his admirer and friend, in return for which,
because he is forsooth a greater wit than his said friend, he thinks it

Motto: Horace, *Satires*, 1. 10. 90–1:
        Demetrius and Tigellius, know your place;
        Go hence, and whine among the schoolboy race.

reasonable to persuade him to marry a young lady, whose virtue, he thinks, will last no longer than till she is a wife, and then she cannot but fall to his share, as he is an irresistible fine gentleman. The falsehood to Mrs. Loveit, and the barbarity of triumphing over her anguish for losing him, is another instance of his honesty, as well as his good nature. As to his fine language; he calls the orange-woman, who, it seems, is inclined to grow fat, 'an over-grown jade, with a flasket of guts before her'; and salutes her with a pretty phrase of, 'How now, Double Tripe?' Upon the mention of a country gentlewoman, whom he knows nothing of, (no one can imagine why) he 'will lay his life she is some awkward, ill-fashioned country toad, who not having above four dozen of hairs on her head, has adorned her baldness with a large white fruz, that she may look sparkishly in the fore-front of the King's box at an old play'. Unnatural mixture of senseless commonplace!

As to the generosity of his temper, he tells his poor footman, 'If he did not wait better'—he would turn him away, in the insolent phrase of, 'I'll uncase you'.

Now for Mrs. Harriet: she laughs at obedience to an absent mother, whose tenderness Busy describes to be very exquisite, for 'that she is so pleased with finding Harriet again, that she cannot chide her for being out of the way'. This witty daughter, and fine lady, has so little respect for this good woman, that she ridicules her air in taking leave, and cries, 'In what struggle is my poor mother yonder? See, see, her head tottering, her eyes staring, and her under-lip trembling.' But all this is atoned for, because 'she has more wit than is usual in her sex, and as much malice, though she is as wild as you would wish her, and has a demureness in her looks that makes it so surprising!' Then to recommend her as a fit spouse for his hero, the poet makes her speak her sense of marriage very ingeniously. 'I think,' says she, 'I might be brought to endure him, and that is all a reasonable woman should expect in an husband.' It is, methinks, unnatural that we are not made to understand how she that was bred under a silly pious old mother, that would never trust her out of her sight, came to be so polite.

Double Tripe: the quotations in this paragraph and the next are all from the opening scene.

fruz: hair ruffled and rumpled in a 'frizzy' mess.

uncase: to strip him of his livery.

that she is so pleased: Act III, scene iii.

In what struggle: Act IV, scene i.

she has more wit: Act I, scene i.

'I think', says she: Act III, scene i.

It cannot be denied, but that the negligence of everything, which engages the attention of the sober and valuable part of mankind, appears very well drawn in this piece: but it is denied, that it is necessary to the character of a fine gentleman, that he should in that manner trample upon all order and decency. As for the character of Dorimant, it is more of a coxcomb than that of Fopling. He says of one of his companions, that a good correspondence between them is their mutual interest. Speaking of that friend, he declares, their being much together 'makes the women think the better of his understanding, and judge more favourably of my reputation. It makes him pass upon some for a man of very good sense, and me upon others for a very civil person.'

This whole celebrated piece is a perfect contradiction to good manners, good sense, and common honesty; and as there is nothing in it but what is built upon the ruin of virtue and innocence, according to the notion of merit in this comedy, I take the shoemaker to be, in reality, the fine gentleman of the play: for it seems he is an atheist, if we may depend upon his character as given by the orange-woman, who is herself far from being the lowest in the play. She says of a fine man, who is Dorimant's companion, 'There is not such another heathen in the town, except the shoemaker'. His pretension to be the hero of the drama appears still more in his own description of his way of living with his lady. 'There is,' says he, 'never a man in town lives more like a gentleman with his wife than I do; I never mind her motions; she never enquires into mine. We speak to one another civilly, hate one another heartily; and because it is vulgar to lie and soak together, we have each of us our several settle-bed.' That of 'soaking together' is as good as if Dorimant had spoken it himself; and, I think, since he puts human nature in as ugly a form as the circumstance will bear, and is a staunch unbeliever, he is very much wronged in having no part of the good fortune bestowed in the last act.

To speak plainly of this whole work, I think nothing but being lost to a sense of innocence and virtue can make any one see this comedy, without observing more frequent occasion to move sorrow and indignation, than mirth and laughter. At the same time I allow it to be nature, but it is nature in its utmost corruption and degeneracy.[n]

Dorimant: the companion is Bellair. The remaining quotations are again from the opening scene.

The Scornful Lady

270   *Wednesday January 9 1712*

Discit enim citius meminitque libentius illud
quod quis deridet quam quod probat . . . . Hor.

I do not know that I have been in greater delight for these many years, than in beholding the boxes at the play the last time *The Scornful Lady*[n] was acted. So great an assembly of ladies placed in gradual rows in all the ornaments of jewels, silks, and colours, gave so lively and gay an impression to the heart, that methought the season of the year was vanished; and I did not think it an ill expression of a young fellow who stood near me, that called the boxes those beds of tulips. It was a pretty variation of the prospect, when any one of these fine ladies rose up and did honour to herself and friend at a distance, by curtseying; and gave opportunity to that friend to show her charms to the same advantage in returning the salutation. Here that action is as proper and graceful, as it is at church unbecoming and impertinent. By the way, I must take the liberty to observe, that I did not see anyone who is usually so full of civilities at church, offer at any such indecorum during any part of the action of the play. Such beautiful prospects gladden our minds, and when considered in general, give innocent and pleasing ideas. He that dwells upon any one object of beauty, may fix his imagination to his disquiet; but the contemplation of a whole assembly together, is a defence against the encroachment of desire: at least to me, who have taken pains to look at beauty abstracted from the consideration of its being the object of desire, at power only as it sits upon another without any hopes of partaking any share of it, at wisdom and capacity without any pretensions to rival or envy its acquisitions: I say to me who am really free from forming any hopes by beholding the persons of beautiful women, or warming myself into ambition from the successes of other men, this world is not only a mere scene, but a very pleasant one. Did mankind but know the freedom which there is in keeping thus aloof from the world, I should have more imitators, than the powerfullest man in the nation has followers. To be no man's rival in love, or competitor in business, is a character which if it does not recommend you as it ought to benevolence among those

Motto: Horace, *Epistles*, 2.1. 262–3:
     For what's derided by the censuring crowd,
     Is thought on more than what is just and good.   CREECH

whom you live with, yet has it certainly this effect, that you do not
stand so much in need of their approbation, as you would if you
aimed at it more, in setting your heart on the same things which the
generality dote on. By this means, and with this easy philosophy, I
am never less at a play than when I am at the theatre; but indeed I
am seldom so well pleased with the action as in that place, for most
men follow nature no longer than while they are in their night-gowns,
and all the busy part of the day are in characters which they neither
become or act in with pleasure to themselves or their beholders. But
to return to my ladies, I was very well pleased to see so great a crowd
of them assembled at a play, wherein the heroine, as the phrase is,
is so just a picture of the vanity of the sex in tormenting their admirers. The lady who pines for the man whom she treats with so
much impertinence and inconstancy, is drawn with much art and
humour. Her resolutions to be extremely civil, but her vanity arising
just at the instant that she resolved to express herself kindly, are
described as by one who had studied the sex. But when my admiration is fixed upon this excellent character, and two or three others in
the play, I must confess I was moved with the utmost indignation at
the trivial, senseless, and unnatural representation of the chaplain.
It is possible there may be a pedant in holy orders, and we have seen
one or two of them in the world; but such a driveller as Sir Roger,[n]
so bereft of all manner of pride, which is the characteristic of a
pedant, is what one would not believe could come into the head of
the same man who drew the rest of the play. The meeting between
Welford and him shows a wretch without any notion of the dignity
of his function; and it is out of all common sense, that he should give
an account of himself 'as one sent four or five miles in a morning on
foot for eggs'. It is not to be denied, but his part and that of the maid
whom he makes love to, are excellently well performed; but a thing
which is blamable in itself, grows still more so by the success in the
execution of it. It is so mean a thing to gratify a loose age with a
scandalous representation of what is reputable among men, not to
say what is sacred, that no beauty, no excellence in an author ought
to atone for it; nay such excellence is an aggravation of his guilt,
and an argument that he errs against the conviction of his own
understanding and conscience. Wit should be tried by this rule, and
an audience should rise against such a scene, as throws down the
reputation of anything which the consideration of religion or decency
should preserve from contempt. But all this evil arises from this one

night-gowns: dressing gowns.
maid: Act IV, scene i.

corruption of mind, that makes men resent offences against their virtue, less than those against their understanding. An author shall write as if he thought there was not one man of honour or woman of chastity in the house, and come off with applause: for an insult upon all the Ten Commandments, with the little critics, is not so bad as the breach of an unity of time or place. Half-wits do not apprehend the miseries that must necessarily flow from degeneracy of manners; nor do they know that order is the support of society. Sir Roger and his mistress are monsters of the poet's own forming; the sentiments in both of them are such as do not arise in fools of their education. We all know that a silly scholar, instead of being below every one he meets with, is apt to be exalted above the rank of such as are really his superiors: his arrogance is always founded upon particular notions of distinction in his own head, accompanied with a pedantic scorn of all fortune and pre-eminence when compared with his knowledge and learning. This very one character of Sir Roger, as silly as it really is, has done more towards the disparagement of Holy Orders, and consequently of virtue itself, than all the wit that author or any other could make up for in the conduct of the longest life after it. I do not pretend, in saying this, to give myself airs of more virtue than my neighbours, but assert it from the principles by which mankind must always be governed. Sallies of imagination are to be overlooked, when they are committed out of warmth in the recommendation of what is praiseworthy; but a deliberate advancing of vice with all the wit in the world, is as ill an action as any that comes before the magistrate, and ought to be received as such by the people.

The Distressed Mother

290   *Friday February 1 1712*

Projicit ampullas et sesquipedalia verba.   Hor.

The players, who know I am very much their friend, take all opportunities to express a gratitude to me for being so. They could not have a better occasion of obliging me, than one which they lately

Motto: Horace, *Ars poetica*, 97.
Forget their swelling and gigantic words.   ROSCOMMON

took hold of. They desired my friend Will Honeycomb to bring me
to the reading of a new tragedy, it is called *The Distressed Mother*.[n]
I must confess, though some days are passed since I enjoyed that
entertainment, the passions of the several characters dwell strongly
upon my imagination; and I congratulate to the age, that they are at
last to see truth and human life represented in the incidents which
concern heroes and heroines. The style of the play is such as becomes
those of the first education, and the sentiments worthy those of the
highest figure. It was a most exquisite pleasure to me, to observe real
tears drop from the eyes of those who had long made it their profession to dissemble affliction; and the player who read, frequently
throw down the book, till he had given vent to the humanity which
rose in him at some irresistible touches of the imagined sorrow. We
have seldom had any female distress on the stage, which did not,
upon cool examination, appear to flow from the weakness rather
than the misfortune of the person represented: but in this tragedy you
are not entertained with the ungoverned passions of such as are
enamoured of each other merely as they are men and women, but
their regards are founded upon high conceptions of each other's
virtue and merit; and the character which gives name to the play,
is one who has behaved herself with heroic virtue in the most
important circumstances of a female life, those of a wife, a widow,
and a mother.[n] If there be those whose minds have been too attentive
upon the affairs of life, to have any notion of the passion of love in
such extremes as are known only to particular tempers, yet in the
above-mentioned considerations, the sorrow of the heroine will
move even the generality of mankind. Domestic virtues concern all
the world, and there is no one living who is not interested that
Andromache should be an imitable character. The generous affection
to the memory of her deceased husband, that tender care for her son,
which is ever heightened with the consideration of his father, and
these regards preserved in spite of being tempted with the possession
of the highest greatness, are what cannot but be venerable even to
such an audience as at present frequents the English theatre. My
friend Will Honeycomb commended several tender things that were
said, and told me they were very genteel; but whispered me, that he
feared the piece was not busy enough for the present taste. To supply
this, he recommended to the players to be very careful in their
scenes, and above all things, that every part should be perfectly new
dressed. I was very glad to find they did not neglect my friend's
admonition, because there are a great many in his class of criticism

Will Honeycomb: one of the members of the Spectator Club, a type of the
(elderly) Restoration rake.

who may be gained by it; but indeed the truth is, that as to the work itself, it is everywhere nature. The persons are of the highest quality in life, even that of princes; but their quality is not represented by the poet with direction that guards and waiters should follow them in every scene, but their grandeur appears in greatness of sentiment, flowing from minds worthy their condition. To make a character truly great, this author understands that it should have its foundation in superior thoughts and maxims of conduct. It is very certain, that many an honest woman would make no difficulty, though she had been the wife of Hector, for the sake of a kingdom, to marry the enemy of her husband's family and country; and indeed who can deny but she might be still an honest woman, but no heroine? That may be defensible, nay laudable, in one character, which would be in the highest degree exceptionable in another. When Cato Uticensis killed himself, Cottius, a Roman of ordinary quality and character, did the same thing; upon which one said, smiling, 'Cottius might have lived though Caesar has seized the Roman liberty.' Cottius's condition might have been the same, let things at the upper end of the world pass as they would. What is further very extraordinary in this work, is, that the persons are all of them laudable, and their misfortunes arise rather from unguarded virtue than propensity to vice. The Town has an opportunity of doing itself justice in supporting the representations of passion, sorrow, indignation, even despair itself, within the rules of decency, honour, and good breeding; and since there is no one can flatter himself his life will be always fortunate, they may here see sorrow as they would wish to bear it whenever it arrives.[n]

Mr. Spectator,

'I am appointed to act a part in the new tragedy, called *The Distressed Mother*: it is the celebrated grief of Orestes which I am to personate; but I shall not act as I ought, for I shall feel it too intimately to be able to utter it. I was last night repeating a paragraph to myself, which I took to be an expression of rage, and in the middle of the sentence there was a stroke of self-pity which quite unmanned me.[n] Be pleased, sir, to print this letter, that when I am oppressed in this manner at such an interval, a certain part of the audience may not think I am out; and I hope with this allowance to do it to satisfaction.

I am,
Sir,
Your most humble servant,
George Powell.'[n]

The Self-Tormentor

502   *Monday October 6 1712*

Melius, pejus, prosit, obsit, nil vident nisi quod lubet.   Ter.

When men read, they taste the matter with which they are entertained according as their own respective studies and inclinations have prepared them, and make their reflections accordingly. Some perusing a Roman writer, would find in them, whatever the subject of the discourses were, parts which implied the grandeur of that people in their warfare or their politics. As for my part, who am a mere spectator, I drew this morning conclusions of their eminence in what I think great, to wit, in having worthy sentiments, from the reading a comedy of Terence. The play was *The Self-Tormentor*. It is from the beginning to the end a perfect picture of human life, but I did not observe in the whole one passage that could raise a laugh. How well disposed must that people be, who could be entertained with satisfaction by so sober and polite mirth! In the first scene of the comedy, when one of the old men accuses the other of impertinence for interposing in his affairs, he answers, 'I am a man, and cannot help feeling any sorrow that can arrive at man.'[n] It is said this sentence was received with an universal applause. There cannot be a greater argument of the general good understanding of a people, than a sudden consent to give their approbation of a sentiment which has no emotion in it. If it were spoken with never so great skill in the actor, the manner of uttering that sentence could have nothing in it which could strike any but people of the greatest humanity, nay people elegant and skilful in observations upon it. It is possible he might have laid his hand on his breast, and with a winning insinuation in his countenance, expressed to his neighbour that he was a man who made his case his own; yet I'll engage a player in Covent Garden[n] might hit such an attitude a thousand times before he would have been regarded. I have heard that the minister of state in the reign of Queen Elizabeth had all manner of books and ballads brought to him, of what kind soever, and took great notice how much they took with the people; upon which he would, and certainly might, very well judge of their present dispositions, and the most proper way of

---

Motto: Terence, *Heauton Timorumenos*, 643: Better or worse, profitable or disadvantageous, they see nothing but what they list.

The Self-Tormentor: *Heauton Timorumenos*, produced in 163 B.C., was adapted from a comedy of the same name by Menander.

applying them according to his own purposes.[n] What passes on the stage, and the reception it meets from the audience, is a very useful instruction of this kind. According to what you may observe there on our stage, you see them often moved so directly against all common sense and humanity, that you would be apt to pronounce us a nation of savages. It cannot be called a mistake of what is pleasant, but the very contrary to it is what most assuredly takes with them. The other night an old woman carried off with a pain in her side, with all the distortions and anguish of countenance which is natural to one in that condition, was laughed and clapped off the stage. Terence's comedy, which I am speaking of, is indeed written as if he hoped to please none but such as had as good a taste as himself. I could not but reflect upon the natural description of the innocent young woman made by the servant to his master.

When I came to the house, [said he] an old woman opened the door, and I followed her in, because I could by entering upon them unawares better observe what was your mistress's ordinary manner of spending her time, the only way of judging any one's inclinations and genius. I found her at her needle in a sort of second mourning, which she wore for an aunt she had lately lost. She had nothing on but what showed she dressed only for herself. Her hair hung negligently about her shoulders. She had none of the arts with which others use to set themselves off, but had that negligence of person which is remarkable in those who are careful of their minds .... Then she had a maid who was at work near her, that was a slattern, because her mistress was careless; which I take to be another argument of your security in her; for the go-betweens of women of intrigue are rewarded too well to be dirty. When you were named, and I told her you desired to see her, she threw down her work for joy, covered her face, and decently hid her tears ....

He must be a very good actor, and draw attention rather from his own character than the words of the author, that could gain it among us for this speech, though so full of nature and good sense.

The intolerable folly and confidence of players putting in words of their own, does in a great measure feed the absurd taste of the audience. But, however that is, it is ordinary for a cluster of coxcombs to take up the house to themselves, and equally insult both the actors and the company. These savages, who want all manner of regard and deference to the rest of mankind, come only to show themselves to us, without any other purpose than to let us know they despise us.

The gross of an audience is composed of two sorts of people, those

When I came: lines 274–307.
The gross: the greater part, the majority.

9*

who know no pleasure but of the body, and those who improve or command corporeal pleasures by the addition of fine sentiments of the mind. At present the intelligent part of the company are wholly subdued by the insurrections of those who know no satisfactions but what they have in common with all other animals.

This is the reason that when a scene tending to procreation is acted, you see the whole pit in such a chuckle, and old lechers, with mouths open, stare at the loose gesticulations on the stage with shameful earnestness, when the justest pictures of human life in its calm dignity, and the properest sentiments for the conduct of it, pass by like mere narration, as conducing only to somewhat much better which is to come after. I have seen the whole house at some times in so proper a disposition, that indeed I have trembled for the boxes, and feared the entertainment would end in the presentation of the rape of the Sabines.

I would not be understood in this talk to argue, that nothing is tolerable on the stage but what has an immediate tendency to the promotion of virtue. On the contrary, I can allow, provided there is nothing against the interests of virtue, and is not offensive to good manners, that things of an indifferent nature may be represented. For this reason I have no exception to the well-drawn rusticities in *The Country-Wake*; and there is something so miraculously pleasant in Dogget's acting the awkward triumph and comic sorrow of Hob in different circumstances, that I shall not be able to stay away whenever it is acted.[n] All that vexes me is, that the gallantry of taking the cudgels for Gloucestershire, with the pride of heart in tucking himself up, and taking aim at his adversary, as well as the other's protestation in the humanity of low romance. That he could not promise the squire to break Hob's head, but he would, if he could, do it in love; then flourish and begin: I say, what vexes me is, that such excellent touches as these, as well as the squire's being out of all patience at Hob's success, and venturing himself into the crowd, are circumstances hardly taken notice of, and the height of the jest is only in the very point that heads are broken. I am confident, were there a scene written, wherein Penkethman should break his leg by wrestling with Bullock, and Dicky come in to set it, without one word said but what should be according to the exact rules of surgery in making

---

Sabines: this legendary event was supposed to have taken place in the reign of Romulus. See Livy's *History* (Book I).

William Penkethman: (or Pinkethman) was a popular droll and showman of the time.

Bullock: for these actors see No. 44 above (p. 223 and note).

this extension, and binding up the leg, the whole house should be in a roar of applause at the dissembled anguish of the patient, the help given by him who threw him down, and the handy address and arch looks of the surgeon. To enumerate the entrance of ghosts, the embattling of armies, the noise of heroes in love, with a thousand other enormities, would be to transgress the bounds of this paper, for which reason it is possible they may have hereafter distinct discourses; not forgetting any of the audience who shall set up for actors, and interrupt the play on the stage; and players who shall prefer the applause of fools to that of the reasonable part of the company.

Miscellaneous Essays

ON LANGUAGE

Est brevitate opus, ut currat sententia . . . .   Hor.

I have somewhere read of an eminent person who used in his private
offices of devotion, to give thanks to Heaven that he was born a
Frenchman: for my own part I look upon it as a peculiar blessing
that I was born an Englishman. Among many other reasons, I
think myself very happy in my country, as the language of it is
wonderfully adapted to a man who is sparing of his words, and an
enemy to loquacity.

As I have frequently reflected on my good fortune in this particular,
I shall communicate to the public my speculations upon the English
tongue, not doubting but they will be acceptable to all my curious
readers.

The English delight in silence more than any other European
nation, if the remarks which are made on us by foreigners are true.[n]
Our discourse is not kept up in conversation, but falls into more
pauses and intervals than in our neighbouring countries; as it is
observed, that the matter of our writings is thrown much closer
together, and lies in a narrower compass than is usual in the works
of foreign authors: for, to favour our natural taciturnity, when we are
obliged to utter our thoughts, we do it in the shortest way we are able,
and give as quick a birth to our conceptions as possible.

This humour shows itself in several remarks that we may make
upon the English language. As first of all by its abounding in monosyllables, which gives us an opportunity of delivering our thoughts
in few sounds. This indeed takes off from the elegance of our tongue,
but at the same time expresses our ideas in the readiest manner, and
consequently answers the first design of speech better than the
multitude of syllables, which makes the words of other languages
more tunable and sonorous. The sounds of our English words are
commonly like those of string music, short and transient, which rise
and perish upon a single touch; those of other languages are like the
notes of wind instruments, sweet and swelling, and lengthened out
into variety of modulation.[n]

In the next place we may observe, that where the words are not

Motto: Horace, *Satires*, 1. 10. 9: Brevity is needed, that the thought may run on.

monosyllables, we often make them so, as much as lies in our power, by our rapidity of pronunciation; as it generally happens in most of our long words which are derived from the Latin, where we contract the length of the syllables that gives them a grave and solemn air in their own language, to make them more proper for dispatch, and more conformable to the genius of our tongue. This we may find in a multitude of words, as *liberty, conspiracy, theatre, orator,* etc.

The same natural aversion to loquacity has of late years made a very considerable alteration in our language, by closing in one syllable the termination of our preterperfect tense, as in the words *drown'd, walk'd, arriv'd,* for *drowned, walked, arrived,* which has very much disfigured the tongue, and turned a tenth part of our smoothest words into so many clusters of consonants. This is the more remarkable, because the want of vowels in our language has been the general complaint of our politest authors, who nevertheless are the men that have made these retrenchments, and consequently very much increased our former scarcity.

This reflection on the words that end in *ed,* I have heard in conversation from one of the greatest geniuses this age has produced. I think we may add to the foregoing observation, the change which has happened in our language, by the abbreviation of several words that are terminated in *eth,* by substituting an *s* in the room of the last syllable, as in *drowns, walks, arrives,* and innumerable other words, which in the pronunciation of our forefathers were *drowneth, walketh, arriveth.* This has wonderfully multiplied a letter which was before too frequent in the English tongue, and added to that hissing in our language, which is taken so much notice of by foreigners; but at the same time humours our taciturnity, and eases us of many superfluous syllables.

I might here observe, that the same single letter on many occasions does the office of a whole word, and represents the *his* and *her* of our forefathers. There is no doubt but the ear of a foreigner, which is the best judge in this case, would very much disapprove of such innovations, which indeed we do ourselves in some measure, by retaining the old termination in writing, and in all the solemn offices of our religion.

As in the instances I have given we have epitomized many of our particular words to the detriment of our tongue, so on other occasions

---

preterperfect: applied to a tense which indicates a past or completed state or action. Now rare or obsolete (*OED*).

geniuses: the reference is almost certainly to Swift.

we have drawn two words into one, which has likewise very much untuned our language, and clogged it with consonants, as *mayn't, can't, sha'n't, wo'n't,* and the like, for *may not, can not, shall not, will not,* etc.

It is perhaps this humour of speaking no more than we needs must, which has so miserably curtailed some of our words, that in familar writings and conversations they often lose all but their first syllables, as in *mob. rep. pos. incog.* and the like; and as all ridiculous words make their first entry into a language by familiar phrases, I dare not answer for these that they will not in time be looked upon as a part of our tongue. We see some of our poets have been so indiscreet as to imitate Hudibras's doggerel expressions in their serious compositions, by throwing out the signs of our substantives, which are essential to the English language. Nay this humour of shortening our language had once run so far that some of our celebrated authors, among whom we may reckon Sir Roger L'Estrange[n] in particular, began to prune their words of all superfluous letters, as they termed them, in order to adjust the spelling to the pronunciation, which would have confounded all our etymologies, and have quite destroyed our tongue.

We may here likewise observe that our proper names, when familiarized in English, generally dwindle to monosyllables, whereas in other modern languages they receive a softer turn on this occasion, by the addition of a new syllable. *Nick* in Italian is *Nicolini, Jack* in French *Janot,* and so of the rest.

There is another particular in our language which is a great instance of our frugality in words, and that is the suppressing of several particles, which must be produced in other tongues to make a sentence intelligible: this often perplexes the best writers, when they find the relatives, *who, which* or *that,* at their mercy whether they may have admission or not, and will never be decided till we have something like an Academy, that by the best authorities and rules drawn from the analogy of languages shall settle all controversies between grammar and idiom.

I have only considered our language as it shows the genius and natural temper of the English, which is modest, thoughtful and sincere, and which perhaps may recommend the people, though it has spoiled the tongue. We might perhaps carry the same thought into other languages, and deduce a great part of what is peculiar to them from the genius of the people who speak them. It is certain

---

pos.: of the abbreviated words mentioned here, *pos.* occurs in a letter in No. 204 and *incog.* is used by Steele in No. 248.

the light talkative humour of the French has not a little infected their tongue, which might be shown by many instances; as the genius of the Italians, which is so much addicted to music and ceremony, has moulded all their words and phrases to those particular uses. The stateliness and gravity of the Spaniards shows itself to perfection in the solemnity of their language; and the blunt honest humour of the Germans sounds better in the roughness of the High Dutch, than it would in a politer tongue.

165   *Saturday September 8 1711*

. . . Si forte necesse est,
fingere cinctutis non exaudita Cethegis,
continget: dabiturque licentia sumpta pudenter.   Hor.

I have often wished, that as in our constitution there are several persons whose business it is to watch over our laws, our liberties and commerce, certain men might be set apart, as superintendents of our language, to hinder any words of a foreign coin from passing among us; and in particular to prohibit any French phrases from becoming current in this kingdom, when those of our own stamp are altogether as valuable.[n] The present war has so adulterated our tongue with strange words, that it would be impossible for one of our great-grandfathers to know what his posterity have been doing, were he to read their exploits in a modern newspaper. Our warriors are very industrious in propagating the French language, at the same time that they are so gloriously successful in beating down their power. Our soldiers are men of strong heads for action, and perform such feats as they are not able to express. They want words in their own tongue to tell us what it is they achieve, and therefore send us over accounts of their performances in a jargon of phrases, which they learn among their conquered enemies. They ought however to be provided with secretaries, and assisted by our foreign ministers, to

Motto: Horace, *Ars poetica*, 48, 50–1:
> But if you would unheard of things express;
> And clothe new notions in a modern dress;
> Invent new words, we can indulge a muse,
> Until the licence rise to an abuse.   CREECH

war: the war of the Spanish Succession.

tell their story for them in plain English, and to let us know in our mother tongue what it is our brave countrymen are about. The French would indeed be in the right to publish the news of the present war in English phrases, and make their campaigns unintelligible. Their people might flatter themselves that things are not so bad as they really are, were they thus palliated with foreign terms, and thrown into shades and obscurity. But the English cannot be too clear in their narrative of those actions, which have raised their country to a higher pitch of glory than it ever yet arrived at, and which will be still the more admired the better they are explained.

For my part, by that time a siege is carried on two or three days, I am altogether lost and bewildered in it, and meet with so many inexplicable difficulties that I scarce know which side has the better of it, till I am informed by the Tower guns that the place is surrendered. I do indeed make some allowances for this part of the war, fortifications having been foreign inventions, and upon that account abounding in foreign terms. But when we have won battles which may be described in our own language, why are our papers filled with so many unintelligible exploits, and the French obliged to lend us a part of their tongue before we can know how they are conquered? They must be made accessory to their own disgrace, as the Britons were formerly so artificially wrought in the curtain of the Roman theatre, that they seemed to draw it up, in order to give the spectators an opportunity of seeing their own defeat celebrated upon the stage: for so Mr. Dryden has translated that verse in Virgil.

> Atque intertexti tollant aulaea Britanni.

> Which interwoven Britons seem to raise,
> And show the triumph that their shame displays.

The histories of all our former wars are transmitted to us in our vernacular idiom, to use the phrase of a great modern critic.[n] I do not find in any of our chronicles, that Edward the Third ever reconnoitred the enemy, though he often discovered the posture of the French, and as often vanquished them in battle. The Black Prince passed many a river without the help of pontoons, and filled a ditch with faggots as successfully as the generals of our times do it

artificially: artistically, skilfully.

Virgil: *Georgics*, 3. 25 ('Purpurea intexti'). Dryden's translation, lines 39–40. For the 'curtain' of the Roman theatre see Margarete Bieber, *The History of the Greek and Roman Theater* (Princeton, 1939), pp. 326–31.

Black Prince. Edward III and his son, the Black Prince, gained the great victories of Crécy (1348) and Poitiers (1356) over the French in the Hundred Years' War.

with fascines. Our commanders lose half their praise, and our people half their joy, by means of those hard words, and dark expressions in which our newspapers do so much abound. I have seen many a prudent citizen, after having read every article, enquire of his next neighbour what news the mail had brought.

I remember in that remarkable year when our country was delivered from the greatest fears and apprehensions, and raised to the greatest height of gladness it had ever felt since it was a nation, I mean the year of Blenheim, I had the copy of a letter sent me out of the country, which was written from a young gentleman in the army to his father, a man of a good estate and plain sense: as the letter was very modishly chequered with this modern military eloquence, I shall present my reader with a copy of it.[n]

Sir,

'Upon the junction of the French and Bavarian armies they took post behind a great morass which they thought impracticable. Our general the next day sent a party of horse to reconnoitre them from a little hauteur, at about a quarter of an hour's distance from the army, who returned again to the camp unobserved through several defiles, in one of which they met with a party of French that had been marauding, and made them all prisoners at discretion. The day after a drum arrived at our camp, with a message which he would communicate to none but the general; he was followed by a trumpet, who they say behaved himself very saucily, with a message from the Duke of Bavaria. The next morning our army being divided into two corps, made a movement towards the enemy: you will hear in the public prints how we treated them, with the other circumstances of that glorious day. I had the good fortune to be in the regiment that pushed the gens d'arms. Several French battalions, who some say were a corps de reserve, made a show of resistance; but it only proved a gasconade, for upon our preparing to fill up a little fossé, in order to attack them, they beat the chamade, and sent us carte blanche. Their commandant, with a great many other general officers, and troops without number, are made prisoners of war, and will I believe give you a visit in England, the cartel not being yet settled. Not questioning but these particulars will be very welcome

---

fascines: 'faggots' (sticks or small branches of trees) is the earlier term; 'fascines' (bundles of brush, used in filling ditches) came into use in the late seventeenth century.

Blenheim: Marlborough's great victory at Blenheim, on the Danube near Höchstädt in Bavaria, occurred on 2 August (13 August, N.S.) 1704.

to you, I congratulate you upon them, and am your most dutiful
Son, etc.'

The father of the young gentleman upon the perusal of the letter
found it contained great news, but could not guess what it was. He
immediately communicated it to the curate of the parish, who upon
the reading of it, being vexed to see anything he could not understand, fell into a kind of passion, and told him, that his son had sent
him a letter that was neither fish, flesh, nor good red herring. I wish,
says he, the captain may be compos mentis, he talks of a saucy
trumpet, and a drum that carries messages: then who is this carte
blanche: he must either banter us, or he is out of his senses. The
father, who always looked upon the curate as a learned man, began
to fret inwardly at his son's usage, and producing a letter which he
had written to him about three posts afore, You see here, says he,
when he writes for money he knows how to speak intelligibly
enough, there is no man in England can express himself clearer, when
he wants a new furniture for his horse. In short, the old man was so
puzzled upon the point, that it might have fared ill with his son,
had he not seen all the prints about three days after filled with the
same terms of art, and that Charles only writ like other men.

red herring: a proverb dating from the sixteenth century.

ON AUTHORS AND WRITING

166 *Monday September 10 1711*

. . . Quod nec Jovis ira, nec ignis,
nec poterit ferrum, nec edax abolere vetustas. Ovid.

Aristotle tells us, that the world is a copy or transcript of those ideas which are in the mind of the first being; and that those ideas which are in the mind of man, are a transcript of the world: to this we may add, that words are the transcript of those ideas which are in the mind of man, and that writing or printing are the transcript of words.

As the Supreme Being has expressed, and as it were printed his ideas in the Creation, men express their ideas in books, which by this great invention of these latter ages may last as long as the sun and moon, and perish only in the general wreck of Nature. Thus Cowley in his poem on *The Resurrection*, mentioning the destruction of the universe, has those admirable lines.

> Now all the wide-extended sky,
> And all the harmonious worlds on high,
> And Virgil's sacred work shall die.

There is no other method of fixing those thoughts which arise and disappear in the mind of man, and transmitting them to the last periods of time; no other method of giving a permanency to our ideas, and preserving the knowledge of any particular person, when his body is mixed with the common mass of matter, and his soul retired into the world of spirits. Books are the legacies that a great genius leaves to mankind, which are delivered down from generation to generation, as presents to the posterity of those who are yet unborn.

All other arts of perpetuating our ideas continue but a short time; statues can last but a few thousands of years, edifices fewer, and colours still fewer than edifices. Michael Angelo, Fontana, and

---

Motto: Ovid, *Metamorphoses*, 15. 871–2: Which nor dreads the rage of tempests, fire, or war, or wasting age. WELSTED

The Resurrection: lines 23–25 ('Then all . . .'). *Poems*, ed. Waller, p. 182.

Fontana: the reference here is probably to the painter of Bologna, Prospero Fontana (1512–97).

Raphael, will hereafter be what Phidias, Vitruvius, and Apelles are at present; the names of great statuaries, architects, and painters, whose works are lost. The several arts are expressed in mouldering materials; Nature sinks under them, and is not able to support the ideas which are impressed upon it.

The circumstance which gives authors an advantage above all these great masters, is this, that they can multiply their originals; or rather can make copies of their works, to what number they please, which shall be as valuable as the originals themselves. This gives a great author something like a prospect of eternity, but at the same time deprives him of those other advantages which artists meet with. The artist finds greater returns in profit, as the author in fame. What an inestimable price would a Virgil or a Homer, a Cicero or an Aristotle bear, were their works like a statue, a building, or a picture, to be confined only in one place, and made the property of a single person?

If writings are thus durable, and may pass from age to age throughout the whole course of time, how careful should an author be of committing anything to print that may corrupt posterity, and poison the minds of men with vice and error? Writers of great talents, who employ their parts in propagating immorality, and seasoning vicious sentiments with wit and humour, are to be looked upon as the pests of society and the enemies of mankind: they leave books behind them (as it is said of those who die in distempers which breed an ill will towards their own species) to scatter infection and destroy their posterity. They act the counterparts of a Confucius or a Socrates; and seem to have been sent into the world to deprave human nature, and sink it into the condition of brutality.

I have seen some Roman Catholic authors, who tell us that vicious writers continue in Purgatory so long as the influence of their writings continues upon posterity: for Purgatory, say they, is nothing else but a cleansing us of our sins, which cannot be said to be done away, so long as they continue to operate and corrupt mankind. The vicious author, say they, sins after death, and so long as he continues to sin, so long must he expect to be punished. Though the

---

Phidias: (*c.* 490–417 B.C.), the Athenian sculptor, famous for his statue of Athena Promachos on the Acropolis and his marble sculpture of the Parthenon.

Vitruvius Pollio: Roman architect and military engineer in the reign of Augustus.

Apelles: Greek painter of the 4th century B.C., noted for his portraits of Philip and Alexander.

counterparts: here in the very unusual sense of 'opposites'.

Confucius (550?–478 B.C.) and *Socrates* (469–399 B.C.): here linked as two of the greatest benefactors of mankind.

Roman Catholic notion of Purgatory be indeed very ridiculous, one cannot but think that if the soul after death has any knowledge of what passes in this world, that of an immoral writer would receive much more regret from the sense of corrupting, than satisfaction from the thought of pleasing his surviving admirers.

To take off from the severity of this speculation, I shall conclude this paper with a story of an atheistical author,[n] who at a time when he lay dangerously sick and had desired the assistance of a neighbouring curate, confessed to him with great contrition, that nothing sat more heavy at his heart than the sense of his having seduced the age by his writings, and that their evil influence was likely to continue even after his death. The curate upon further examination finding the penitent in the utmost agonies of despair, and being himself a man of learning, told him, that he hoped his case was not so desperate as he apprehended, since he found that he was so very sensible of his fault, and so sincerely repented of it. The penitent still urged the evil tendency of his book to subvert all religion, and the little ground of hope there could be for one whose writings would continue to do mischief when his body was laid in ashes. The curate finding no other way to comfort him, told him, that he did well in being afflicted for the evil design with which he published his book; but that he ought to be very thankful that there was no danger of its doing any hurt. That his cause was so very bad and his arguments so weak, that he did not apprehend any ill effects of it. In short, that he might rest satisfied his book could do no more mischief after his death, than it had done whilst he was living. To which he added, for his further satisfaction, that he did not believe any besides his particular friends and acquaintance had ever been at the pains of reading it, or that anybody after his death would ever enquire after it. The dying man had still so much the frailty of an author in him, as to be cut to the heart with these consolations; and without answering the good man, asked his friends about him (with a peevishness that is natural to a sick person) where they had picked up such a blockhead? And whether they thought him a proper person to attend one in his condition? The curate finding that the author did not expect to be dealt with as a real and sincere penitent, but as a penitent of importance, after a short admonition withdrew; not questioning but he should be again sent for if the sickness grew desperate. The author however recovered, and has since written two or three other tracts with the same spirit, and very luckily for his poor soul, with the same success.

ON GENIUS

. . . Cui mens divinior, atque os
magna sonaturum, des nominis hujus honorem.   Hor.

There is no character more frequently given to a writer, than that of being a genius. I have heard many a little sonneteer called a 'fine genius'. There is not an heroic scribbler in the nation, that has not his admirers who think him a 'great genius'; and as for your smatterers in tragedy, there is scarce a man among them who is not cried up by one or other for a 'prodigious genius'.

My design in this paper is to consider what is properly a great genius, and to throw some thoughts together on so uncommon a subject.

Among great geniuses, those few draw the admiration of all the world upon them, and stand up as the prodigies of mankind, who by the mere strength of natural parts, and without any assistance of art or learning, have produced works that were the delight of their own times and the wonder of posterity. There appears something nobly wild and extravagant in these great natural geniuses, that is infinitely more beautiful than all the turn and polishing of what the French call a *bel esprit*, by which they would express a genius refined by conversation, reflection, and the reading of the most polite authors. The greatest genius which runs through the arts and sciences, takes a kind of tincture from them, and falls unavoidably into imitation.

Many of these great natural geniuses that were never disciplined and broken by rules of art, are to be found among the Ancients, and in particular among those of the more eastern parts of the world. Homer has innumerable flights that Virgil was not able to reach, and in the Old Testament we find several passages more elevated and sublime than any in Homer. At the same time that we allow a greater and more daring genius to the Ancients, we must own

Motto: Horace, *Satires*, 1. 4. 43–4:
> On him confer the poet's sacred name,
> Whose lofty voice declares the heavenly flame.

rules of art: Du Bos, in his *Réflexions critiques sur la poésie et la peinture* (1719) quotes this passage (Pt. ii, sect. xxxix).

that the greatest of them very much failed in, or, if you will, that they were much above the nicety and correctness of the Moderns. In their similitudes and allusions, provided there was a likeness, they did not much trouble themselves about the decency of the comparison: thus Solomon resembles the nose of his beloved to the Tower of Lebanon which looketh toward Damascus; as the coming of a thief in the night is a similitude of the same kind in the New Testament. It would be endless to make collections of this nature: Homer illustrates one of his heroes encompassed with the enemy, by an ass in a field of corn that has his sides belaboured by all the boys of the village without stirring a foot for it; and another of them tossing to and fro in his bed, and burning with resentment, to a piece of flesh broiled on the coals. This particular failure in the Ancients, opens a large field of raillery to the little wits, who can laugh at an indecency but not relish the sublime in these sorts of writings.[n] The present Emperor of Persia, conformable to this eastern way of thinking, amidst a great many pompous titles, denominates himself the Sun of Glory and the Nutmeg of Delight. In short, to cut off all cavilling against the Ancients, and particularly those of the warmer climates, who had most heat and life in their imaginations, we are to consider that the rule of observing what the French call the *bienséance* in an allusion, has been found out of latter years and in the colder regions of the world; where we would make some amends for our want of force and spirit, by a scrupulous nicety and exactness in our compositions. Our countryman Shakespeare was a remarkable instance of this first kind of great geniuses.

I cannot quit this head without observing that Pindar was a great genius of the first class, who was hurried on by a natural fire and impetuosity to vast conceptions of things, and noble sallies of imagination. At the same time, can anything be more ridiculous than for men of a sober and moderate fancy to imitate this poet's way of writing in those monstrous compositions which go among us under the name of pindarics?[n] When I see people copying works, which, as Horace has represented them, are singular in their kind and inimitable; when I see men following irregularities by rule, and by the little tricks of art straining after the most unbounded flights of nature, I cannot but apply to them that passage in Terence.

Damascus: S. of S., 7:4.
thief: 1 Thess. 5:2; 2 Pet. 3:10.
Homer: *Iliad*, 11. 558–65.
coals: *Odyssey*, 20. 25–30.
bienséance: decorum, propriety.
Horace: *Odes*, 4. 2. 1–4.

> . . . incerta haec si tu postules
> ratione certa facere, nihilo plus agas,
> quam si des operam, ut cum ratione insanias.

In short a modern pindaric writer compared with Pindar, is like a sister among the Camisars compared with Virgil's Sybil: there is the distortion, grimace, and outward figure, but nothing of that divine impulse which raises the mind above itself, and makes the sounds more than human.

There is another kind of great geniuses which I shall place in a second class, not as I think them inferior to the first, but only for distinction's sake as they are of a different kind. This second class of great geniuses are those that have formed themselves by rules, and submitted the greatness of their natural talents to the corrections and restraints of art. Such among the Greeks were Plato and Aristotle, among the Romans Virgil and Tully, among the English Milton[n] and Sir Francis Bacon.

The genius in both these classes of authors may be equally great, but shows itself after a different manner. In the first it is like a rich soil in a happy climate, that produces a whole wilderness of noble plants rising in a thousand beautiful landscapes without any certain order or regularity. In the other it is the same rich soil under the same happy climate, that has been laid out in walks and parterres, and cut into shape and beauty by the skill of the gardener.

The great danger in these latter kind of geniuses, is, lest they cramp their own abilities too much by imitation, and form themselves altogether upon models, without giving the full play to their own natural parts. An imitation of the best authors, is not to compare with a good original; and I believe we may observe that very few writers make an extraordinary figure in the world, who have not something in their way of thinking or expressing themselves that is peculiar to them and entirely their own.

It is odd to consider what great geniuses are sometimes thrown away upon trifles.

incerta: 'You may as well pretend to be mad and in your senses at the same time, as to think of reducing these uncertainties into certainties by reason.' *Eunuchus*, 61–3.

the Camisars: (properly Camisards) were Calvinists from the Cévennes who, during the war of the Spanish Succession, revolted and were put down by force. Many fled to England, where they were also known as the French Prophets (cf. D'Urfey's play of this title). Guiscard, who had stabbed Harley in Mar. 1711, was said to have had a hand in the Camisard rebellion.

Sybil: *Aeneid*, 6. 42 ff.

different kind: this qualifying sentence Addison inserted in the first collected editions of the *Spectator*.

I once saw a shepherd, says a famous Italian author, who used to divert himself in his solitudes with tossing up eggs and catching them again without breaking them: in which he had arrived to so great a degree of perfection, that he would keep up four at a time for several minutes together playing in the air, and falling into his hand by turns. I think, says the author, I never saw a greater severity than in this man's face; for by his wonderful perseverance and application, he had contracted the seriousness and gravity of a privy counsellor; and I could not but reflect with myself, that the same assiduity and attention had they been rightly applied, might have made him a greater mathematician than Archimedes.

Italian author: he has not been identified.
Archimedes: (*c.* 287–212 B.C.). The greatest mathematician of the ancient world.

ON METHOD IN WRITING AND SPEAKING

... lucidus ordo. Hor.

Among my daily papers, which I bestow on the public, there are some which are written with regularity and method, and others that run out into the wildness of those compositions, which go by the name of essays. As for the first, I have the whole scheme of the discourse in my mind, before I set pen to paper. In the other kind of writing, it is sufficient that I have several thoughts on a subject, without troubling myself to range them in such order, that they may seem to grow out of one another, and be disposed under the proper heads. Seneca and Montaigne are patterns for writing in this last kind, as Tully and Aristotle excel in the other. When I read an author of genius, who writes without method, I fancy myself in a wood that abounds with a great many noble objects, rising among one another in the greatest confusion and disorder. When I read a methodical discourse, I am in a regular plantation, and can place myself in its several centres, so as to take a view of all the lines and walks that are struck from them. You may ramble in the one a whole day together, and every moment discover something or other that is new to you, but when you have done you will have but a confused imperfect notion of the place; in the other, your eye commands the whole prospect, and gives you such an idea of it, as is not easily worn out of the memory.

Irregularity and want of method are only supportable in men of great learning or genius, who are often too full to be exact, and therefore choose to throw down their pearls in heaps before the reader, rather than be at the pains of stringing them.

Method is of advantage to a work, both in respect to the writer and the reader. In regard to the first, it is a great help to his invention. When a man has planned his discourse, he finds a great many thoughts rising out of every head, that do not offer themselves upon the general survey of a subject. His thoughts are at the same time more intelligible, and better discover their drift and meaning, when they are placed in their proper lights, and follow one another in a regular series, than when they are thrown together without order and connexion. There is always an obscurity in confusion, and the

Motto: Horace, *Ars poetica*, 41: His method will be clear. CREECH.
Seneca: the philosopher and author of moral discourses (5 or 4 B.C.–A.D. 65).

same sentence that would have enlightened the reader in one part of a discourse, perplexes him in another. For the same reason likewise every thought in a methodical discourse shows itself in its greatest beauty, as the several figures in a piece of painting receive new grace from their disposition in the picture. The advantages of a reader from a methodical discourse, are correspondent with those of the writer. He comprehends everything easily, takes it in with pleasure, and retains it long.

Method is not less requisite in ordinary conversation, than in writing, provided a man would talk to make himself understood. I, who hear a thousand coffee-house debates every day, am very sensible of this want of method in the thoughts of my honest countrymen. There is not one dispute in ten, which is managed in those schools of politics, where, after the three first sentences, the question is not entirely lost. Our disputants put me in mind of the cuttle-fish, that when he is unable to extricate himself, blackens all the water about him, till he becomes invisible. The man who does not know how to methodize his thoughts, has always, to borrow a phrase from *The Dispensary*, 'a barren superfluity of words'. The fruit is lost amidst the exuberance of leaves.

Tom Puzzle is one of the most eminent immethodical disputants of any that has fallen under my observation. Tom has read enough to make him very impertinent: his knowledge is sufficient to raise doubts, but not to clear them. It is pity that he has so much learning, or that he has not a great deal more. With these qualifications Tom sets up for a free-thinker, finds a great many things to blame in the constitution of his country, and gives shrewd intimations that he does not believe another world. In short, Puzzle is an atheist as much as his parts will give him leave. He has got about half-a-dozen commonplace topics, into which he never fails to turn the conversation, whatever was the occasion of it: though the matter in debate be about Douai or Denain, it is ten to one but half his discourse runs upon the unreasonableness of bigotry and priestcraft. This makes Mr. Puzzle the admiration of all those who have less sense than himself, and the contempt of all those who have more. There is none in town whom Tom dreads so much as my friend Will

---

The Dispensary: by Samuel Garth, ii. 94–5:
> Hourly his learn'd impertinence affords
> A barren superfluity of words.

Douai: one of the four fortress towns captured by the Allies in 1710, capitulated to Marlborough and Prince Eugene on 14 June 1710. At Denain, on 24 July N.S. 1712, Villars outmanœuvred Prince Eugene and inflicted on him a crushing defeat; the French thereupon recaptured Douai.

Dry. Will, who is acquainted with Tom's logic, when he finds him running off the question, cuts him short, with a 'What then? we allow all this to be true, but what is it to our present purpose?' I have known Tom eloquent half an hour together, and triumphing, as he thought, in the superiority of the argument, when he has been nonplussed, on a sudden, by Mr. Dry's desiring him to tell the company, what it was that he endeavoured to prove. In short, Dry is a man of a clear methodical head, but few words, and gains the same advantages over Puzzle, that a small body of regular troops would gain over a numberless undisciplined militia.

Notes

WIT AND HUMOUR

True and False Wit

p. 1 Longinus thus criticizes Caecilius, the Sicilian rhetorician, as writing in a humbler style than the argument demands.

p. 2 Poems in typographical shapes are discussed in Puttenham's *Art of English Poesie* (1589), Book II, Ch. xi [xii], ed. Gladys D. Willcock and Alice Walker (Cambridge, 1936), pp. 91–112. In this chapter Puttenham also discusses anagrams (pp. 108–11). See Margaret Church, 'The First English Pattern Poems', *PMLA* 61 (1946): 636–50. The order of examples (egg, wings, axe, shepherd's pipe, and altar) and the details of each follow Ralph Winterton's anthology (Cambridge, 1635), *Poetae Minores Graeci*.

p. 3 Winterton (pp. 328–9) describes the altar as by Simias of Rhodes 'or, according to others', by Theocritus. (None of the Technopaegnia are now attributed to Theocritus. See Gow's note to the *Syrinx* in Vol. ii of his edn., pp. 553–4.)

p. 3 George Herbert has several poems in typographical shapes, such as 'Easter Wings'.

p. 3 *Du Bartas.* Joshua Sylvester, in his translation of the *Divine Weeks and Works* (1608), includes in the Dedication several 'Anagrammata regia': 'IACOBVS STVART: Justa Scrutabo', 'IAMES STVART: A just Master', etc. Among the other preliminary pieces is 'An Acrostick Sonnet, to his friend M. Iosva Silvester, by R.N.'

p. 3 When Samuel Sorbière came to St. John's College at Oxford he entered 'a large wainscotted gallery, wherein I found no other ornament than the picture of King Charles I, which they took out of a cover, and showed here for a rarity, because the hair of his head was made up of Scripture lines, wrought wonderfully small, and more particularly of the Psalms of David in Latin' (*A Voyage to England*, 1709, pp. 42–3). R. Plot, *Natural History of Oxfordshire* (Oxford, 1677), pp. 276–7, also mentions this and a similar picture of King James as 'pretty curiosities'.

p. 4 Pindaric odes, particularly the irregular odes made fashionable by Cowley, were popular during the latter part of the seventeenth century.

p. 5 Proverbial for far-fetched etymologies. According to Quintilian (1.6.34), *Lucus*, a grove, is so called because, from the dense shade, there is very little light there (*Lucus, quia umbra opacus, parum luceat*).

p. 6 The owl, associated with Pallas Athene, was used on the coins of Athens.

p. 6 Blenheim Palace was at this time still uncompleted. The figure of the lion and cock is still to be seen over the entrance. The 'truly ingenious architect' was Sir John Vanbrugh, and the 'statuary' Grinling Gibbons.

p. 7   *Colloquia Familiaria* (Lyons, 1533), pp. 490–2. The Echo poem consists of a dialogue between Iuvenis and Echo, on the subject of studies. Echo answers in Latin and Greek, though not in Hebrew.

p. 8   The *Epigrammatum selectorum libri v* (Antwerp, 1616) of the Jesuit poet Bernard van Bauhuysen (or Bauhusius) contains (p. 74) an inscription to the Virgin Mary concluding with this line, which, according to its author, could be arranged in 1,022 ways, without impairing the sense or metre.

p. 8   'The Anagrame, or poesie transposed' is discussed in Puttenham (1589) (see note to No. 58, above) and there is a section on anagrams in Camden's *Remains* (ed. 1674, pp. 216–27). For contemporary examples of anagrams and acrostics see W. Winstanley, *New Help to Discourse* (4th edn., 1695), pp. 185–9.

p. 9   The acrostic, like the anagram, is found before the Middle Ages. Cicero gives examples in *De Divinatione*, 2. 54. 111–12.

p. 10   The chronogram seems to have arisen in the seventeenth century. See James Hilton's *Chronograms, 5,000 and more in number* (1882) and *Chronograms continued and concluded* (1885).

p. 10   A monthly periodical founded in 1672, with literary and theatrical news, fugitive pieces in verse and prose, etc. The editor from 1710 to 1714 was Charles Rivière Dufresny.

p. 11   Bysshe's *Art of English Poetry* (Ch. ii, sect. iii), cites Dryden's opinion that double rhymes should seldom be used in heroic verse. Bysshe adds: 'but they are very graceful in the lyric, to which, as well as to the burlesque, those rhymes more properly belong' (8th edn., 1737, i. 22). (Bysshe uses these two couplets from *Hudibras* by way of illustration.)

p. 12   *Tatler* 32 calls punning 'an enormity which has been revived (after being long oppressed)', and the *Spectator* generally considers the pun only an example of false wit (cf. the censure of Milton's puns in No. 297), though Addison himself occasionally puns, as in the play on the words *pie* and *piety* in No. 85, and many of his friends were addicted to the practice, particularly Swift.

p. 13   Rowe, in his 'Account of Shakespeare' (1709), makes a similar comment: 'As for his jingling sometimes, and playing upon words, it was the common vice of the age he lived in: and if we find it in the pulpit, made use of as an ornament to the sermons of some of the gravest divines of those times; perhaps it may not be thought too light for the stage' (p. xxiii).

p. 13   'Honest Mr. Swan' as a maker of puns and clenches, is mentioned by Dryden in the *Discourse concerning Satire* (1693) (*Essays*, ed. Watson, ii. 139). Wycherley addressed a 'panegyric on quibbling' to him (*Works*, ed. Summers, ii. 163–5).

p. 14   The university was Cambridge. Cf. John Henley, 'An Oration on Grave Conundrums and Serious Buffoons': 'All schools, especially Westminster, train up scholars to declaim in an ironical manner, and make sharp and burlesque epigrams and poems. Colleges are famous for the like; puns are a main education

in Cambridge; and practised and professed in all exercises and conversation'
(*Oratory Transactions*, no. vi (1729), p. 12).

p. 14   The earliest example in *OED* of the phrase 'revival of letters' for 'the
Renaissance in its literary aspect' is dated 1785.

p. 14   'last winter's productions': the recently revived 'enormity called punning' is discussed in *Tatler* 32 (23 June 1709) and there are frequent references to it,
as well as to other examples of false wit in the earlier paper. For Nick Crosse-
grain 'who writes anagrams' see *Tatler* 58 (23 Aug. 1709).

p. 15   'Witch's Prayer': see *Hudibras*, I. iii. 343–4; Congreve, *Love for Love*,
IV. xxi; Blackmore, *Satyr against Wit*, 348–9; etc.

p. 15   'paw of a lion': cf. L'Estrange, *Fables of Aesop*, No. 14.

p. 17   Anagrams, chronograms, acrostics and doggerel rhymes are discussed in
No. 60; lipograms and echo poems in No. 59; puns in No. 61; and poems in typographical shapes in No. 58.

p. 17   Cowley, Waller, Dryden, Milton, and Spenser are all treated in Addison's
early poem, 'An Account of the Greatest English Poets' (1694), where Cowley's
fault is described as 'only wit in its excess'.

p. 17   The 'Hero and Leander' ascribed to Musaeus is printed in Winterton,
Poetae Minores Graeci, pp. 330–47. It was written, not by the early mythical
singer Musaeus, but by Musaeus Grammaticus, the epic poet (late fifth century
A.D.).

p. 17   The examples of Cowley's mixed wit are taken from his collection, *The
Mistress*. Burning-glasses: 'The Vain Love', lines 1–4. The Torrid Zone: 'The
Request', stanza 4. His Letter: 'Written in Juice of Lemon', stanza 4. When
she weeps: 'Weeping', stanza 4. When she is absent: 'The Parting', stanza 3.
His ambitious love: 'My Fate', stanzas 1, 3. When it does not let him sleep:
'Sleep', stanza 1. When it is opposed: 'Counsel' (ii), stanza 2. Upon the Dying
of a Tree: 'The Tree', stanza 1. When he resolves: 'Love given over', stanza 4.
An Aetna: 'The Monopoly', stanza 1. Throwing Oil: 'The Incurable', stanza 4.
The Fire of Love: 'The Parting', stanza 6. Love . . . cooks Pleasure: 'Answer
to the Platonics', 11–12. The Poet's Heart: 'The Heart Fled Again', stanza 4.
A Ship set on Fire: 'Love Given Over', stanza 2.

p. 18   *Dryden on wit:*, 'a propriety of thoughts and words; or, in other terms,
thoughts and words elegantly adapted to the subject' (*Apology* prefixed to
The State of Innocence, 1677; Watson, i. 207).

p. 19   Dominique Bouhours (1628–1702). The Jesuit grammarian and critic.
His influential *Manière de bien penser dans les ouvrages d'esprit* was published
in 1687 (2nd edn., revised and corrected, Amsterdam, 1692). It consists of
four dialogues between Eudoxe, the exponent of good taste and admirer of
the Ancients, and Philanthe, who prefers the more showy literature of the
Spanish and Italians.

p. 19   In the Preface to the 1701 edition of his *Works* Boileau writes: 'What is a new, brilliant, extraordinary thought? It is not, as the ignorant persuade themselves, a thought which nobody ever had, nor ought to have. But on the contrary, a thought which everybody ought to have had, and which someone bethinks himself of expressing the first. *Wit* is not *wit*, but as it says something everybody thought of, and that in a lively, delicate, and new manner' (Works, 1711–12, i, pp. ii–iii).

Humour

p. 26   This paper, the first of the critical essays in the *Spectator*, is preliminary to the series on true and false wit (Nos. 58–63). Here, however, the emphasis is on the needless cruelty inflicted by writers of lampoon and satire. The genealogy of true and false wit introduces a device very popular in Addison's day, with relationships humorously depicted by means of a family tree. Swift had drawn up a similar genealogy of true and false merit, in *Examiner* 30, just a few weeks earlier (1 March 1711).

p. 26   Bedlam, the hospital of St. Mary of Bethlehem, had occupied since 1675 a new structure in Moor-fields. Edward Hatton's *New View of London* (1708) describes the hospital, with apartments 'for 150 lunatic persons'. An account of a visit there is to be found in Ward's *London Spy* (Part III, 1706).

p. 26   Shadwell had died in 1692. The breaking of windows is a frequent theme of satire in Shadwell's description of the rakes of his day: *The Woman-Captain, The Squire of Alsatia, The Scowrers, Epsom Wells*, etc.

p. 29   In the Middle Ages and later, professional fools were a recognized class at court and in the families of the wealthy. The Earl of Suffolk's jester, Dicky Pearce, is the subject of an epitaph by Swift. Many examples are given in John Doran's *History of Court Fools* (1858).

p. 29   *Satire* iv (to the Abbé Le Vayer). In his reply, 'To the Spectator upon his paper on the 24th of April', published with his *Essay on Shakespear* (1712), John Dennis admits the authorship of the ridiculous couplet, but states that he had written it thirty years before, when he was 'a very boy', and regrets that Steele (who was generally believed to be Mr. Spectator at this time) did not quote some of his more mature work, such as his 'Battle of Ramillia'. In the *Critical Specimen* (by Pope?) of 1711 one of the jibes at Dennis is: 'How he writ upon occasion (*vide Spect.* 47) two good lines, being the most wonderful and surprising adventure in the whole book' (Pope, *Prose Works*, ed. Ault, i. 15).

p. 30   On the custom of April Fools see A. R. Wright, *British Calendar Customs: England*, vol. ii, ed. T. E. Lones (1938), pp. 171–6, where the earliest reference given is from *Dawks's News Letter*, 2 April 1698: 'yesterday being the 1st of April, several persons were sent to the Tower Ditch to see the lions washed.' When or how the custom originated, writes Mr. Lones, may never be known. The earliest quotation in *OED* is dated 1687.

p. 31   A biter is described in *Tatler* 12 as 'a dull fellow, that tells you a lie with a grave face, and laughs at you for knowing him no better than to believe him'.

Cf. Swift, letter to the Rev. William Tisdall (16 Dec. 1703): 'I will teach you a way to outwit Mrs. Johnson: it is a new-fashioned way of being witty, and they call it a *bite*. You must ask a bantering question, or tell some damned lie in a serious manner, and then she will answer or speak as if you were in earnest; and then cry you, "Madam, there's a *bite*"' (*Correspondence*, ed. H. Williams, i. 40).

p. 32 Cureau de la Chambre in *The Characters of the Passions* (1650), p. 227, discusses 'Why, of all creatures, Man only laughs'. For risibility as 'the proper affection of man' see also Dr. Thomas Willis, *Anatomy of the Brain*, Ch. xvii (*Four Treatises*, 1681, p. 117).

p. 33 A reminiscence of Addison's tour on the Continent. In a letter to Henry Newton (from Blois, Feb. 1700), in which he comments on the austerities of the French convents, Addison wrote: 'I can't forbear on this occasion telling you an odd opinion of a Holy Father, a Capucin, who in a discourse on the vanity of mirth, told us that he did not question but laughter was the effect of Original Sin and that Adam was not risible before the Fall' (*Letters*, ed. Graham, p. 20).

p. 34 For a fuller development of this distinction see Fielding's Preface to *Joseph Andrews*. In the Dedication to his translation of Boileau's *Lutrin* in 1708 (*Works of Boileau*, 1711–12, i, sig. A3ᵛ) John Ozell wrote: 'If I distinguish right, there are two sorts of Burlesque; the first where things of mean figure and slight concern appear in all the pomp and bustle of an epic poem; such is this of the *Lutrin*. The second sort is where great events are made ridiculous by the meanness of the character, and the oddness of the numbers, such is the *Hudibras* of our excellent Butler.'

p. 34 Lucian (A.D. 115–*c*. 200), the Greek satirist, wrote a series of dialogues ridiculing the myths about the gods.

p. 34 *The Dispensary*, by Samuel Garth, was published in 1699; Butler's *Hudibras* in 1663, 1664, 1678. On this subject see R. P. Bond, *English Burlesque Poetry* (Cambridge, Mass., 1932), pp. 29–41.

POETRY

The Ballad

p. 36 See Boileau 'Critical Reflections on … Longinus', i: ''Tis said, Malherbe read his verses to his servant maid; and I remember, Molière has often shown me an old maid of his, to whom, he told me, he read his comedies; assuring me, that when any part of the pleasantry did not strike her, he corrected it; because he frequently found at his theatre, that those very places did not succeed' (*Works*, 1711–12, ii. 89).

p. 37 Jonson's conversations with Drummond were first printed in this year (1711) at Edinburgh, in the *Works* of William Drummond, edited by Bishop John Sage and Thomas Ruddiman (pp. 224–7), but this statement of Jonson does not occur in it. A transcript of the conversations, made by the Edinburgh antiquary, Sir Robert Sibbald, and preserved in the National Library of Scotland, contains a sentence about Southwell somewhat similar: 'That Southwell was hanged yet so he had written that piece of his the Burning Babe he would have been content to destroy many of his' (*Works* of Jonson, ed. Herford and Simpson, i. 137). As Herford and Simpson suggest, Addison may be recalling this verdict of Jonson on Southwell and transferring it to 'Chevy Chase'.

p. 37   *Apology for Poetry* (ed. Geoffrey Shepherd, 1965), p. 118.

p. 37   Addison is right: the weight of seventeenth-century critical opinion was solidly in support of the view that art should serve the ends of morality (cf. René Bray, *La Formation de la doctrine classique en France*, 1927, pp. 63–84), but the formulations he makes and the examples he gives show that he is following the critic who gave the most extreme expression to the theory of heroic poetry as 'moral instruction disguised under the allegory of an action', viz. Le Bossu. Book i, Ch. vii of the *Traité du poème épique* (1675) deals with the method of composing a fable. The first thing, says Le Bossu, is 'to choose the instruction, and the point of morality, which is to serve as its foundation . . .' (edn. of 1719, i. 28–9). For the extraordinary reputation of Le Bossu at this period—from the time of Dryden through the greater part of the eighteenth century—see A. F. B. Clark, *Boileau and the French Classical Critics in England, 1660–1830* (Paris, 1925), pp. 243–61.

p. 37   Le Bossu (Book i, Ch. viii) makes this point about Homer. 'He saw the Grecians, for whom he designed his poems, were divided into as many states as they had capital cities. Each was a body politic, and had its form of government independent from all the rest. And yet these distinct states were very often obliged to unite together in one body against their common enemies . . . Homer then has taken for the foundation of his fable this great truth; viz. *That a misunderstanding between princes is the ruin of their own states*' (1719 edn., i. 34–5).

p. 37   The historical inaccuracy is refuted by Nichols, Chalmers, and other editors of the *Spectator*.

p. 38   Valerius Flaccus' epic poem, the *Argonautica*, was left unfinished at the time of his death (*c*. A.D. 92). The *Thebais* of Statius was completed about A.D. 91.

p. 41   Karl Nessler (*Geschichte der Ballade Chevy Chase*, p. 110) compares Dryden's remarks on the vulgar words and low expressions in Shakespeare (in 'The Grounds of Criticism in Tragedy' and elsewhere) which may have influenced Addison. The best account of Addison's treatment of 'Chevy Chase' and 'The Children in the Wood' (No. 85) is by A. B. Friedman, *The Ballad Revival* (Chicago, 1961), Ch. iv.

p. 42   Horace, *Odes*, 1. 2. 23–4:
    The youth shall hear that impious steel
    Against our selves we madly drew, . . .   CREECH

p. 42   Virgil, *Georgics*, 3. 43–5:
    Cytheron loudly calls me to my way;
    Thy hounds, Taygetus, open and pursue their prey.

High Epidaurus urges on my speed,
Famed for his hills, and for his horses' breed:
From hills and dales the cheerful cries rebound:
For echo hunts along; and propagates the sound. DRYDEN

p. 43   Virgil, *Aeneid*, 11. 605–6; 7. 682–4, 712–15:
Advancing in a line, they couch their spears;
And less and less the middle space appears.
His own Praeneste sends a chosen band,
With those who plough Saturnia's Gabine land:
Besides the succour which cold Anien yields,
The rocks of Hernicus, and dewy fields.
              Besides a band
That followed from Velinum's dewy land:
And Amiternian troops, of mighty fame,
And mountaineers, that from Severus came.
And from the craggy cliffs of Tetrica,
And those where yellow Tiber takes his way,
And where Himella's wanton waters play.
Casperia sends her arms, with those that lie
By Fabaris, and fruitful Foruli. DRYDEN

p. 43   *Aeneid*, 9. 47, 269–70:
The fiery Turnus flew before the rest.
Thou saw'st the courser by proud Turnus pressed. DRYDEN

p. 43   *Aeneid*, 12. 318–20:
Thus while he spoke, unmindful of defence,
A winged arrow struck the pious prince.
But whether from some human hand it came,
Or hostile god, is left unknown by fame. DRYDEN

p. 44   *Aeneid*, 2. 426–8:
Then Ripheus followed, in th' unequal fight;
Just of his word, observant of the right;
Heaven thought not so. DRYDEN

p. 44   *Hudibras*, I. iii. 94–6:
And being down still laid about;
As Widdrington in doleful dumps
Is said to fight upon his stumps.

p. 45   *Aeneid*, 12. 229–31:
For shame, Rutulians, can you bear the sight,
Of one exposed for all, in single fight?
Can we, before the face of Heaven, confess
Our courage colder, or our numbers less? DRYDEN

p. 46   The Turks 'are so careful in showing their reverence to the name of God,
that if they find the least bit of paper in the way, they take it up, and put it into
some hole of a wall . . .' (Jean de Thévenot, *Travels into the Levant*, Part i (1687),
p. 43). Cf. also *Letters writ by a Turkish Spy*, vol. vi, Book i, Letter 7 (1702 edn.),
vi. 25).

p. 46   Christmas pies (and plum puddings) would be looked upon by Puritans and dissenters as 'superstitious viands' associated with Popery.

p. 47   There is a reference to the use of printed papers on walls in Etherege's *Comical Revenge* (IV. iii): 'Thou shalt be witness . . . how many bellmen I'll rob of their verses, to furnish a little apartment in the back side of my lodging.'

p. 47   'The Children in the Wood' (*Oxford Book of Ballads*, ed. Quiller-Couch, No. 174) was one of the best-known broadside 'vulgar' ballads—those narrating a rather long connected story, often (as here) giving an account of a murder or some other sensational deed. The tune 'Rogero' associated with it became even more popular a few years later, when Gay used it for one of the most affecting songs in the first act of *The Beggar's Opera* (Air xii).

p. 48   Horace, *Odes*, 3. 4. 9–13.
> In lofty Vultur's rising grounds
> Without my nurse Apulia's bounds
> When young, and tired with sport and play,
> And bound with pleasing sleep I lay,
> Doves covered me with myrtle boughs
> And with soft murmurs sweetened my repose.   CREECH

p. 48   Charles Sackville, sixth Earl of Dorset (1643–1706). Hearne wrote in his diary on 8 June, the day following the publication of this essay:

> The late Earl of Dorset had a very large collection of old ballads, which he used oftentimes to read, with very great delight, much admiring the simplicity and nakedness of the style; and yet he was a man of admirable sense and understanding. I heard the late Dean of Christ Church, Dr. Aldrich say, the last time I was with him, that he would give a good sum of money for a collection of such ballads, whenever he could meet with one (*Collections*, ed. Doble, iii. 173).

Since this is probably based on Addison's essay, it does not offer much confirmatory evidence, except that Hearne tends to take issue with the *Spectator* whenever possible. Mr. Brice Harris, in his *Charles Sackville, Sixth Earl of Dorset* (Univ. of Illinois Studies in Language and Literature, vol. xxvi, 1940, nos. 3–4), mentions Addison's statement and also Hearne's, and adds that 'nothing further is known' about 'this reputed collection' (pp. 31–2). The statement about Lord Dorset, as well as the one in the following sentence about Dryden and others, may well rest, as Addison says, on oral report.

p. 48   In *Le Misanthrope* (I. ii) Alceste, after quoting an old song, declares its superiority to a new modish sonnet:

> La rime n'est pas riche, et le style en est vieux:
> Mais ne voyez-vous pas que cela vaut bien mieux
> Que ces colifichets dont le bon sens murmure,
> Et que la passion parle là toute pure?   (401–4.)

The Fable

p. 49   The widespread popularity of the verse fable in the early eighteenth century was due primarily to La Fontaine. His *Fables* were first published in 1668 (six books), other parts appearing in 1671, 1678, 1679, and the twelve books in

1694. Aesop, in a Latin version, had of course been used for generations in the schools. Sir Roger L'Estrange brought out in 1692 a large collection, which went through a number of editions. Lady Winchilsea wrote a great many fables, many of them imitated from the French. Shortly after the *Spectator* John Gay published two famous collections (1727 and 1738), which remained popular throughout the century. In *Guardian* 152 Addison discusses the fable or allegory and praises Spenser for his accomplishments in this genre.

p. 49   See Judges 9:8–15.

p. 49   Aesop, the traditional composer of animal fables, is thought to have lived in the sixth century B.C.

p. 49   The fable of the interdependence of the parts of the body (Livy, *History*, 2. 32, and elsewhere) had been used recently by Defoe in the *Review* (1 May 1711) to illustrate the dependence of the landed interest upon trade.

p. 49   Although Horace did not write fables as such, his poems inculcated moral truths through anecdote and story, in the fashion described here, as in the tale of the country mouse and the city mouse (*Satires*, 2. 6, 77–117).

p. 49   Boileau does not discuss the fable in his *Art poétique* (1674), although La Fontaine's first collection of fables had appeared by that date. Boileau himself wrote two short fables, *La Mort et le bûcheron* (1668) and *L'Huître et les deux plaideurs* (1699).

p. 49   Horace (*Epistles*, 1. 2) makes this point about the *Iliad* and *Odyssey*. Dacier, in his notes to Aristotle's *Poetics* Ch. ix, published in 1705, observes that when Homer wrote of Achilles 'he had no design to describe that man alone who bore that name, but to set before our eyes, what violence and anger could make all men of that character, say, or do. Achilles is then an universal person, general and allegorical . . .' (p. 144).

p. 53   *Absalom and Achitophel*, by Dryden, was published in November 1681, at the height of the agitation aroused by fears of a 'Popish plot'. Quotations from the poem appear in *Spectator* 77, 162, and 222.

p. 53   The story told here is 'The Fable of the Two Owls' in the *Turkish Tales* (Tonson, 1708), pp. 174–6. Addison had quoted from this collection in No. 94.

p. 54   Pliny, *Natural History*, 10. 137. See Bayle's *Dictionnaire historique*, art. 'Democritus', Remark H: 'Here follow some other idle fancies of Democritus. He said that the blood of some birds, which he named, being mixed together, would bring forth a serpent of such an admirable virtue, that whosoever did eat it might understand what the birds said to each other. Pliny is in the right to laugh at this chimera.'

Modern Poetry

p. 55   This is the volume of *Miscellaneous Poems and Translations by Several Hands* published by Lintot, containing 'The Rape of the Lock', the 'Epistle to

Miss Blount, with the Works of Voiture', and other shorter pieces of Pope, advertised in No. 383 (20 May 1712) as 'This Day . . . Published'.

p. 55   Tickell's poem is advertised in No. 521, two days before the publication of this number as 'This day . . . Published'.

p. 56   Cf. No. 62 (p. 19): 'Bouhours . . . has taken pains to show that it is impossible for any thought to be beautiful which is not just, and has not its foundation in the nature of things. . . .'

p. 56   Perhaps a compliment to Pope's 'Rape of the Lock', first published in the *Miscellany* mentioned above.

p. 56   *Mr. Philips.* The pastorals of Ambrose Philips had been praised (by Steele) earlier in No. 400.

Pope's *Essay on Criticism*

p. 58   Gaius Cornelius Gallus was a friend of Virgil. The poems in which he may have praised Virgil are not extant, but Virgil refers to him in *Eclogues* 6 and 10. Lucius Varius Rufus and Plotius Tucca were friends to whom Virgil bequeathed his unfinished writings, and who afterwards published the *Aeneid*. For the praise of Propertius see *Elegies*, 2. 34. 61 ff. Horace praises the work of Virgil in various places; Ovid praises the *Aeneid* in *Ars amatoria*, 3. 337-8. Bavius and Maevius, minor poets, are pilloried by Virgil in a famous passage (*Eclogue* 3. 90).

p. 59   See the Preface to the 1701 edition of Boileau's works: 'Qu'est-ce qu'une pensée neuve, brillante, extraordinaire? Ce n'est point, comme se le persuadent les ignorans, une pensée que personne n'a jamais eue, ni dû avoir: c'est au contraire une pensée qui a dû venir à tout le monde, et que quelqu'un s'avise le premier d'exprimer. Un bon mot n'est bon mot qu'en ce qu'il dit une chose que chacun pensait, et qu'il la dit d'une manière vive, fine et nouvelle (*Œuvres*, ed. Berriat-Saint-Prix, 1837, i. 19-20).

p. 60   On 10 Oct. 1714 Pope wrote to Addison suggesting that this phrase should be altered. 'I happened to find the same in Dionysius of Halicarnassus's Treatise, περὶ Συνθέσεος ὀνομάτων, who treats very largely upon these verses. I know you will think fit to soften your expression, when you see the passage, which you must needs have read, though it be since slipped out of your memory' (*Correspondence*, ed. Sherburn, i. 263-4). Addison apparently deleted this passage, since it is omitted from Tickell's edition of 1721. In the same letter Pope requested Addison to point out the 'strokes of ill-nature' which Addison had seen in the *Essay on Criticism*. Whether Addison complied with this request does not appear.

p. 61   *The Essay on Translated Verse*, by Wentworth Dillon, Earl of Roscommon, appeared in 1684. The '*Essay on the Art of Poetry*' is the *Essay* on *Poetry* by John Sheffield, Earl of Mulgrave (Duke of Buckinghamshire), published in 1682.

PARADISE LOST

p. 62 In his *Discourse concerning Satire* (1693) Dryden maintained that Milton's subject 'is not that of an heroic poem, properly so called. His design is the losing of our happiness; his event is not prosperous, like that of all other epic works; his heavenly machines are many, and his human persons are but two' (*Essays*, ed. Watson, ii. 84).

p. 62 For the relationship of 'fable' to 'action' in English criticism at this time see H. T. Swedenberg, Jun., *The Theory of the Epic in England, 1650–1800* (University of California Publications in English, vol. xv, 1944, Ch. vii). Addison here seems to be thinking of fable in the sense in which Le Bossu had defined it, 'a discourse invented to form men's manners by instructions disguised under the allegories of one single action' (Book I, Ch. vi). In No. 297 (p. 83), on the other hand, he uses the term 'fable', simple and implex, where it seems synonymous with action, and follows Le Bossu's qualifications for epic action (Book II, Ch. vii).

p. 62 Aristole, *Poetics*, 23. 1 ('ought to include one only action, entire, perfect, and finished' (Dacier's translation, p. 390)). Le Bossu (Book II, Ch. vii) had enumerated four qualifications for epic action: unity, integrity, importance, and duration. Unity requires the use of episodes kept in proper subordination to the main action (Chs. vii, viii); integrity means that the action should be entire, perfect, and complete (Chs. ix–xvii); duration allows a longer action in epic poems than in dramatic (Ch. xviii); and importance requires the epic poet to surprise 'the minds of his readers by admiration, and by the *importance* of the things he treats of; and [by] taking for his subject a great, noble, and important action' (Ch. xix). Addison obviously has these points of Le Bossu in mind, since he discusses duration along with greatness toward the end of the essay. Addison's criteria for action are what almost any well-read critic of his day would subscribe to. Dryden, at the beginning of his Dedication of the *Aeneis*, had used the same formula: the action of the heroic poem 'is always one, entire, and great' (ed. Watson, ii. 224); and Dennis, in his *Remarks on Prince Arthur* (1696), holds that the action of an epic poem should be one, important, and entire (ed. Hooker, i. 59). For Dacier see p. 281 (note to p. 210).

p. 65 Dacier, in a note on the *Poetics* 24. 7, writes (p. 418):

> Epic poem cannot subsist without narration, since 'tis the narration that gives its form, and distinguishes it from tragedy; but as narration, properly speaking, is not an imitation, or at most an imperfect one, an epic poem ought to be a true imitation. [Homer] uses in his poem only so much of the narration, as is necessary to preserve its form; and when he has said some small matter himself, makes his persons appear who are really actors. This is what Aristotle, with good reason too, thought so praiseworthy. Virgil knew perfectly well this address of Homer, and made a wonderful use of it.

p. 65 In his *Discourse concerning Satire* Dryden mentions the action in the *Iliad* as forty-eight days (Watson, ii. 96), and in the *Parallel of Poetry and Painting* he writes: ''Tis true, Homer took up only the space of eight-and-forty days for his

Iliads; but whether Virgil's action was comprehended in a year, or somewhat more, is not determined by Bossu' (Watson, ii. 188). (Le Bossu discusses the duration of the action in Book II, Ch. xviii, and in Book III, Ch. xii.) In the Dedication of the *Aeneis* Dryden dismisses the matter: 'Indeed, the whole dispute is of no more concernment to the common reader, than it is to a ploughman, whether February this year had 28 or 29 days in it' (*Essays*, ed. Ker, ii. 204; a passage omitted from Watson's edn. cited elsewhere). Dacier, in a note to the *Poetics*, 5. 4, observes that Homer confined the action of the *Iliad* to forty-seven days, since the theme was one of violence and passion, but that he allowed eight-and-a-half years to the *Odyssey*, where the theme was the wisdom and conduct of Ulysses. 'Virgil', he concludes, 'knew very well this prudence and wisdom of the Greek poet; for to the action of his *Aeneids*, whose character is piety, and good nature, he gives seven years; in confining that poem, to the narrow limits of the *Iliads*, he would have been no less blameable than Homer, if he had given to his *Iliads* the whole extent of his *Odysses*' (p. 67).

p. 66   Although he follows 'Aristotle's method' in considering manners in the second place, Addison somewhat over-simplifies in equating manners with characters. Strictly speaking, 'Manners characterize men, and denote their inclinations, either good, or bad' (Dacier, p. 85). Le Bossu (Book IV, Ch. i) defines them as 'all the natural or acquired inclinations, which carry us on to good, bad, or indifferent actions'. In No. 309 (pp. 96–100) Addison illustrates the general points he makes here by analysing the characters of the fallen angels.

p. 68   Dennis, in *The Grounds of Criticism in Poetry* (1704), remarked that 'Milton was the first, who in the space of almost 4000 years, resolved, for his country's honour and his own, to present the world with an original poem; that is to say, a poem that should have his own thoughts, his own images, and his own spirit' (Hooker, i. 333).

p. 68   Addison criticizes Sin and Death more fully in No. 357 (pp. 155–7).

p. 68   Garth's *Dispensary* was published in 1699; Boileau's *Lutrin* in 1674 and 1681.

p. 68   Dacier (pp. 430–2) has a long note on this, concluding (p. 432): 'Thus this absurdity which is found in the fable, when 'tis examined alone, is hidden by the beauties that surround it, and 'tis this the poets ought to imitate: this is more adorned with fictions, than any place of Homer, and whose style is most wrought up, it signifies little to have this account of it; read it and you'll find that Homer is the greatest charmer in the world.'

p. 69   Uriel: one of the seven archangels in rabbinical lore, the 'Regent of the Sun' (*PL*, iii. 690). Gabriel: the archangel traditionally thought of as God's chief messenger, in Hebrew and Mohammedan lore. Michael: the prince of all the angels and leader of the celestial armies (Rev. 12:7, 8). Raphael: the 'affable archangel' (*PL*, vii. 40) and the companion of Tobias in the apocryphal Book of Tobit.

p. 69   The material in this and the following paragraph follows very closely a passage in Addison's *Discourse on Ancient and Modern Learning*, first published

in 1739 (Guthkelch, ii. 456–7). It has been suggested that the *Discourse* is an early
work drawn upon by Addison for this number (and No. 416). See E. K. Broadus,
M.L.N. 22 (1907): 1–2.

p. 69   Aristotle, *Poetics*, 13. 2–3. As translated by Dacier, it reads: 'We must
not choose to make a very honest man fall from prosperity into adversity; for
instead of exciting terror and compassion, it will give horror, which is detested by
all' (p. 186). Addison's reference to the *Aeneid* is probably influenced by Le
Bossu's discussion (Book II, Ch. xvii) of sad endings as appropriate to tragedy
and happy endings as appropriate to the epic. 'The Romans would have been
disgusted and offended, if [Virgil] had ill-used their founder and ancestors: and
besides in the *Odyssey* and the *Aeneid* the poets would have been unjust, and the
readers dissatisfied, if such brave princes and such noble souls as Ulysses and
Aeneas had been suffered to sink under any misfortune' (1719 edn., i. 211–12).

p. 71   Rapin (*A Comparison of Homer and Virgil*, Ch. viii) criticizes Homer for
the meanness of his sentiments, but concludes that 'the weaknesses of this poet
are not so much to be imputed to him as to the age he lived in, which was not
capable of any greater refinement, either in thoughts or in morals' (*Whole
Critical Works*, 1706, i. 160). Le Bossu (Book VI, Ch. iii) takes the same position.
'What is base and ignoble at one time and in one country, is not always so in
others' (1719 edn., ii, 259).

p. 71   In treating imagination as the poetic power which creates something
'out of nature' and 'original', Addison is somewhat in advance of his time.
Shadwell, in the Preface to *The Lancashire Witches* (1682), had praised Shakespeare for creating witchcraft 'for the most part out of his own imagination', and
Rowe in 1709 thought Shakespeare's genius most apparent where 'he gives his
imagination an entire loose, and raises his fancy to a flight above mankind and
the limits of the visible world' (Preface, p. xxiii); but to most critics of the
seventeenth and early eighteenth centuries the poet's imagination worked with
visible materials, and invention consisted generally in simply making new
combinations from existing data. Dryden, in 'The Grounds of Criticism in
Tragedy' (1679), had praised Shakespeare's Caliban, but on the ground that the
character 'is not wholly beyond the bounds of credibility, at least the vulgar still
believe it' (Watson, i. 253). The most that Rowe can say of the 'extravagant
character of Caliban' is that it is 'mightily well sustained, shows a wonderful
invention in the author, who could strike out such a particular wild image, and is
certainly one of the finest and most uncommon grotesques that was ever seen'
(Preface, p. xxiv).

p. 72   The general view. Cf. Sir W. Temple 'Of Poetry' (Spingarn, iii.82).

p. 72   Of the four Latin poets mentioned here, Ovid (43 B.C.–A.D. 17?) was best
known for the *Metamorphoses*; Lucan (39–65) was author of the epic poem
Bellum Civile in ten books (usually known as *Pharsalia*); Statius (*c.* 45–96)
published the epic poem *Thebais* (*c.* A.D. 91); Claudian (*fl.* 395–404) wrote
various epics and short occasional poems. For the reputation of the Italian poet
Tasso, author of *Jerusalem Delivered*, see A. F. B. Clark, *Boileau and the French
Classical Critics in England* (Paris, 1925), pp. 337–60; and C. P. Brand, *Torquato
Tasso: A Study of the Poet and his Contribution to English Literature* (Cambridge,
1965). Ovid, Lucan, Statius and Claudian are frequently grouped together as

11 + C.E.T.S.

writers of 'false wit' at this time. Dryden couples Lucan and Statius as 'men of an unbounded imagination, but who often wanted the poise of judgement' (Preface to *The State of Innocence*, 1677; Watson, i. 201). In No. 333 Addison cites an example of Claudian's 'puerilities'.

p. 75   For Dryden's views see Watson, i. 199; ii. 46, 150. The letter 'to Mr. T. S.' in vindication of Milton, printed in Gildon's *Miscellaneous Letters and Essays* of 1694 (Spingarn, iii. 198–200), defends Milton's '*ancient* and consequently *less intelligible* words, phrases, and similes'. On the whole subject see R. D. Havens, *The Influence of Milton on English Poetry* (Cambridge, Mass., 1922), pp. 64–8.

p. 75   Addison here follows Aristotle, *Poetics*, 22. 1.

p. 79   For Dryden's criticism of Milton's revival of 'antiquated' words (in the *Discourse of Satire*) see Watson, ii.150.

p. 81   Cf. Pope, *Essay on Criticism*, 408–9.
Some ne'er advance a judgement of their own,
But catch the spreading notion of the town.

p. 82   Addison's position is close to that of Dryden, who wrote in the Preface to *The State of Innocence* (1677): 'They wholly mistake the nature of criticism who think its business is principally to find fault. Criticism, as it was first instituted by Aristotle, was meant a standard of judging well; the chiefest part of which is to observe those excellencies which should delight a reasonable reader' (Watson, i. 196–7).

p. 82   Contemporary readers doubtless saw in this a reference to John Dennis, the 'critic of the woeful countenance' of the *Critical Specimen* (1711), probably by Pope, and the butt of much contemporary sarcasm (see Hooker, ii. pp. lvii–lviii). Hooker quotes from the *Examiner* of 10 Jan. 1712 a reference to Dennis as 'an old sour dry critic'.

p. 83   Dryden in the passage from the Preface to *The State of Innocence* cited above had also referred to Longinus, who 'has judiciously preferred the sublime genius that sometimes errs to the middling or indifferent one which makes few faults, but seldom or never rises to any excellence' (Watson, i. 197).

p. 83   Dryden (Dedication of *Aeneis*) thought Milton would have had a better place among the list of heroic poets 'if the giant had not foiled the knight and driven him out of his stronghold, to wander through the world with his lady errant' (Watson, ii. 233).

p. 84   In the epic, writes Le Bossu (Book II, Ch. xvii), 'all the poets seem to conspire for a happy catastrophe' (i. 211).

p. 84   Dennis (in *The Grounds of Criticism*, 1704) also thought 'the Devil is properly his hero, because he gets the better' (*Works*, ed. Hooker, i. 334).

p. 87   Le Bossu (Book VI, Ch. vi) warns against pedantry and undue display of learning. 'The desire of appearing learned makes a poem smell of it from one end to the other' (ii. 283).

p. 88   Cf. No. 61 (pp. 12–15), where punning is described as 'a jingle of words'. In his notes on Ovid's *Metamorphoses* Addison remarks that Homer, Virgil, and Horace all scorned mixed wit and that 'one would wonder therefore how so sublime a genius as Milton could sometimes fall into it, in such a work as an epic poem. But we must attribute it to his humouring the vicious taste of the age he lived in, and the false judgment of our unlearned English readers in general, who have few of them a relish of the more masculine and noble beauties of poetry' (Guthkelch, i. 144).

p. 88   Hobbes, in his *Answer to Davenant* (1650), had objected to 'metaphors or comparisons as cannot come into men's thoughts but by mean conversation and experience of humble or evil arts, which the person of an epic poem cannot be thought acquainted with' (Spingarn, ii. 54). In the Preface to *Annus Mirabilis* (1667) Dryden approves of their use (Watson, i. 96), but in the Dedication of *Aeneis* (1697) he admits that he has not written in 'the proper terms of navigation, land-service, or in the cant of any profession'. Virgil, he continues, 'writ not to mariners, soldiers, astronomers, gardeners, peasants, etc., but to all in general, and in particular to men and ladies of the first quality, who have been better bred than to be too nicely knowing in the terms. In such cases, 'tis enough for a poet to write so plainly that he may be understood by his readers; to avoid impropriety, and not affect to be thought learned in all things' (Watson, ii. 254).

p. 89   Simplicity and modesty, according to Le Bossu (Book III, Ch. iii), are the two characteristics of the propositions in the *Odyssey*, the *Aeneid*, and even the *Iliad*. For the precept of Horace see *Ars poetica*, 136–45.

p. 92   In a note on Ovid (Book III, Fable ii) Addison comments on these catalogues of proper names:

> The smoothness of our English verse is too much lost by the repetition of proper names, which is otherwise very natural and absolutely necessary in some cases; as before a battle, to raise in our minds an answerable expectation of the event, and a lively idea of the numbers that are engaged. For had Homer or Virgil only told us in two or three lines before their fights, that there were forty thousand of each side, our imagination could not possibly have been so affected, as when we see every leader singled out, and every regiment in a manner drawn up before our eyes (Guthkelch, i. 142–3).

p. 92   *A Journey from Aleppo to Jerusalem at Easter, A.D. 1697*, by Henry Maundrell, 'Chaplain to the Factory at Aleppo', was published at Oxford in 1703. The brief account of his journey is in the form of a journal, and the passage quoted is under the dates 16–17 Mar. (p. 34). The stream he identifies with the Adonis was called by the Turks, according to Maundrell, Ibrahim Bassa.

p. 100   In No. 114 of the *Tatler* Addison had praised this passage for its 'excellent turns'. Milton 'describes the Fallen Angels engaged in the intricate disputes of predestination, free-will, and fore-knowledge; and to humour the perplexity, makes a kind of labyrinth in the very words that describe it'. Addison also quotes these lines in *Spectator* 237, as descriptive of the vain pursuit of knowledge on the part of those excluded from the bliss of Heaven.

p. 103   Cf. Dryden, Preface to *Sylvae* (1685): 'Milton's *Paradise Lost* is admirable; but am I therefore bound to maintain that there are no flats amongst his elevations, when 'tis evident he creeps along sometimes for above an hundred lines together?' (Watson, ii. 32.)

p. 106   According to Le Bossu (Book III, Ch. ix) the passion most peculiar to the epic is admiration. 'We admire with joy things that surprise us pleasingly, and we admire with terror and grief such things as terrify and make us sad' (ii. 56). Dennis, in his *Advancement and Reformation of Modern Poetry* (1701), calls admiration 'the reigning passion in epic poetry' (*Works*, ed. Hooker, i. 229); he means, however, approval of the hero 'heightened by revelations, by machines, and the ministration of the gods'. Addison is clearly thinking of astonishment and the marvellous. On the two meanings of the term see the references collected by Hooker (i. 455). Dacier, in a note on Chapter ix of the *Poetics*, observes that admiration is too soft for tragedy: 'Tragedy employs only terror and compassion, and leaves admiration for an epic poem, to which it is more necessary and proper, and where it has more time to act on habitudes and manners' (p. 153).

p. 107   Cf. Le Bossu (Book V, Ch. iii):

> Now the Episodes of Circe, the Sirens, Polypheme, and the like, are necessary to the action of the *Odysseis*, and yet they are not humanly probable. Homer artificially brings them under the *human probability*, by the simplicity of those before whom he causes these fabulous recitals to be made. . . . But even here the poet is not unmindful of his more understanding readers. He has in these fables given them all the pleasure that can be reaped from *moral truths*, so pleasantly disguised under these miraculous allegories (ii. 223–4).

p. 108   Cf. Cowley's note on *Davideis* (iv. 359): 'According to the old senseless opinion, that the heavens were divided into several orbs or spheres, and that a particular Intelligence or Angel was assigned to each of them, to turn it round . . . to all eternity' (*Poems*, ed. Waller, p. 398).

p. 109   In No. 418 (p. 197) Addison cites Milton's description of Paradise as more 'refreshing to the imagination' than his description of Hell.

p. 110   *Poetics*, 24. 11: 'Thus ought we to reserve all the ornaments of the diction for these weak parts: those that have either good sentiments, or manners, have no occasion for them. A brilliant, or glorious expression, damages them rather, and serves only to hide their beauty' (Dacier's trans., pp. 408–9).

p. 116   Addison's reference shows that he is citing Boileau's version; in the original it is section 27. The notation from Homer is *Iliad*, 15. 346–9.

p. 119   As Newton pointed out (1749) in his note on this passage in *Paradise Lost*, the reference is more likely to be 'Homer's making the gates of Heaven open of their own accord to the deities who passed through them, *Iliad* V. 749.'

p. 119   For Scaliger's criticism and Dacier's defence of Homer see the latter's note on Aristotle's *Poetics*, 25. 17: 'If Vulcan had made ordinary trevits, they would not have been fit for a poem [i.e. an epic], and had not answered the greatness, power, and skill of a god' (p. 480).

p. 125 *Greeks.* Addison makes this point also in the *Discourse on Ancient and Modern Learning*: the habitations of the ancients 'lay among the scenes of the *Aeneid*; they could find out their own country in Homer, and had every day perhaps in their sight the mountain or field where such an adventure happened, or such a battle was fought' (Guthkelch, ii. 455).

p. 132 In his *Essay on Virgil's Georgics* (1697) Addison had praised Virgil's art in clothing precepts of morality and objects of natural philosophy with beautiful descriptions and images, 'which are the spirit and life of poetry' (Guthkelch, i. 4).

p. 135 The reference is to Sir Richard Blackmore's poem in seven books, *Creation*, advertised in *Spectator* 313 as 'this day' published (28 Feb. 1712). For the generally favourable reception of the poem see Albert Rosenberg, *Sir Richard Blackmore* (Lincoln, Nebr., 1953), pp. 100–4.

p. 135 On the same date on which this essay appeared Defoe wrote in the *Review*: 'If anything could heighten the imagination, or move the passions and affections in the subject which Milton wrote upon, more than reading Milton himself, I should think the world beholden to the Spectator, for his extraordinary notes upon that sublime work.'

p. 136 See Le Bossu, Book II, Ch. ii–vi. Le Bossu defines episodes as 'necessary parts of the action, extended by probable circumstances' (II. vi). Dennis, who quotes this definition without acknowledgement in his *Remarks on Prince Arthur* (1696), goes on to name the three qualities which episodes must have (again borrowing from Le Bossu): they are to be derived from the first plan of the action, they are to have a necessary or probable dependence one upon another, and they are not to be complete in themselves (*Works*, ed. Hooker, i. 58). Rapin calls the episode 'a kind of digression from the subject' and stipulates that it be proportionately short, closely related to the subject, and not used too often ('A Comparison of Homer and Virgil', Ch. vi. *Whole Critical Works*, 1706, i. 151).

p. 141 Addison had quoted lines 546–59 in *Tatler* 102; lines 546–54 he quotes later in *Freeholder* 32, adding: 'If there is such a native loveliness in the sex, as to make them victorious even when they are in the wrong, how resistless is their power when they are on the side of truth!'

p. 155 Addison here discusses at some length the objection which he had briefly mentioned earlier, in Nos. 273, 297, 309, and 315 (pp. 68, 85, 101, 107). 'This unskilful allegory appears to me one of the greatest faults of the poem' (Johnson, *Life of Milton*, World's Classics edn., i. 134).

p. 156 Cf. Le Bossu, Book V, Ch. iv, on this point.

p. 156 This does not appear to be in Homer; Addison may be recalling *Iliad*, 5. 835–41, where Pallas Athene accompanies Diomedes.

p. 156 *Prometheus Bound.* Although there are references in the play to 'strong necessity', the two figures who are introduced as leading in Prometheus are Strength and Force. (The Folio reading, 'Strength and Violence', is more accurate.)

p. 156   Dacier's note on Aristotle's *Poetics* 14, criticizes poets who endeavour to excite passions by monstrous decorations:

> Nothing can be farther from true tragedy than this means. Aeschylus has a great share in this censure, for as his imagination was vast and quick, but extravagant and irregular, he often ventured at those things, which were not only contrary to art, but nature too. His *Prometheus* is full of these monsters, which Aristotle condemns, for what can be more such, than his punishment of that god, where Force and Violence, two persons nail him to the rock with vast hammers? (p. 238.)

p. 158   At the end of the *Oedipus* of Dryden and Lee a stage direction reads: 'He [Oedipus] flings himself from the window: the Thebans gather about his body.'

p. 163   Cowley, commenting on this passage in Ovid (in the notes to Book I of *Davideis*), calls the latter part of the verse 'superfluous, even to ridiculousness' (*Poems*, ed. Waller, p. 270).

p. 164   Addison may be thinking of Dennis (*Grounds of Criticism in Poetry*, 1704), who remarked that Milton in the first eight books of *Paradise Lost* 'divinely entertained us with the wondrous works of God', but that 'in the latter end of his poem, and more particularly, in the last Book, he makes an angel entertain us with the works of corrupted Man' (*Critical Works*, ed. Hooker, i. 351).

p. 168   Heliodorus. *Aethiopian History*, Book 3. Translated as *The Trimphs of Love and Constancy* (2nd edn., 1687, p. 118): 'Yet by their going [gods and divine spirits] may be better known [than by their eyes]; for their pace is not made by stepping or transposition of the feet, but by a certain airy violence and quick even motion, that they rather sail or cut, than pass the air.'

p. 169   In the second edition of *Paradise Lost* (1674) Milton divided Books vii and x (not Book xi) into two books each.

p. 169   Book I, Ch. vii: The Method of Composing a Fable. According to Le Bossu, the first step in composing a fable is 'to choose the instruction and the point of morality which is to serve as its foundation' (i. 28–9).

p. 170   Again Addison is doubtless thinking of Le Bossu, who, in Book II, Ch. v, traces the number of months and days in these epics (i. 130), a matter he takes up again in Book II, Ch. xviii, and Book III, Ch. xii. Addison had referred to this earlier, at the end of No. 267. *Tatler* 6 recounts an attempt to put the action of the *Iliad* into an exact journal, with the events distributed into days.

p. 171   Cf. Addison's comments on the 'mixed embellishments' of Tasso (No. 279, p. 72).

TASTE AND THE PLEASURES OF THE IMAGINATION

p. 173   The greatest Roman historians: Livy (59 B.C.–A.D. 17), author of a history of Rome, of which only parts survive; Sallust (*c.* 86–35 B.C.), a partisan of Caesar and author of *Catilina* and *Jugurtha*; Tacitus (A.D. 55?–117), author of many works, including *Germania, Historiae,* and *Annales* (only portions of the last two extant). See below, No. 420 (p. 202), for Addison's praise of Livy.

p. 173 Perhaps Newton.

p. 174 Rome in the Augustan age (30 B.C.–A.D. 14), Greece in the time of Socrates (469–399 B.C.), and France in the reign of Louis XIV—three frequently cited periods in which the arts of civilization flourished. Addison names the three great dramatists of the French seventeenth century, Corneille (1606–84), Racine (1639–99), and Molière (1622–73); its two great poets, Boileau (1636–1711) and La Fontaine (1621–95), and the influential author of *Les Caractères,* Jean de la Bruyère (1645–96). The last two names are those of critics whose work Addison knew and admired—René Le Bossu (1631–80), Superior of the Abbey of St. Jean de Chartres and author of the *Traité du poëme épique* (1675), and the two Daciers, André (1651–1722), translator of Aristotle's *Poetics* and other classics for Monseigneur the Dauphin (*in usum Delphini*), and his wife Anne, *née* Lefebvre (1654–1720), translator of Homer and other Greek authors into French.

p. 174 *Longinus on the Sublime,* a Greek treatise of unknown date and authorship, but probably dating from the first or second century A.D.

p. 174 In this and the following three sentences Addison reminds his readers of his papers on wit (Nos. 58–63, pp. 1–25), on the ballads (Nos. 70, 74, 85, pp. 36–48) and on Milton (Nos. 267, &c., pp. 62–171).

p. 175 Johnson may be echoing this phrase in his comment on Addison's *Campaign*: 'The rejection and contempt of fiction is rational and manly' (World's Classics edn., i. 446).

p. 176 In adopting the terms 'primary' and 'secondary' for pleasures Addison probably has in mind Locke's distinction between primary and secondary qualities (*Essay,* Book II, Ch. viii).

p. 177 *Polite imagination.* A point of view frequently expressed by neo-classical critics: although taste might be dependent in theory on the appeal to universality, in practice it was likely to be found among the most 'polite' in the most polite ages.

p. 177 *Bacon,* Essay 30, 'Of Regiment of Health' (*Essays,* ed. W. A. Wright, 1892, p. 132).

p. 179 In Chapter vi of his *Remarks on Prince Arthur* (1696) Dennis had commented unfavourably on the 'wearisome uniformity' of Blackmore's poem, in language similar to Addison's:

> For the mind does not care for dwelling too long upon an object, but loves to pass from one thing to another; because such a transition keeps it from languishing, and gives it more agitation. Now agitation only can give it delight. For agitation not only keeps it from mortifying reflections, which it naturally has when it is not shaken, but gives it a force which it had not before, and the consciousness of its own force delights it (*Critical Works,* ed Hooker, i. 109).

In *The Advancement and Reformation of Modern Poetry* (1701; Ch. vi) Dennis again speaks of the advantages in having the imagination fired with the motion and 'violent agitation' of images (ibid. i. 218).

p. 179   Addison does not define 'beauty', beyond saying that there are 'several modifications of matter' which the mind instantly recognizes as beautiful or deformed, although he distinguishes between beauty as raising sexual desire and beauty deriving from colours, symmetry, and arrangements.

p. 180   The Latin verses are by Addison and appear in the MS. in his own hand, with his corrections. In the 1744 12mo edition of the *Spectator* they are translated:

> The feathered husband, to his partner true,
> Preserves connubial rites inviolate.
> With cold indifference every charm he sees,
> The milky whiteness of the stately neck,
> The shining down, proud crest, and purple wings:
> But cautious with a searching eye explores
> The female tribes, his proper mate to find,
> With kindred colours marked. Did he not so,
> The grove with painted monsters would abound,
> Th'ambiguous product of unnatural love.
> The blackbird hence selects her sooty spouse;
> The nightingale her musical compeer,
> Lured by the well-known voice: the bird of night,
> Smit with his dusky wings, and greenish eyes,
> Woos his dun paramour. The beauteous race
> Speak the chaste loves of their progenitors;
> When, by the spring invited, they exult
> In woods and fields, and to the sun unfold
> Their plumes, that with paternal colours glow.

p. 181   The 'efficient cause' in Aristotelian philosophy is the impetus or instrument by which a thing is produced. Since we cannot understand what causes the imagination to be affected pleasurably by the great, the new, or the beautiful (the 'efficient' cause), Addison turns to consider why we are so affected (the 'final' cause).

p. 182   Cf. Seneca, *Dialogues*, 8. 5. 3.

p. 183   Book II, Ch. viii: 'Some farther considerations concerning our simple ideas.'

p. 184   On the antithesis of nature and art, and the shifting concepts of nature at this period, see A. O. Lovejoy, '"Nature" as aesthetic norm', *Modern Language Notes*, 42 (1927): 444–50.

p. 184   Horace, *Epistles*, 2. 2. 77:
> Each writer hates the town and woods approves.   CREECH

p. 184   Virgil, *Georgics*, 2. 467–70:
> Unvexed with quarrels, undisturbed with noise,
> The country king his peaceful realm enjoys:

Cool grots, and living lakes, the flowery pride
Of meads, and streams that through the valley glide;
And shady groves that easy sleep invite,
And after toilsome days, a soft repose at night.   DRYDEN

p. 185   Addison probably has in mind the scene obtained by a camera obscura,
or possibly that produced by the projection of two on opposite walls. There was
such a camera obscura at Greenwich Park. Hugh Blair, in his lectures at Edinburgh in the 1760s, recalled the experiment:

> The scene, which I am inclined to think Mr. Addison here refers to, is
> Greenwich Park, with the prospect of the Thames, as seen by a Camera
> Obscura, which is placed in a small room in the upper story of the Observ-
> atory; where I remember to have seen, many years ago, the whole scene
> here described, corresponding so much to Mr. Addison's account of it in
> this passage, that, at the time, it recalled it to my memory. As the Observatory
> stands in the middle of the Park, it overlooks, from one side, both the river
> and the park; and the objects afterwards mentioned, the ships, the trees, and
> the deer, are presented in one view, without needing any assistance from
> opposite walls (*Lectures on Rhetoric and Belles Lettres*, 1783, i. 469).

Several 'moving pictures' were being exhibited at the time the *Spectator* was
published. One of these, exhibited at the Duke of Marlborough's Head in Fleet
Street in 1710 and 1711, is advertised in *Tatler* 127. In the *Daily Courant* of
20 Feb. 1709/10 it is described as follows: 'It is a most noble landscape finely
painted by the best hand, it contains the prospect of a city with a harbour; a
large extent of land with a river winding and running into the sea; a bridge
leading to the city; and near 70 figures in lively motion: viz. several stately ships
and vessels sailing; a coach and 4 horses; a gentleman in a chair saluting the
company. . . .' This seems to be similar to one which Swift describes to Stella on
27 March 1713: 'You see a sea ten miles wide, a town on t'other end, and ships
sailing in the sea, and discharging their cannon. You see a great sky with moon
and stars, &c.' (ed. H. Williams, p. 647). Addison's account, however, must have
been written much earlier, and more likely refers to the scene produced by the
camera obscura, probably at Greenwich.

p. 185   Addison here contrasts the formal gardens of England, owing something
to the Dutch influence introduced at the time of William III, with the private
gardens of France and Italy—not, of course, the great gardens of Le Nôtre at
Versailles. Later in the century it is the *jardin à l'anglaise* which is to become
popular on the Continent.

p. 185   The English garden at this time was a combination of orchard and
vegetable garden with flower gardens. See Sir William Temple's 'Upon the
Gardens of Epicurus; or, of Gardening, In the Year 1685', in *Miscellanea*, Part
II (*Works*, 1720), i. 181–3.

p. 185   Sir William Temple's essay just referred to (*Works*, Pt. II, i. 186) is
clearly the source of Addison's statements here:

> Among us, the beauty of building and planting is placed chiefly in some
> certain proportions, symmetries, or uniformities; our walks and our trees

11*

ranged so, as to answer one another, and at exact distances. The Chineses scorn this way of planting, and say a boy that can tell an hundred, may plant walks of trees in straight lines, and over-against one another, and to what length and extent he pleases. But their greatest reach of imagination is employed in contriving figures, where the beauty shall be great, and strike the eye, but without any order or disposition of parts, that shall be commonly or easily observed. And though we have hardly any notion of this sort of beauty, yet they have a particular word to express it; and where they find it hit their eye at first sight, they say the *Sharawadgi* is fine or is admirable, or any such expression of esteem.

p. 187   Herodotus (*History*, 1. 178) describes the wall of Babylon as of 50 royal cubits of thickness and 200 cubits height. The Hanging Gardens, according to Diodorus Siculus (*Library of History*, 2. 10. 1), was built not by Semiramis but by a later Syrian king (actually Nebuchadnezzar, 605–562 B.C.).

p. 187   Semiramis built dykes on the plain, but it was the second queen, Nitocris, who changed the course of the Euphrates (Herodotus, 1. 184–5).

p. 187   According to Diodorus Siculus (2. 17. 1.) the army consisted of 3,000,000 foot soldiers, 200,000 cavalry, and 100,000 chariots.

p. 187   According to Herodotus (1. 179) they made bricks from the earth and used hot bitumen for cement, the bitumen derived from the river Is, a tributary of the Euphrates. See also Quintus Curtius, 5. 1. 12.

p. 188   An error for Stasicrates (Plutarch, *Life of Alexander*, 72. 4). See also Plutarch 'On the Fortune of Alexander' (*Moralia*, 335C).

p. 188   The Pantheon, or Rotunda, and St. Peter's were the two buildings which Addison especially sought out on his first visit to Rome. 'I must confess the eye is better filled at first entering the *Rotund*, and takes in the whole beauty and magnificence of the temple at one view. But such as are built in the form of a cross, give us a greater variety of noble prospects. Nor it is easy to conceive a more glorious show in architecture, than what man meets with in St. Peter's, when he stands under the Dome' (*Remarks on Italy*, 1705, p. 177).

p. 188   In the *Remarks on Italy* Addison, praises St. Peter's in contrast to the Gothic churches: 'The proportions are so very well observed, that nothing appears to an advantage, or distinguishes itself above the rest. It seems neither extremely high, nor long, nor broad, because it is all of them in a just equality. As on the contrary in our Gothic cathedrals, the narrowness of the arch makes it rise in height, or run out in length; the lowness often opens it in breadth, or the defectiveness of some other particular makes any single part appear in greater perfection' (pp. 174–5).

p. 188   *Fréart*. The *Parallèle de l'architecture antique et de la moderne* (1650) by Roland Fréart, Sieur de Chambray, was translated by John Evelyn in 1664. The passage quoted is from Chapter ii ('Of the Doric Order').

p. 189   Of the dome of St. Peter's Addison wrote: 'If he looks upward he is astonished at the spacious hollow of the cupola, and has a vault on every side of him, that makes one of the beautifullest vistas that the eye can possibly pass through' (*Remarks on Italy*, p. 177).

p. 190   The combinatory powers of the imagination had long been recognized, without any suggestion of a creative faculty in the 'romantic' sense of the phrase. M. W. Bundy (*Theory of Imagination*, Urbana, Ill., 1927, p. 85 n.) quotes an example from Philoponus, a sixth-century commentator on Aristotle.

p. 192   In his early essay on Virgil's *Georgics* (1697) Addison had praised this as Virgil's masterpiece, 'where we receive more strong and lively *ideas* of things from his words, than we could have done from the objects themselves: and find our imaginations more affected by his descriptions, than they would have been by the very sight of what he describes' (Guthkelch, ii. 8).

p. 194   Descartes, in *Les Passions de l'âme* (1649), art. xxi (Eng. trans., 1650, pp. 18–19), states that imaginations 'proceed from nothing but this, that the spirits being agitated several ways, and meeting the traces of divers impressions preceding them in the brain, they take their course at haphazard through some certain pores, rather than others. Such are the illusions of our dreams, and those dotages we often are troubled with waking, when our thought carelessly roams without applying itself to any thing of its own.'

p. 195   Homer, *Iliad*, 1. 528–30:

> This said, his kingly brow the sire inclined;
> The large black curls fell awful from behind,
> Thick-shadowing the stern forehead of the god:
> Olympus trembled at th' almighty nod.   TICKELL

p. 195   Virgil, *Aeneid*, 1. 402–5:

> Thus having said, she turned and made appear
> Her neck refulgent, and dishevelled hair;
> Which flowing from her shoulders, reached the ground,
> And widely spread ambrosial scents around:
> In length of train descends her sweeping gown,
> And by her graceful walk, the Queen of Love is known.   DRYDEN

p. 195   *Aeneid*, 1. 590–1:

> And gave his rolling eyes a sparkling grace,
> And breathed a youthful vigour on his face.   DRYDEN

p. 198   Virgil, *Aeneid*, 8. 264–7:

> The wondering neighbourhood, with glad surprise,
> Behold his shagged breast, his giant size,
> His mouth that flames no more, and his extinguished eyes.   DRYDEN

p. 198   In his remarks on Chapter vi of Aristotle's *Poetics* Dacier comments: tragedy 'disposes the most miserable to think themselves happy when they compare their own misfortunes with those which tragedy has represented to them. In whatever condition a man may be, yet when he shall see an Oedipus, a Philoctetes, an Orestes, he can but think his own afflictions light in comparison with theirs' (p. 79).

p. 199   In No. 279 Addison had praised Milton for depicting characters which 'lie out of nature, and were to be formed purely by his own invention'.

p. 199   In his dedication (to the Marquis of Halifax) of *King Arthur* (1691) Dryden speaks of 'that fairy kind of writing, which depends upon the force of the imagination'.)

p. 200   Horace, *Ars poetica*, 244-6:

> A satyr that comes staring from the woods,
> Must not at first speak like an orator:
> But, though his language should not be refined,
> It must not be obscene and impudent.   ROSCOMMON

p. 200   In No. 12 Addison had written: 'I am apt to join in opinion with those who believe that all the regions of nature swarm with spirits. . . .'

p. 201   On these and other supernatural evidences see Robert Plot, *Natural History of Staffordshire* (Oxford, 1686), pp. 9–19. Addison refers to the fairy circles in his early poem, *Machinae Gesticulantes*.

p. 201   In the account of Shakespeare prefixed to the edition of the plays brought out by Tonson in 1709 Rowe comments that 'the greatness of this author's genius does nowhere so much appear as where he gives his imagination an entire loose and raises his fancy to a flight above mankind and the limits of the visible world' (i, p. xxiii). 'His magic has something in it very solemn and very poetical . . .' (p. xxiv).

p. 202   Cf. Rapin, *Reflections upon History*, Chapter x: 'It is now about two thousand years, that the majesty of this historian has commanded the respect and admiration of all the world. Nothing so fills my soul, as that excellent choice of words, which are always proportioned to his thoughts, and that genuine expression of his thoughts, which are always conformable to his subject' (*Whole Critical Works*, 1706, ii, 273). Cf. No. 409 (p. 173), where Livy's 'manner of telling a story' is contrasted with the special excellences of Sallust and Tacitus.

p. 204   The traditional view was that, since the imagination is closely tied to sense-representations, we can only imagine what we are capable of picturing to ourselves. Descartes (*Six Metaphysical Meditations*, 1680, p. 84), illustrates this by the thousand-angled figure, or chiliogon, which can be understood to be a figure of a thousand sides as easily as a triangle can be understood to be a figure of three sides; 'but I do not in the same manner imagine, or behold as present those thousand sides, as I do the three sides of a triangle'. Many English writers had adopted the same position, e.g. Hobbes (*Leviathan*, Ch. iii).

p. 206   Virgil, *Aeneid*, 4. 469–73 (in Virgil line 473 begins *Cum fugit*):

Like Pentheus, when distracted with his fear,
He saw two suns, and double Thebes appear:
Or mad Orestes, when his mother's ghost
Full in his face infernal torches tossed;
And shook her snaky locks: he shuns the sight,
Flies o'er the stage, surprised with mortal fright;
The Furies guard the door; and intercept his flight.   DRYDEN

DRAMA

English Tragedy

p. 210   Addison here follows Aristotle (*Poetics* 26); seventeenth-century critics, especially in France, had generally placed the epic above tragedy.

p. 210   *Poetics*, 4. 14: 'Iambics are of all sorts of verse the most proper for conversation; this is a certain sign of it that we often make iambics in talking to one another' (*Aristotle's Art of Poetry: translated from the original Greek, according to Mr. Theodore Goulston's Edition, together with Mr. D'Acier's notes translated from the French*, 1705, p. 34). Citations from the *Poetics*, unless otherwise noted, are from this edition.

p. 210   The question of blank verse or rhyme in tragedy had been discussed frequently in the seventeenth century. Dryden argues the advantages of rhyme in the Epistle Dedicatory of *The Rival Ladies* (1664) and discusses the relative merits of rhyme and blank verse in the *Essay of Dramatic Poesy* (1668). Sir Robert Howard (Preface to *Four New Plays*, 1665) and Dryden (*Defence of an Essay of Dramatic Poesy*, 1668) consider the matter further.

p. 211   Cf. Saint-Évremond ('A Dissertation on Racine's Tragedy, called The Grand Alexander'): 'Some of his thoughts are strong and bold; his expressions equal the force of his thoughts' (*Works*, 1714, i. 272).

p. 212   Cf. Dryden, Preface to *The State of Innocence* (1677): 'Virgil and Horace, the severest writers of the severest age, have made frequent use of the hardest metaphors, and of the strongest hyperboles . . .' (*Essays*, ed. Watson, i. 200).

p. 212   *Poetics*, 24. 11: 'Thus ought we to reserve all the ornaments of the diction for these weak parts: those that have either good sentiments, or manners, have no occasion for them. A brilliant or glorious expression damages them rather, and serves only to hide their beauty' (pp. 408–9). Dacier's note on this passage is: 'Those places which have beautiful sentiments have no occasion for the ornaments of the diction, because these ornaments would only obscure them' (p. 432).

p. 213   Thomas Otway (1652–85). For his reputation in the eighteenth century see Aline Mackenzie Taylor, *Next to Shakespeare: Otway's Venice Preserved and The Orphan and their History on the London Stage* (Durham, N. C., 1950). As to

Otway's 'following nature', Dryden, in the Preface to Du Fresnoy's *Art of Painting* (1695), thought that the passions were truly touched in *Venice Preserved*, 'though perhaps there is somewhat to be desired, both in the grounds of them, and in the height and elegance of expression; but nature is there, which is the greatest beauty' (*Essays*, ed. Watson, ii. 201). Mrs. Taylor, who quotes this passage, adds: 'During the eighteenth century, however, Addison's criticism, not Dryden's, was quoted in handbooks and prefaces for the readers of Otway's plays' (p. 250).

p. 213   *Venice Preserved, or a Plot Discovered* was first acted in 1682, just after the excitement of the 'Popish Plot', which it, of course, satirizes. The play had in consequence long been a great favourite with the Tories, and Addison's comment here states the Whig view of the play admirably. 'By the middle of the century', writes Mrs. Taylor, 'Addison's charge had become one of the clichés of criticism' (p. 40 n.).

p. 214   With the exception of *Theodosius*, all the plays in this list were a part of the current repertory at Drury Lane. *The Orphan, or the Unhappy Marriage*, by Otway, had been given on 27 Feb., with Mrs. Bradshaw in the role of Monimia. *Venice Preserved* (cf. No. 39, p. 213) was produced on 16 Jan. *The Rival Queens, or the Death of Alexander the Great*, by Lee, was still a standard piece in the repertory at Drury Lane, and had had three performances in 1710. *Theodosius, or the Force of Love*, also by Lee, is mentioned by Addison in No. 92 as a great favourite with the ladies. *All for Love, or the World Well Lost*, by Dryden, had been last given on 2 May 1709. *Oedipus*, by Dryden and Lee, had performances at Penkethman's Theatre on 3 and 31 Aug. 1710. *Oroonoko*, by Thomas Southerne, had been given on 9 and 19 Dec. 1710, and *Othello* on 18 Jan. 1711, with Booth in the title-role. Dennis's comment on this list is that 'there are not two of those which he commends, whose principal characters can be said to be innocent, and consequently there are not two of them where there is not a due observance of poetical justice' (Hooker, ii. 21). As Hooker notes, the one exception would be *Oedipus*.

p. 214   Tate's adaptation had been given at Drury Lane on 30 Nov. 1710, with Powell as Lear.

p. 215   *The Mourning Bride*, by Congreve, had been given at Drury Lane on 18 Jan. 1710. For its reputation at this time see Emmett Avery, *Congreve's Plays on the Eighteenth-Century Stage* (New York, 1951). *Tamerlane* and *Ulysses* are both by Rowe; the former was given at Drury Lane on 7 Mar. 1710 and at Penkethman's Theatre in Greenwich on 30 Sept. 1710; the latter had not been performed since 1705. *Phaedra and Hippolitus*, by Edmund Smith, was produced at the Haymarket on 21 Apr. 1707. The Prologue was written by Addison.

p. 215   Addison may be recalling the attack on this 'drama of our own invention' by Lisideius in Dryden's *Essay of Dramatic Poesy* (*Essays*, ed. Watson, i. 45).

p. 215   In Dryden's *Essay of Dramatic Poesy* Neander offers a similar justification: Our plays, 'besides the main design, have under-plots or by-concernments, of less considerable persons and intrigues, which are carried on with the motion of the main plot . . .' (*Essays*, ed. Watson, i. 59).

p. 215   Granville's Preface to *Heroick Love* (1698) concludes:

> It often indeed happens, that the audience is best pleased where the author is most out of countenance, and that part of the performance which the writer suspects, the spectator chiefly approves. When we observe how little notice is taken of the noble and sublime [thoughts] and expressions of Mr. Dryden in *Oedipus*, and what applause is given to the rants and the fustian of Mr. Lee, what can we say, but that madmen are only fit to write, when nothing is esteemed great and heroic but what is unintelligible' (p. 5).

Colley Cibber devotes a long passage in the *Apology* (Ch. iv) to 'the furious fustian and turgid rants' in *The Rival Queens*. 'The unskilful actor, who imagined all the merit of delivering those blazing rants lay only in the strength and strained exertion of the voice, began to tear his lungs upon every false or slight occasion to arrive at the same applause' (Everyman edn., p. 61).

p. 215   George Powell (d. 1714), 'that famous and heroic actor' (*Tatler* 3) created the role of Orestes in Ambrose Philips's *Distressed Mother* at Drury Lane on 17 Mar. 1712 and that of Portius in Addison's *Cato*. For his acting see Cibber's (unfavourable) comments in the *Apology* (Ch. vii).

p. 216   The two passages from *Oedipus* are quoted with several verbal changes. In *The Drummer* Addison closes Act I with a tag facetiously chosen from the second act of *Oedipus*:

> Clasped in the folds of love, I'd meet my doom,
> And act my joys, though thunder shook the room.

p. 216   *Conquest of Mexico*. This performance of Dryden's *Indian Emperor*, with Powell as Cortez, is advertised in *Spectator* 41.

p. 217   In *Tatler* 42 Addison had in a similar vein of raillery described the costumes and stage equipment at Drury Lane. The 'inventory' of the movables of Christopher Rich, 'who is breaking up house-keeping', included such items as 'an imperial mantle, made for Cyrus the Great, and worn by Julius Caesar, Bajazet, King Harry the Eighth, and Signor Valentini', and 'a plume of feathers, never used but by Oedipus and the Earl of Essex'.

p. 218   Roscommon, in a note to Horace's *Ars poetica* 96, cites Aristophanes' *Frogs* (IV, ii), where Aeschylus says to Euripides: 'You dress kings in rags to move pity.'

p. 218   The inventory of the movables of Christopher Rich cited above concludes: 'There are also swords, halberds, sheep-hooks, cardinals' hats, turbans, drums, gally-pots. . . .'

p. 218   In *The Rehearsal*, V. i, Bayes says, 'I sum up my whole battle in the representation of two persons only—no more—and yet so lively that, I vow to gad, you would swear ten thousand men were at it, really engaged.'

p. 219   Since 20 Nov. 1710 the Haymarket Theatre had been used exclusively for opera, and Addison's examples refer to the tragedies at Drury Lane. Unless this is an oversight, it suggests that the essay may have been written some time earlier.

p. 219   *Spectator* 36 prints a letter signed 'Salmoneus of Covent Garden', who claims to have been for many years 'Thunderer to the Play-house' and to 'have descended and spoke on the stage as the bold Thunder in the *Rehearsal.*'

p. 219   Pope has a note on 'Tolling Bell' in his *Dunciad* (1729), ii. 220: 'A mechanical help to the pathetic, not unuseful to the modern writers of tragedy.'

p. 220   In the scene of parting between Jaffeir and Belvidera (Act V) the passing-bell tolls for Pierre.

p. 221   Possibly an allusion to Dryden's *All for Love*, Act III, where Octavia enters, 'leading Antony's two little daughters'.

p. 221   Rapin (*Reflections on Aristotle's Treatise of Poesie*, 1694, Part II, Chs. xx, xxiii) notes that the English 'love blood in their sports, by the quality of their temperament', and that 'The English have more genius for tragedy than other people, as well by the spirit of their nation which delights in cruelty, as also by the character of their language which is proper for great expressions' (*Whole Critical Works*, 1706, ii. 210, 219–20). Steele, who quotes this in *Tatler* 134, adds: 'I must own, there is something very horrid in the public executions of an English tragedy. Stabbing and poisoning, which are performed behind the scenes in other nations, must be done openly among us to gratify the audience.' The point is frequently made by foreign observers, particularly the French. See Georges Ascoli, *La Grande-Bretagne devant l'opinion française au XVIIᵉ siècle* (Paris, 1930), i. 434–5.

p. 222   Rowe, in his 'Account of the Life of Shakespeare' prefixed to the *Works* (1709), makes a similar comparison between the behaviour of Hamlet and Orestes. The death of Clytemnestra off stage is frequently cited in illustration of the classical 'rule', e.g. by Corneille in his *Discours de la tragédie*, 1660 (*Œuvres*, ed. C. Marty-Laveaux, i. 78). Actually, in Sophocles' *Electra*, it is not Orestes but Electra who says that Clytemnestra 'showed no mercy to his father'.

p. 223   Cf. Dacier's comment (p. 276):

> There are things which the audience ought to see, and there are others which they ought only to hear related. If this order is inverted, and that is related which ought be be seen, and that is exposed to the sight, which ought to be only related, 'tis such a fault as will certainly spoil the poem. A poet has need of a great deal of judgement, and ingenuity, not to leave any of those incidents behind the scene, which will affect the audience by being seen: and to hide those which might offend by reason of their cruelty, or be found fault with for the want of probability.

p. 223   William Bullock (1657?–1740?) is described in *Tatler* 7 as well qualified for the part of Biskett in *Epsom Wells* because he 'has a peculiar talent of looking like a fool'. His height is mentioned in *Tatler* 188. Henry Norris (1665–1730?), the comic actor, became famous as Dicky in Farquhar's *Constant Couple, or a Trip to the Jubilee,* and was thereafter known as 'Jubilee Dicky'. Bullock and Norris are paired in one of Penkethman's drolls at Southwark Fair in 1714: 'The Constant Lovers; or, Sir Paul Slouch, alias, Sir Timothy Little-Wit. With the comical humours of his Man Trip. The parts of Sir Tomothy and his Man to be acted by Bullock and Jubilee-Dicky, and the part of Old Buzzard by Penkethman himself' (*Daily Courant,* 2 Sept. 1714).

p. 223 Dufoy, 'a saucy impertinent Frenchman', in Etherege's *Comical Revenge, or Love in a Tub* (IV. vi, vii; V. i).

p. 224 This paper, unsigned in all three of the earliest texts, is assigned to Addison by both Morley and Aitken. (Gregory Smith makes no attribution.) The style and subject-matter both sound like Addison, and it would be characteristic of him to add the final paragraph, which was not in the original folio version. Though in the form of a letter, it is purportedly written on the 27th, the preceding day, which is unlikely for a genuine letter.

p. 224 No. 548 printed a number of advertisements, in the style of the medical advertisements of the time, testifying to the cures of 'ill-nature, pride, party-spleen', etc., effected by the reading of the *Spectator.*

p. 224 The following may be the advertisement referred to; it occurs frequently (23 times in all) in the *Spectator,* beginning in No. 75 and ending in No. 543:

> An incomparable pleasant tincture to restore the sense of smelling, though lost for many years. A few drops of which being snuffed up the nose, infallibly cures those who have lost their smell, let it proceed from what cause soever: it admirably opens all manner of obstructions of the olfactory or smelling nerves, comforts and strengthens the head and brain, and revives the smelling faculty to a miracle, effectually removing whatever is the cause of the disorder of that sense, and perfectly cures, so as to cause the person to smell as quick and well, as any one in the world. Price 2*s.* 6*d.* a bottle. Sold only at Mr. Payne's Toyshop at the Angel and Crown in St. Paul's Church Yard near Cheapside, with directions.

p. 226 Cf. Cowley, note to *Davideis,* ii. 725: 'Weeping seems to depend so much upon the eyes as to make the expression *poetically true,* though not *literally*' (*Poems,* ed. Waller, p. 320); Dryden, Dedication of *Aeneis*: 'By this example [Achilles], the critics have concluded that it is not necessary the manners of the hero should be virtuous. They are poetically good, if they are of a piece . . .' (Watson, ii. 228). Dacier, in a note to his translation of *Aristotle's Art of Poetry* (1705), remarks that when Aristotle speaks of the goodness of the manners ''Tis not a moral, but a poetical goodness; which consists in expressing the manners, and so well making them known, that we may be able at the same time to perceive what they will produce' (p. 243).

p. 226 Virgil, *Aeneid,* 2. 426–8:

> Then Ripheus followed, in the unequal fight;
> Just of his word, observant of the right;
> Heaven thought not so. DRYDEN

p. 226   *Aeneid*, 2. 429–30:
  Nor Pantheus, thee, thy mitre not the bands
  Of awful Phoebus, saved from impious hands.   DRYDEN

Critiques on Plays, by Richard Steele

p. 228   Etherege's comedy, *The Man of Mode, or Sir Fopling Flutter* (1676), had
been given at Drury Lane on 20 Apr., with the following cast: Sir Fopling, Cibber;
Dorimant, Wilks; Medley, Mills; Old Bell-Air, Penkethman; Young Bell-Air,
Bullock Junior; Shoe-maker, Bowen; Loveit, Mrs. Oldfield; Belinda, Mrs.
Rogers; Harriet, Mrs. Santlow; Emilia, Mrs. Porter.

p. 230   Dennis replied to this paper in his *Defence of Sir Fopling Flutter* in 1722
(*Critical Works*, ed. Hooker, ii. 241–50), arguing that while Dorimant might not
be 'the pattern of genteel comedy' by present-day standards, Etherege was
writing according to Restoration standards of conduct and hence 'was obliged to
accommodate himself to that notion of a fine gentleman which the Court and the
Town both had at the time of the writing of this comedy' (ii. 244).

p. 231   *The Scornful Lady*, by Beaumont and Fletcher, had been given at Drury
Lane on the preceding Friday, 4 Jan., with Mrs. Oldfield in the title-role.

p. 232   Sir Roger's part was taken by Colley Cibber. Welford was played by
Barton Booth. The meeting between Sir Roger and Welford occurs in the opening
scene. The chaplain is made to say, 'Yes, I do take the air many mornings on
foot, three or four miles, for eggs.'

p. 234   *The Distressed Mother*, a version of Racine's *Andromaque* by Ambrose
Philips, was first acted on 17 Mar. 1712 at Drury Lane and had an initial run of
eight performances. It was published on 28 Mar., with a Dedication to the
Duchess of Montague, in which her illustrious father the Duke of Marlborough is
compared to Hector. The part of Pyrrhus was taken by Barton Booth and that of
Andromache by Mrs. Anne Oldfield. The Prologue was written by Steele and the
Epilogue by Budgell, possibly with the help of Addison.

p. 234   The Preface notes that the life of Astyanax is a little prolonged in the
play in order 'to heighten in Andromache the character of a tender mother, an
affectionate wife, and a widow full of veneration for the memory of her deceased
husband'.

p. 235   *A Modest Survey of that Celebrated Tragedy, The Distrest Mother, so
often and so highly applauded by the Ingenious Spectator* (printed and sold by
William Redmayne in Jewen Street and John Morphew near Stationers Hall,
1712) criticizes Philips's play for thinness of thought and style, unnaturalness of
characterization, and clumsiness of plot—all the more surprising, says the author,
after 'so profuse a recommendation given it, so long before its public appearance,
by the most ingenious *Spectator*' (p. 3). The anonymous critic pays tribute to the
far-reaching effect of Mr. Spectator's judgement on plays; even this *Modest
Survey*, he says, 'shall appear not so much an affront to his judgement, as a
congratulation of his POWER, when a stroke of his ingenious pen could carry so

universal a sway o'er the town in favour to that play' (p. 7). The *Modest Survey* was published on 22 May 1712 (advertisement in *Post Boy*).

p. 235   George Powell, who took the part of Orestes, is probably referring here to III. i, the scene between Orestes and his friend Pylades (played by John Mills).

p. 236   Lines 75–7. Menedemus is the accuser (and the 'self-tormenter'), and it is Chremes who answers with the celebrated line, *Homo sum: humani nil a me alienum puto*. The present passage in the *Spectator* (this sentence and the four following) is quoted in *Guardian* 59 apropos of Addison's *Cato*: the warm reception given this play has removed from the English 'the imputation which a late writer had thrown upon them in his 502d *Speculation*'.

p. 236   The allusion to 'Covent Garden' is to the general theatre district—to Drury Lane Theatre near by, and possibly to Martin Powell's puppet theatre in the Piazzas. Covent Garden Theatre was not built until 1732.

p. 237   Nichols' edition of the *Spectator* refers to Andrew Fletcher of Saltoun, who is reported to have said: 'I knew a very wise man who believed that if a man were permitted to make all the ballads, he need not care who should make the laws of a nation.'

p. 238   *The Country-Wake*, by Doggett, was produced at Lincoln's Inn Fields Theatre in 1696, with the author in the part of Young Hob. It was revived, in altered form, as a farce at Drury Lane on 6 Oct. 1711 (advertisement in No. 189), with Doggett as Hob, Bullock as Sir Thomas Testy, Pack as Friendly, and Mrs. Santlow as Flora. It was frequently given thereafter, and had just been performed on the Thursday (2 Oct.) preceding the publication of this paper.

Thomas Doggett was an Irish actor, who came to England about 1690 with a travelling company, and in 1702 had a booth at Bartholomew Fair. Besides the part of Hob in his own play, he was famous for his playing of Fondlewife in *The Old Bachelor* and Ben in *Love for Love*, a part which Congreve is said to have written for him. In 1709–11 he was partner with Cibber, Wilks, and Swiney in the management of the Haymarket Theatre.

In spite of the similar title and similar characters, the two plays are different. The earlier play, *The Country-Wake*, is a comedy; *Hob* is a one-act farce. *Hob, or The Country Wake*, with 'the famous song performed by Mr. Pack, called London City's Triumph; or, my Lord Mayor's Show', was published on 15 Feb. 1714/15 (advertisement in *Post Boy*).

MISCELLANEOUS ESSAYS

On Language

p. 240   One traveller, Henri Misson de Valberg, thought it might be the general use of tobacco which makes most Englishmen 'so taciturn, so thoughtful, and so melancholy' (*Mémoires et observations faites par un voyageur en Angleterre*, La Haye, 1698, p. 312). Guy Miege, in *The Present State of Great Britain* (1707), also comments on the Englishman's 'natural taciturnity':

The English are generally averse to rambling and frothy discourses, to affected eloquence, and mimical gesticulations, so much used beyond sea. They love to hear one keep close to the subject, argue with solidity, and express himself in a nervous style. Without raising and falling their voices from one extreme to another, they endeavour not so much to move the hearer's affections, as to convince his reason. In short, as men of sense, they stand more upon the strength of arguments, than upon the gaudy part and pomp of rhetoric (p. 312).

p. 240   Swift, in a letter to the *Tatler* (No. 230), had deplored 'the continual corruption of our English tongue' and offered a sample letter showing the fashionable 'refinements' which had come in. Among other things he commented on

the abbreviations and elisions, by which consonants of most obdurate sound are joined together, without one softening vowel to intervene; and all this only to make one syllable of two, directly contrary to the example of the Greeks and Romans; altogether of the Gothic strain, and a natural tendency towards relapsing into barbarity, which delights in monosyllables, and uniting of mute consonants; as [is] observable in all the Northern languages. And this is still more visible in the next refinement, which consists in pronouncing the first syllable in a word that has many, and dismissing the rest; such as *phizz, hipps, mobb, poz. rep.* and many more; when we are already overloaded with monosyllables, which are the disgrace of our language.

He returns to the subject in his letter to the Lord Treasurer, *A Proposal for Correcting, Improving and Ascertaining the English Tongue*, published on 12 May 1712 (*Post Boy*), in which he proposes the establishment of an Academy to correct and fix the English language. Here he repeats many of the points from the *Tatler* letter and those made in this essay. Near the end he writes:

I would willingly avoid repetition, having about a year ago communicated to the public much of what I had to offer upon this subject, by the hands of an ingenious gentleman who for a long time did thrice a week divert or instruct the kingdom by his papers; and is supposed to pursue the same design at present under the title of *Spectator*. This author, who hath tried the force and compass of our language with so much success, agrees entirely with me in most of my sentiments relating to it . . . (pp. 36-7).

p. 242   Sir Roger L'Estrange (1616-1704), the prolific translator, journalist, and pamphleteer, chiefly against the Whigs and Dissenters.

p. 243   Addison had discussed the importation of French fopperies in an earlier *Spectator* (No. 45). The present paper may be regarded as a sequel to No. 135 (pp. 240-3), on corruptions of the language.

p. 244   According to Nichols this was Richard Bentley. In his reply to Boyle, in the *Dissertation upon the Epistles of Phalaris* (1699), Bentley gives a list of words which Boyle had objected to in Bentley's earlier book, including the word *idiom*: 'every one of which were in print, before I used them; and most of them, before I was born' (p. lxxxv).

p. 245   Of the fifteen French words or phrases in this letter, two (*corps* and *maraud*) are quoted from this paper as the first examples in English in the *OED*. *Hauteur*, in the sense of a height, is also dated 1711 in *OED*, but the example is from the London *Gazette*. Other recent importations in the list (with the earliest date in *OED*) are *reconnoitre* (1707), *defiles* (1685), *corps de reserve* (1704), *gasconade* (1709), *fossé* (1708), *chamade* (1684), *charte blanche* (1707), and *cartel* (1692). *Carte blanche* is used, however, by Dryden in *Don Sebastian* (1690), III. ii. The remainder are older: *at discretion* (1630), *drum* (1577), *trumpet* (1390), and *gens d'arms* (c. 1550). On the word *corps* the *OED* notes:

> As short for *corps d'armée*, it is found in French before 1700, and appears to have come up in English during Marlborough's campaigns. Here it was probably at first pronounced like English *corps*, CORPSE; but before the end of the eighteenth century the French pronunciation generally prevailed, and with this the French spelling was retained, while for the senses with the English pronunciation the spelling *corpse* was established.'

As noted above, *corps de reserve* is found in English a little earlier, in 1704. 'It is remarkable', wrote Hurd (Addison's *Works*, 1811), 'that most of the French terms inserted in this letter, in order to expose the affectation of the writer, are now grown so familiar among us, that few men would think of expressing themselves, on the like occasion, in any other.'

On Authors and Writing

p. 249   Nichols suggested that this 'might perhaps be Mr. Toland'. The article on Toland in the *Biographia Britannica* does not mention this paper. The point of view here is that of *Tatler* 111, which considered under 'Infidels' not only deists and atheists but also free-thinkers. The latter are described thus:

> These are the wretches, who, without any show of wit, learning, or reason, publish their crude conceptions with an ambition of appearing more wise than the rest of mankind, upon no other pretence, than that of dissenting from them. One gets by heart a catalogue of title-pages and editions: and immediately to become conspicuous, declares that he is an unbeliever. Another knows how to write a receipt, or cut up a dog, and forthwith argues against the immortality of the soul.

On Genius

p. 251   Rapin ('A Comparison of Homer and Virgil', Ch. x) says of the ass simile in the *Iliad* that it 'is become so famous for its indecency and meanness, that all the world have heard of it' (*Whole Critical Works*, 1706, i. 163). Le Bossu (Book VI, Ch. iii) defends both similes (2nd edn., London, 1719, ii. 259–60).

p. 251   Addison's (and Steele's) comments on these poems are almost always adverse. A 'receipt for Pindarics' is given in *Tatler* 106. Cf. also the ironic reference to 'those admirable English authors who call themselves Pindaric writers' in the concluding sentence of No. 58 (p. 4).

p. 252   In placing Milton among the learned geniuses Addison takes a position opposed to Dennis, who in *The Grounds of Criticism in Poetry* (1704) called Milton 'one of the greatest and most daring geniuses that has appeared in the world', and *Paradise Lost* 'the most lofty, but most irregular poem, that has been produced by the mind of man' (*Critical Works*, ed. Hooker, i. 333).

Index